EVERYDAY OBJECTS

Roller Skate 84
Mug 86
Teacup 88
Teapot 90
Flower Vase 92
Watering Can 94
Bow 95
Candle 96
Sun 98
Weather 100

HOLIDAYS

Christmas Tree 104
Gift Boxes 106
Ugly Christmas Sweater 108
Christmas Ornament 110
Bell Ornament 111
Santa Claus 112
Thanksgiving Gourds 113
Jack-o'-Lantern 114
Witchy Ghost 115
Cute Monster 116
Valentine's Letter in a Bottle 118
Valentine's Love Birds 120

LETTERING

Floral-Decorated Letters 124
Letters Wrapped with Vines 126
Collage-Style Letters 127
Patchwork Letters 128
C as a Cat 130
R as a Rabbit 132
E as an Elephant 134
A as an Alligator 136
T as a Tiger 138

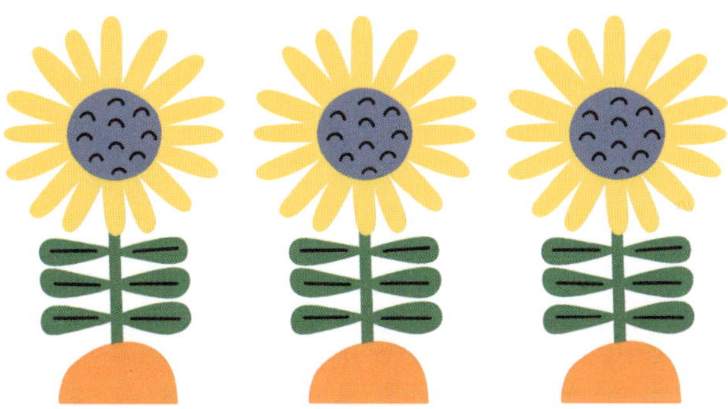

BRING YOUR ART TO LIFE

Mix & Match 140
Make It Yours 141
Creative Applications 141
Acknowledgments 143
About the Author 143

INTRODUCTION

MY STORY

Hi I'm Sandra, a surface pattern designer and illustrator based in Vienna, Austria. I create joyful art full of vibrant colors, bold shapes, and a touch of playfulness.

My creative journey started when I was little, with a love for color, cutting paper, and making things with my hands. I always loved drawing playful shapes, using colors that pop, and creating artwork that had a hand-drawn feel—a little wobbly, a little imperfect, but full of personality. That naturally led me to pattern design. I loved finding ways to repeat my quirky little drawings and turn them into something bigger.

What began as a creative hobby slowly grew into my full-time job, and I'm so grateful for that. These days, I get to see my artwork on puzzles, greeting cards, home décor, and even dog accessories. And honestly? It still feels just as exciting every time.

This book brings together the spirit of what I love most about making art and puts it in your hands. I created it as a space where you can explore freely, try out bold colors, and bring your own creative voice to life. Whether you're using markers, an iPad, or a pair of scissors and some glue, you're in the right place.

My Art Style

The style you'll find in this book is inspired by folk art, children's book illustrations, vintage patterns, nature, and the imperfect beauty of handmade things. You'll notice lots of flat, simple shapes, bright color combinations, and hand-drawn details that give each drawing its own personality. I like it when things feel a little different—not too perfect or polished. That's what gives each drawing its charm.

Encouragement for Creativity

This book isn't about drawing perfectly. It's about having fun, trying things out, and letting yourself be creative, even if it feels messy sometimes. You can follow the steps exactly, or you can change things up. Add a face. Try a wild color. Cut it out and collage it. Whatever feels exciting to you—go with it!

MODERN FOLK ART

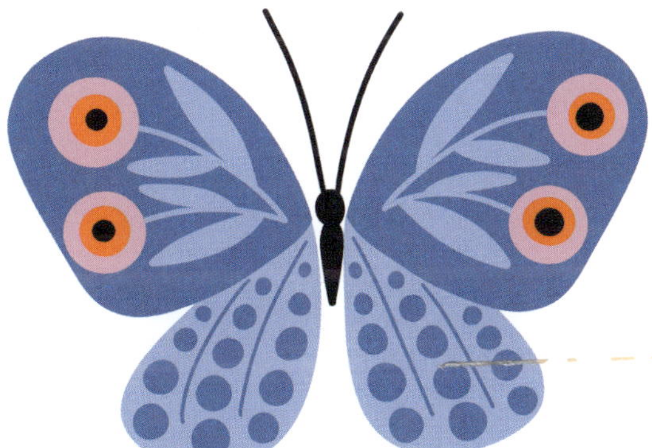

Draw 75 Charming Animals, Botanicals, Patterns, and More

SANDRA HUTTER

ROCK POINT

CONTENTS

INTRODUCTION

My Story 4
How to Use This Book 5
Drawing Techniques 6
Using Color. 7
Creativity, Mistakes & Play 9

FLORALS & BOTANICALS

Tulip. 12
Sunflower. 13
Daisy 14
Line Art Flower 16
Dandelions 18
Palm Tree. 20
Potted Cactus 21
Cactus. 22
Mushroom 23
Mushroom Cluster 24
Hanging Plant 25
Hanging Vines. 26
Flower Meadow 28
Sunset Flower 30
Crown Flower 31

FRUITS, VEGGIES & SNACKS

Apple 34
Lemon. 36
Papaya 37
Cherries 38
Strawberries 39
Tomatoes 40
Popsicle. 41
Bubble Tea 42
Cupcake 43
Cake. 44

FRIENDLY CREATURES

Butterfly 48
Moth. 50
Beetle 52
Lady Bug 54
Folk Art Bird 56
Peace Dove 58
Hummingbird 60
Toucan 62
Cute Bird 64
Snake 65
Cat. 66
Dachshund 68
Poodle. 70
Bunny 72
Chicken. 74
Sheep 76
Bear 77
Fish 78
Lobster 80

I hope this book gives you the confidence to draw more often, worry less, and express your creativity in ways that feel joyful and fun.

HOW TO USE THIS BOOK

Following some tips and tricks to crafting your very own folk art, this book includes seventy-five step-by-step tutorials in six chapters: Florals & Botanicals; Fruits, Veggies, & Snacks; Friendly Creatures; Everyday Objects; Holidays; and Lettering. Once you've completed the tutorials, the back of the book teaches you how to take everything you've learned and start making your very own folk art! So grab your pencil or stylus, and let's get started!

My Favorite Tools

You don't need fancy materials to start drawing. I draw most of my artwork digitally in Procreate on my iPad, but I also love working by hand. Everything in this book can be created with whatever tools you already have, such as pencils, markers, paper, or an iPad, or you can cut out shapes from crafting paper.

Digital Tools

The digital tools I used to create the artwork in this book were an iPad and an Apple Pencil, which makes smooth, pressure-sensitive lines. My preferred software is Procreate. On Procreate, I most often use the following brushes:

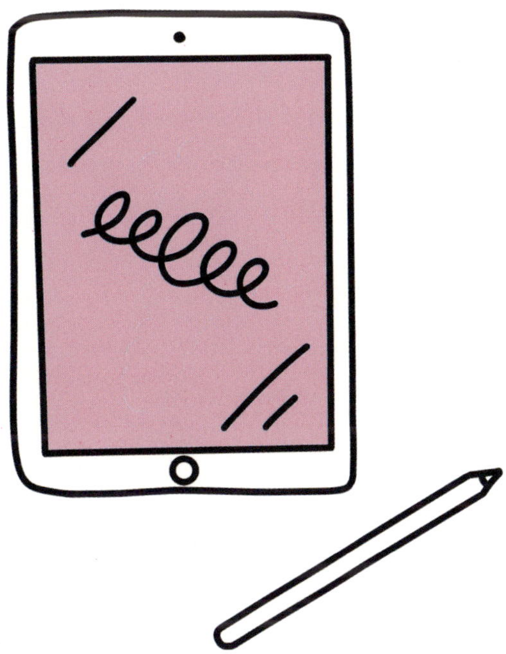

- **Monoline:** For clean shapes and fills, but also for line art details
- **Dry Ink:** For textured outlines and quirky details
- **Syrup:** For flowing lines and lettering
- **6B Pencil:** Perfect for sketching ideas digitally

Analog Tools

When I'm not working on my iPad, the traditional tools I love to use are:

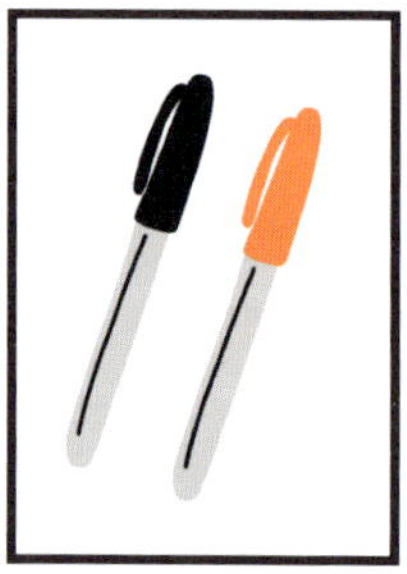

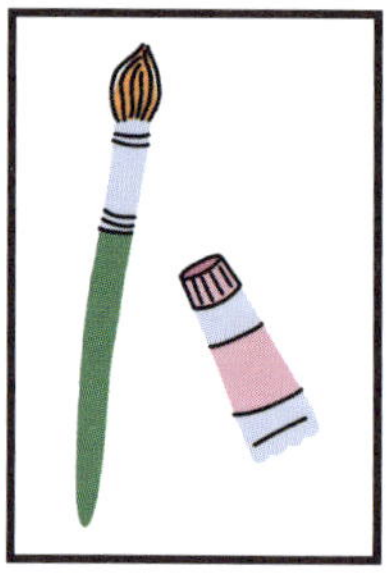

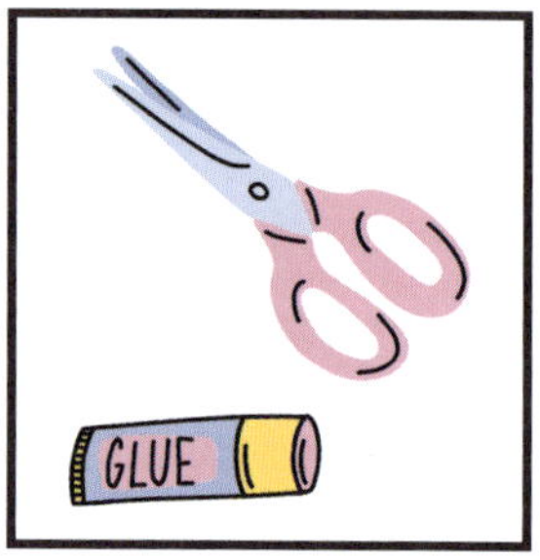

- **Scrap Paper or a Sketchbook:** For doodling
- **Pencils:** For loose sketches
- **Black Marker or Sharpie:** For outlines and line art details
- **Colored Markers or Crayons:** For bold and fun colors
- **Gouache or Acrylics:** For color with that matte, handmade look
- **Scissors and Glue Sticks:** For playful collage days

DRAWING TECHNIQUES

There are a lot of ways to draw, so choose what methods feel best to you. You don't need to be an expert at sketching. You'd be surprised how much you can create with just a few basic shapes.

Most of my drawings begin with simple building blocks, such as circles, ovals, rectangles, triangles, and teardrops. You can flip them, repeat them, or stretch them into something unexpected, and before you know it, you've got a fun little flower or even a cute cat!

Once I've mapped out the line art, I fill in the shapes with color. This is the step where things really start to come to life! I love using bold colors to make each design pop.

Some motifs in this book use bold outlines, like the mushroom cluster. Others, like the sun, are made up of solid color shapes with no outlines at all. Both techniques are great, but try them out and see what feels right for you!

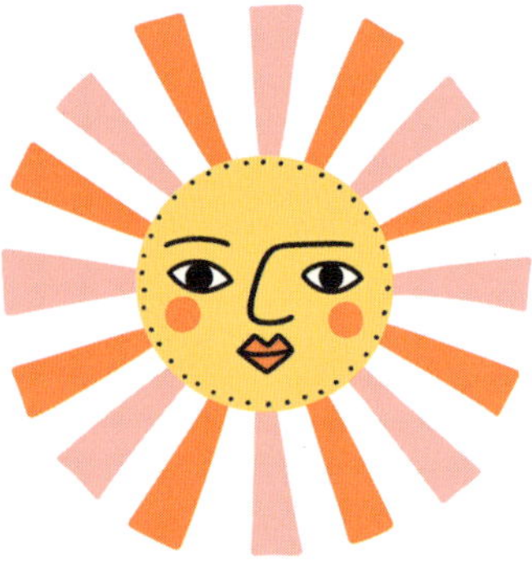

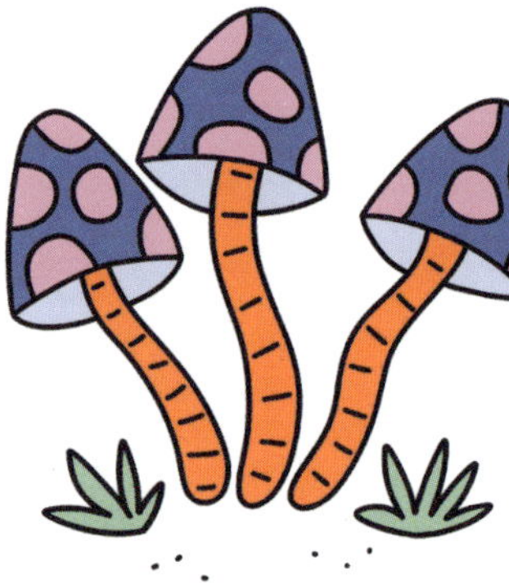

Bonus Tip: If you're working digitally in Procreate, the Symmetry tool can be a fun one to try! It's especially helpful for motifs like insects, hearts, or anything that's mirrored on both sides. But if you prefer to just eyeball it, that's perfectly fine too. A little asymmetry adds charm and makes your work feel more human.

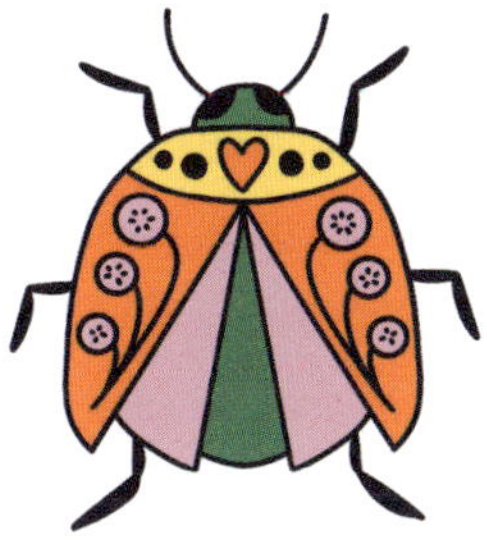

As a final step, I often add hand-drawn linear details, such as little dots, lines, and markings that bring everything together and give the drawing its unique texture and personality.

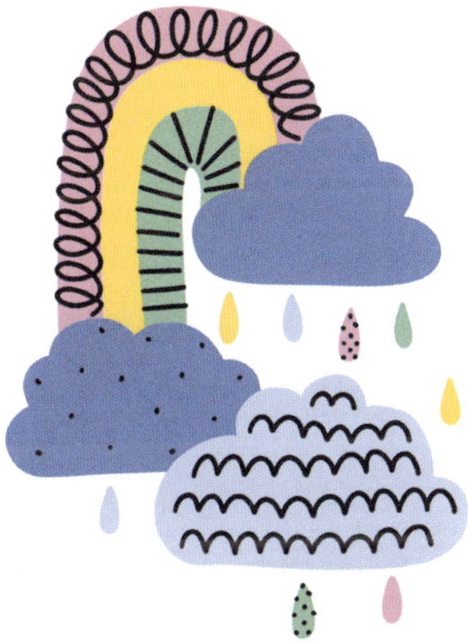

USING COLOR

Color is one of my favorite parts of the creative process—it's where the joy really kicks in! I love colors that pop. Bright pinks, juicy oranges, bold blues, happy yellows—anything that brings instant energy and charm. I usually stay away from muted tones, but that's just my style. If softer shades are more your thing, go for it! The important part is finding what feels right to you and experimenting with your creativity.

When I start a new design, I usually choose three to five main colors to work with. Limiting your palette can make the whole process feel more focused and make your artwork more balanced. If you're not sure where to start, try a color palette generator (like www.coolors.co) or look around you for inspiration in a favorite piece of clothing, a mug you love, or a poster that makes you smile.

Color is emotional. Some combinations feel bold and happy, while others are calm or quirky. There's no "right" way to use color. Experiment and follow what lights you up.

On the next page, you'll find a space to create your own color palettes. Choose colors that make you feel excited, happy, or calm. Use your palettes as a starting point for the motifs in this book, and come back to it whenever you need inspiration.

My Color Palettes

Let's create three different color palettes to explore your style! Color in the empty circles to create your go-to color palette. Use the template below to make your first palette based on the colors you added in the circles above.

You can base them on a feeling, a season, or a favorite object. You also can choose colors that make you smile. Don't overthink it, just play!

Name your colors if you'd like (e.g., sunshine yellow, bubblegum pink, soft lilac) or simply fill them in and start drawing!

PALETTE 1

Theme or mood (optional):

Color 1: ....

Color 2: ....

Color 3: ....

Color 4 (optional):

....

Color 5 (optional):

....

PALETTE 2

Theme or mood (optional):

Color 1: ....

Color 2: ....

Color 3: ....

Color 4 (optional):

....

Color 5 (optional):

....

PALETTE 3

Theme or mood (optional):

Color 1: ....

Color 2: ....

Color 3: ....

Color 4 (optional):

....

Color 5 (optional):

....

CREATIVITY, MISTAKES & PLAY

I've said it a couple of times already, but let's say it once more, just to be sure: Not every drawing has to be perfect. In fact . . . it shouldn't be. Some of my favorite motifs started out as messy doodles or "mistakes" that turned into something much better than I had planned. A wobbly petal, a strange face, a color that didn't make sense. These are all instances where things can get interesting.

This book is here to help you loosen up and have fun. Follow the steps if that feels right to you or do your own thing. Change the colors. Add a silly twist. Scribble outside the lines. Invent something totally new. The more you play, the more confident you will become.

Throughout this book, you'll find little "Be Bold!" prompts. These are here to encourage you to experiment, personalize, or break the rules a bit. I encourage you to give them a try! There's no one way to be creative. The only goal here is to enjoy the process.

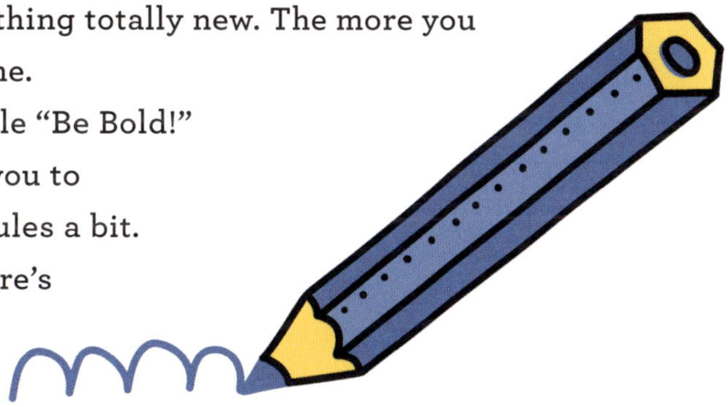

Be Bold!

Now try these three just-for-fun exercises to help you loosen up.

1. Doodle Time

Fill a page with swirls, humps, loops, bumps, and wobbly circles. No planning. No judgment. Just move your hand and let the shapes appear.

2. Use Your Nondominant Hand

Yes, really! Try drawing a flower, a bird, or even your name with your "wrong" hand. It's weird, it's wobbly, and it's fun. (You might be surprised by how playful and loose it looks.)

3. Draw Something Bad on Purpose

Set a timer for two minutes and draw the absolute silliest version of anything from this book without fixing lines or erasing. The more ridiculous, the better!

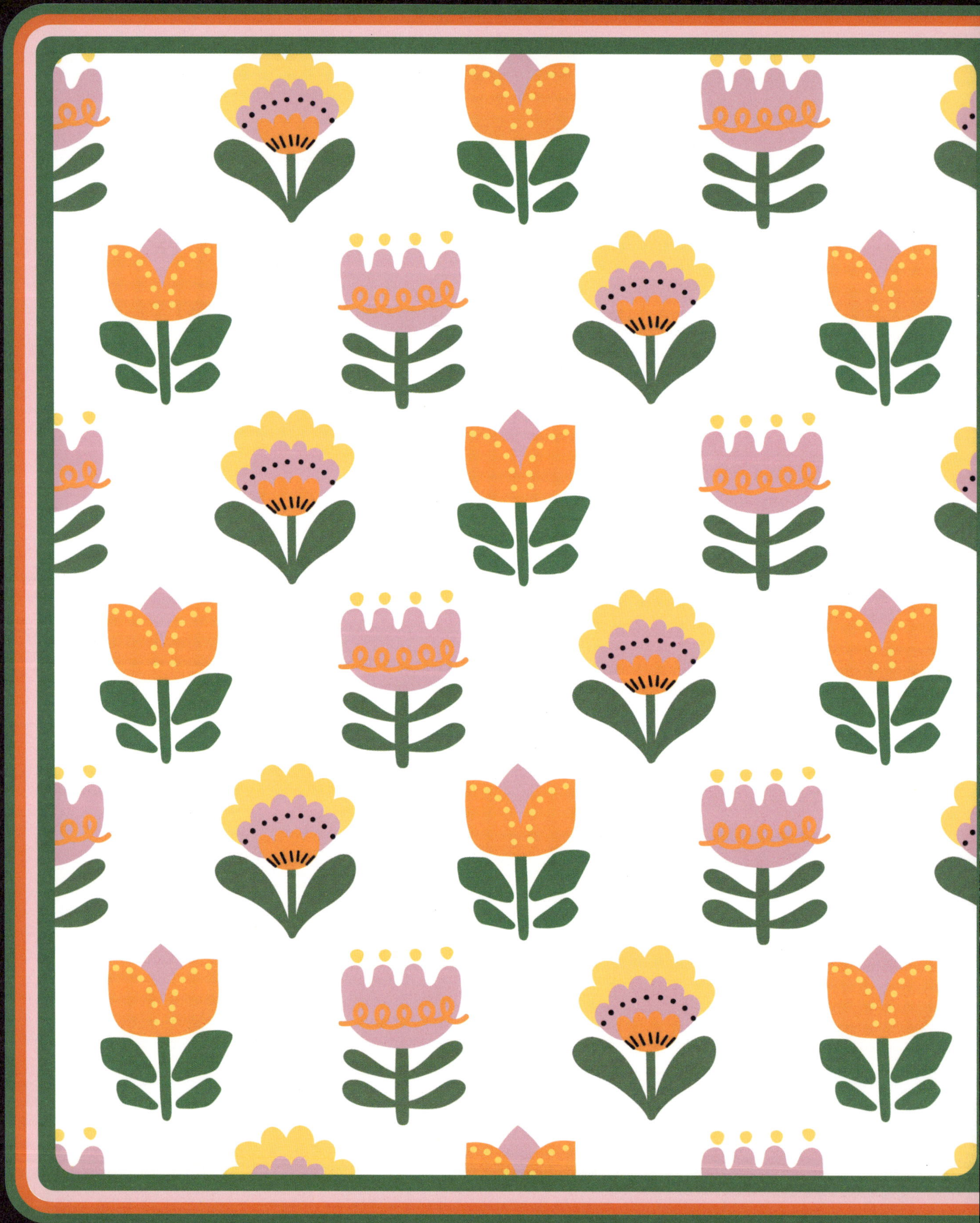

FLORALS & BOTANICALS

TULIP

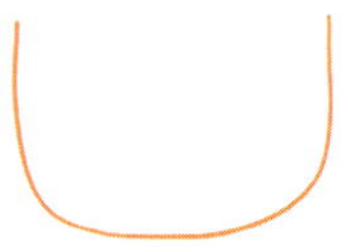

1. Start with a large, wide U shape for the base of the tulip flower head.

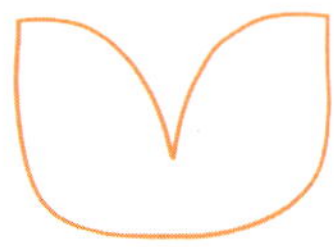

2. Add two curved petal shapes with curved lines at each side of the U. Connect them in the middle.

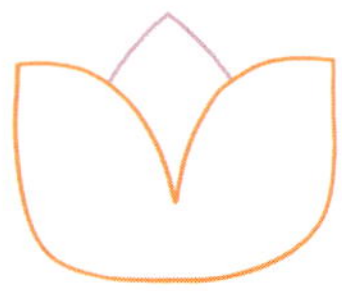

3. Draw a tall, pointed petal between the two front petals.

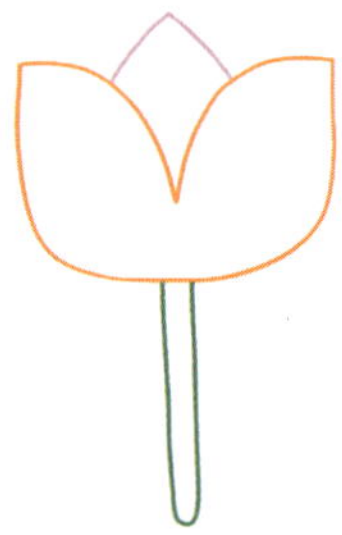

4. Draw a thin U-shaped line under the middle of the flower for the stem.

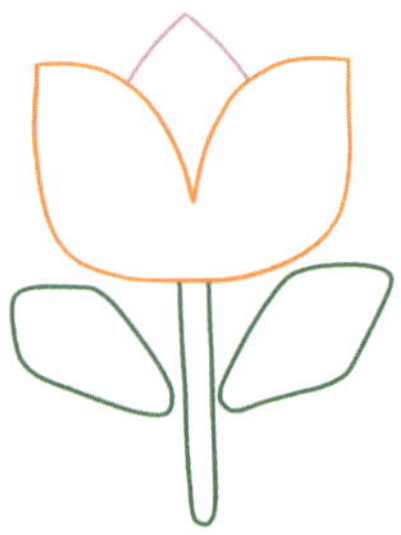

5. Add a pair of rounded, diamond-shaped leaves on each side of the stem.

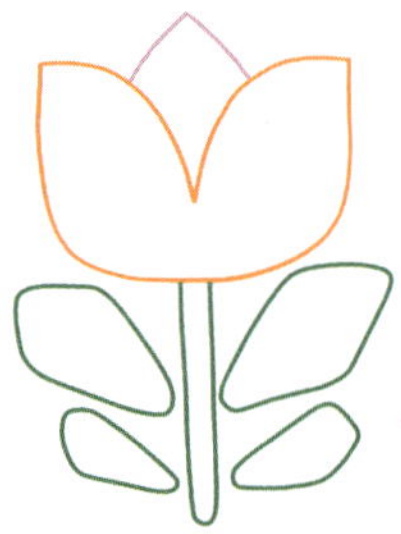

6. Add another pair of slightly smaller leaves below the first pair. Shift their angle or size for a more playful, organic feel.

7. Bring your tulip to life with color!

8. Decorate with a row of small round dots along the inside edge of each front petal.

9. Add a few loose vertical lines under the stem to create a playful grassy base.

BE BOLD!

Keeping the leaves detached from the stem gives a more modern, playful twist. You also can experiment with petal width or the angle of the leaves to give your tulip its own personality.

SUNFLOWER

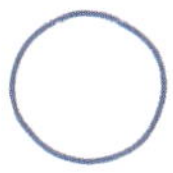

1. Start with a circle in the center of your page.

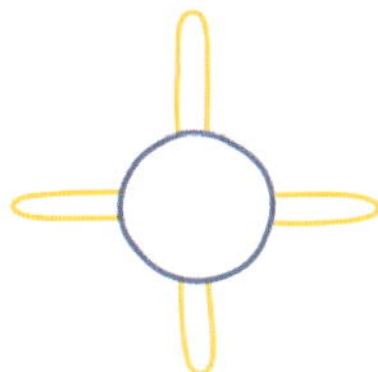

2. Add four thin U-shaped lines in the formation of a cross.

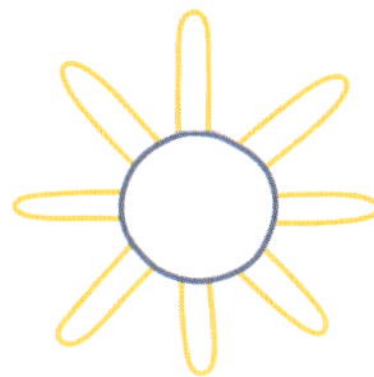

3. Add more petal lines in between the first four, so you have eight lines total.

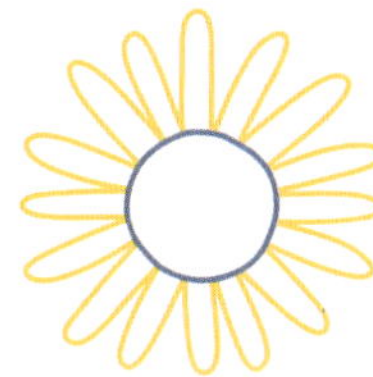

4. Keep adding more petals around the center until you've created a full round flower shape.

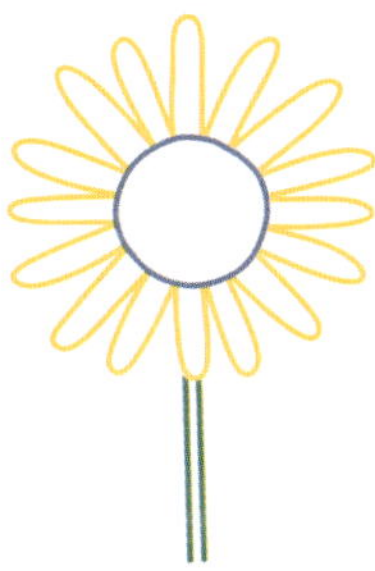

5. Draw two vertical lines for the stem.

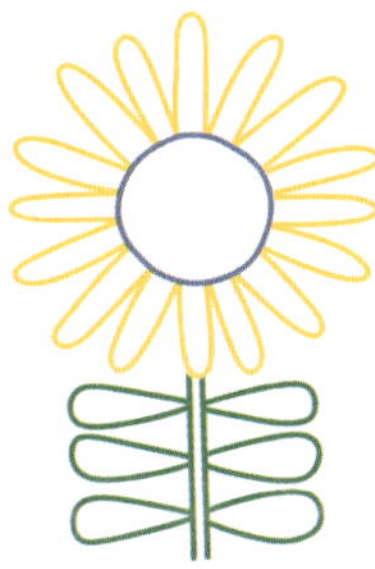

6. Add three teardrop-shaped leaves on each side of the stem.

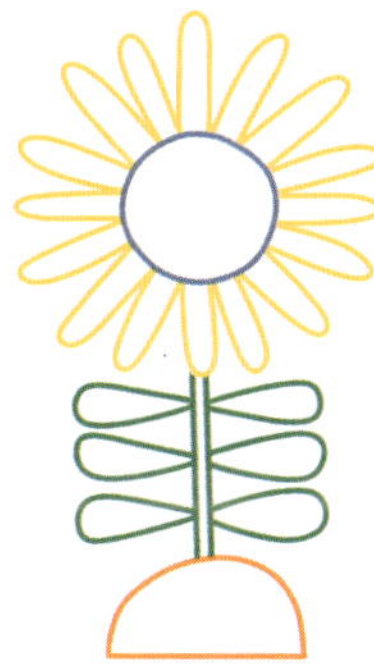

7. Add a semicircle at the bottom to anchor the flower.

8. Bring your sunflower to life with color!

9. Decorate with small curved lines in the center in a circular layout and straight lines in the leaves.

BE BOLD!

Alternate coloring your petals in two different yellows or go bold with unexpected combinations like blue and coral!

DAISY

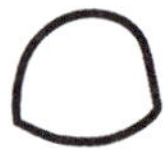

1. Start with a small arch with a rounded bottom.

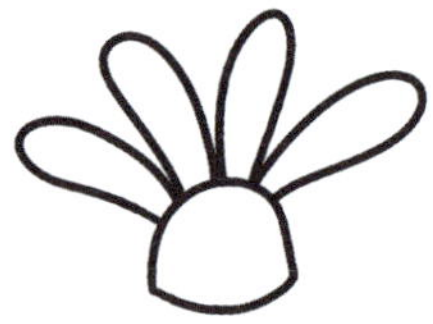

2. Add rounded petals curving upward and outward with four U-shaped lines. Make the ends slightly thicker.

3. Draw more petals underneath, in varying U-shaped lines, with the ends curving gently downward.

4. Draw two vertical lines to create the stem.

5. Add a leaf on each side of the stem using long, pointed ovals.

6. Draw the top edge of the flowerpot with a wide rectangle.

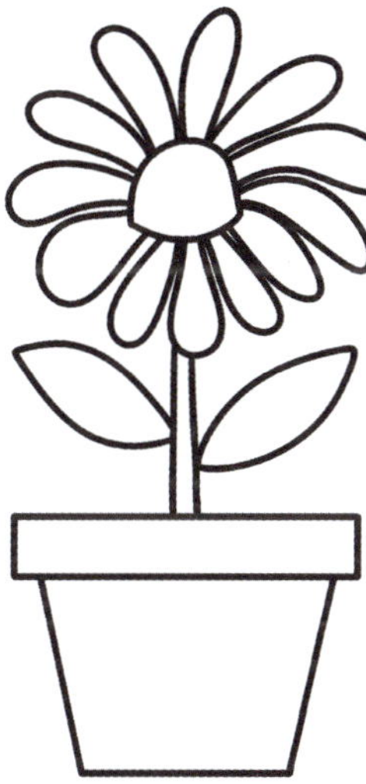

7. Sketch the pot with a flat U shape.

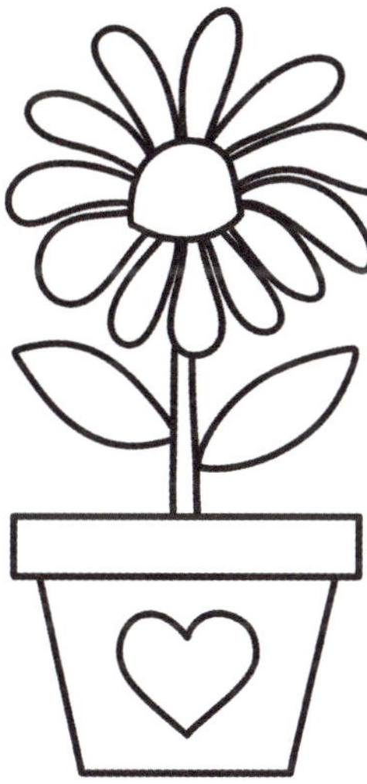

8. Add a heart to the center of the pot for an extra cute touch.

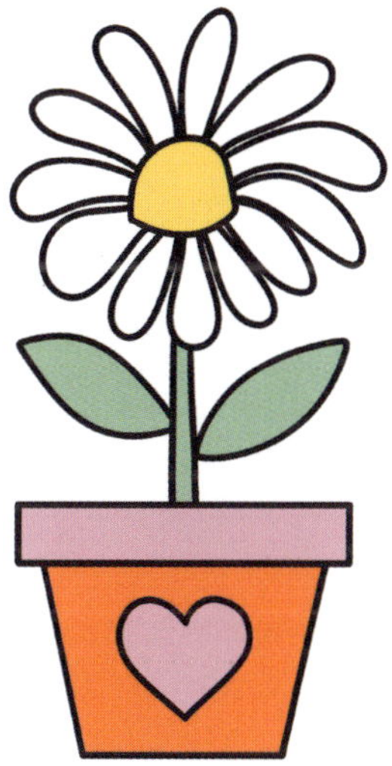

9. Bring your daisy to life with color!

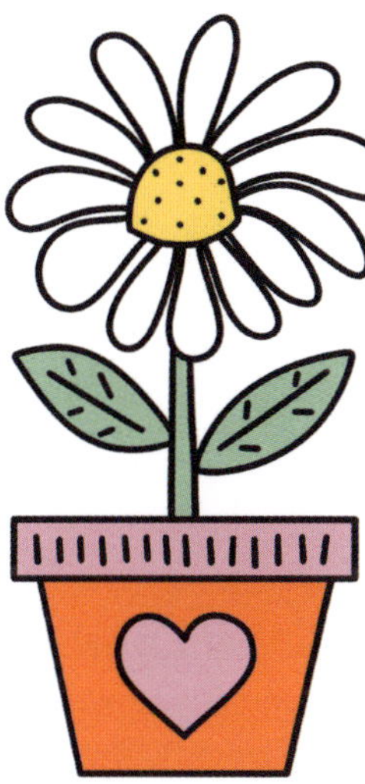

10. Decorate with small dots on the flower center and lines on the leaves and rim of the pot.

BE BOLD!

Not into hearts? Customize your flowerpot with stripes, polka dots, or smiley faces—whatever feels fun and you!

LINE ART FLOWER

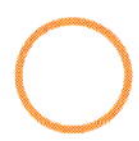

1. Start by drawing a small circle near the top right of your page.

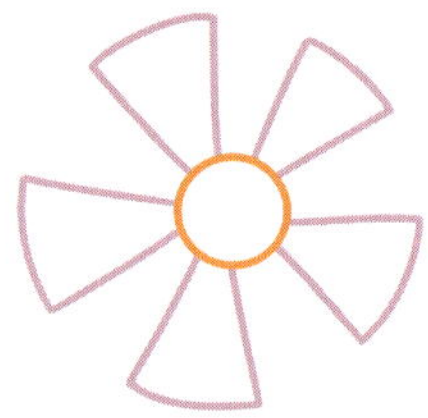

2. Add five wide petal shapes, of varying sizes, that taper toward the circle.

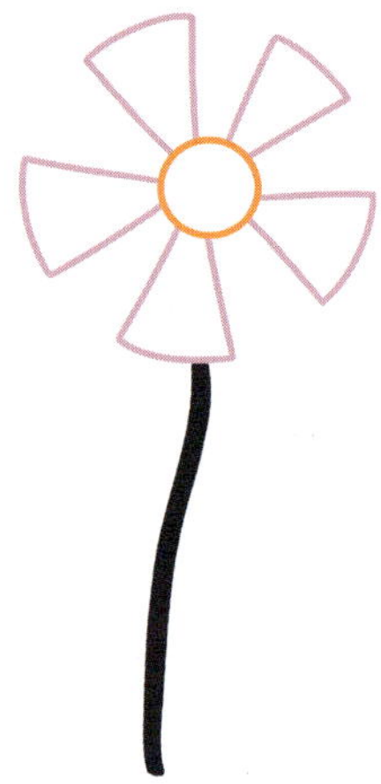

3. Using a thick solid line, draw a long, slightly curved stem under the flower.

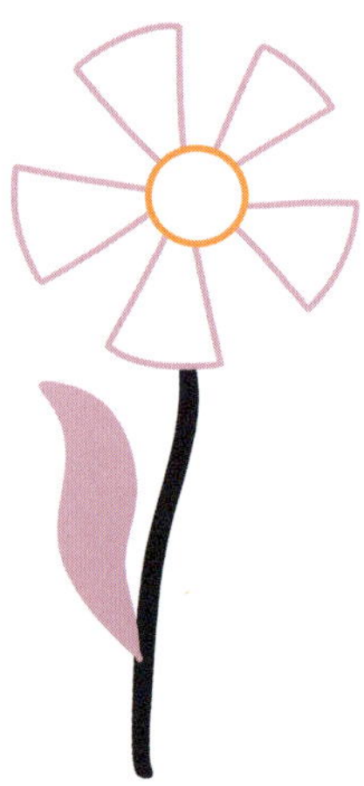

4. Add a pointed wavy leaf on the left side of the stem.

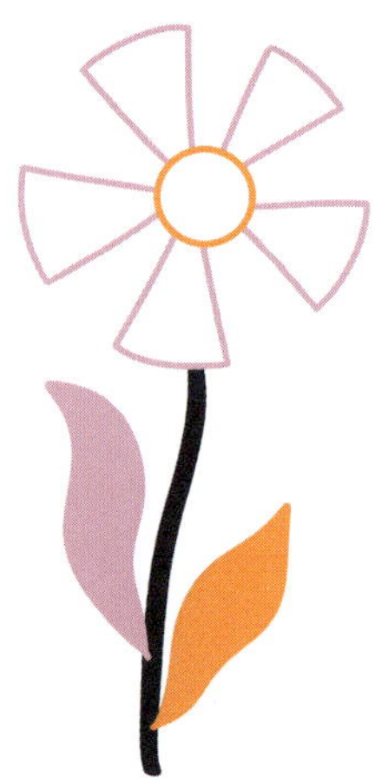

5. Add a second leaf lower on the right side of the stem.

6. Add a third leaf on the right above the other leaf, with simple black lines and a line through the middle.

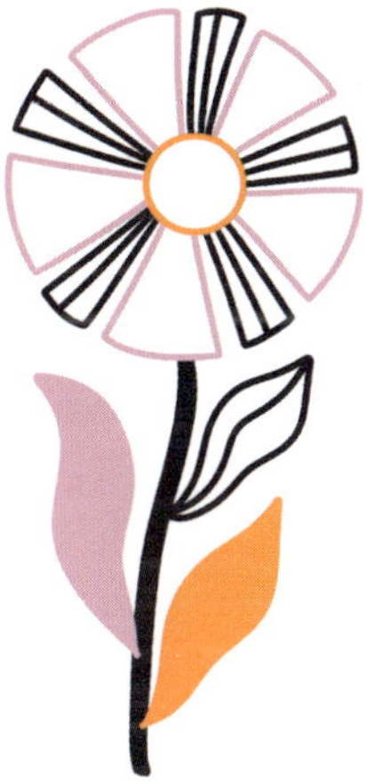

7. Add five thin black line petals between the wide petals with a line down the center.

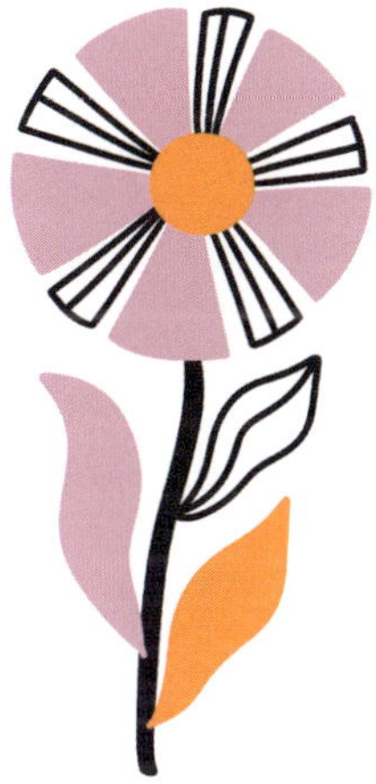

8. Color the wide petals and the flower center.

9. Decorate the circular center with small black circles.

10. Add wavy black lines in the leaves and short black lines around the base of the stem to create a grassy ground.

BE BOLD!

Try mixing together unexpected petal colors or adding extra line details to give your flower a unique graphic feel.

DANDELIONS

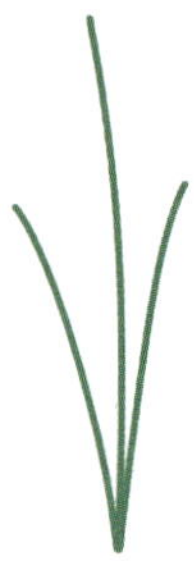

1. Start with three thin stems that connect at the bottom and curve away from each other.

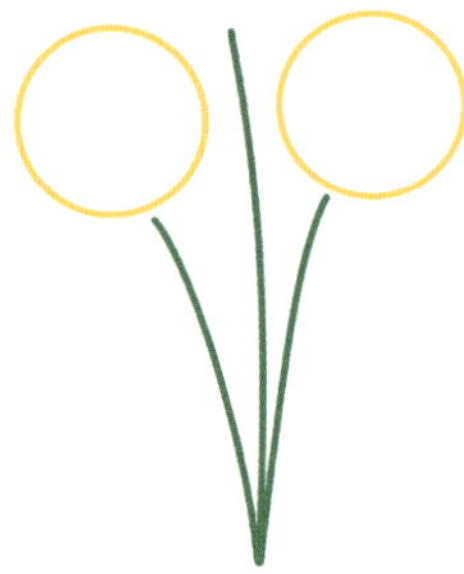

2. Draw a circle at the top of the two outer stems.

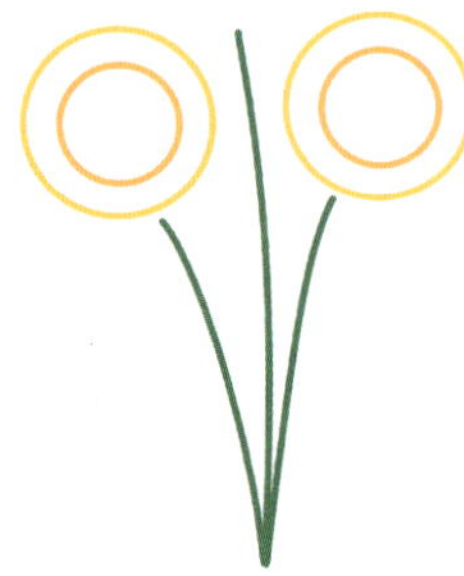

3. Add smaller circles in the centers of the circles.

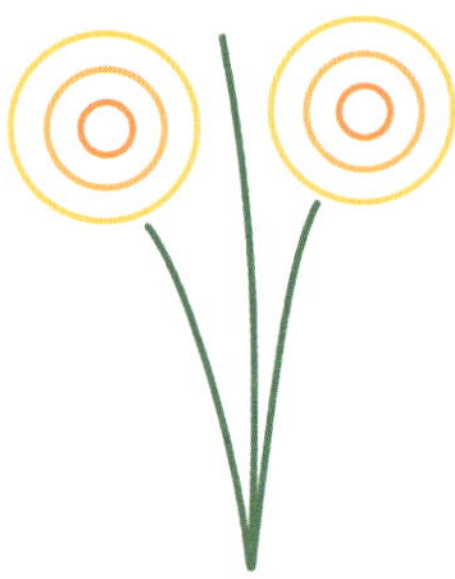

4. Add even smaller circles in the centers of the second circles.

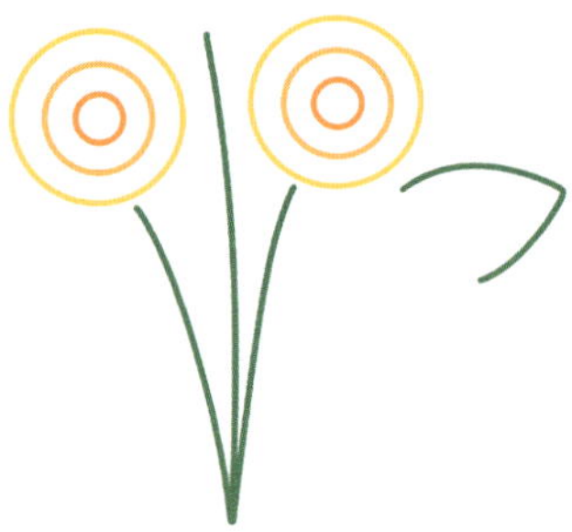

5. Draw the top of a leaf with a curved V shape on the right.

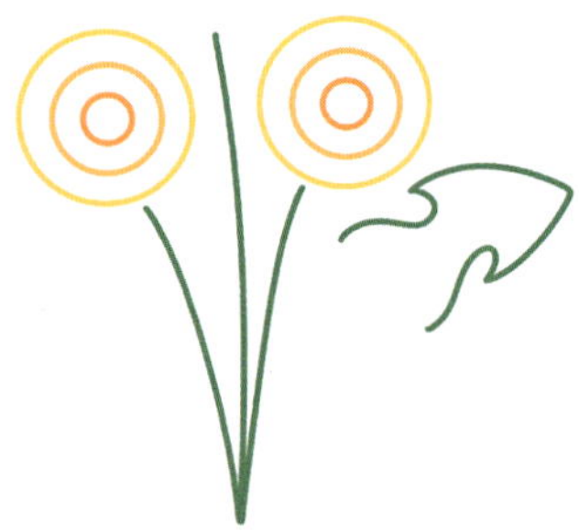

6. From each edge of the V shape, draw a wavy line toward the stems.

BE BOLD!

Every patch of dandelions is unique, so play around with the placement and number of flowers to create a whole field of dandelions.

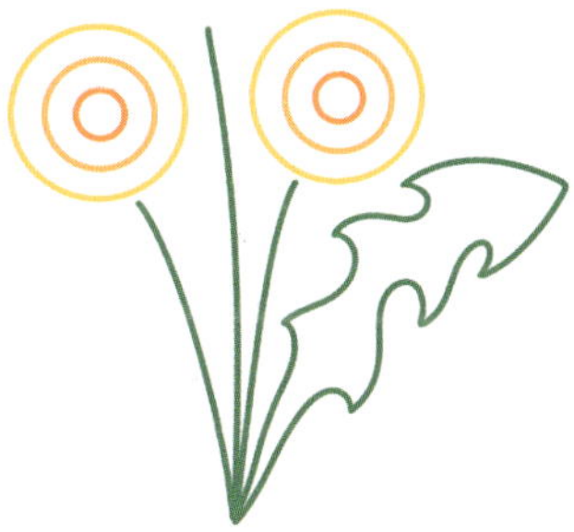

7. Repeat step 6 on each side of the leaf twice, making the wave longer each time, and connect to the base of the stems.

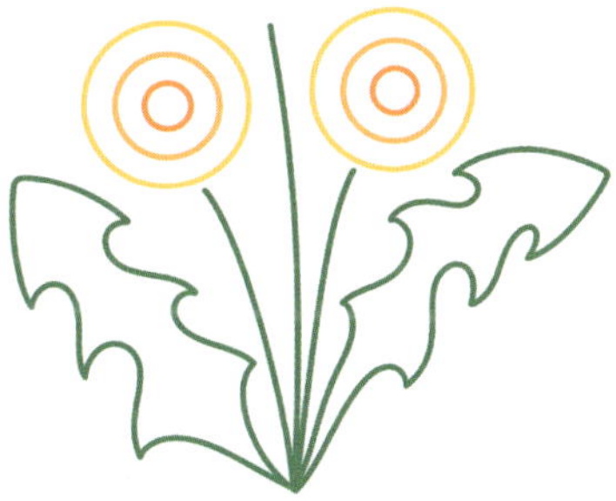

8. Draw a leaf on the left side by repeating steps 5 to 7.

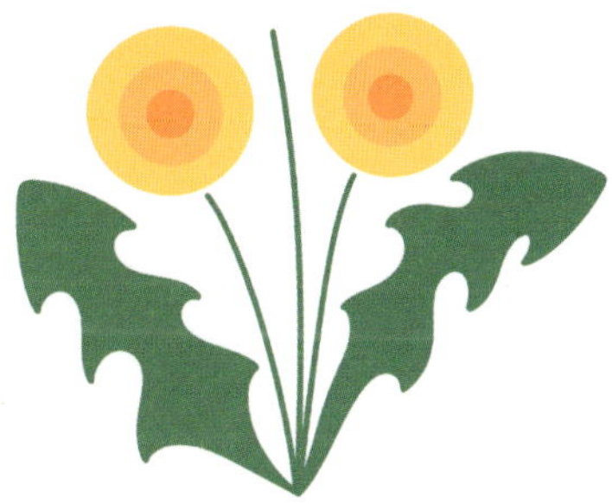

9. Fill in the dandelion flowers and leaves with color.

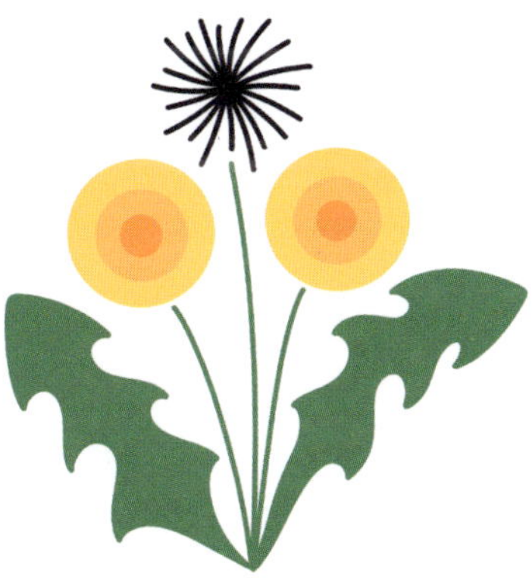

10. Above the center stem, draw curved black lines of varying lengths in a circular shape.

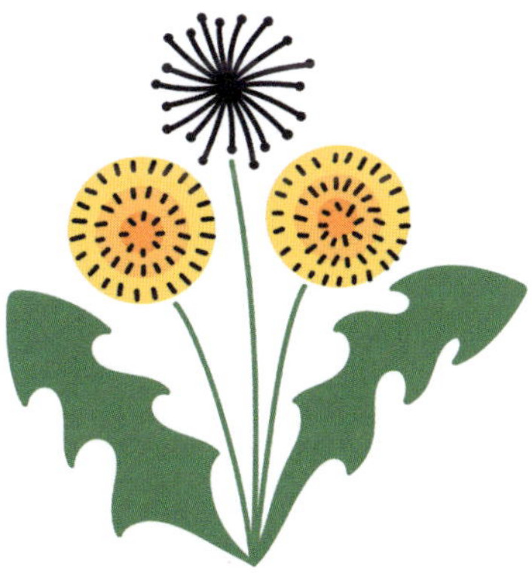

11. Decorate the dandelion flowers with small black dashes in each circle and add dots to the tips of the black lines of the center flower.

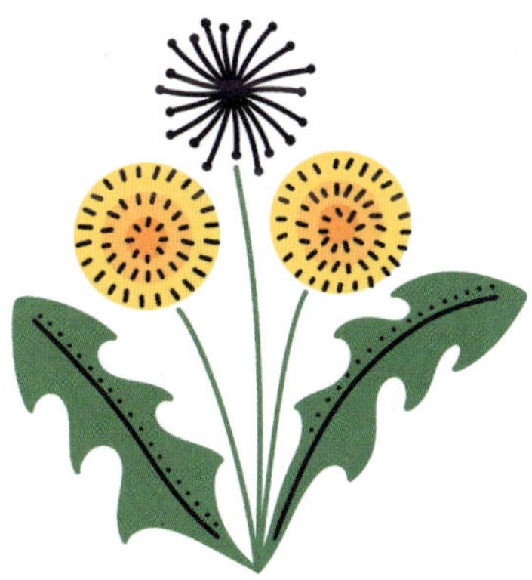

12. Decorate the leaves with a black line and dots along the top of the line.

PALM TREE

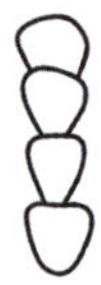

1. Start by drawing four stacked, rounded triangles for the trunk of your palm tree.

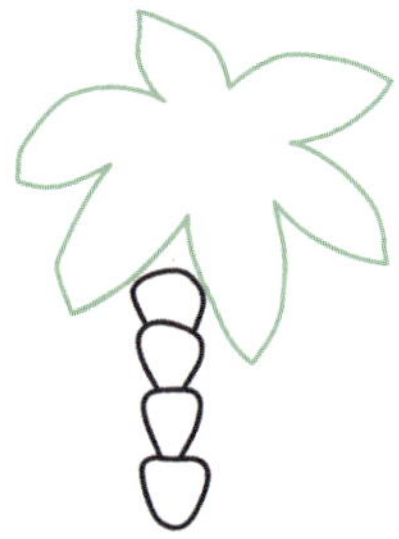

2. Add six large, pointed leaf shapes like a playful star. Angle and bend them in different directions.

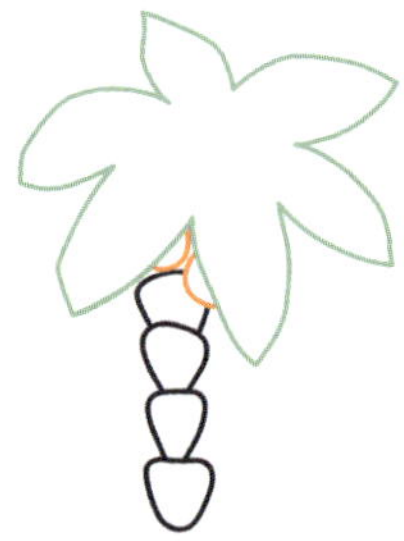

3. Draw two coconuts just below the leaves with two curved lines.

4. Color the trunk, coconuts, and leaves.

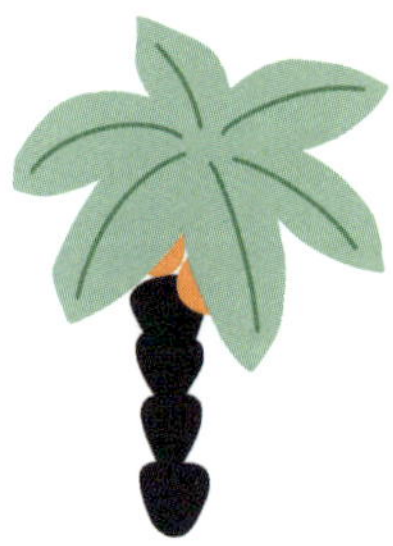

5. Draw slightly curved lines inside each leaf.

6. Add three lines to each trunk segment alternating the curve left and right to mimic the natural texture of palm bark.

7. Ground your tree with a few small, curved hill shapes at the bottom.

BE BOLD!

Make your palm tree lean to one side or stretch out extra tall. You can also draw tiny flowers or dots in the sand to create a beachy scene!

POTTED CACTUS

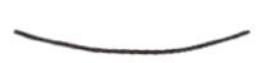

1. Start with a curved horizontal line near the center of the page.

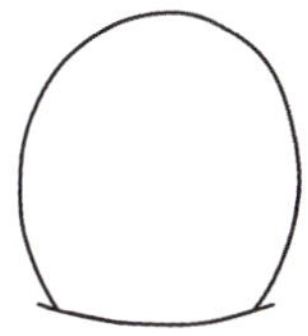

2. Draw an upside-down U shape on top of the horizontal line, leaving the ends of the line sticking out.

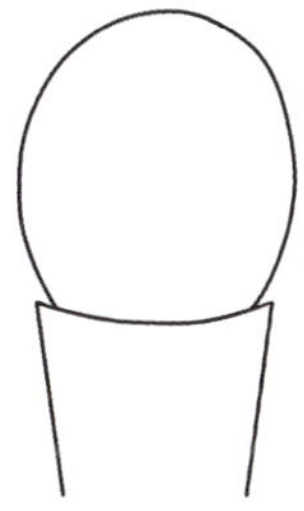

3. Draw two parallel lines down from the ends of the horizontal line.

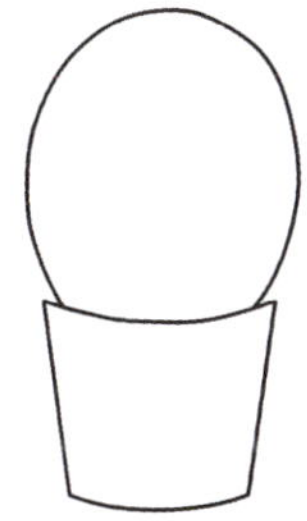

4. Connect the bottom of the two lines with a slightly curved horizontal line.

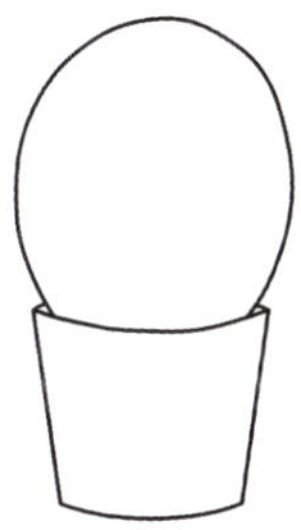

5. Add two short, curved lines from the top tips of the pot to the cactus bulb.

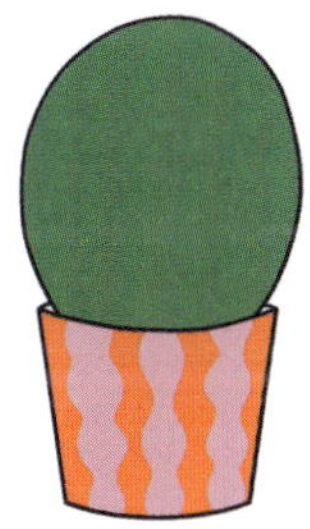

6. Fill in the cactus with color and make the pot two colors with wavy lines.

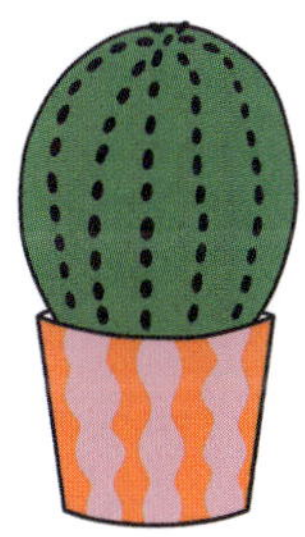

7. Add a series of oval dashes in curved vertical lines along the cactus bulb to create the cactus spikes.

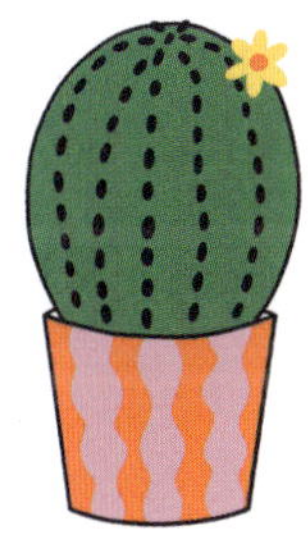

8. Draw and color a small flower with six petals on the top right of the cactus.

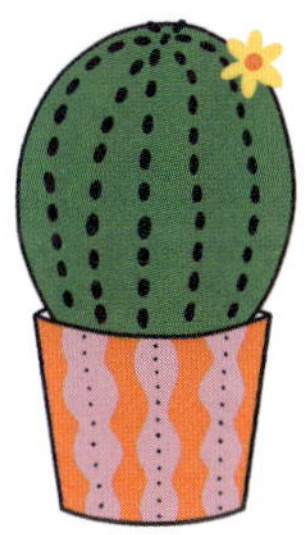

9. Add three lines of small black dots down the middle of the wavy stripes on the pot.

BE BOLD!

Make your cactus taller or thicker by adjusting the size of the cactus bulb. Or get creative with color and create your own unique pot decorations.

CACTUS

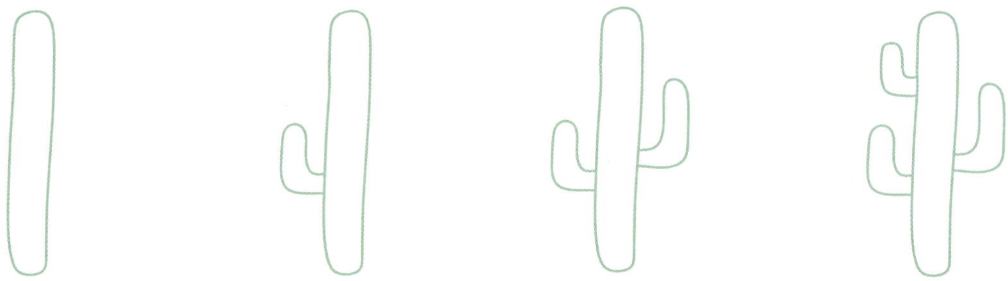

1. Start by drawing a tall, rounded oval for the cactus trunk.
2. Add a short L-shaped arm to the left of the trunk.
3. Add a taller arm with a backwards L above and on the right to balance the shape.
4. Add a smaller arm on the upper left side for extra character.

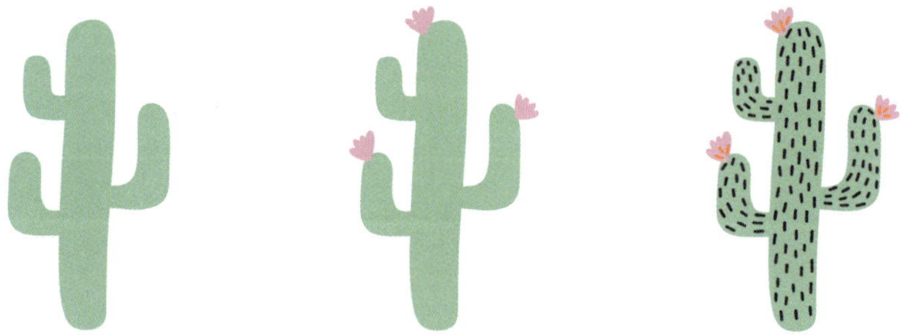

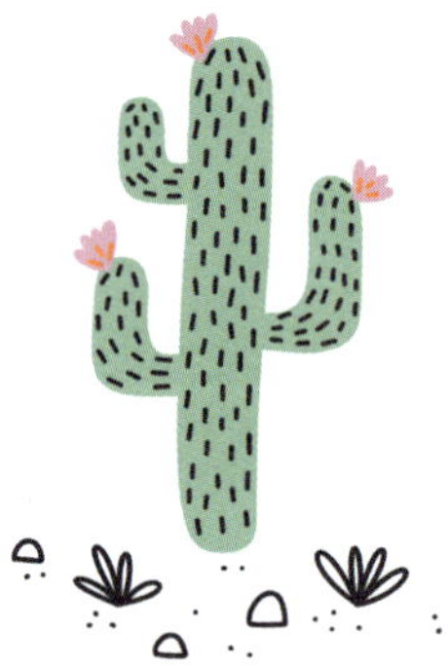

5. Color the full cactus shape in one solid shade.
6. Add small four-petal flowers on top of the bottom two arms and the main trunk.
7. Decorate the cactus with short black dashes that follow the direction of the trunk and arms for the spikes.
8. Add semicircle rocks, dots, and four-leaf desert plants around the base to decorate the ground.

BE BOLD!

Add more cactus arms or use bright colors for the flowers to make your desert scene pop.

MUSHROOM

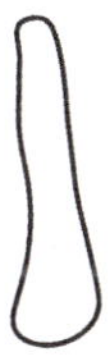

1. Start by drawing the mushroom stem with a long, wobbly oval that's wider at the base.

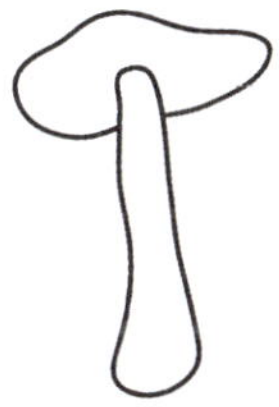

2. Add the top of the mushroom with a wide, wavy oval.

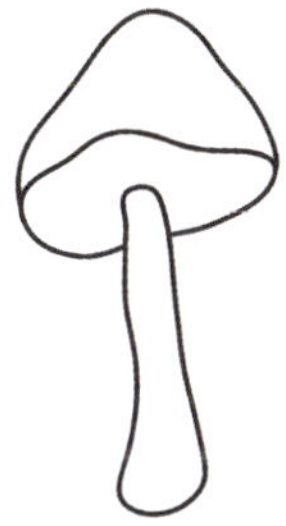

3. Add the cap with a bumpy, triangular shape.

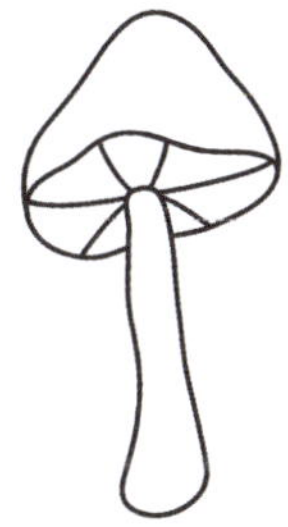

4. Draw the gills using straight lines under the cap, spreading out from the stem.

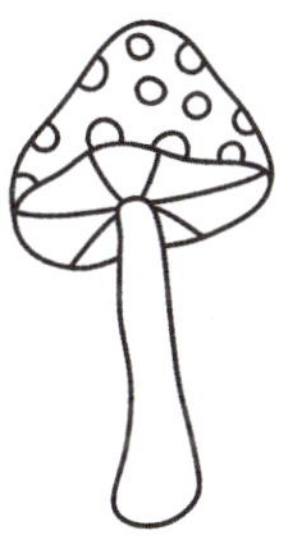

5. Draw small circles and partial circles on the cap of the mushroom.

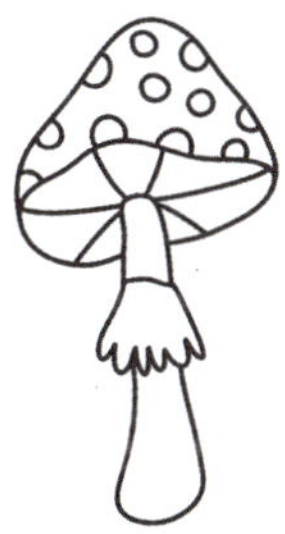

6. Near the upper third of the stem, draw a trapezoid with a bunch of U shapes on the bottom.

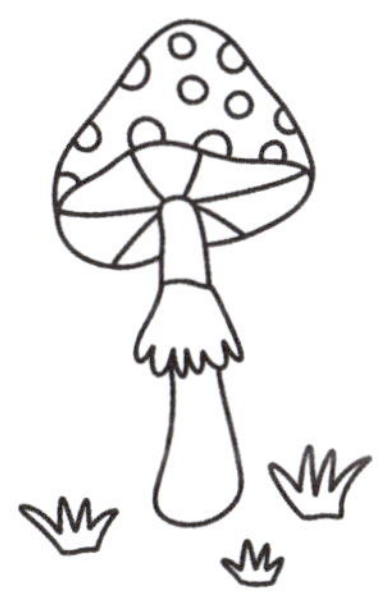

7. Add small tufts of grass in varying sizes with four spikes and a flat base.

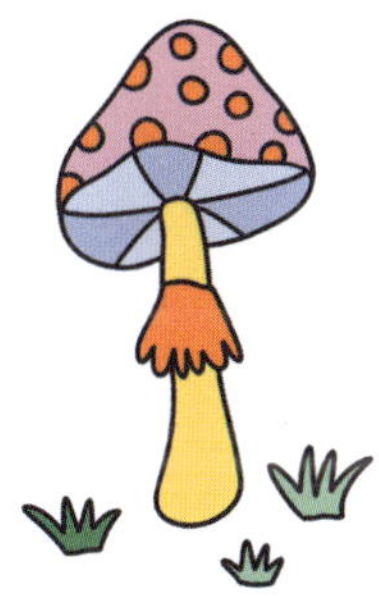

8. Color the cap, stem, and gills—don't be afraid to go bright!

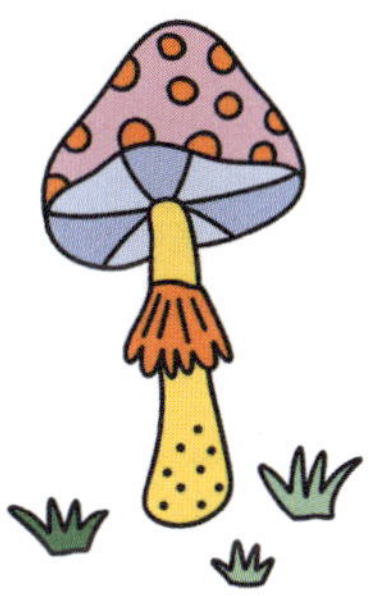

9. Decorate with some lines on the trapezoid and dots on the bottom of the stem.

BE BOLD!

Give your mushroom a magical twist by adding sparkles or even tiny windows to turn it into a fairy house!

MUSHROOM CLUSTER

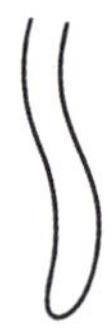

1. Start by drawing the stem with a long, wobbly oval that's open at the top.

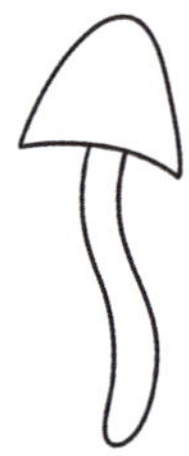

2. Add a curved triangle to make the mushroom top.

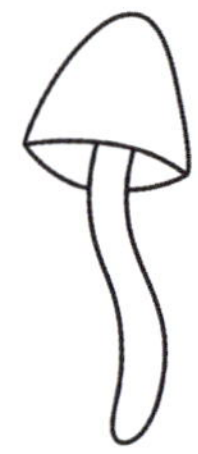

3. Add two curved lines under the mushroom top that connect to the mushroom stem.

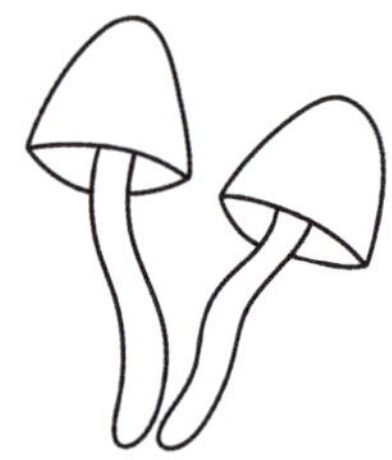

4. Repeat steps 1 to 4 to draw a second mushroom on the right.

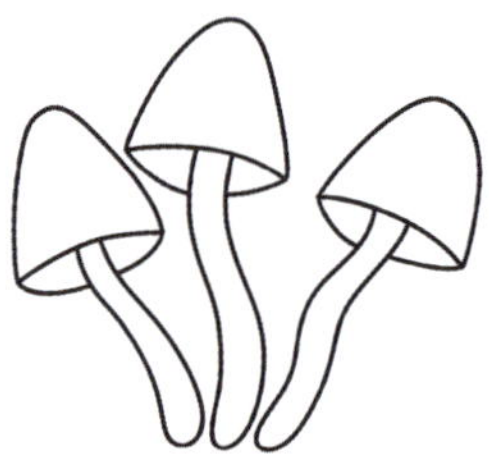

5. Repeat steps 1 to 4 to draw a third mushroom on the left.

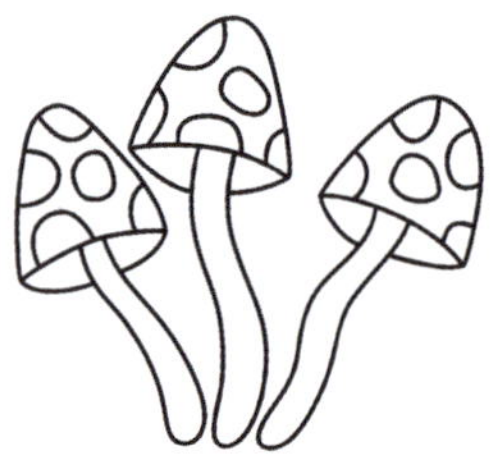

6. Add a bunch of wobbly ovals and semicircles to the mushroom tops.

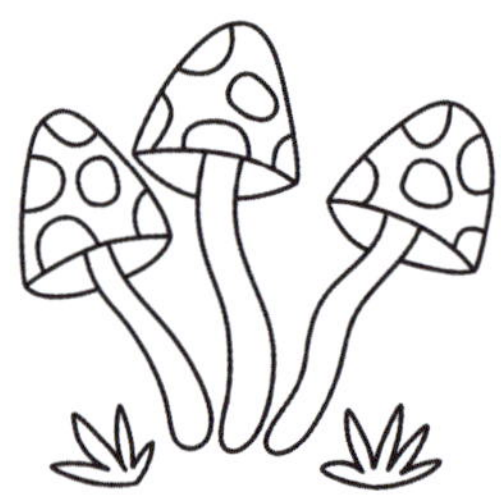

7. Draw little tufts of grass around the base of the stems.

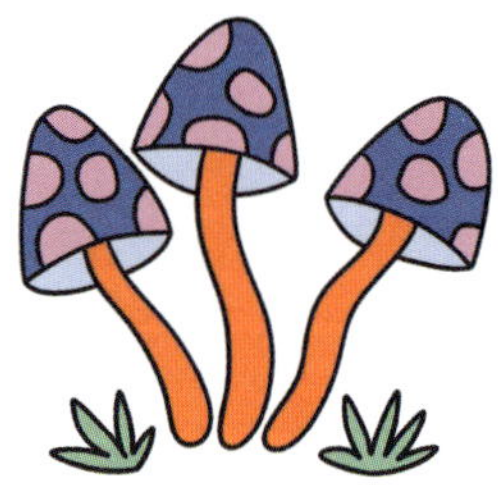

8. Fill in with color!

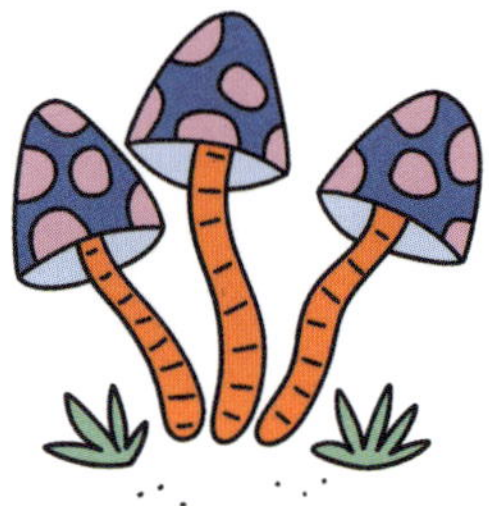

9. Decorate the mushroom stems with dashes and add dots on the ground.

BE BOLD!

Fill in your mushroom scene with a little snail on top of a mushroom or bugs on the ground.

HANGING PLANT

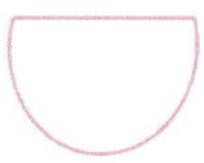

1. Start with a semicircle for the planter.

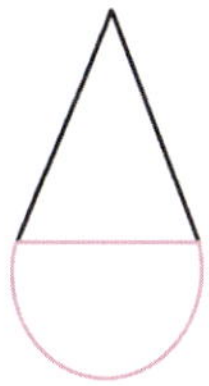

2. Draw an upside-down V shape on top of the semicircle.

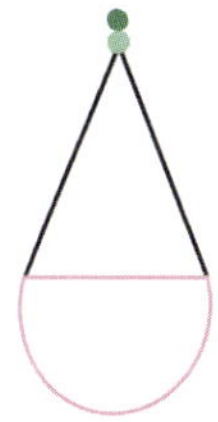

3. Add two stacked circles on top of the V point.

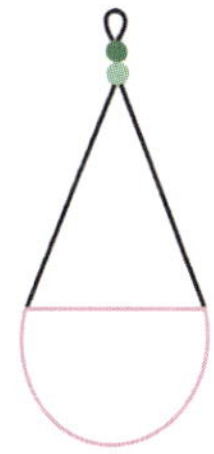

4. Draw an upside-down teardrop shape above the circles.

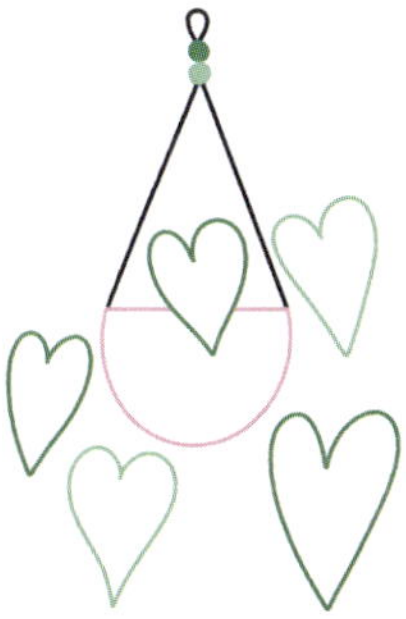

5. Draw five heart-shaped leaves of varying sizes around the planter.

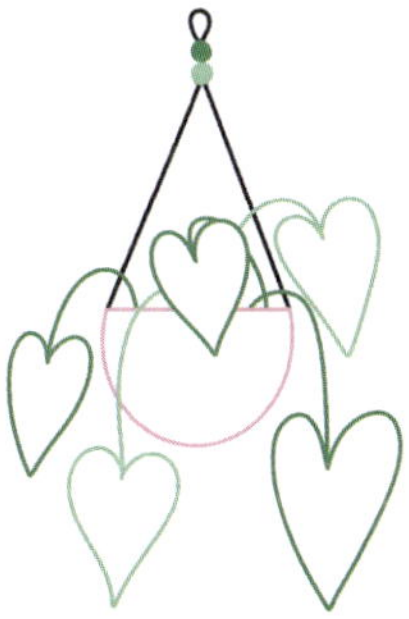

6. Connect the leaves to the top of the planter with curved lines.

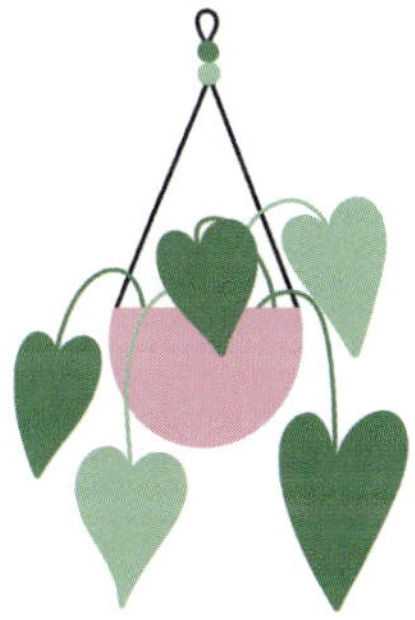

7. Fill in the planter and leaves with color!

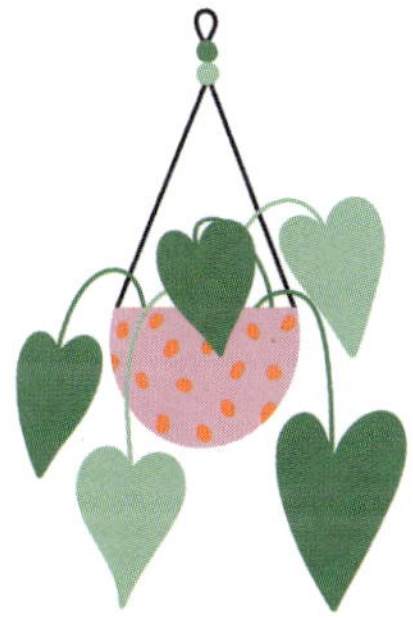

8. Decorate the planter with ovals.

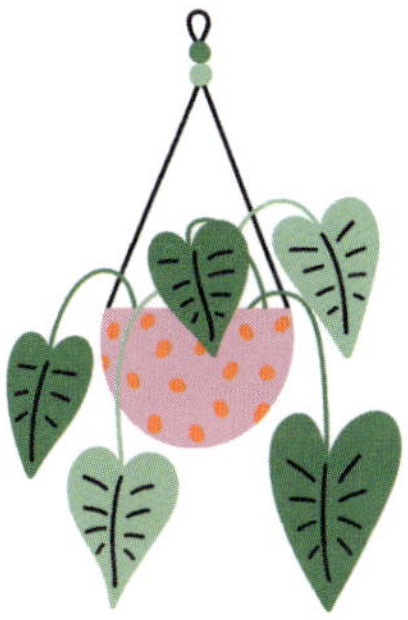

9. Decorate the leaves with a vertical line down the center and short horizontal dashes along the sides.

BE BOLD!

Decorate your leaves with dots like a spotted pothos plant or create your own decorations on the planter with the colors of your choice.

HANGING VINES

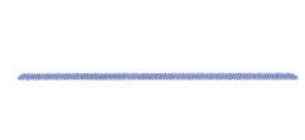

1. Start with a horizontal line in the center of the page.

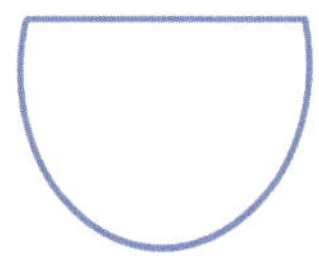

2. Draw a curved U shape under the line to create a semicircle.

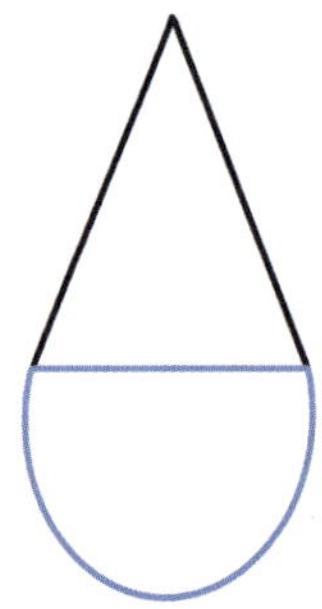

3. Add an upside-down V on top of the semicircle.

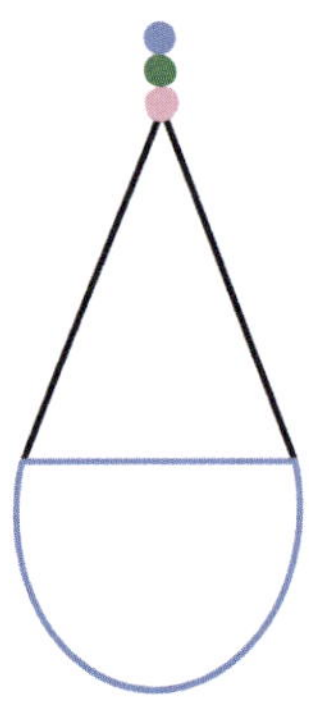

4. Add three stacked circles on top of the V point.

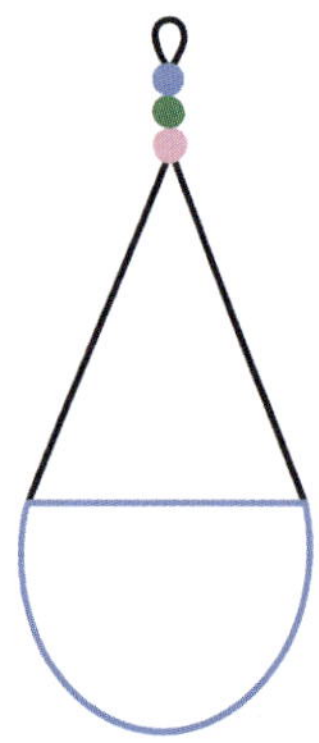

5. Draw an upside-down teardrop above the circles.

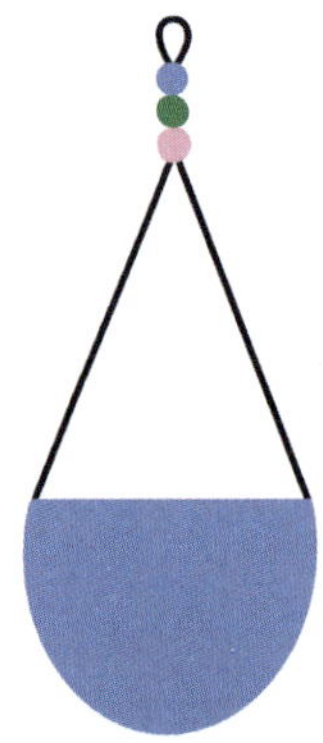

6. Fill in the planter pot with color.

BE BOLD!

Create your own plant by drawing different leaf shapes for your vines. Try pointed leaves, big leaves, heart-shaped leaves, and more!

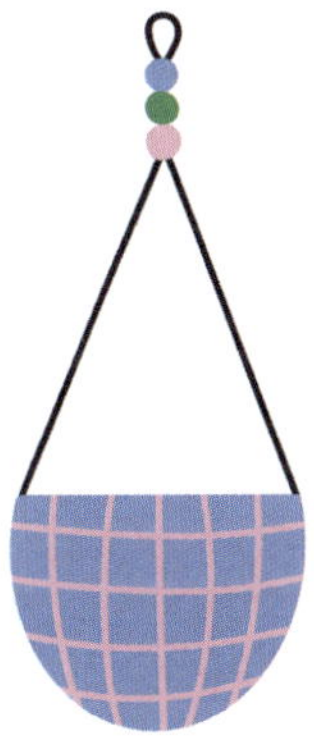

7. Decorate the planter pot with horizontal and vertical lines to make a grid pattern.

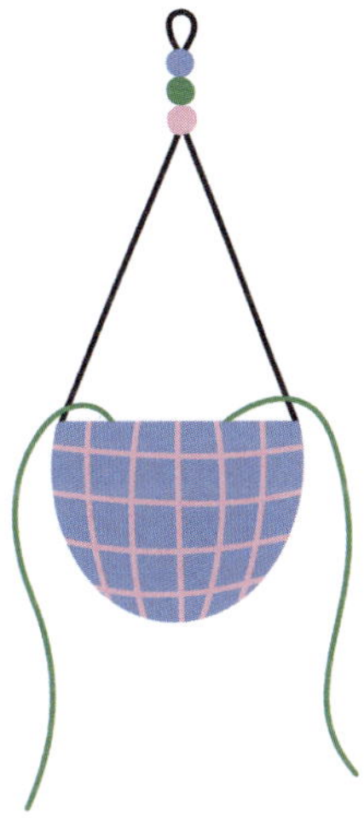

8. Draw two wavy lines that trail down from the top of the planter.

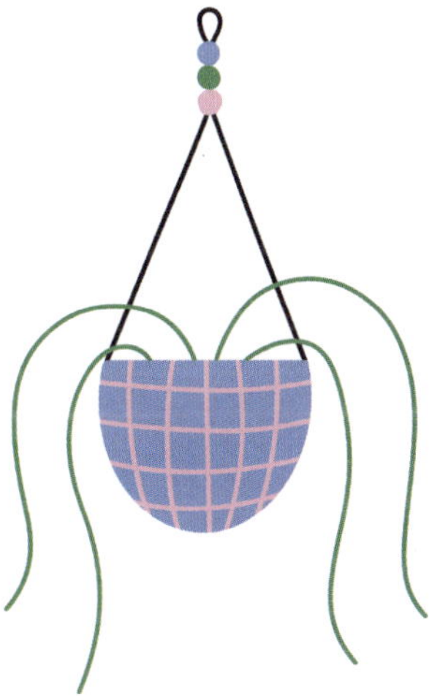

9. Draw two more wavy lines above the first two, starting near the center of the planter.

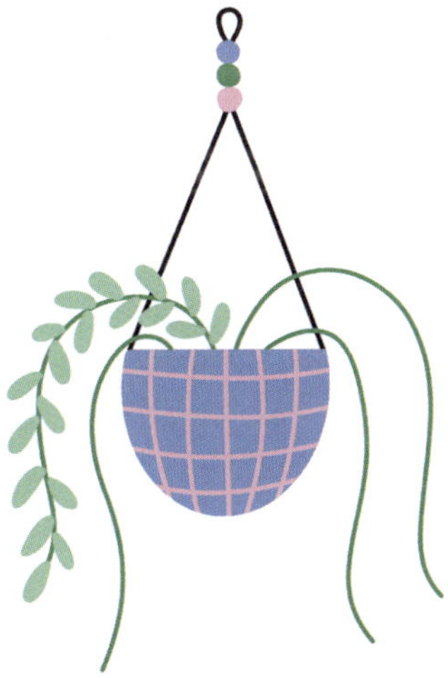

10. Draw a series of small teardrop-shaped leaves along one wavy vine.

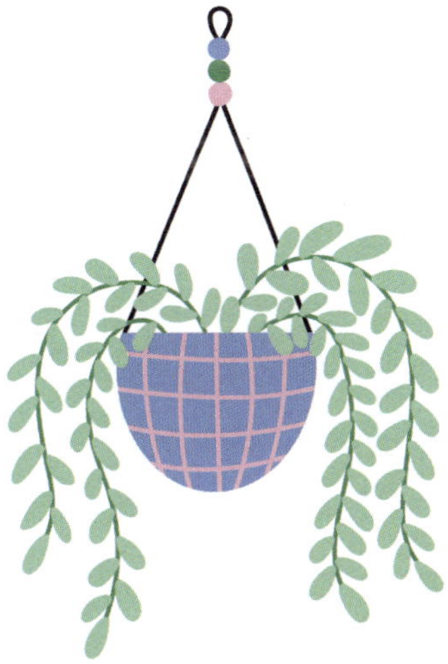

11. Repeat step 10 for the rest of the vines.

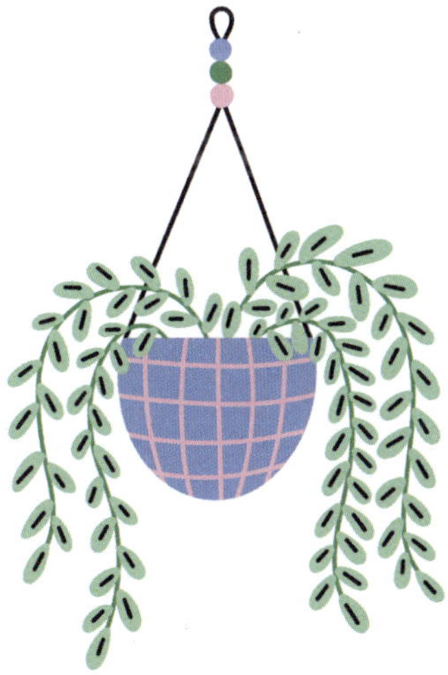

12. Decorate the leaves with a black line down the middle.

FLOWER MEADOW

1. Start with a long horizontal line near the bottom of the page.

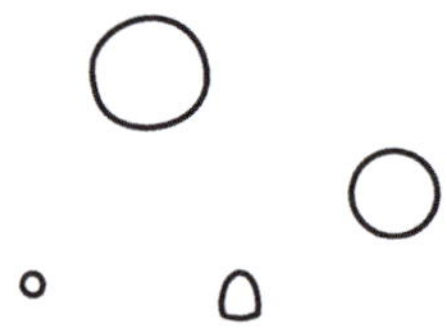

2. Draw three circles—one big, one medium, and one tiny. Then add a small semicircle.

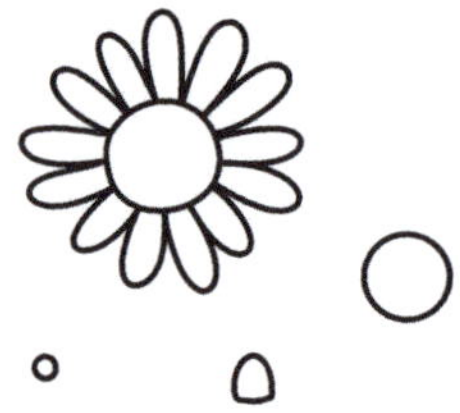

3. Surround the big circle with long oval petals of varying lengths.

4. Draw thinner petals around the medium circle.

5. Draw big petals around the tiny circle that are all different sizes and taper at the end.

6. Draw oval petals around only the curved edge of the semicircle.

BE BOLD!

Make your flower field extra colorful by using a wide range of colors or make different types of flowers in your field by experimenting with the petal and center shapes and sizes.

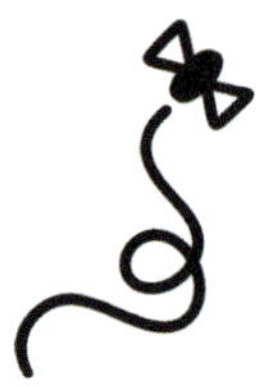

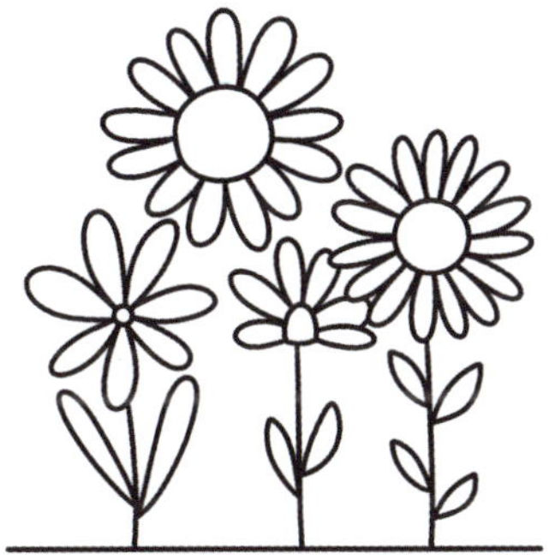

7. Give the three lower flowers stems, each with two to four unique leaves.

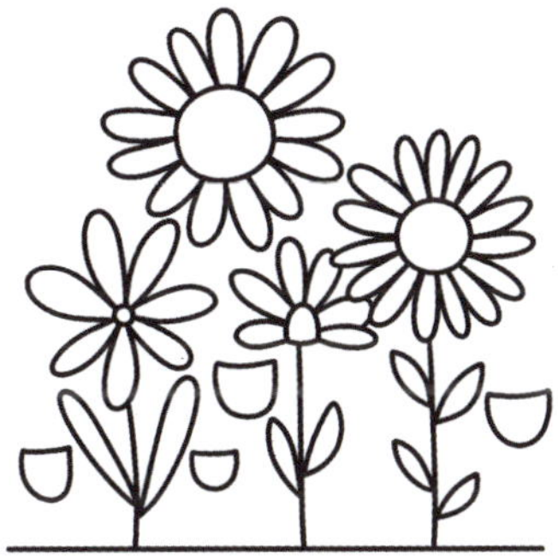

8. Add four small semicircles around the three stems.

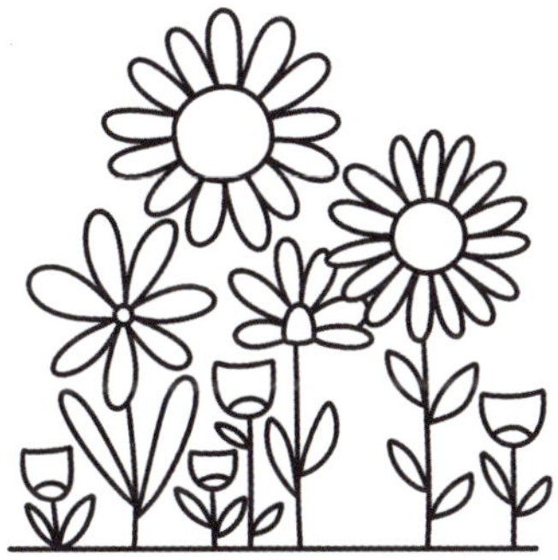

9. Draw a downward curved line at the bottom of each semicircle. Then give each a stem and some little leaves.

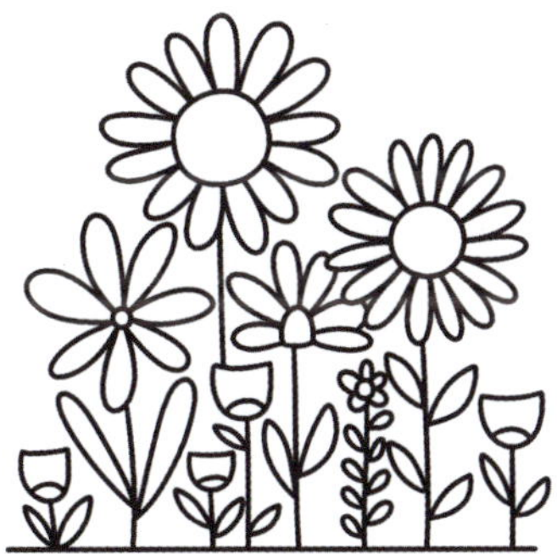

10. Add a stem to the largest and tallest flower. Then create a short five-petal flower to the left of the two right-most flowers with lots of leaves on its stem.

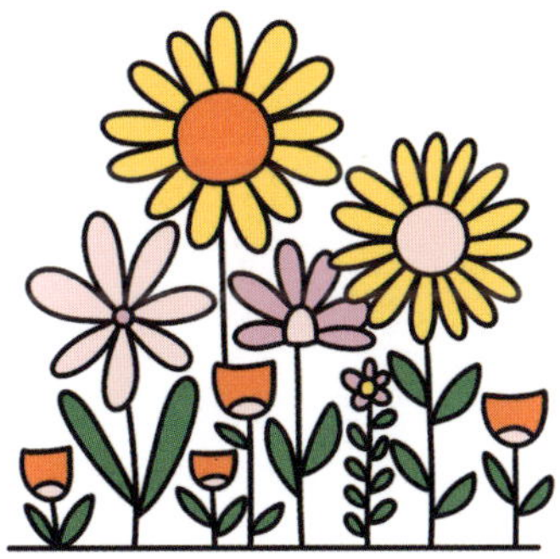

11. Color in all the flowers and leaves!

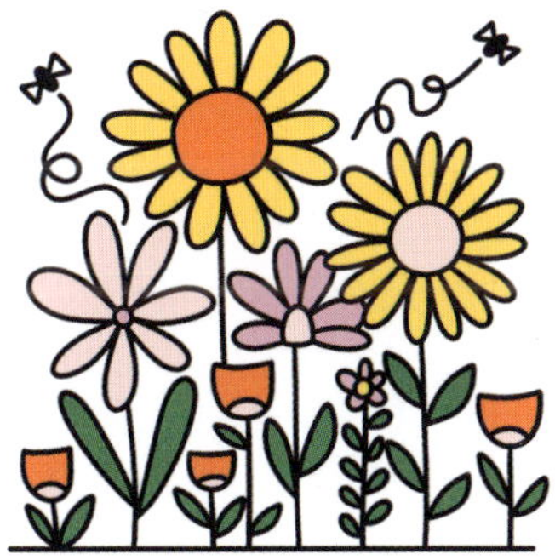

12. Add two black ovals with little triangle wings and squiggly doodle lines underneath to make little bees flying above the flowers.

SUNSET FLOWER

1. Start by drawing a U shape with four scallops on top.

2. Add a second, wider scalloped layer with six scallops around the first.

3. Draw a third and even wider scalloped layer, again with six scallops.

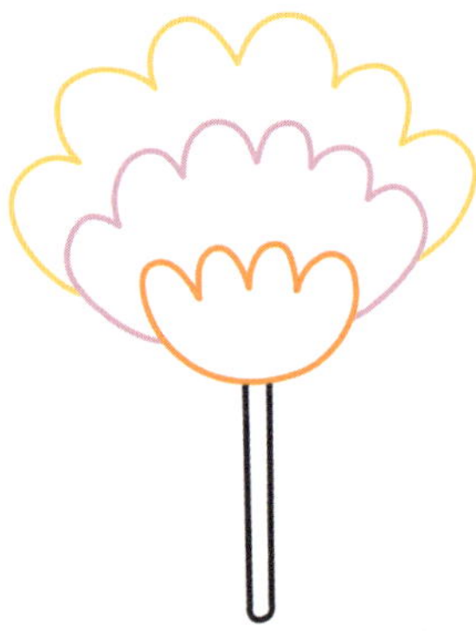

4. Add a thin, U-shaped line for the stem.

5. Sketch two large teardrop-shaped leaves on each side of the stem, curving slightly outward.

6. Bring your flower to life with color!

7. Decorate the flower with dots and lines.

BE BOLD!

Vary the number of scallops in each petal layer or tilt the whole flower to one side for a fresh look.

CROWN FLOWER

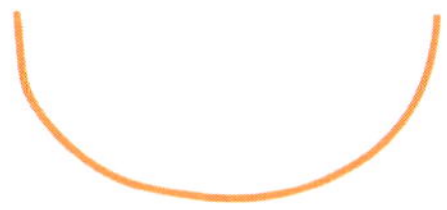

1. Draw a wide U shape for the bottom of the flower.

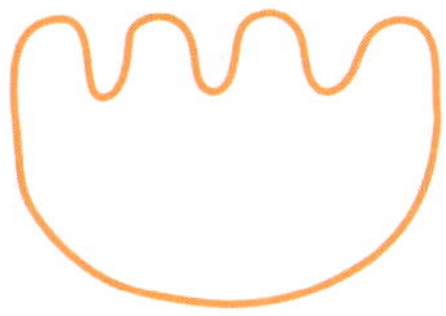

2. Close the U shape with four soft bumps across the top to form the crown shape.

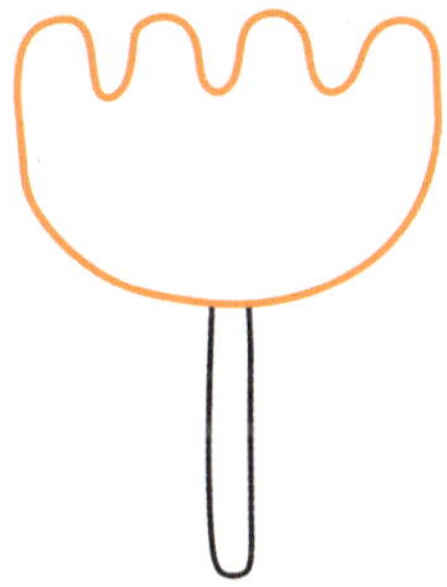

3. Draw a U-shaped line for the stem.

4. Add a rounded leaf on each side of the stem.

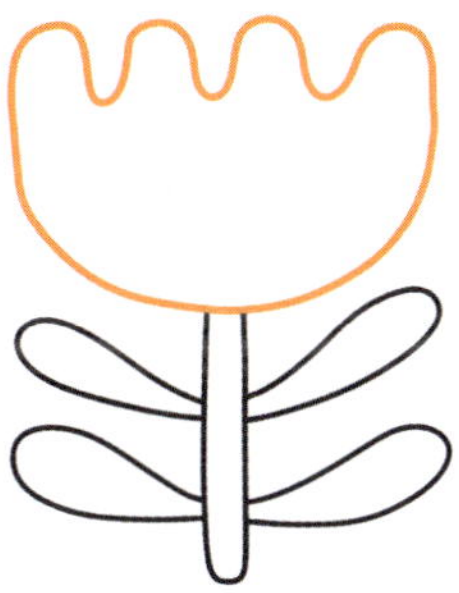

5. Draw another, slightly larger pair of leaves below the first pair.

6. Bring your flower to life with color!

7. Draw four dots floating above each crown point like little jewels.

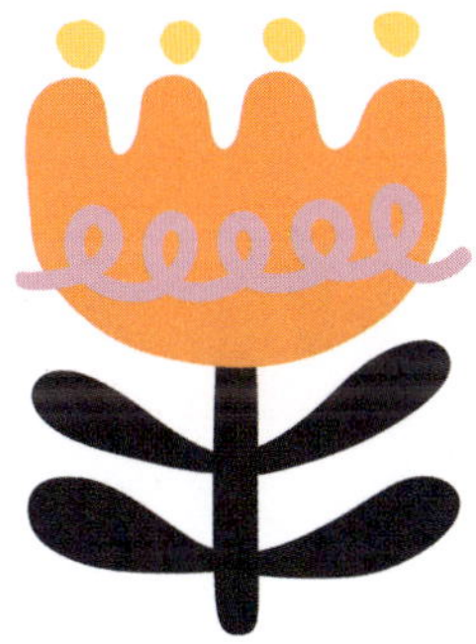

8. Decorate with a looping line across the middle of the flower for that fun folk style.

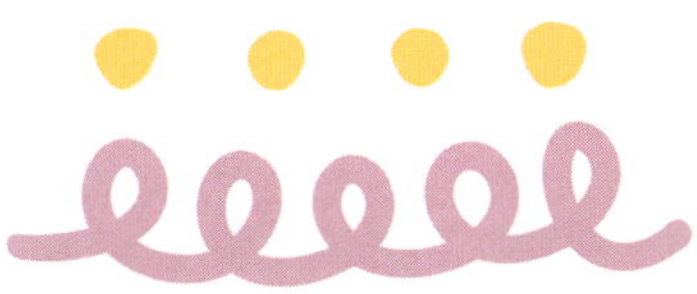

BE BOLD!

Play with different line styles—try zigzags, double loops, or a row of dots instead of the looped line.

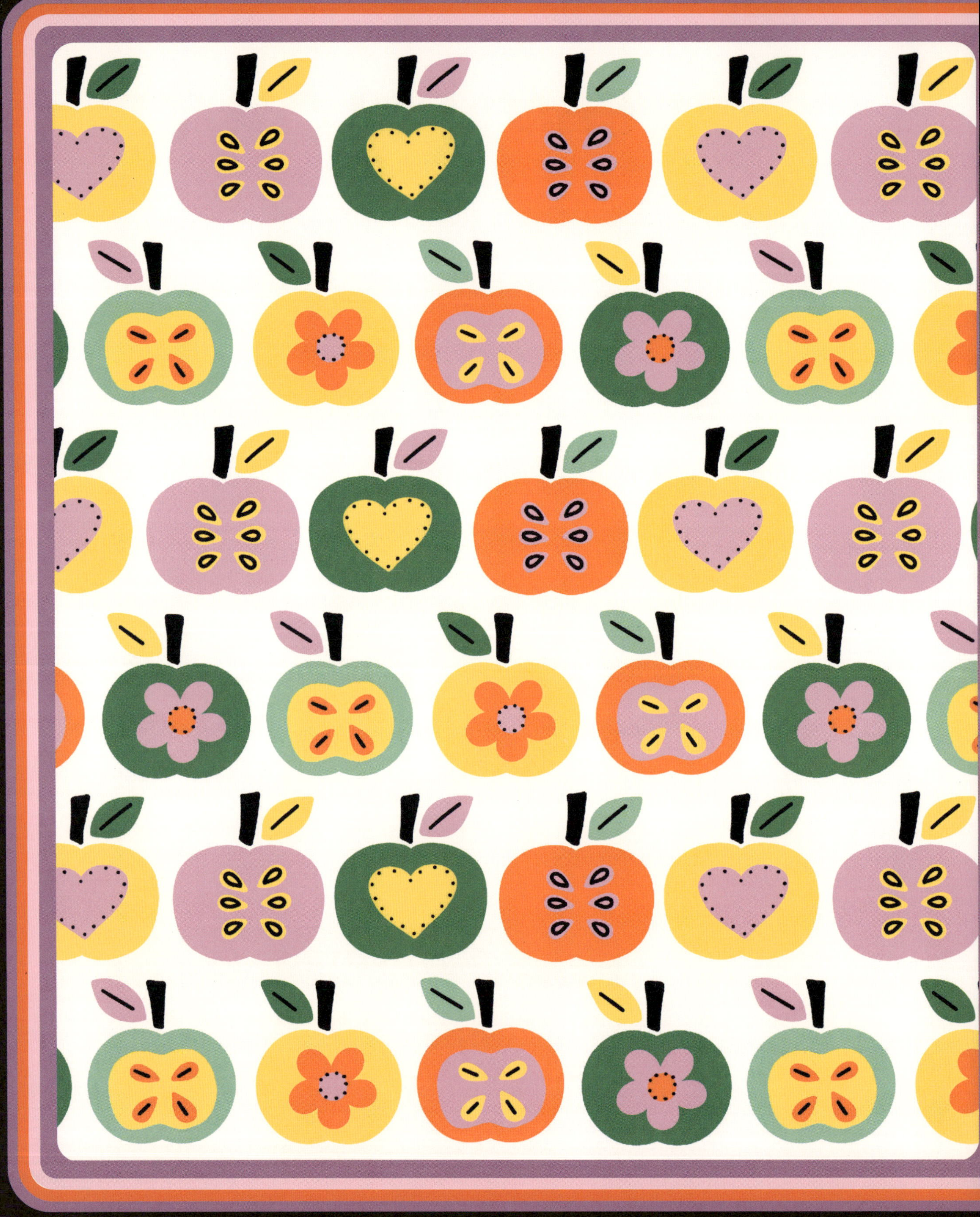

FRUITS, VEGGIES & SNACKS

APPLES

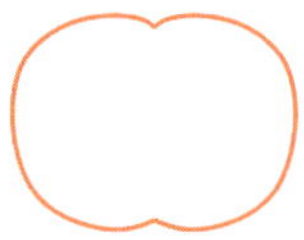

1. Start with an oval shape, with a divot in the center top and bottom, on the left of the page.

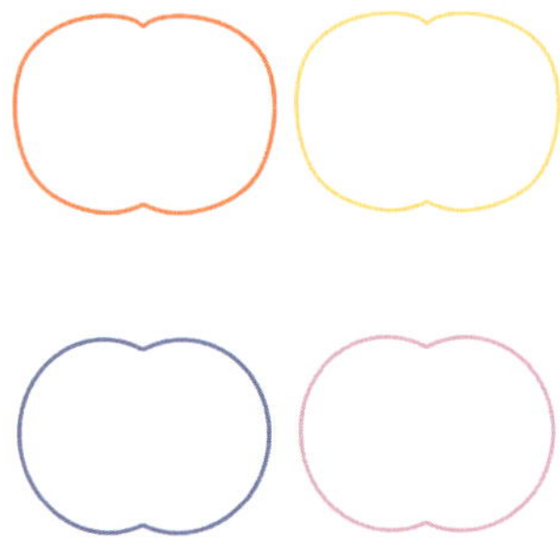

2. Repeat step 1 three times to create two rows of two apples, for a total of four apples.

3. Color in the apples!

4. Add six teardrop-shaped seeds to the top left apple with their points facing the center.

5. Draw a heart in the center of the top right apple.

6. Draw a five-petal flower in the bottom left apple.

BE BOLD!

Create different folk-art–inspired decorations for your apples with multicolor lines, stripes, birds, or even little happy faces.

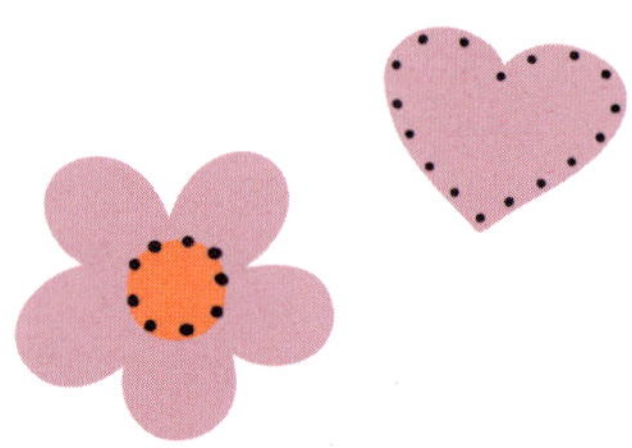

7. Add a wobbly oval shape in the center of the bottom right apple.

8. Add four teardrop-shaped seeds to the bottom right apple with their points facing the center.

9. Draw a thick black stem on the top of each apple.

10. Draw a pointed leaf on each apple, with the top two on the right of the stem and the bottom two on the left.

11. Add details like a line through the center of each leaf, lines and teardrop shapes inside the seeds, and dots around the heart and flower center.

LEMON

1. Start with a large uneven oval near the center of the page.

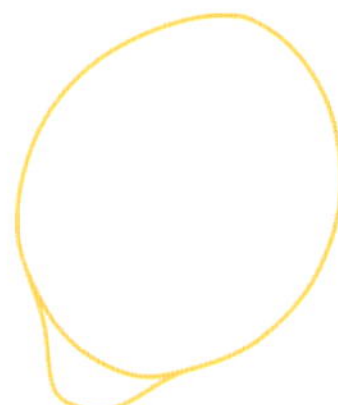

2. Add a slightly pointed curve to the bottom end.

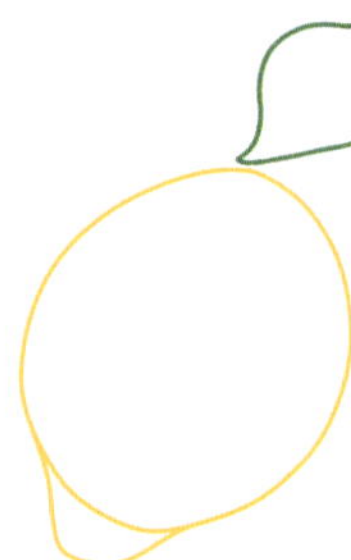

3. Draw a curvy leaf that comes to a point at both ends on the top of the lemon.

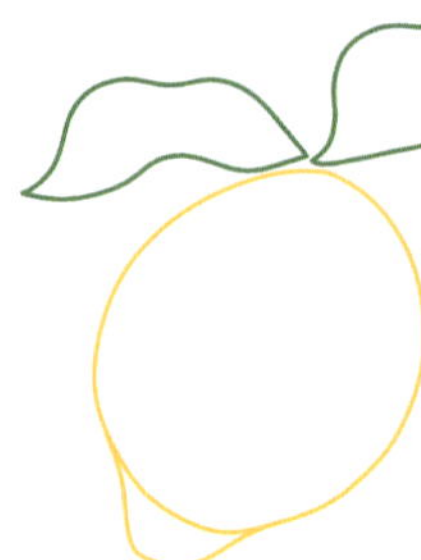

4. Add a longer wavy leaf to the left of the first leaf.

5. Fill in the colors!

6. Add a black stem between the two leaves.

7. Add four long wobbly shapes in varying sizes at the top of the lemon for highlights.

8. Draw a small five-petal flower with pointed tips under the right leaf.

9. Add texture details with wavy black lines through the center of each leaf, small circles at the bottom of the lemon, and dashes around the center of the flower.

BE BOLD!

Draw a whole branch of lemons by creating a black wavy branch across your page and filling it in with lemons, leaves, and blossoms.

PAPAYA

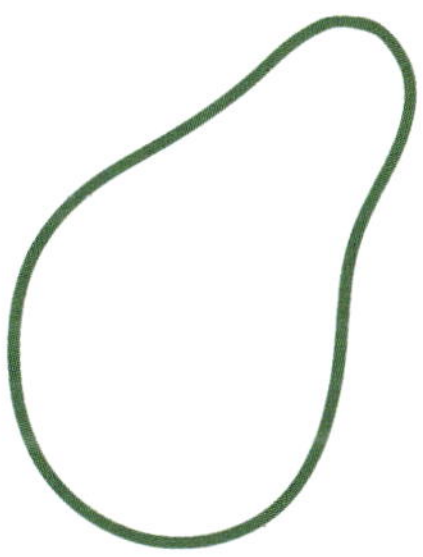

1. Start with a wavy teardrop shape with the top tilted to the right.

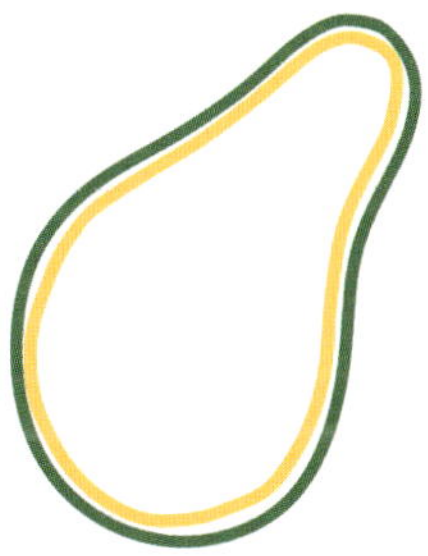

2. Draw a slightly smaller teardrop within the teardrop.

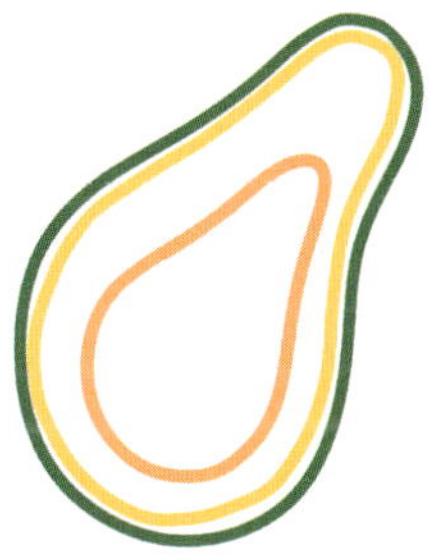

3. Draw a much smaller teardrop within the second teardrop.

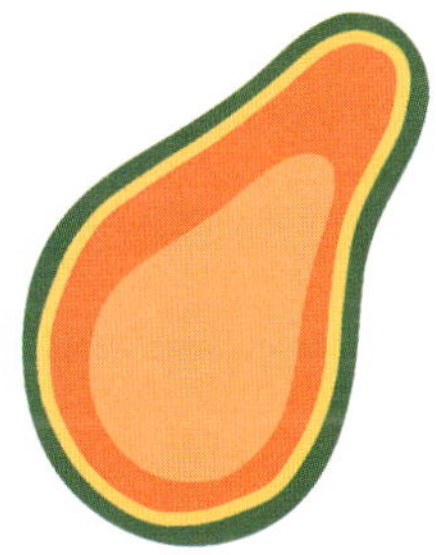

4. Fill in the layers with colors.

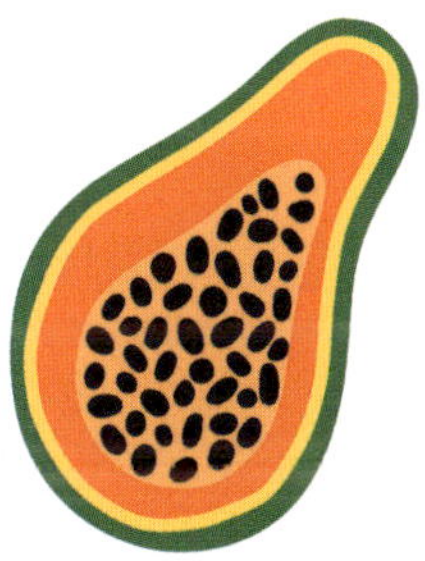

5. Within the center teardrop, draw a bunch of little black ovals and circles for the seeds.

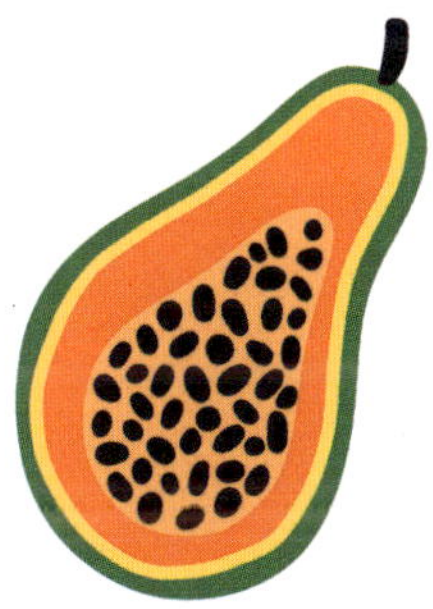

6. Add a curved black stem, that is wide at the top and narrow at the bottom, to the top of the papaya.

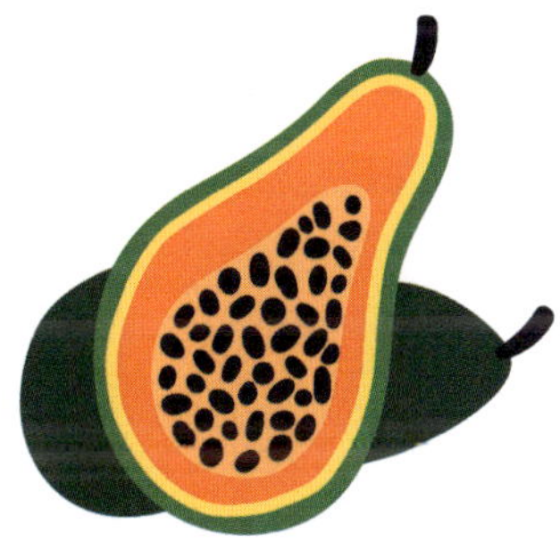

7. Draw an oval with a black stem for a second papaya that is partially hidden behind the first.

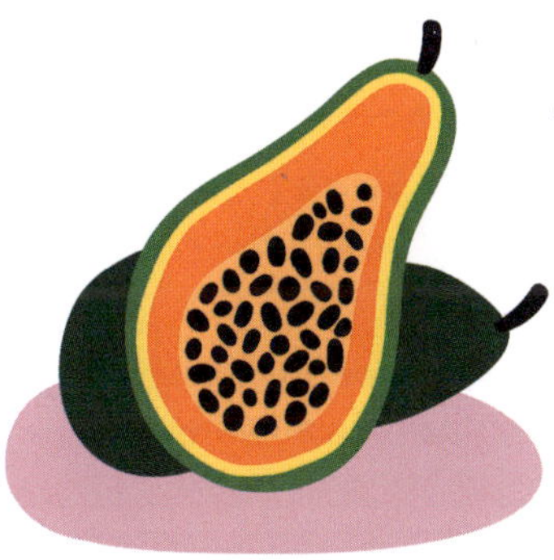

8. Add colorful details like a circular shadow below the papayas.

BE BOLD!

Use bright, unnatural colors for your papayas for a funky and groovy look.

CHERRIES

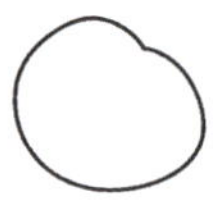

1. Start with a circular shape with a divot in the top right on the bottom left of the page.

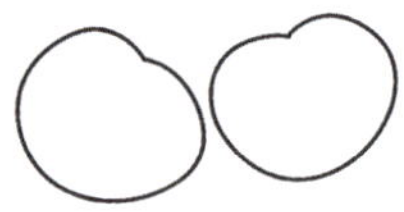

2. Draw the same shape mirrored on the right.

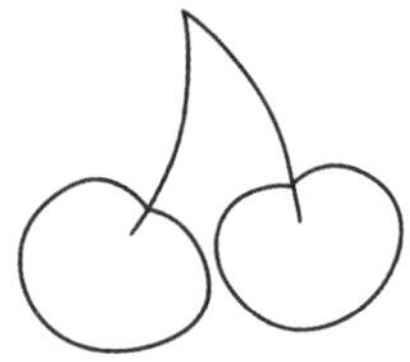

3. Draw two curved stems that go through the center of the divots and meet at the top.

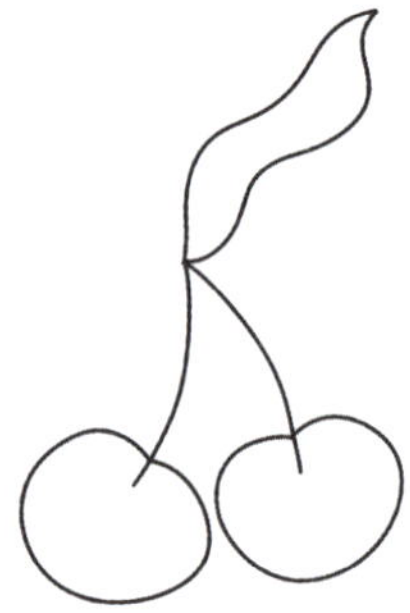

4. Add a large wavy leaf at the top of the stem.

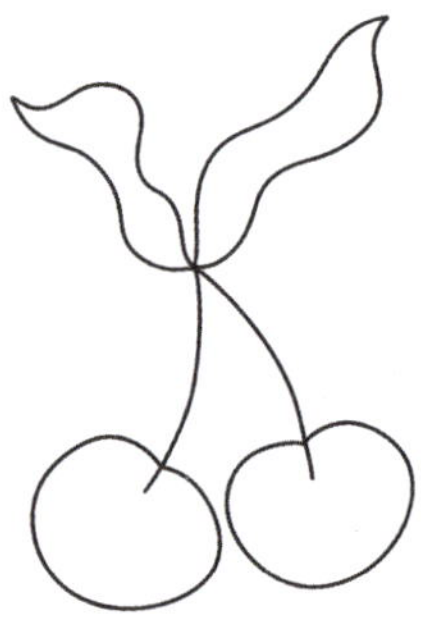

5. Draw another leaf on the left.

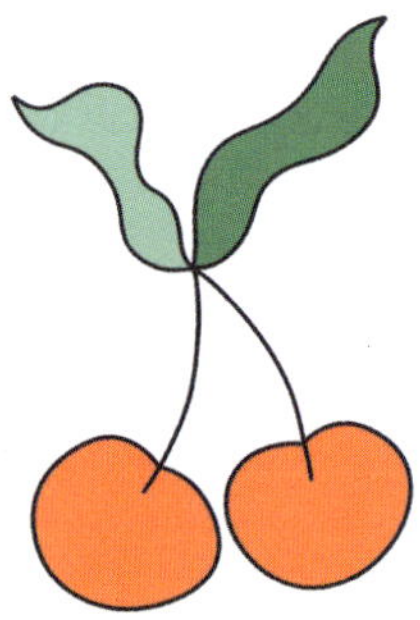

6. Fill in the cherries with color.

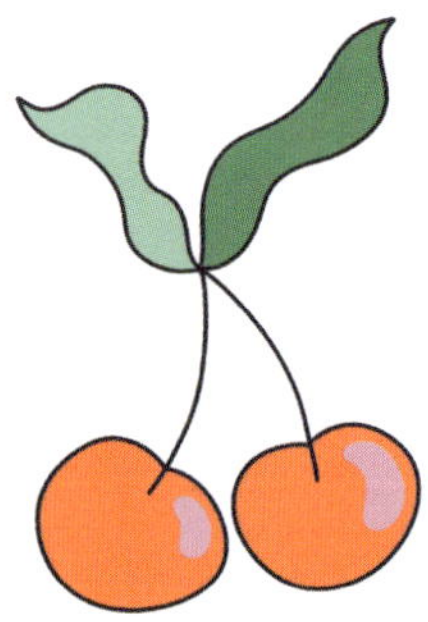

7. Add bean-shaped highlights to the cherries.

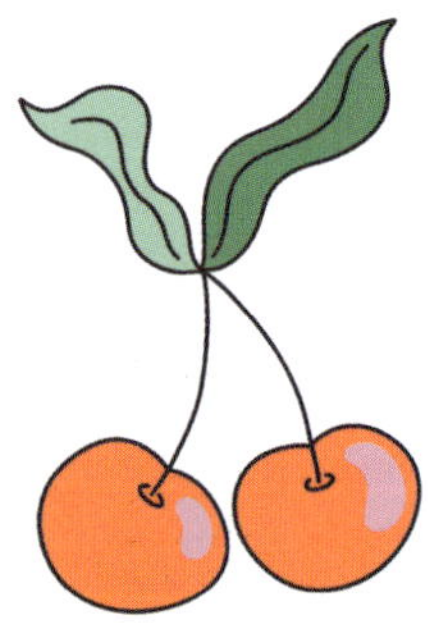

8. Draw a black wavy line through the center of each leaf and a black C-shaped line around the base of the stem of each cherry.

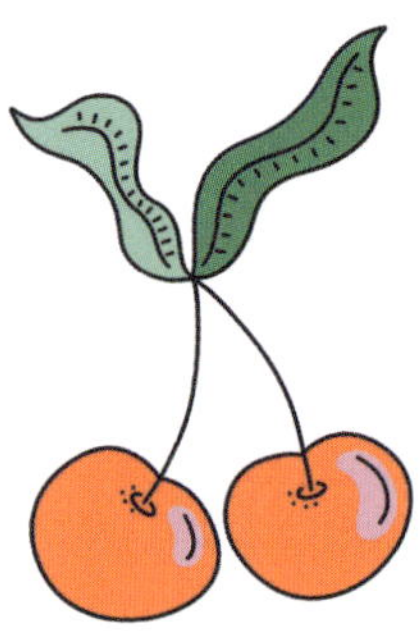

9. Add extra details with dashes inside the leaves and dots around the base of the stems. Add dimension with a black curved line near the edge of the cherry highlights.

BE BOLD!

Cherries come in lots of shades and colors. Make your cherries an extra dark red or color them in with a yellow and red gradient like Rainier cherries.

STRAWBERRIES

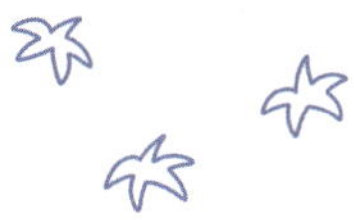

1. Draw three wonky star-shaped calyxes.

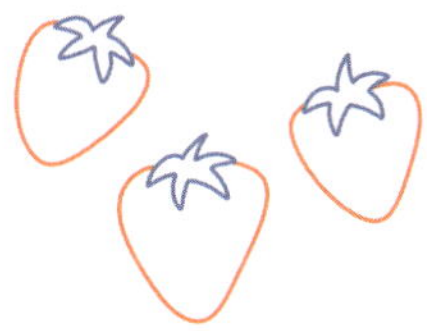

2. Connect rounded triangles to each calyx.

3. Fill in the colors!

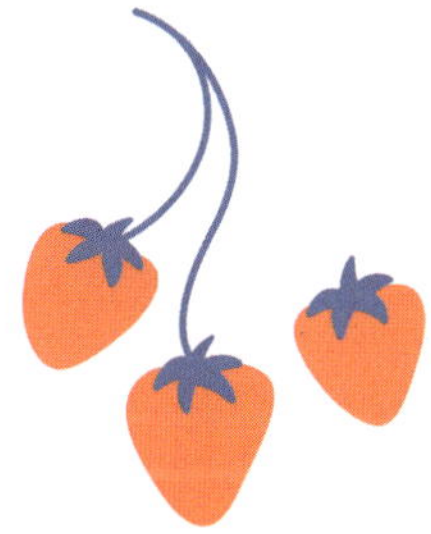

4. Draw two wavy lines starting from the center of the middle and left strawberries and connecting at the end.

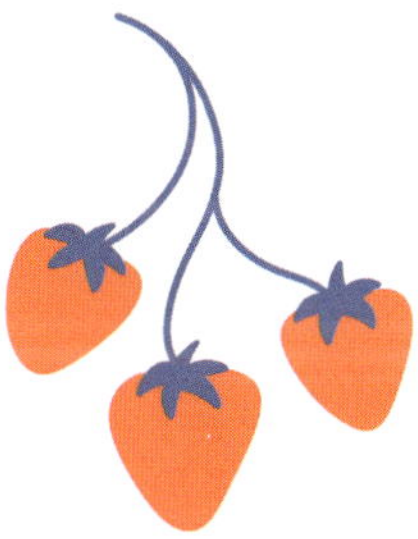

5. Draw a wavy line from the center of the right strawberry and connect it to the middle stem.

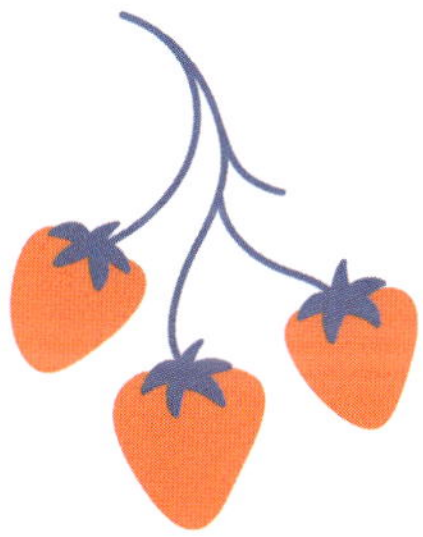

6. Draw a short stem just above the right stem.

7. Draw a five-petal flower at the end of the short stem, with a second flower above.

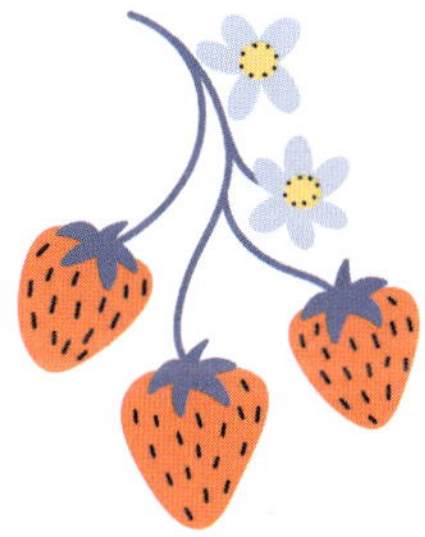

8. Add texture details like short black dashes for the strawberry seeds and black dots around the flower centers.

BE BOLD!

Gardens are full of little creatures that love strawberries. Add a tiny bug snacking on the berries or a butterfly visiting the flowers.

TOMATOES

1. Start with three wonky star-shaped calyxes.

2. Draw a circle below and attached to each calyx.

3. Fill in the tomatoes with colors!

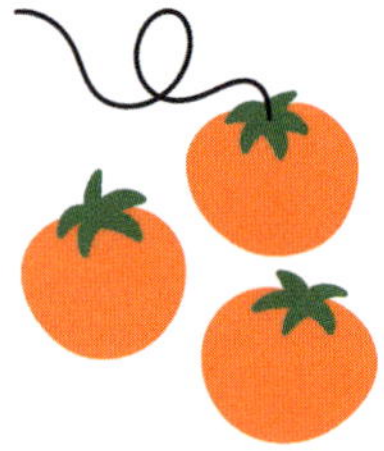

4. Draw a swirling black line from the top right tomato.

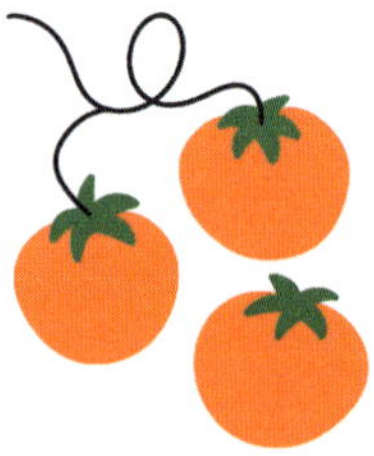

5. Draw a curved black line from the left tomato and connect it to the first.

6. Draw another swirling black line from the leaves of the bottom right tomato.

7. Add two fringed leaf shapes to the top tomato vines.

8. Add a black line through the center of each leaf as well as curved highlights and black dots to each tomato.

BE BOLD!

Make your tomatoes different sizes or a variety of colors like yellow, orange, or green. Or, see how many tomatoes you can draw on a single vine.

POPSICLE

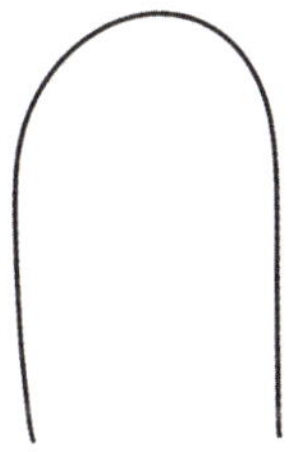

1. Start with an upside-down U shape.

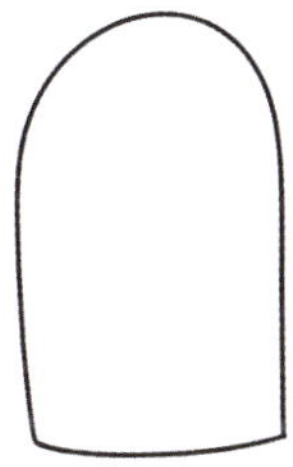

2. Close the bottom of the U shape with a slightly curved horizontal line.

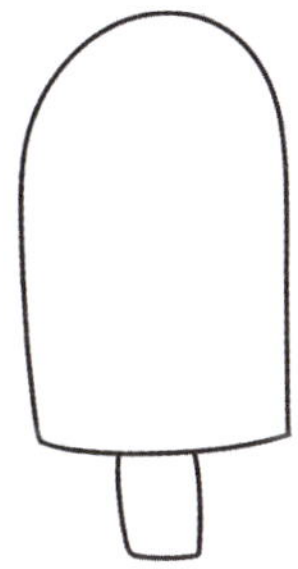

3. Add a rectangular stick under the Popsicle.

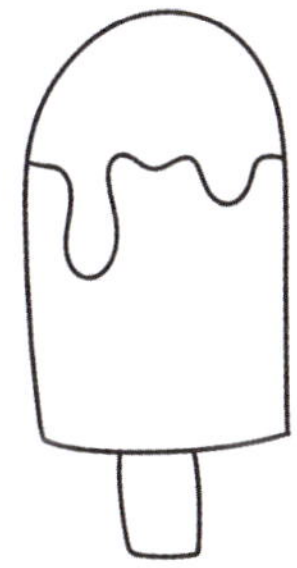

4. Draw a squiggly line of drips across the top of the Popsicle.

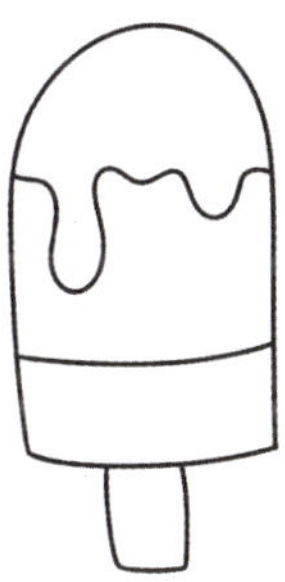

5. Add a slightly curved horizontal line across the lower half of the Popsicle.

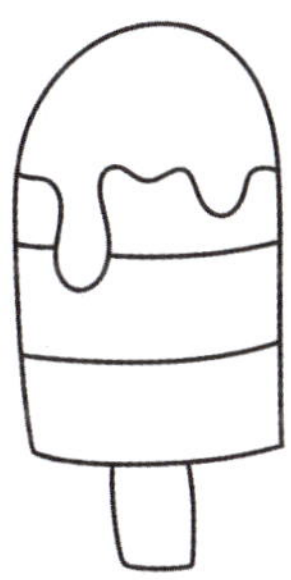

6. Add another slightly curved horizontal line across the top half, behind the drips.

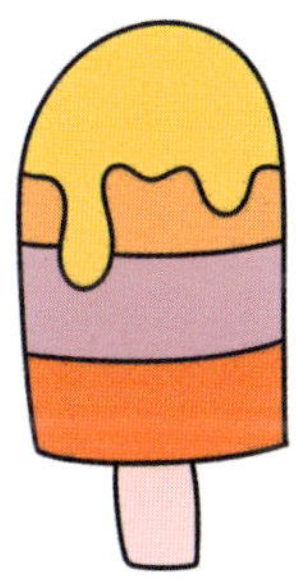

7. Fill in the colors, using a different color for each segment of the Popsicle.

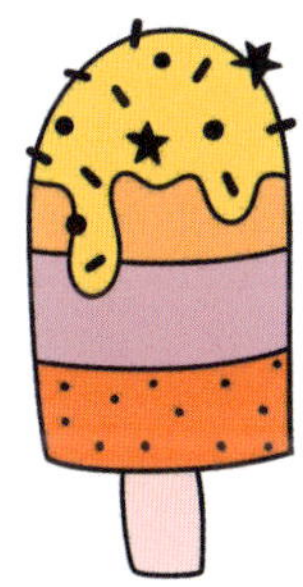

8. Add details like stars, sprinkles, and little dots for texture.

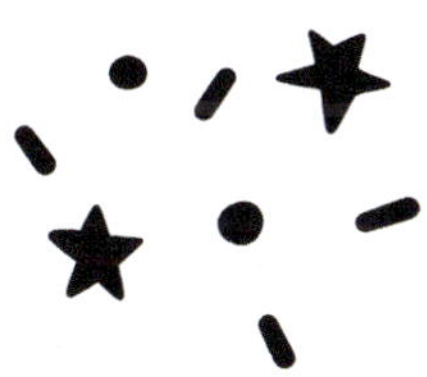

BE BOLD!

Use different colors to create different popsicle flavors or draw different textures in your Popsicle segments for things like fruit or candy inclusions.

BUBBLE TEA

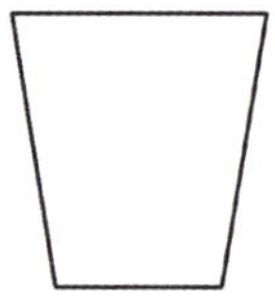

1. Start with a tall trapezoid-shaped cup.

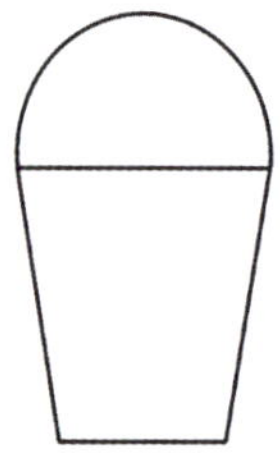

2. Draw a semicircle lid on top.

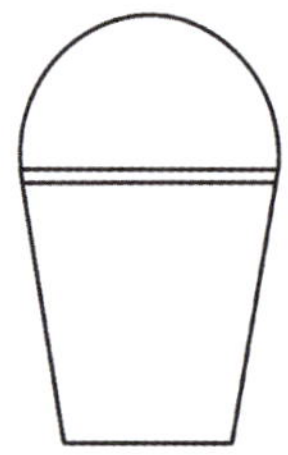

3. Draw a horizontal line just below the top horizontal line.

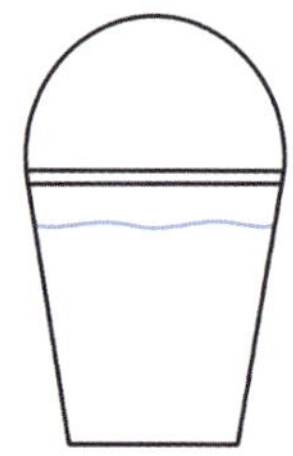

4. Draw a wavy horizontal line slightly below the second horizontal line.

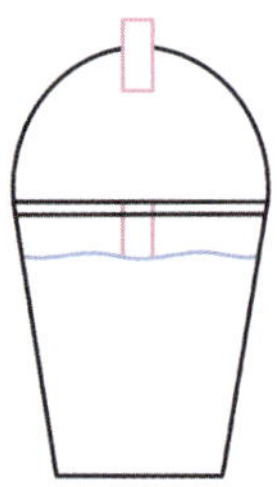

5. To make the straw, draw two vertical lines at the center of the cup from the wavy line to the top horizontal line, then add a short rectangle near the top of the lid.

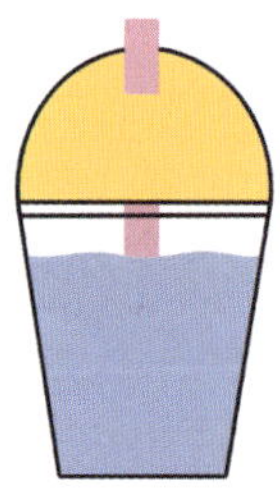

6. Color in the straw, the semicircle lid, and the tea under the wavy line.

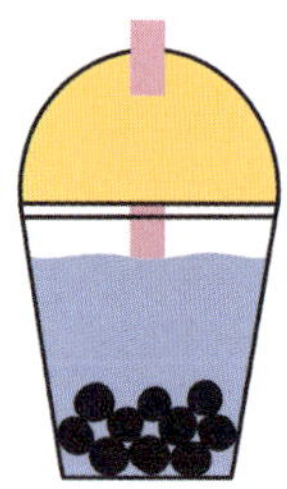

7. Add a bunch of large black circles at the bottom of the cup for the bubble tea pearls.

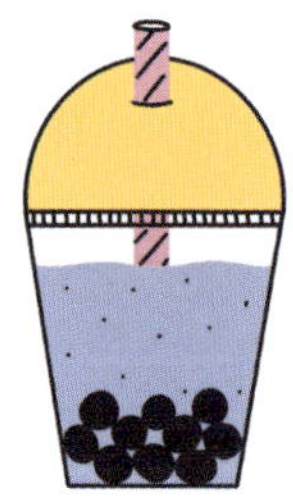

8. Add an oval at the top of the straw to create an opening and a curve at the bottom for the lid opening. Then add texture lines and dots to the straw, cup rim, and tea.

BE BOLD!

Use different colors for different tea flavors or add bubble tea extras to your cup like white rectangular shapes for coconut jelly or a cloud shape for a creamy foam or pudding topping.

CUPCAKE

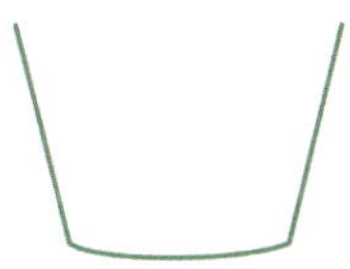

1. Draw a wide U shape with slanted sides for the cupcake wrapper.

2. Add a bumpy cloud shape on top for the frosting.

3. Fill in the colors!

4. Add two blue circular shapes on top of the pink cloud shape.

5. Draw a black line star shape in the center of each blue circle.

6. Draw scattered dashes across the pink shape to make sprinkles on the icing.

7. Draw four yellow hearts along the bottom of the cupcake wrapper.

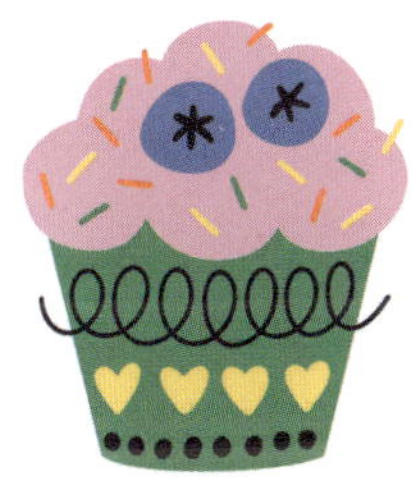

8. Add additional texture details to the wrapper like a swirling line and little black dots.

BE BOLD!

Use different colors of icing or base to make different cupcake flavors, or, instead of blueberries, draw different fruits or treats on top of your cupcake.

CAKE

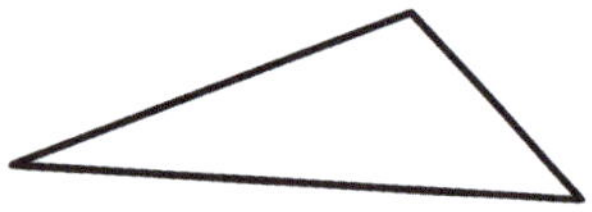

1. Start with a stretched triangle near the center of the page.

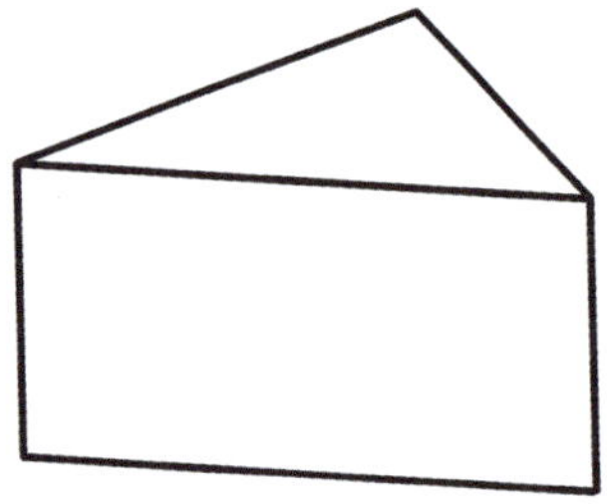

2. Draw a rectangle underneath the triangle.

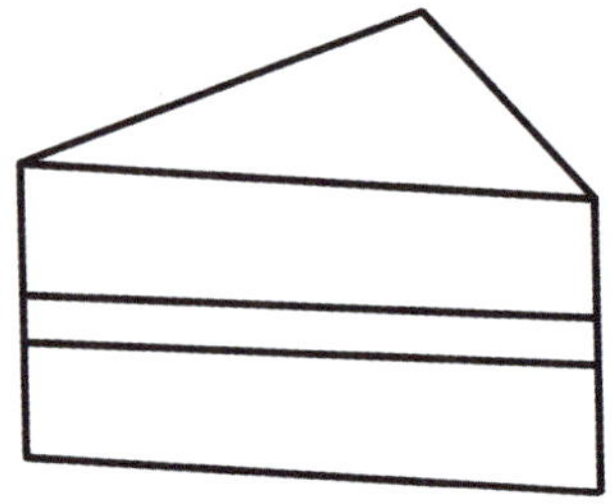

3. Draw a stripe using two horizontal lines through the center of the rectangle.

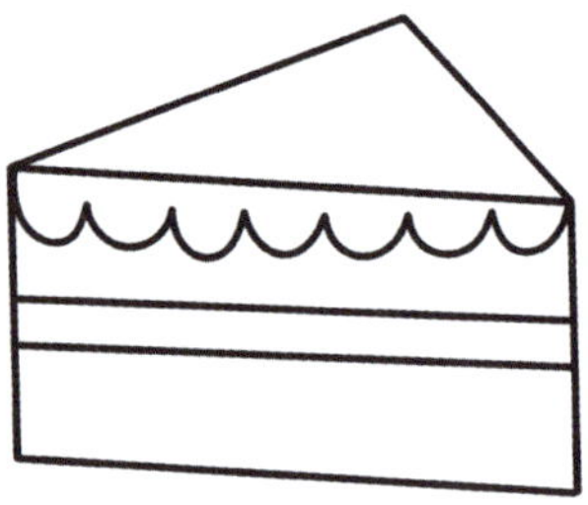

4. Draw a scalloped line along the top edge of the rectangle.

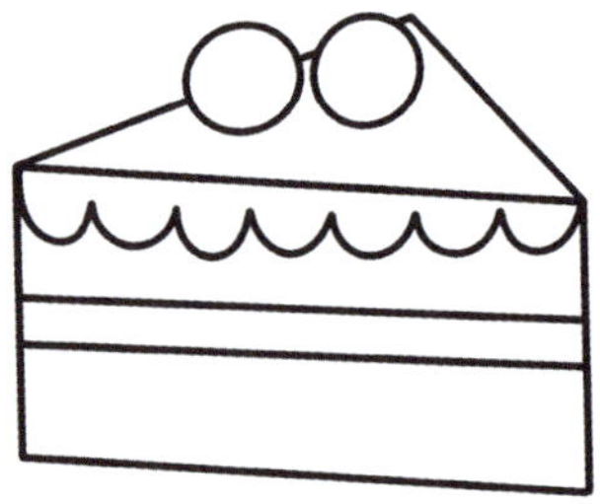

5. Add two circles to the top of the cake.

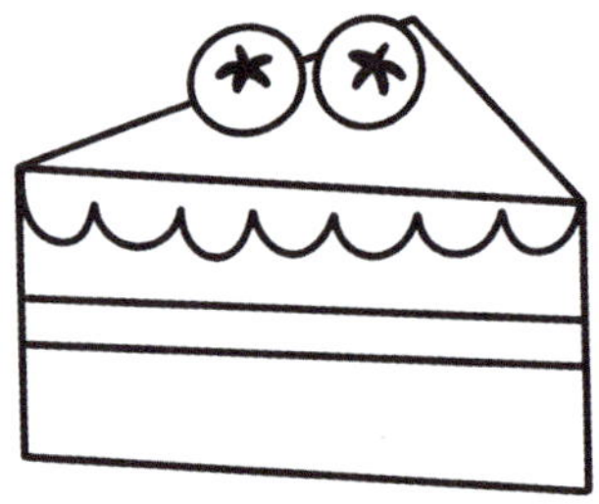

6. Draw a star shape in the center of each circle to make blueberries.

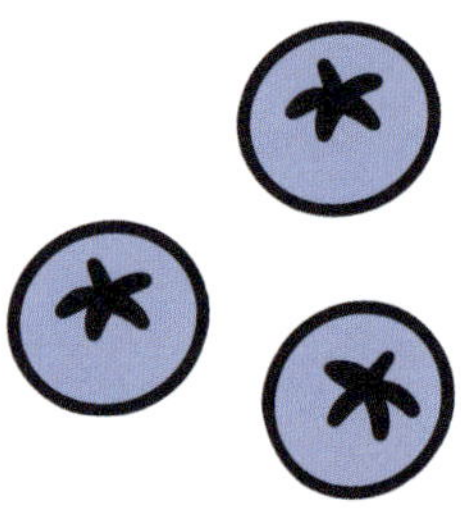

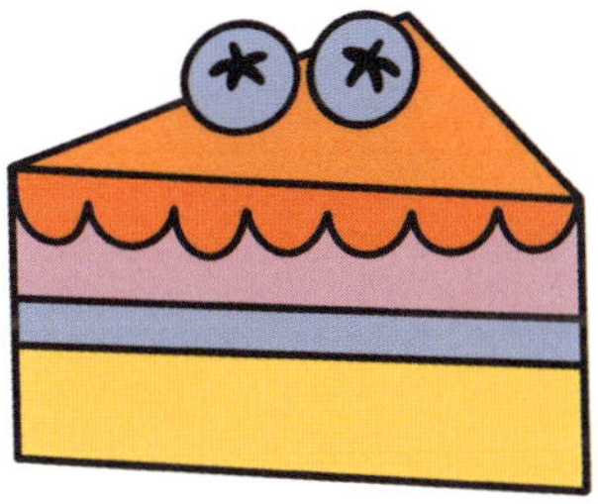

7. Fill in the colors for the cake, icing, filling, and blueberries.

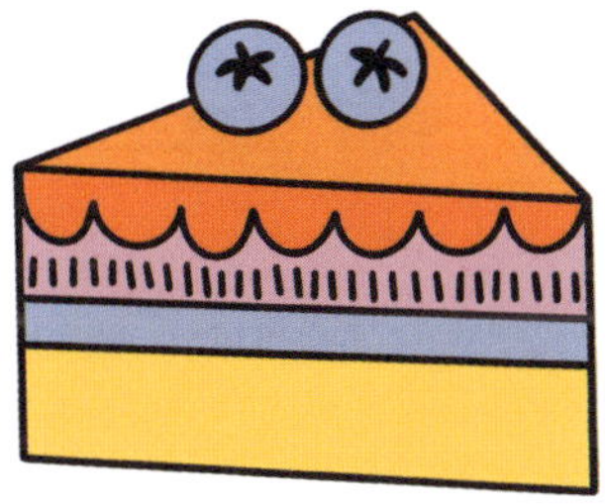

8. Add a horizontal line of vertical dashes to the top cake layer.

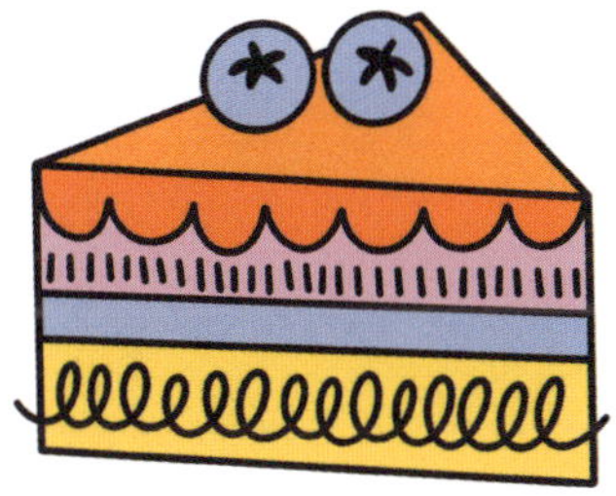

9. Draw a swirling line of loops to the bottom cake layer.

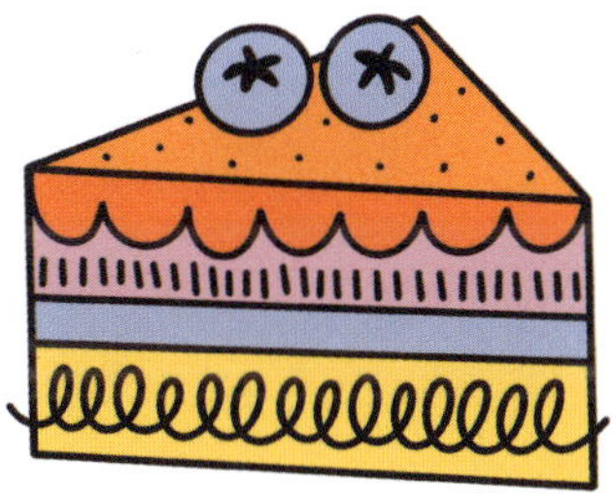

10. Add little dots to the top icing layer.

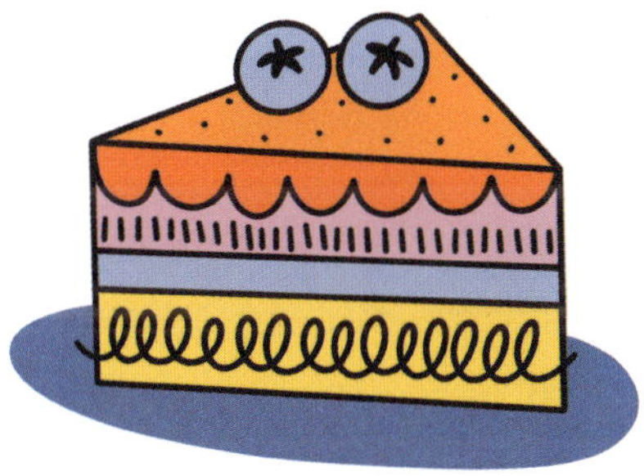

11. Draw an oval underneath the cake to create a plate.

BE BOLD!

Create your dream cake by playing with different colors or switch the blueberries for your favorite fruits.

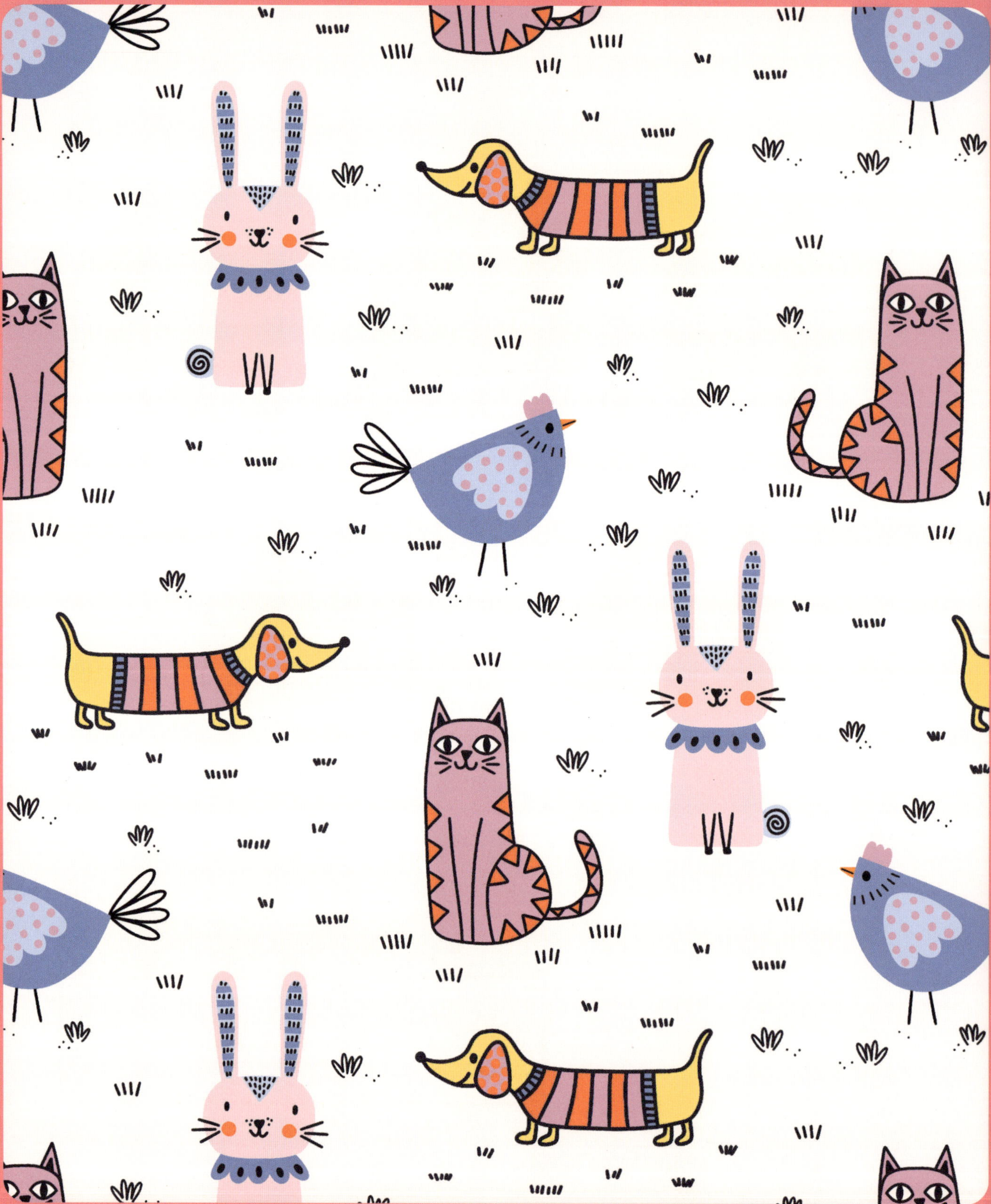

FRIENDLY CREATURES

BUTTERFLY

1. Start with a small black oval that is open at the bottom in the center of the page.

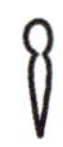

2. Add an upside-down teardrop shape to the bottom of the oval.

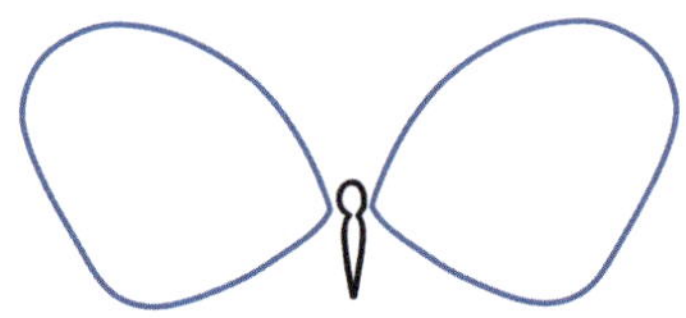

3. Draw two oblong wings on each side of the oval. Make the corners nearest to the oval pointed.

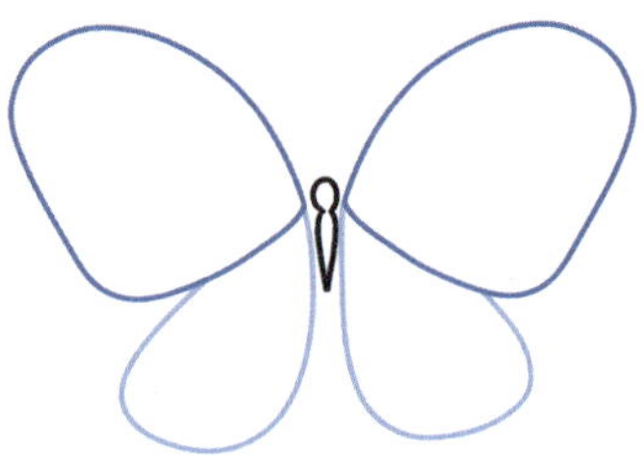

4. Draw two teardrop shapes that extend from the bottom of the wings.

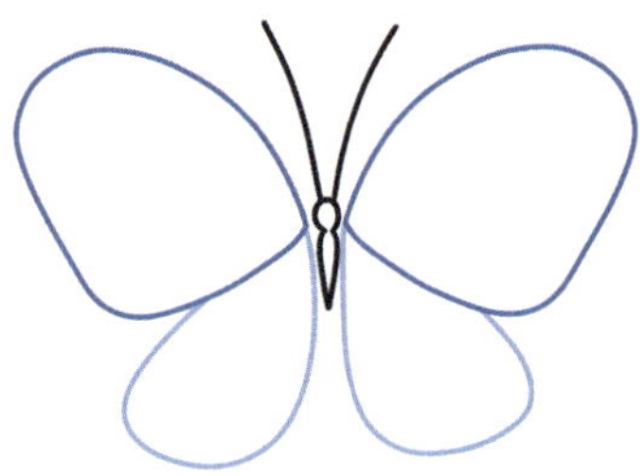

5. Draw two long black antennae that extend out and upward from the oval.

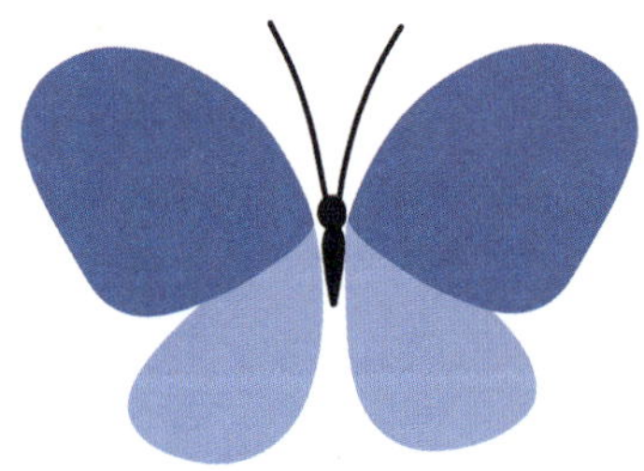

6. Fill in the colors.

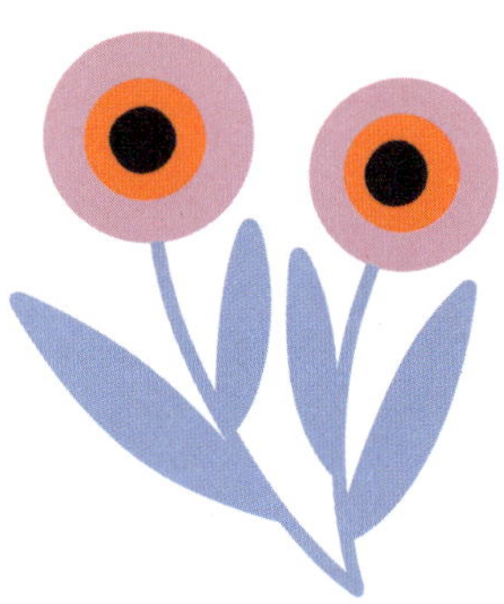

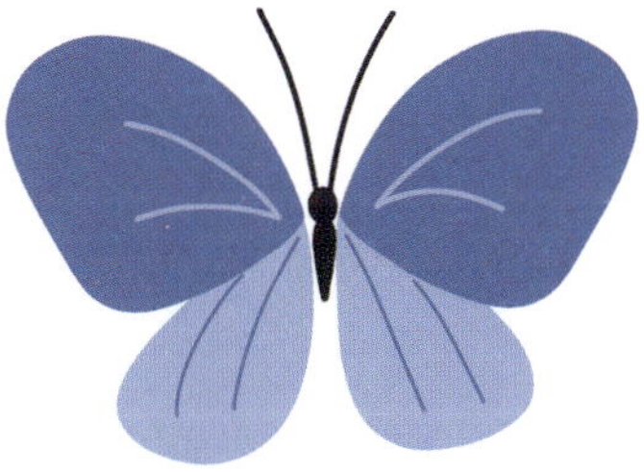

7. Add a curved V-shaped detail to the top wings and two straight lines in the bottom wings.

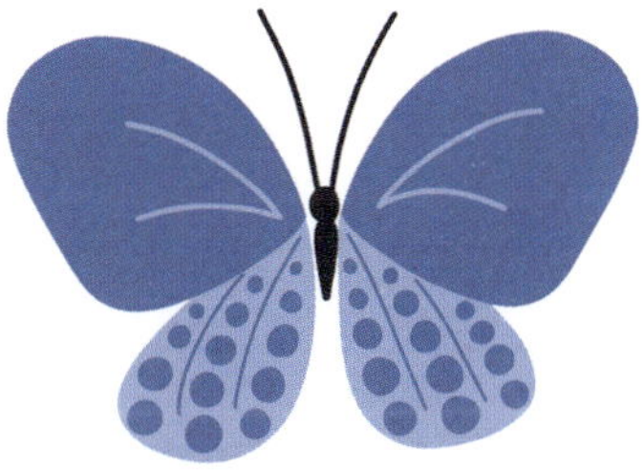

8. Add a series of blue dots between the lines on the bottom wings.

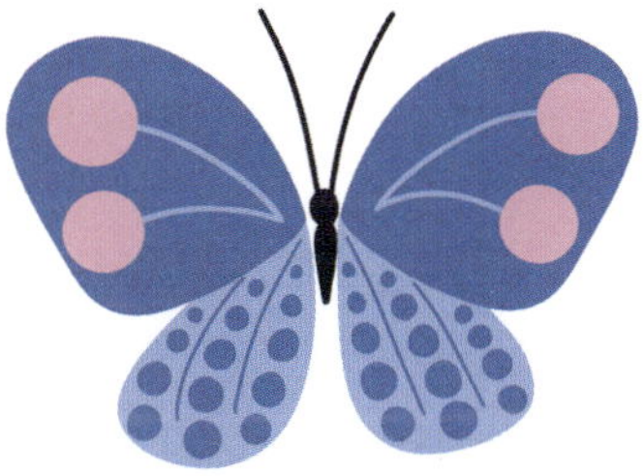

9. Add circles to the ends of the V-lines in the top wings.

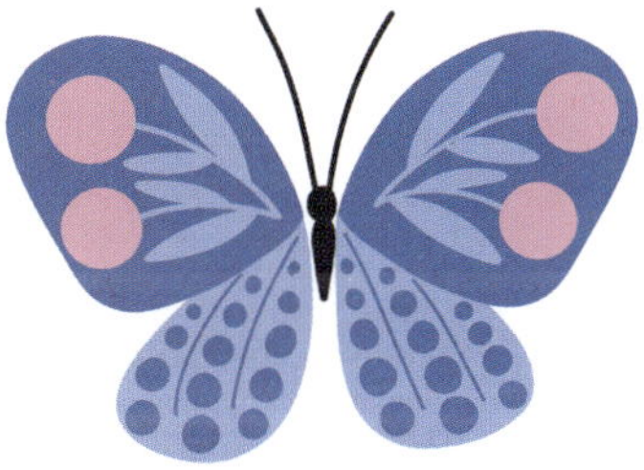

10. Draw pointed leaf shapes along the lines in the top wings.

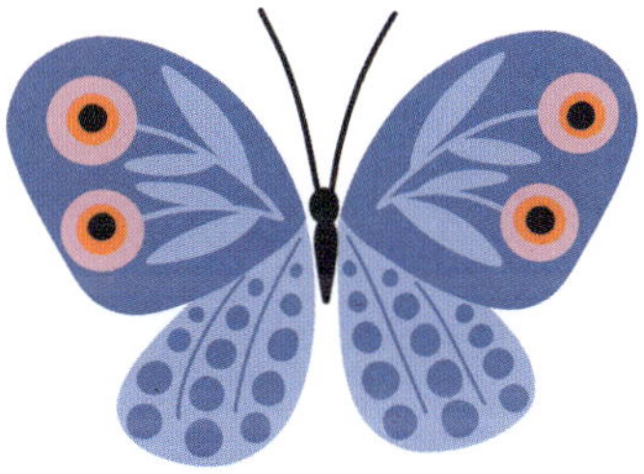

11. Add two circles inside the first circles using different colors.

BE BOLD!

Decorate your butterfly's wings with all kinds of designs like swirls, dashes, hearts, and more to make each butterfly beautiful and special.

MOTH

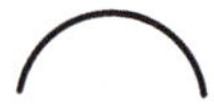

1. Start with an upside-down curve near the center of the page.

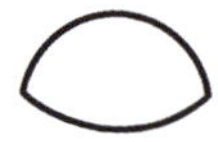

2. Connect the ends with a slightly upturned curved line.

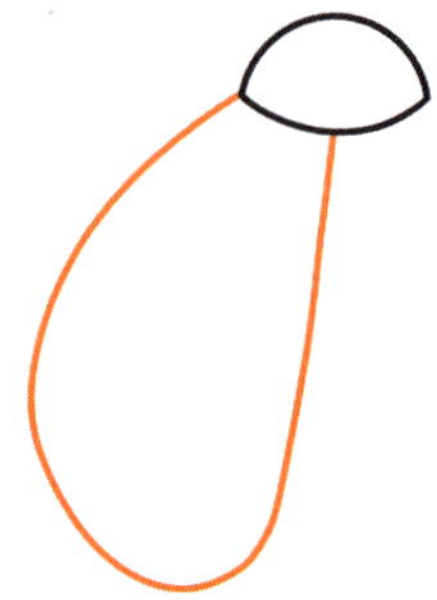

3. Add a large, long, U-shaped wing to the bottom left of the curve.

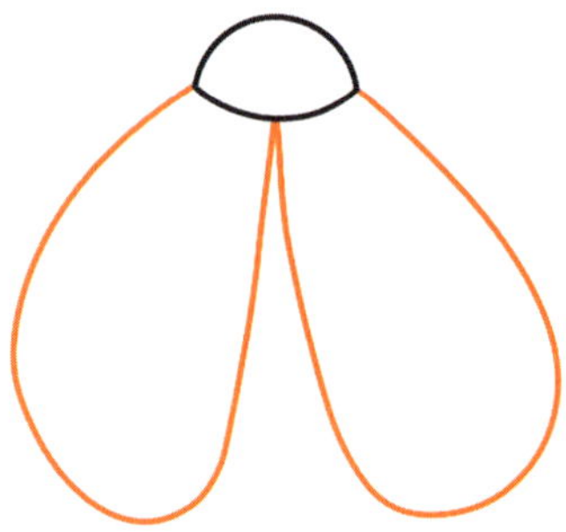

4. Repeat step 3 on the right side.

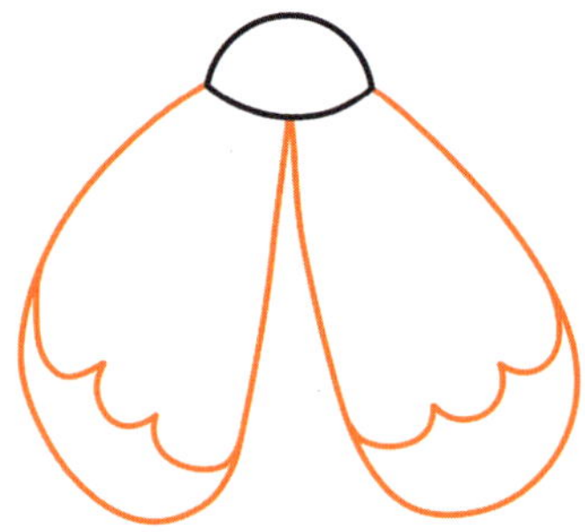

5. Add a scalloped line across the bottom of each wing.

BE BOLD!

Moths can be very simple or very ornate. Try changing the texture or color of the wings and add more or less details. For something extra special, adjust the shape and size of the wings.

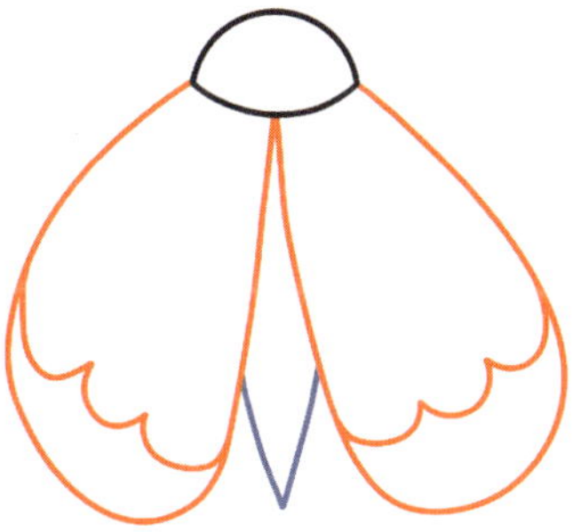

6. Draw a V between the two wings.

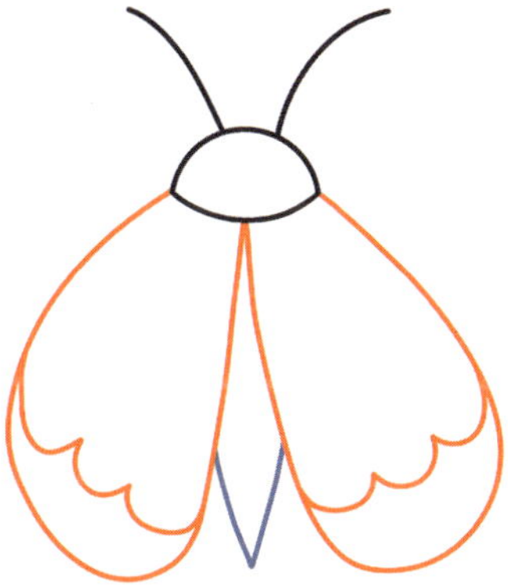

7. Draw two curved lines from the top of the moth's head for antennae.

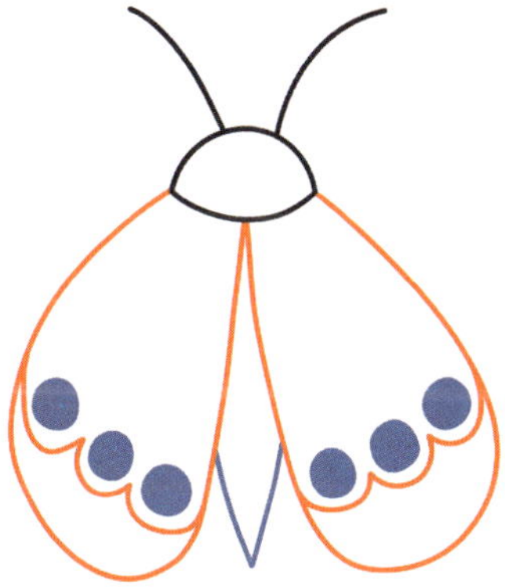

8. Add a large dot to the center of each scallop in the wings.

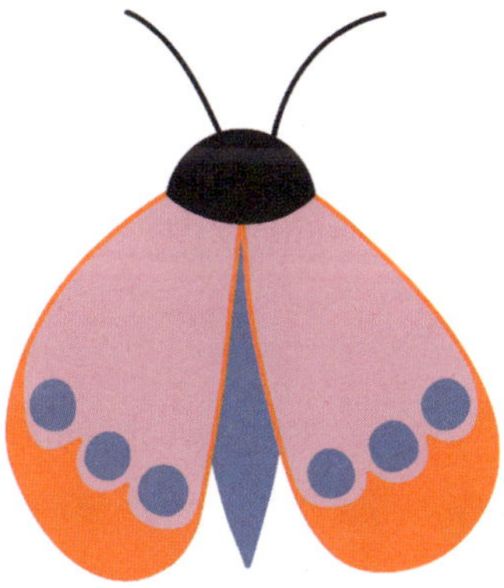

9. Fill in the moth with color!

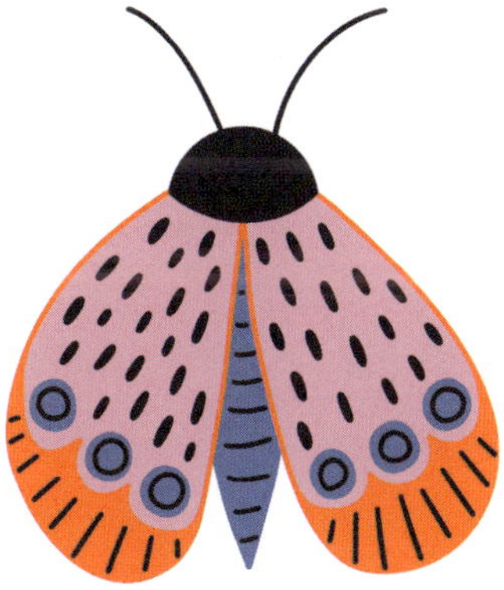

10. Decorate the moth wings with a series of black lines, circles, and dashes.

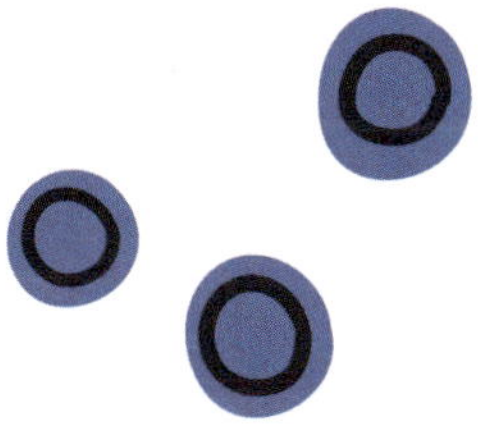

BEETLE

1. Start with a long oval that's flat on top and pointed at the bottom in the center of the page.

2. Add a curved line to the top of the oval.

3. Draw a smaller curved line on top of the first curved line.

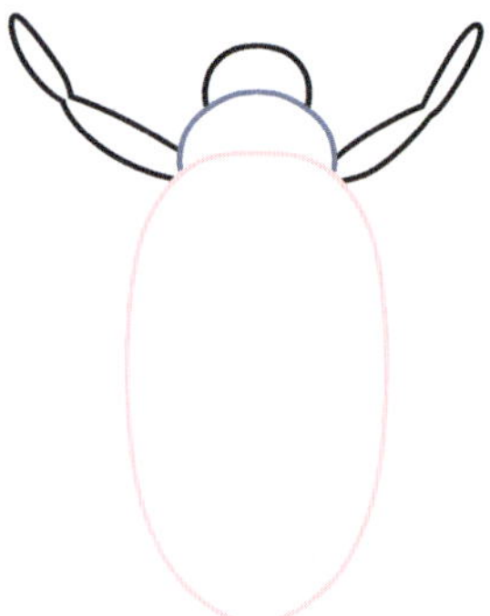

4. Draw two legs, with long noodle shapes and with a divot near the center on both sides.

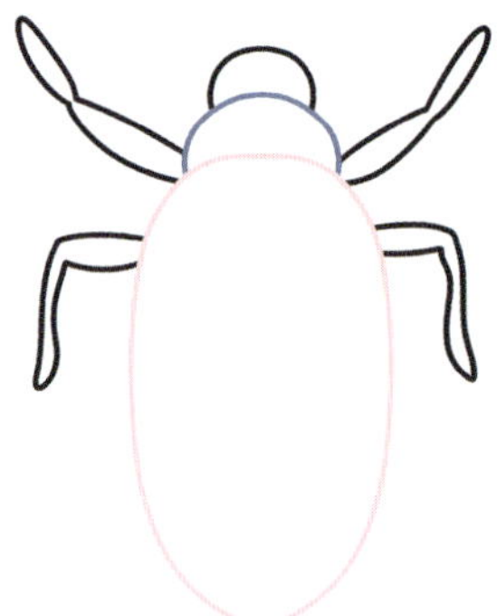

5. Draw two more legs that bend downward on either side of the large oval.

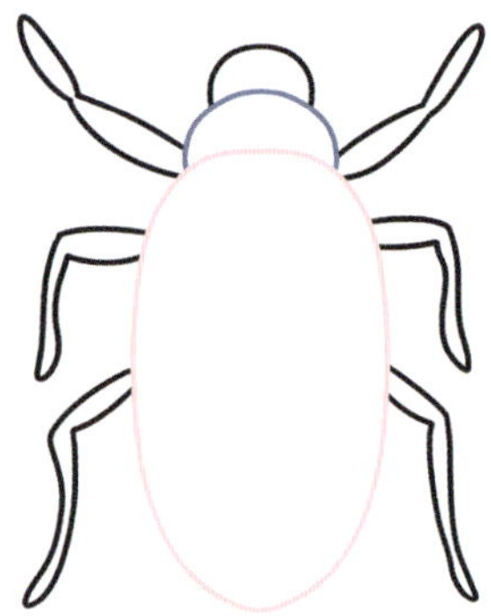

6. Draw two longer legs below the last pair that curve and bend slightly.

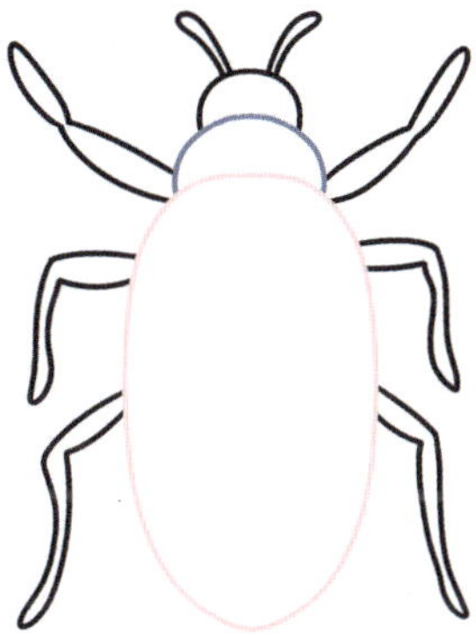

7. Draw two elongated ovals for the antennae on top of the head.

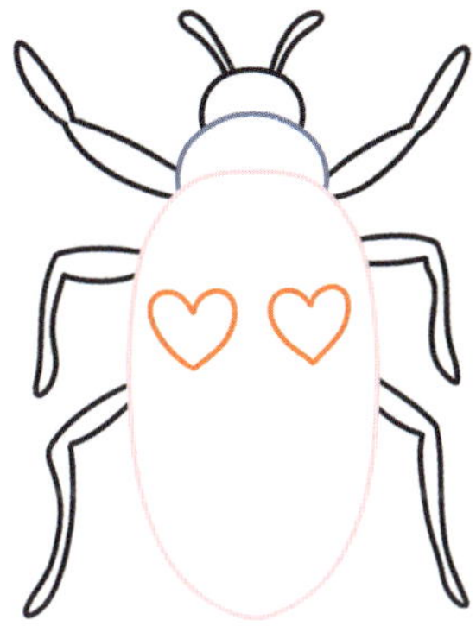

8. Add two heart shapes side by side near the center of the body.

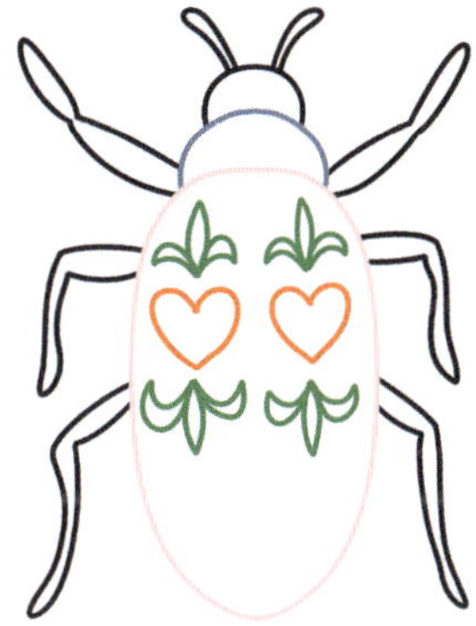

9. Draw a trio of leaves, similar to a fleur de lis, above and below each heart.

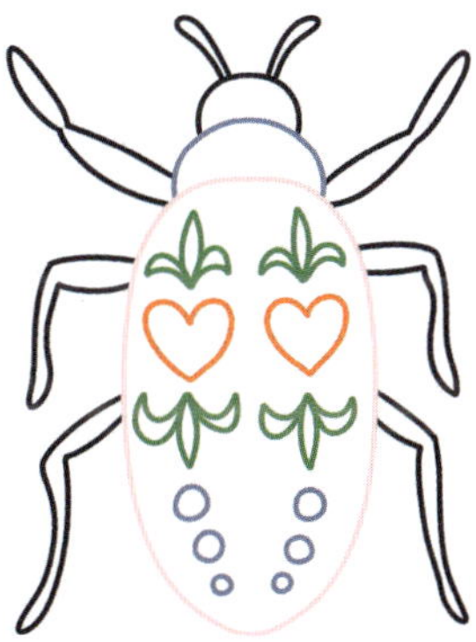

10. Add three circles that get smaller toward the bottom of the body.

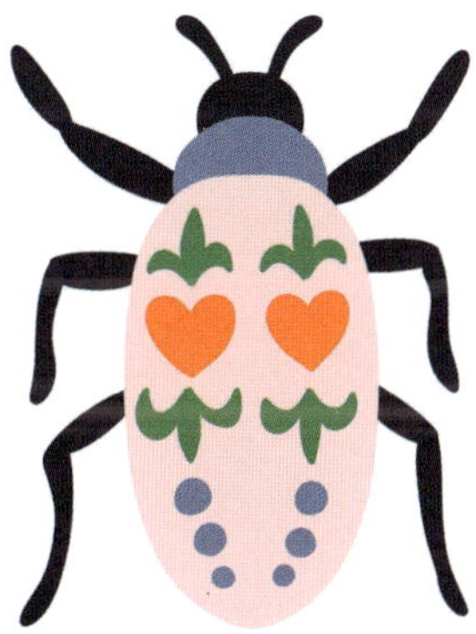

11. Fill in the colors!

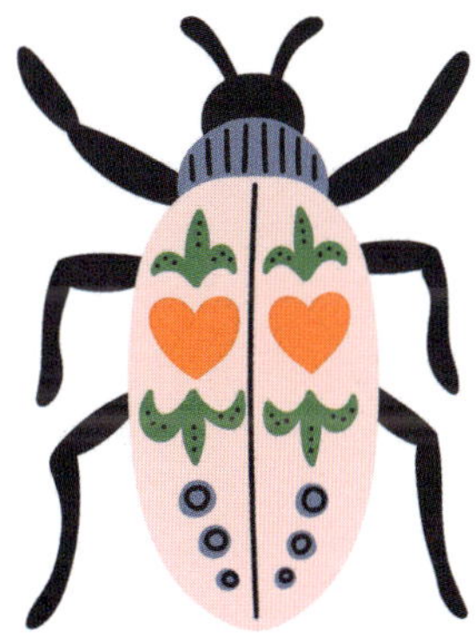

12. Add a line down the center of the oval for the shell and decorate your beetle with lines, dots, and circles.

BE BOLD!

Make your beetle super cute by using bright or pastel colors and sweet decorative elements. Or make it extra spooky by extending the legs and using dark colors and creepy decorative elements.

LADY BUG

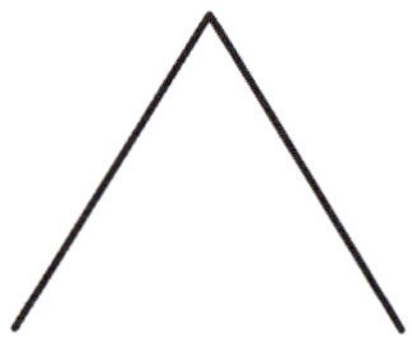

1. Start with a large upside-down V near the center of the page.

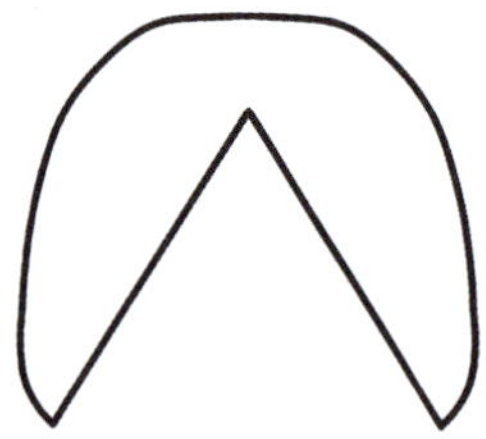

2. Connect a large U shape that is slightly flat on top over the V.

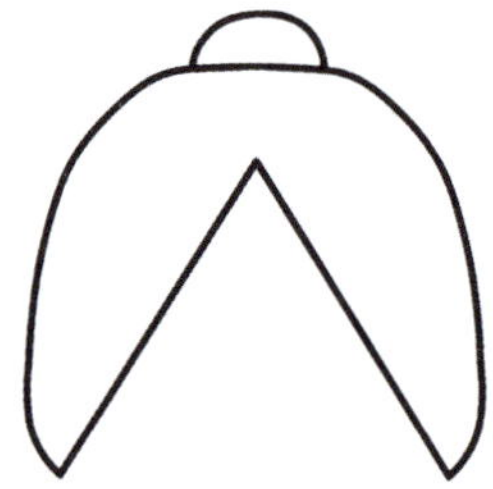

3. Draw a curved line on top of the U shape.

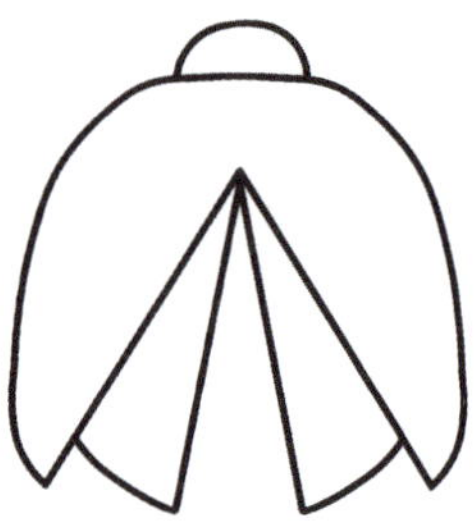

4. Draw two narrow triangles inside of the V.

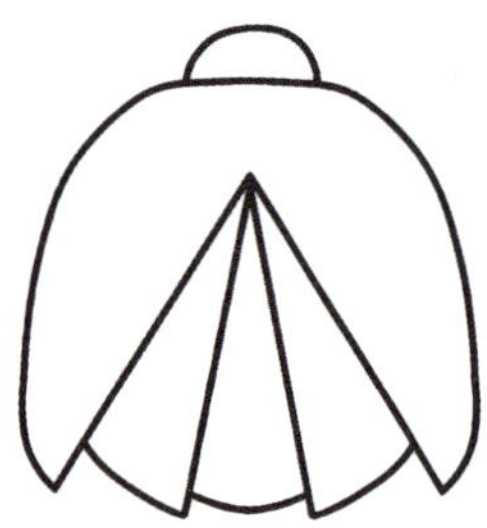

5. Add a curved line between the triangles to connect them.

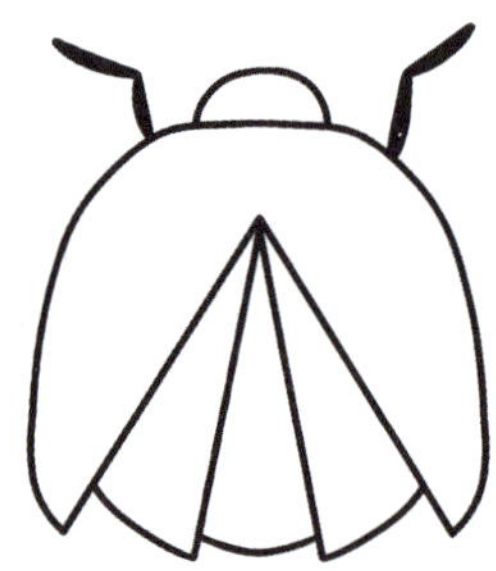

6. Draw two angled legs on either side of the head.

BE BOLD!

Play around with the shapes of your bug. Make the wings more curved, elongate the antennae, make your bug extra long or extra wide. Slightly adjusting the shapes can create an entirely different look!

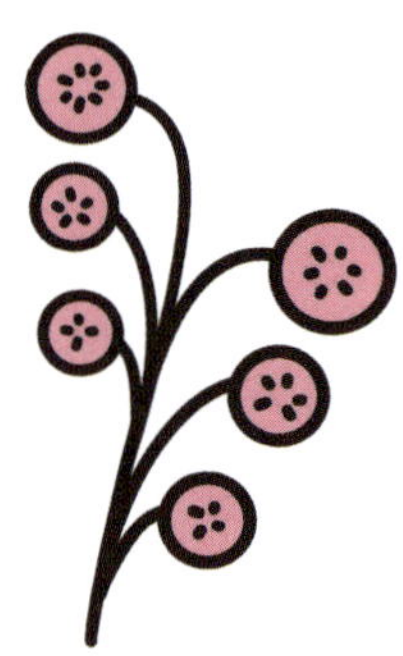

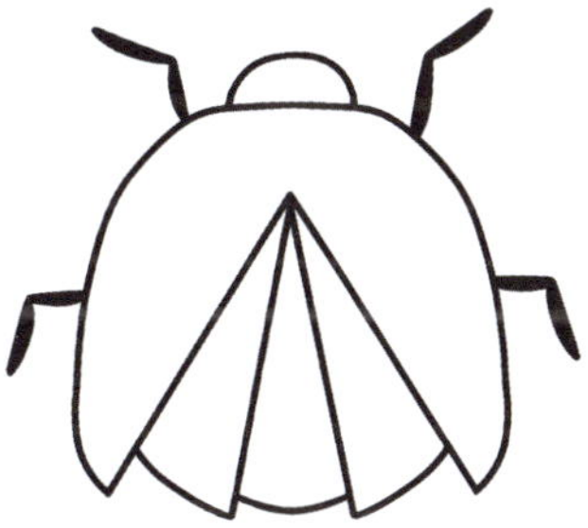

7. Draw two more legs angled down on either side of the body.

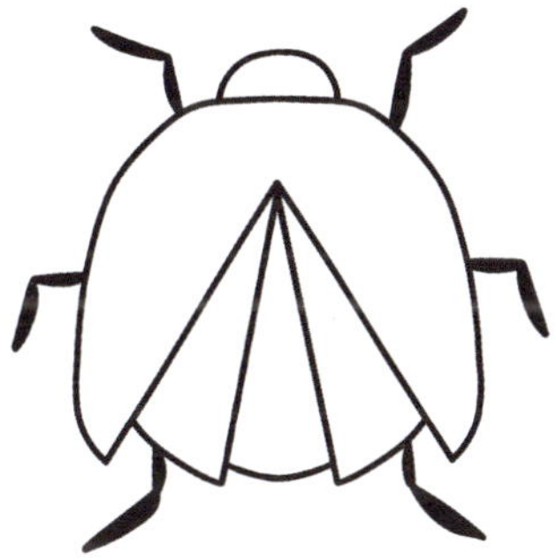

8. Add two more angled legs under the body.

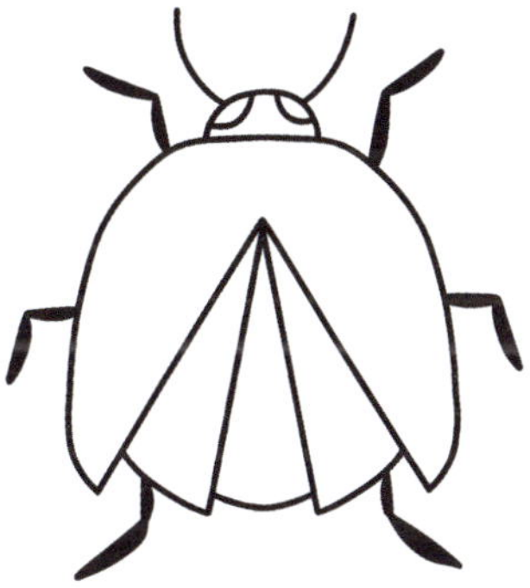

9. Draw two curved lines inside the head for eyes and two curved antennae on top.

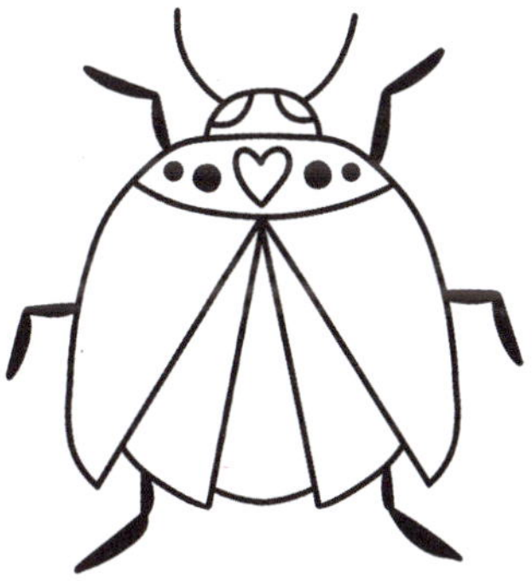

10. Add a horizontal curved line across the top of the body that touches the point of the center triangle. Add a heart and dots.

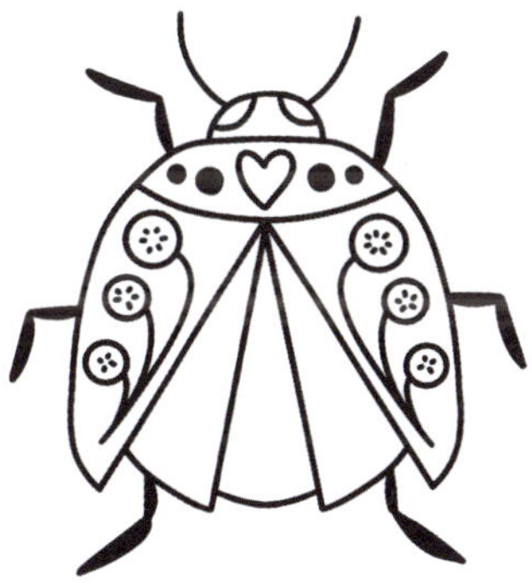

11. Decorate the shell with a simple floral motif using circles, curved lines, and dots.

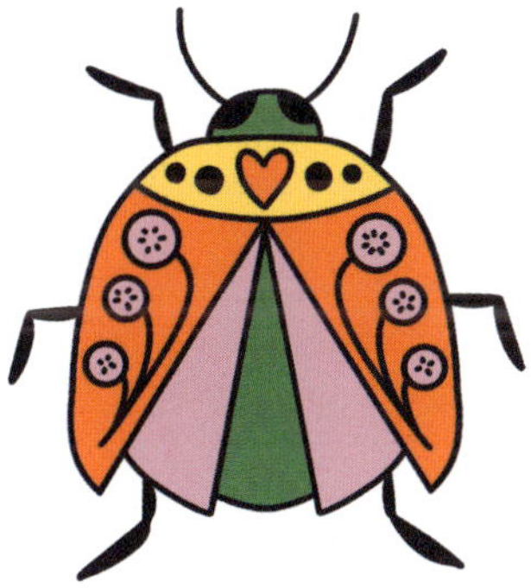

12. Fill in the lady bug with the colors of your choice!

FOLK ART BIRD

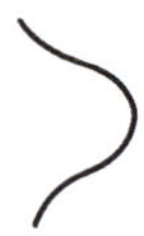

1. Start with a curved line on the right side of the page.

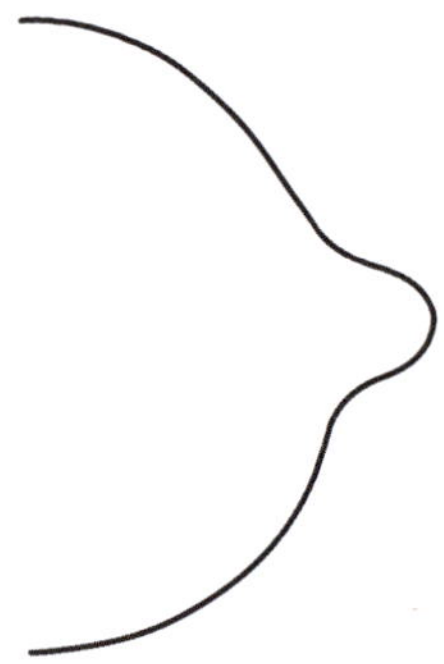

2. Extend each side of the curved line with long, curved lines to make the wings.

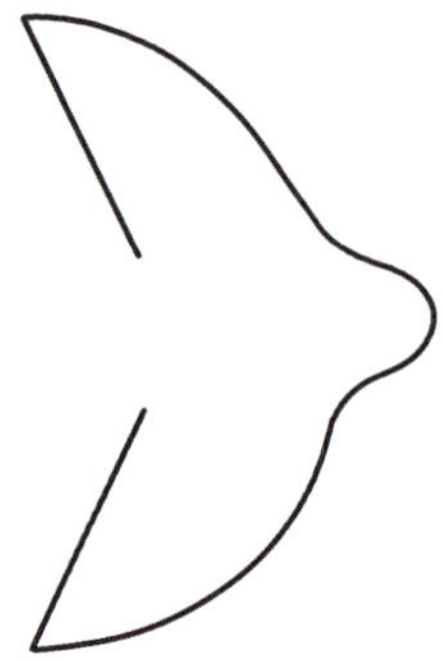

3. Draw a straight line from the end of each wing toward the center.

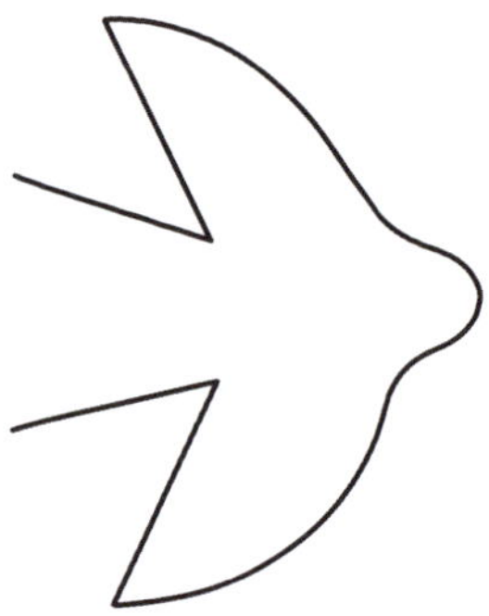

4. Draw two more straight lines to start the tail.

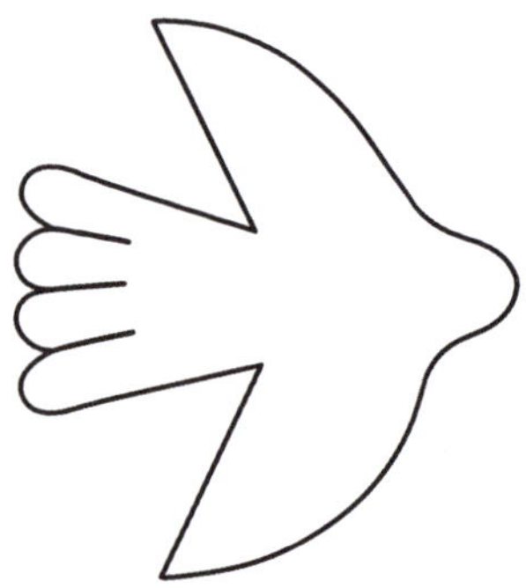

5. Draw long scallops to make the tail feathers.

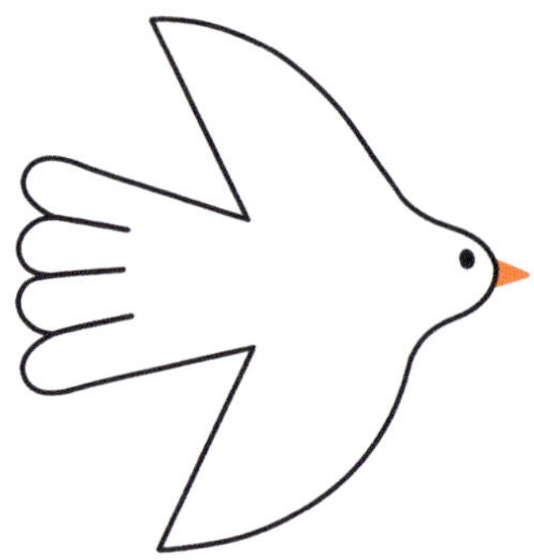

6. Add a black dot for the eye and a triangle beak to the head.

BE BOLD!

Different colors can mean different things. Change the colors on the decorative elements of the bird to express your desired feelings or emotions.

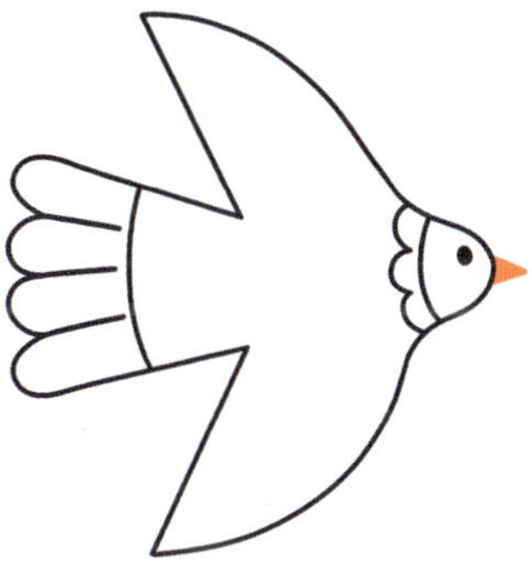

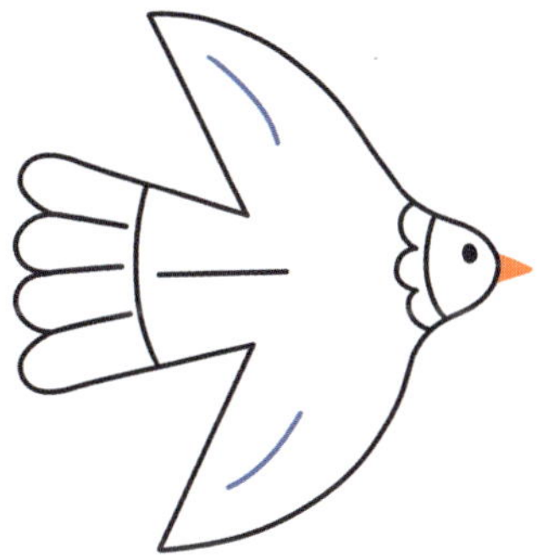

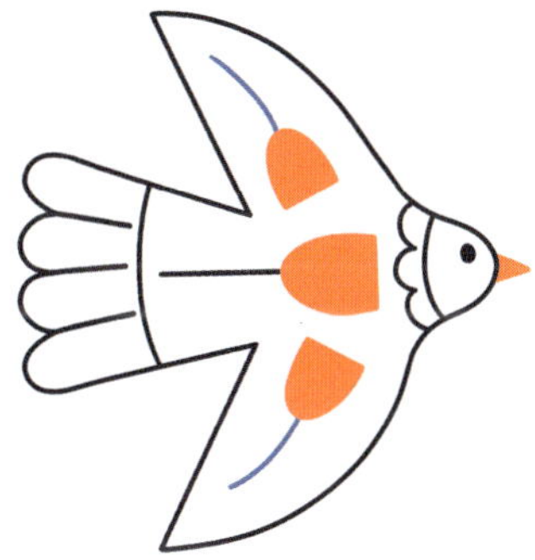

7. Add a curved line at the tail and neck. Add a scalloped line to the neck.

8. Add a horizontal black line in the center of the bird and two curved lines in the wings.

9. Draw three semicircles, one in each wing and one in the center of the body.

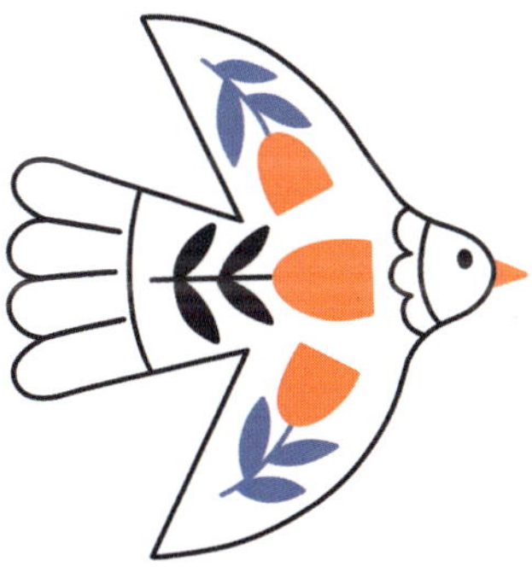

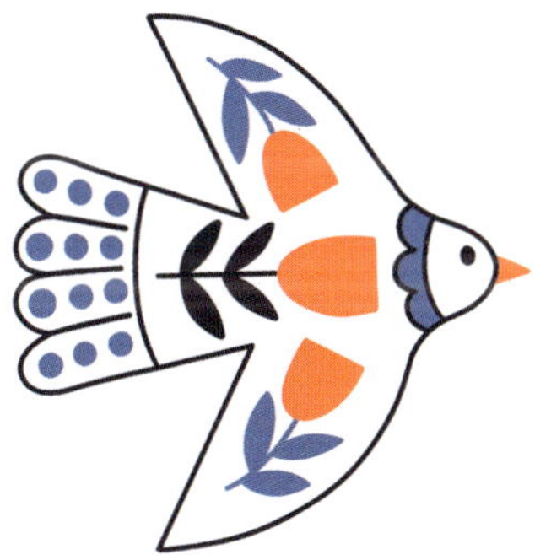

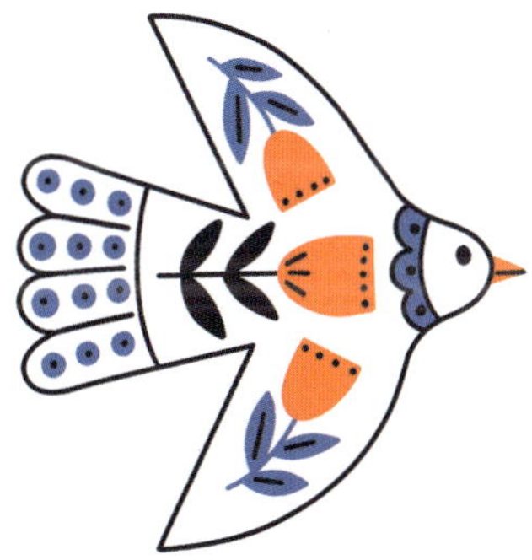

10. Add four pointed leaves to the horizontal black line and three pointed leaves to each line in the wings.

11. Add three dots in a row on each tail feather. Color the scalloped collar around the neck.

12. Create texture by adding dots and dashes to the beak, collar, tail feathers, and flowers.

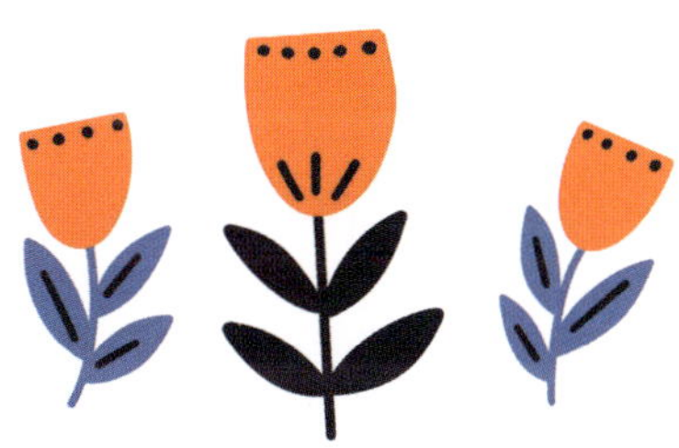

PEACE DOVE

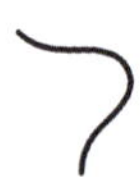

1. Start with a curved line on the right of the page.

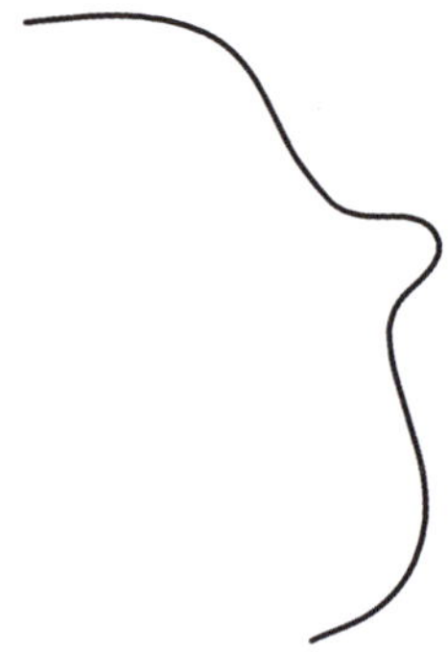

2. Extend the edges of the line with long, curved lines to make the wings.

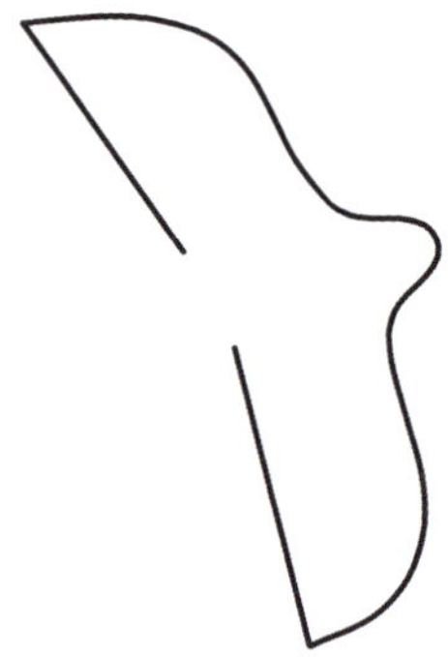

3. Draw a straight line from the end of each wing going in toward the center of the bird.

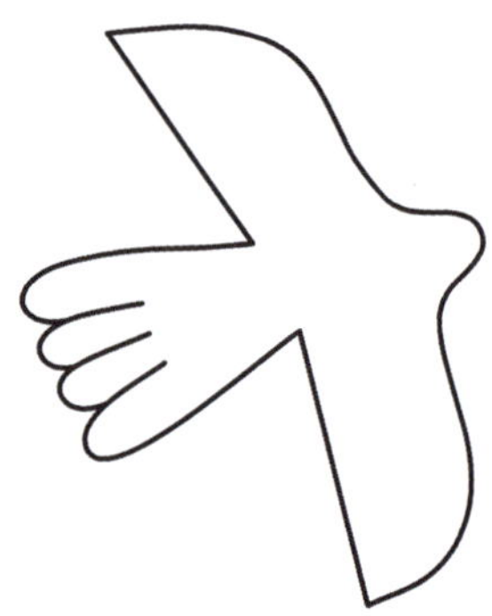

4. Connect the ends of the wings with an elongated tail with four long scallops for the feathers.

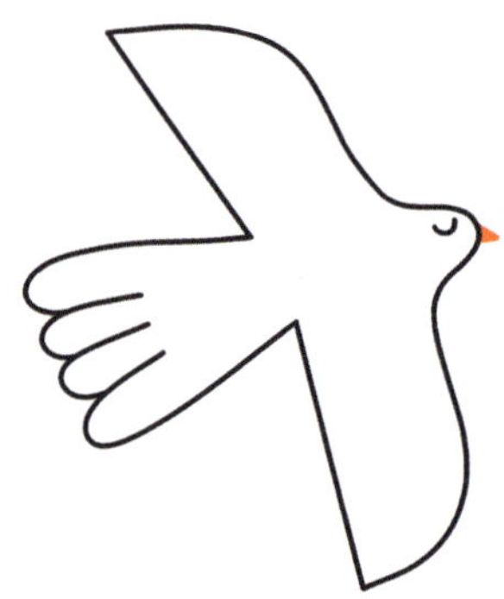

5. Add a black curve for the eye and a triangle beak.

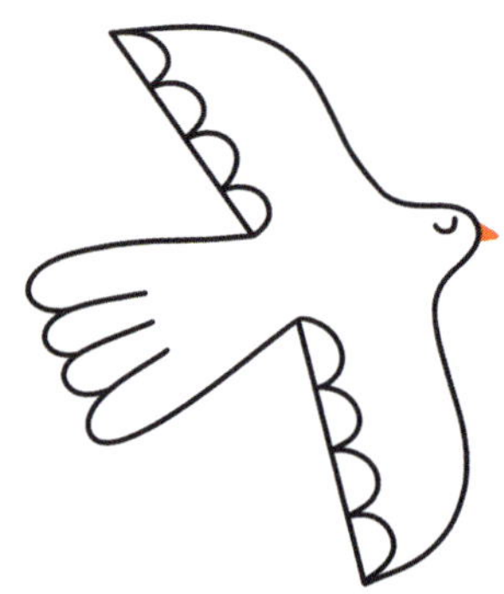

6. Add four semicircles to the inner edge of each wing.

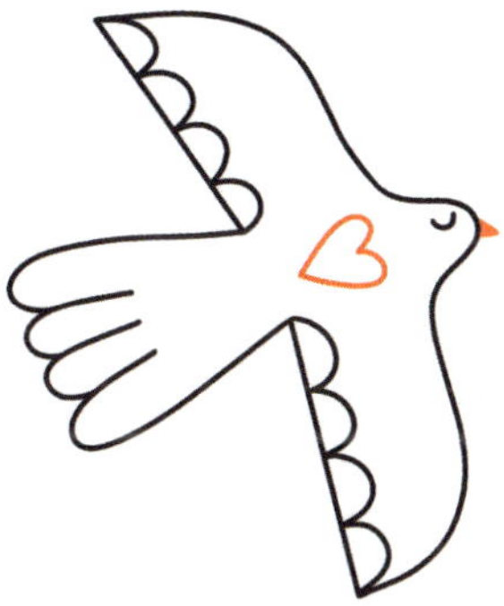

7. Draw a heart in the center of the dove.

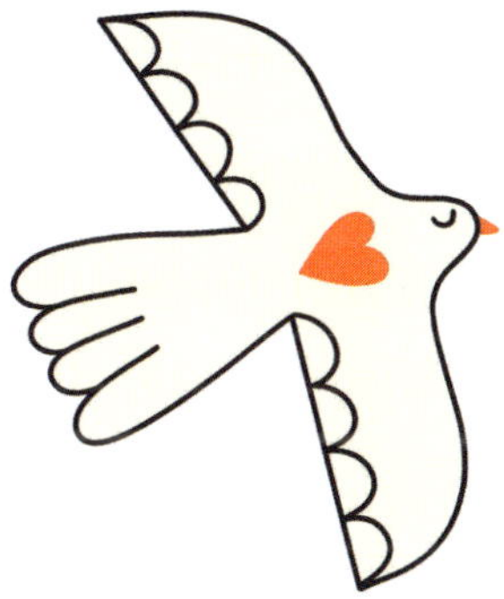

8. Color in the heart and dove!

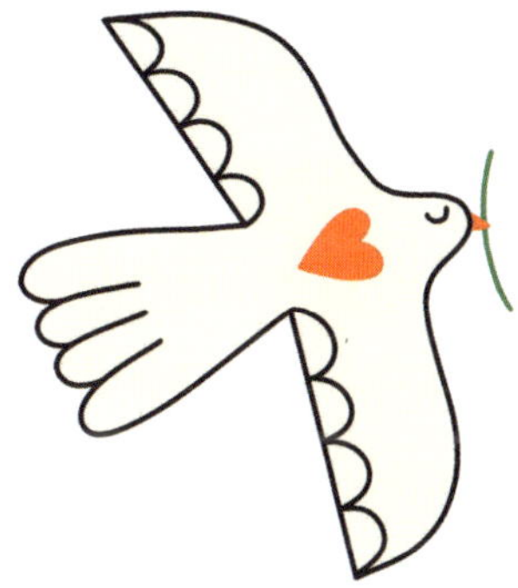

9. Draw a curved line at the end of the dove's beak.

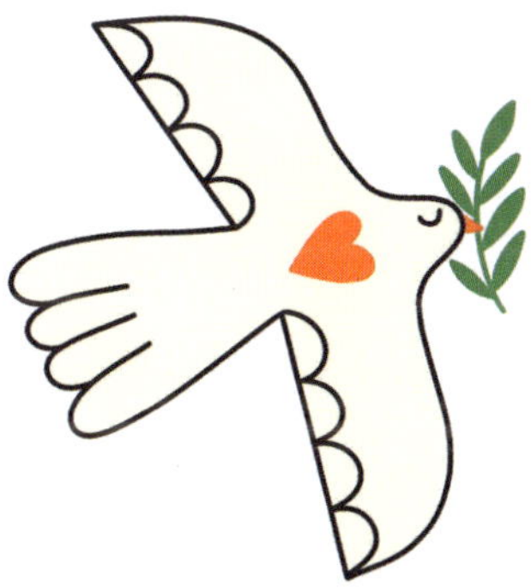

10. Add pointed leaves along the curved line to make a stem and leaves.

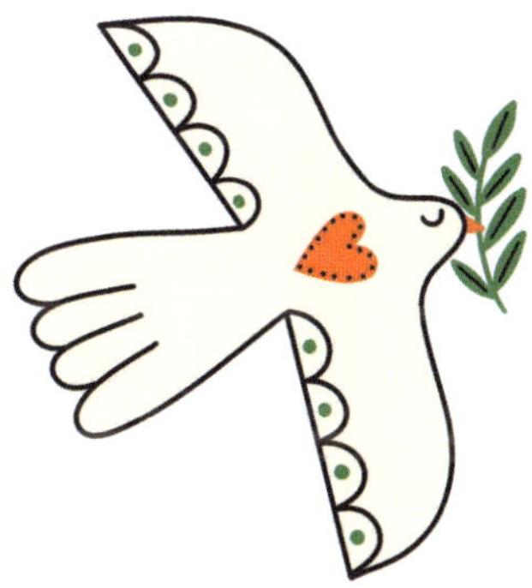

11. Decorate the dove with dots in the semicircles and around the heart, and lines through the center of each leaf.

BE BOLD!

Create a flock of doves all carrying symbols of peace like white poppies, a peace bell, or mistletoe.

HUMMINGBIRD

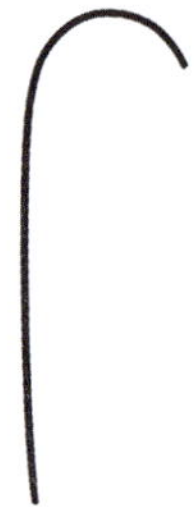

1. Start with a long line that hooks at the top like a lowercase R.

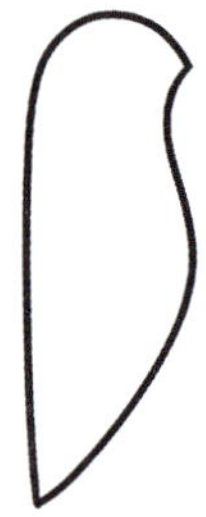

2. Connect a wavy line to close the shape of the body. It should be a teardrop or bean-like shape.

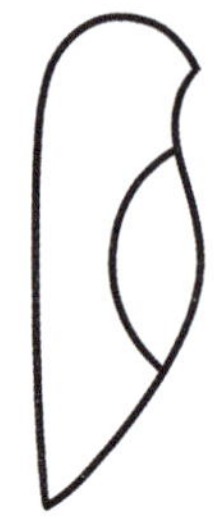

3. Add a curved line inside to mark the belly area.

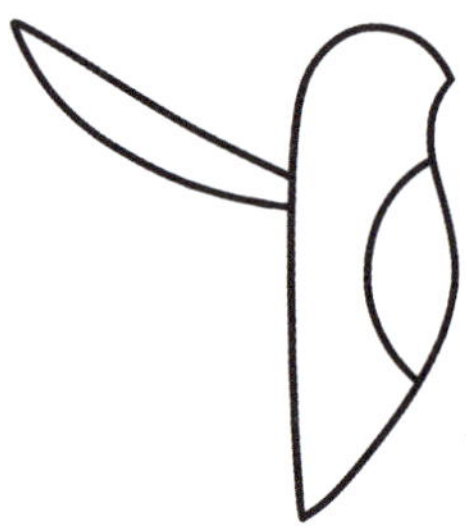

4. Draw a pointed and slightly curved wing extending from the bird's back.

5. Add a second wing below the first.

6. Add a third wing below the second wing.

7. Draw a fourth wing.

8. Add a thin, long, curved beak.

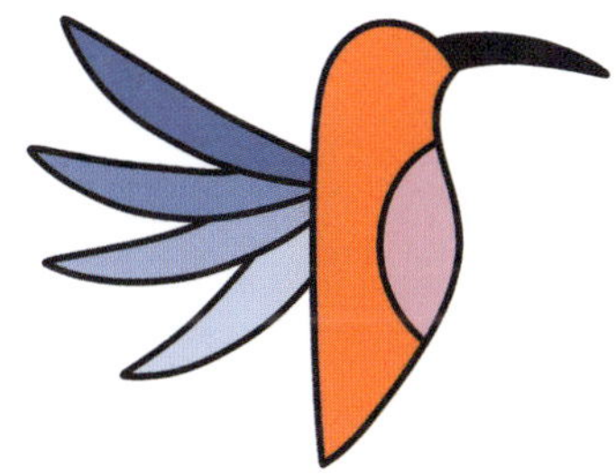

9. Color the bird. For the wings, use four shades of one color to make a gradient—this helps to add a sense of movement.

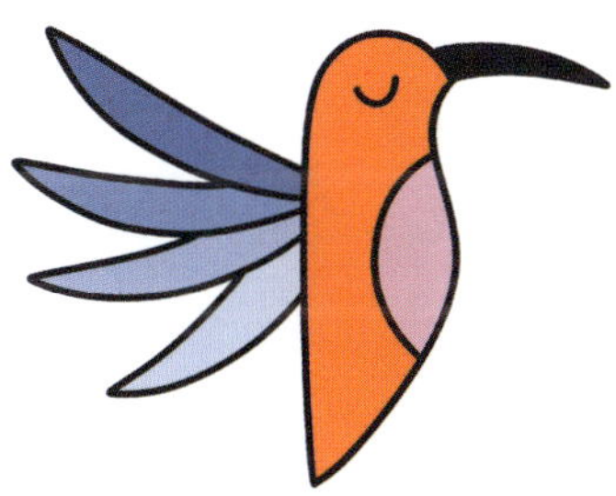

10. Draw a U for the eye.

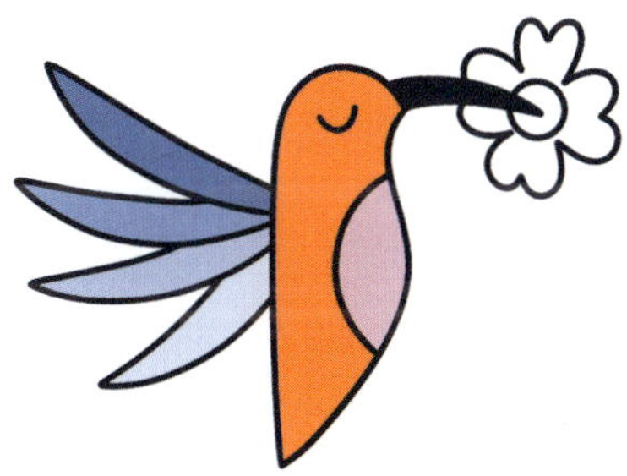

11. Add a tiny flower near the beak with a circle and four petals with two scallops on the end of each.

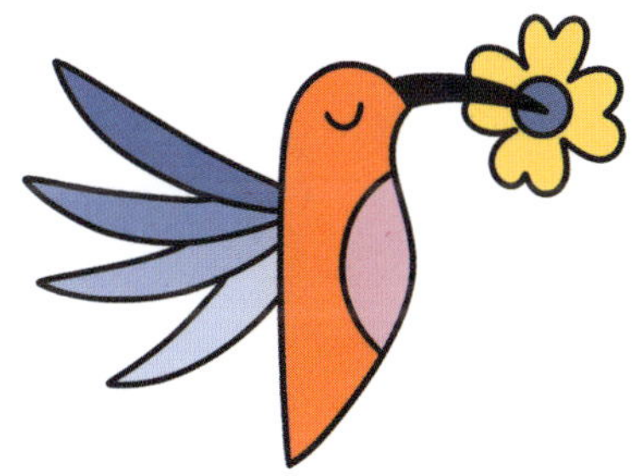

12. Finish by coloring in the flower.

BE BOLD!

Give your bird a different personality just by changing the eye—try a wide circle for a surprised look or a dot with lashes for a playful one.

TOUCAN

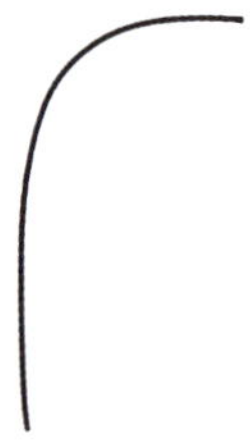

1. Start with a curved black line on the left.

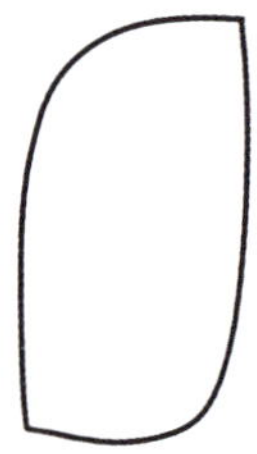

2. Connect the two ends with a curved line mirrored against the first one to make the body.

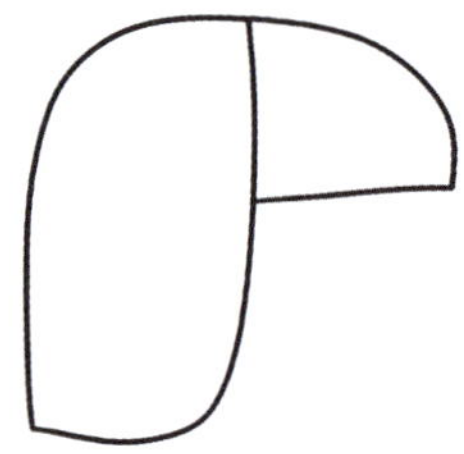

3. On the top right of the shape, add a quarter circle to make the beak.

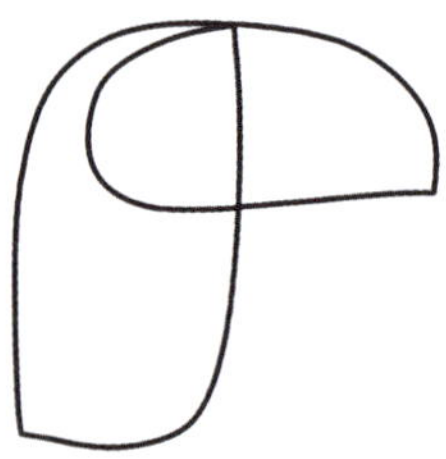

4. Draw a curved line behind the beak.

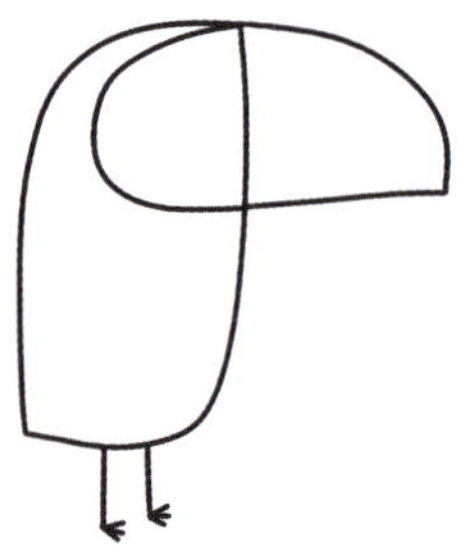

5. Draw two vertical lines under the body with three short lines extending out from each.

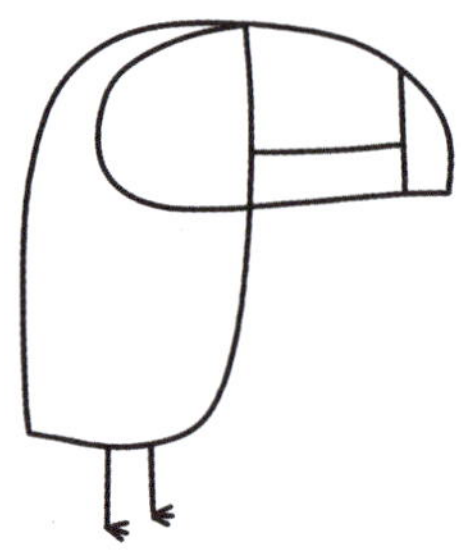

6. In the beak, draw a vertical line near the pointed end and then a horizontal line closer to the bottom.

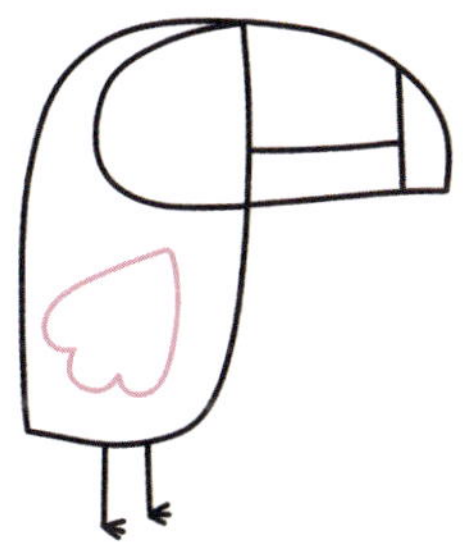

7. Add a teardrop-shaped wing with three scallops on the bottom.

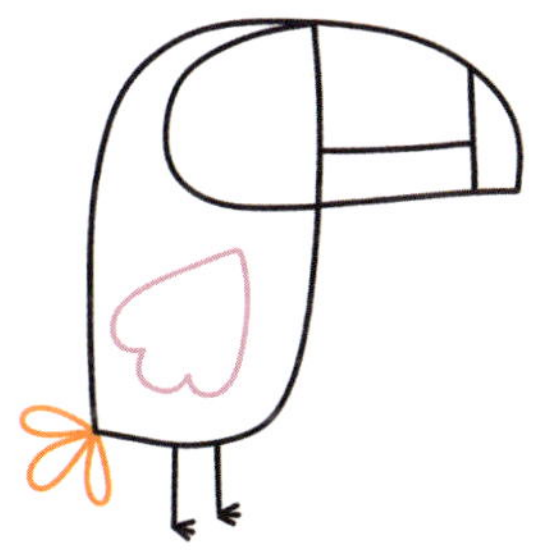

8. On the lower left corner of the body, draw three thin teardrop shapes for the tail feathers.

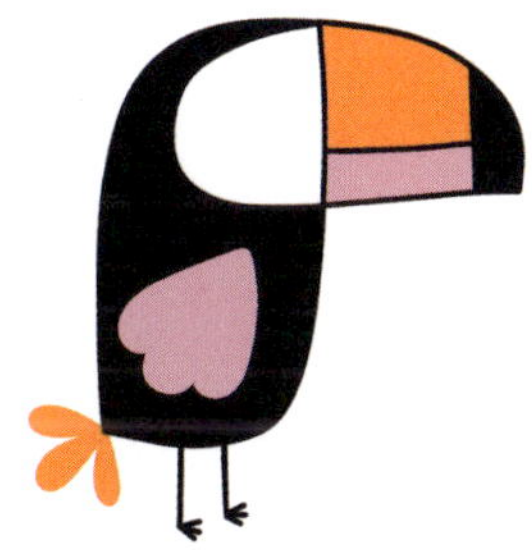

9. Fill in the toucan with color!

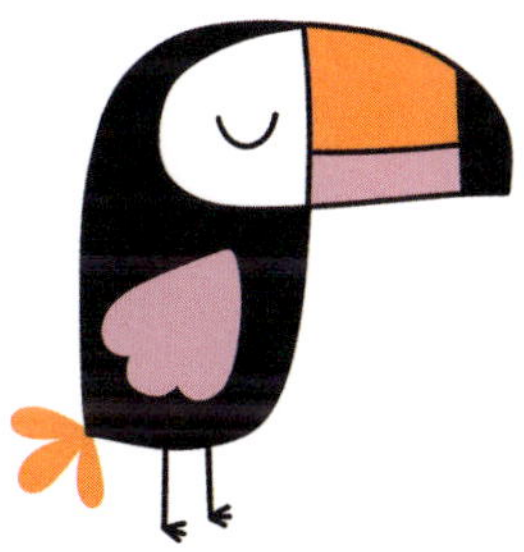

10. Add a curve for an eye.

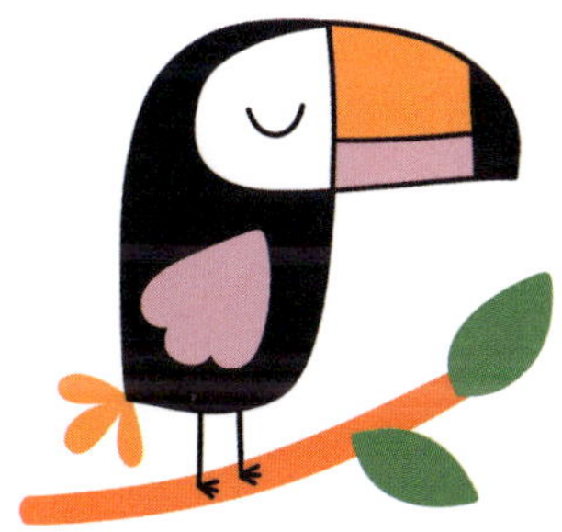

11. Draw a curved, thick line under the feet to make a branch. Add two pointed leaf shapes to the branch.

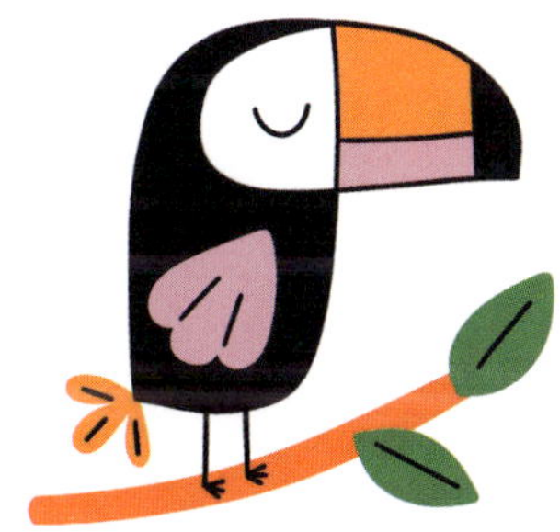

12. Decorate by adding black lines to the center of the tail feathers, wing, and leaves.

BE BOLD!

Toucans are colorful birds that love fruit! Color in your toucan with different colors and give him a little snack growing on his branch. You can find lots of fruit in the Fruits, Veggies & Snacks section of this book.

CUTE BIRD

1. Start with a stretched pink teardrop shape for the body.

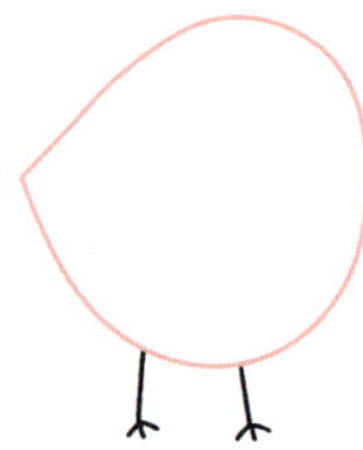

2. Add two black vertical lines under the body with three short lines extending from each.

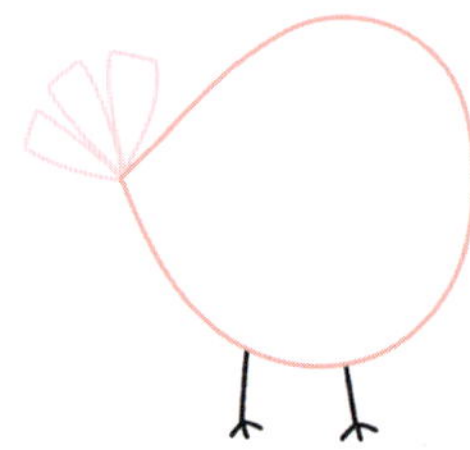

3. Draw three thin triangles at the point of the body to make the tail.

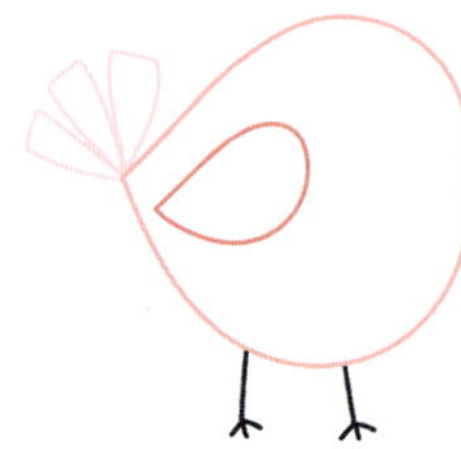

4. Draw a smaller teardrop to create a wing.

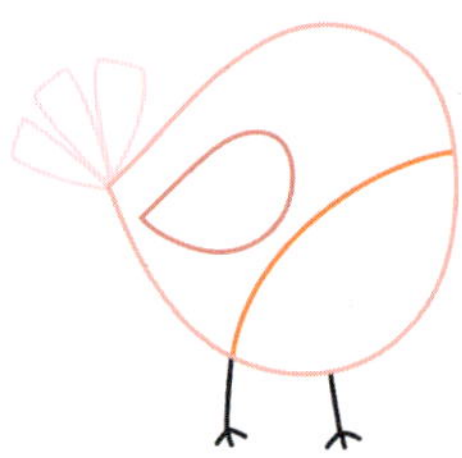

5. Add a curved line on the bottom right of the body.

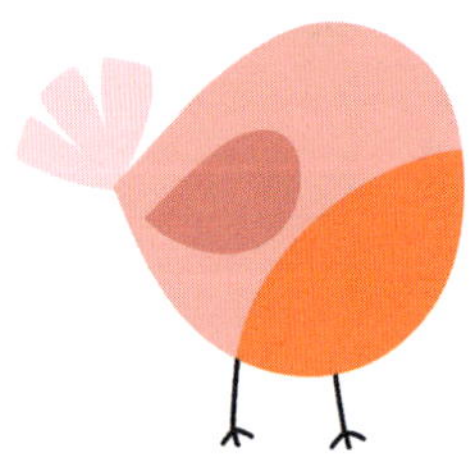

6. Fill in all the colors!

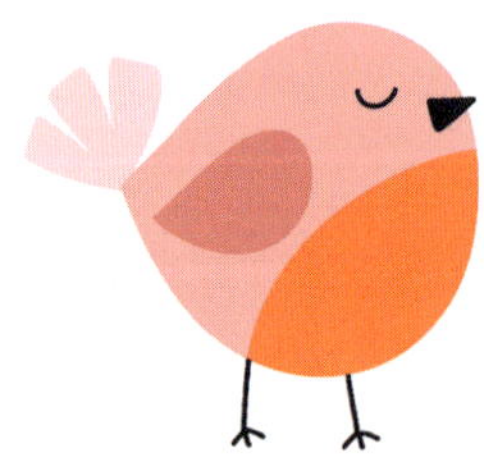

7. In the top right of the bird, add a small, curved eye and a black triangle beak.

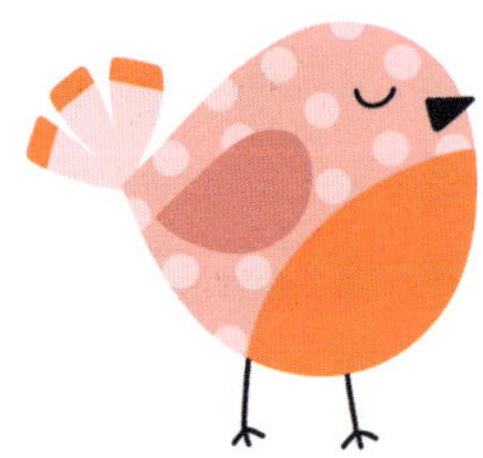

8. Decorate with polka dots on the body and stripes at the ends of the tail feathers.

BE BOLD!

Birds come in all shapes and colors. Get creative with your color choices or play with patterns like stripes or scallops to make your own special bird.

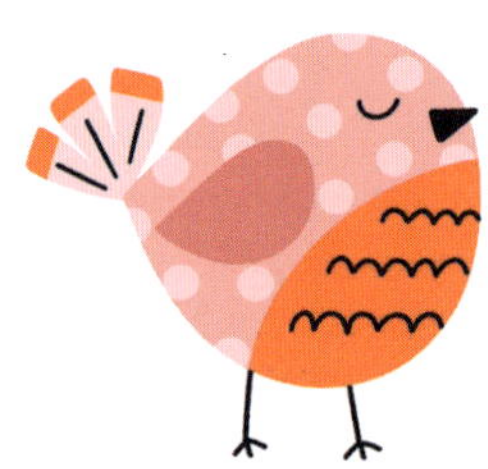

9. Add texture to the bird with black lines through the center of each tail feather and scalloped feather lines to the chest.

SNAKE

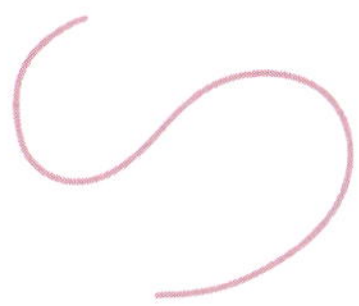

1. Start with a swirly S-line in the top center of the page.

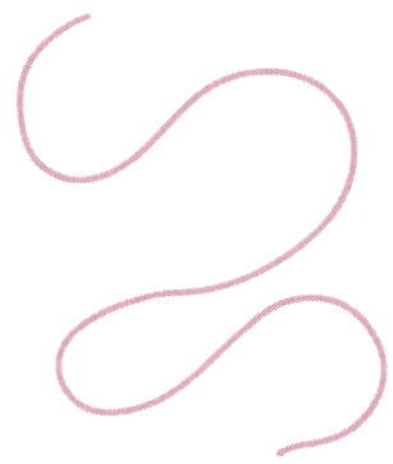

2. Add another swirly S-line to the end of the first one.

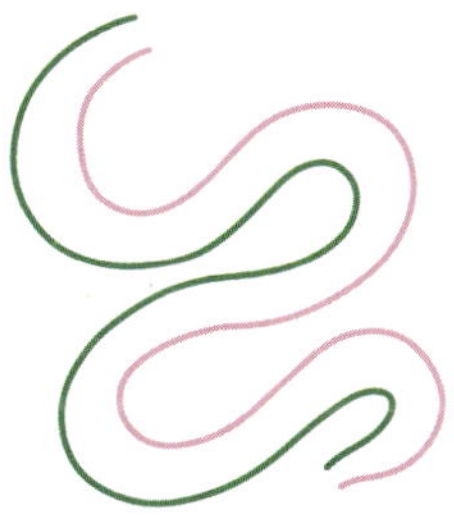

3. Draw a swirly line on the left side that follows the first line.

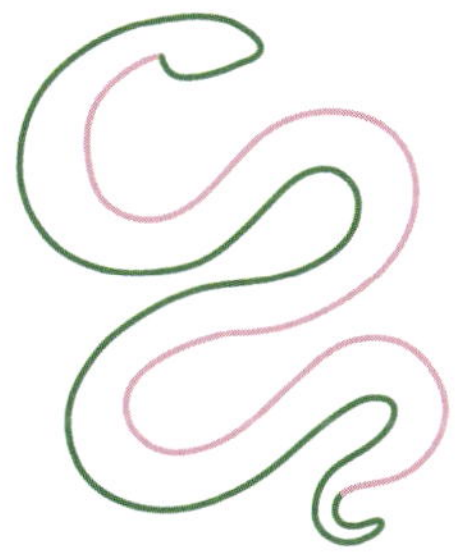

4. Close the line at the top with a triangular head and at the bottom with a pointed tail.

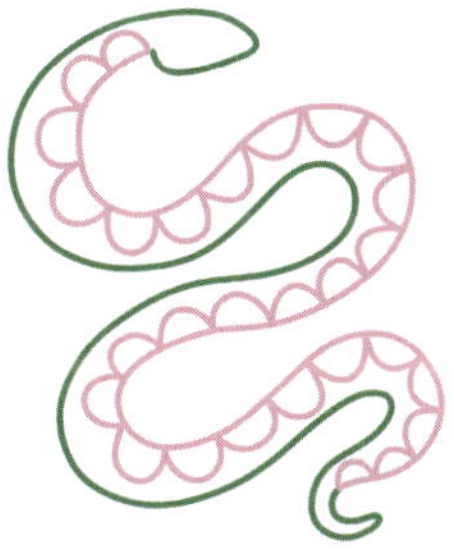

5. Draw a bunch of semicircles along the pink line.

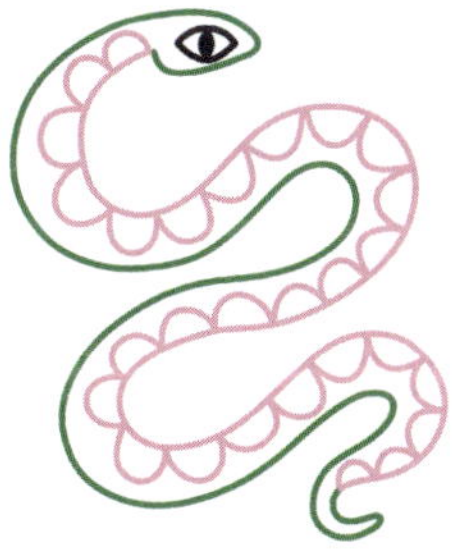

6. Draw a large, pointed eye with an oval in the middle.

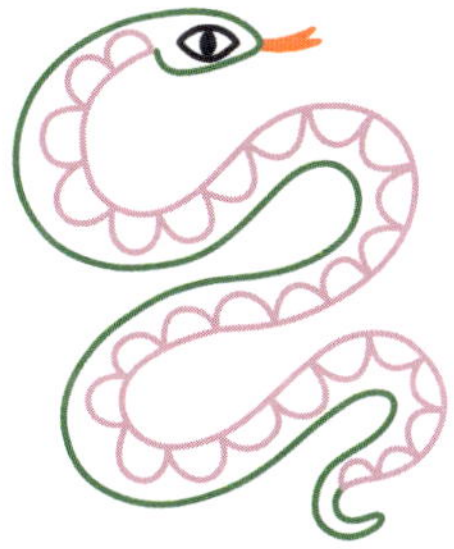

7. Add a forked tongue.

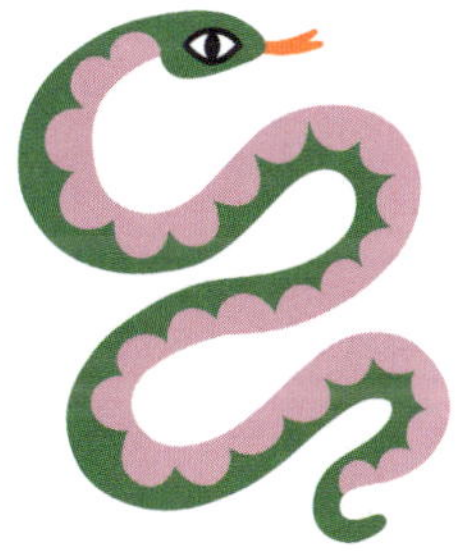

8. Fill in the snake with two colors!

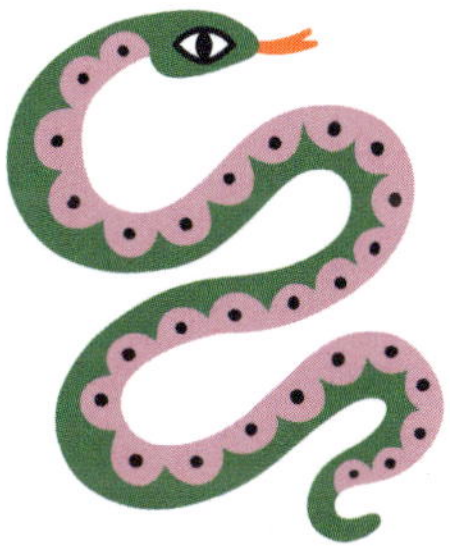

9. Add black dots to the center of each scallop.

BE BOLD!

Some snakes can be very ornate. Include additional colors or textures like triangle scales, dashes, or cute shapes like hearts and stars to make a new type of snake.

CAT

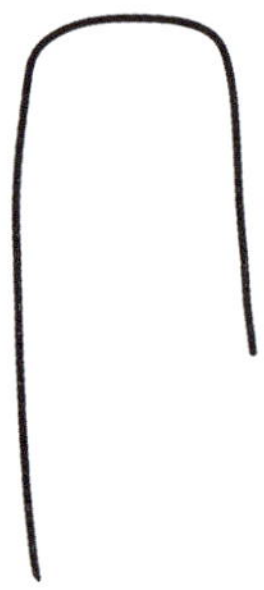

1. Start with a long upside-down U shape that is shorter on the right side.

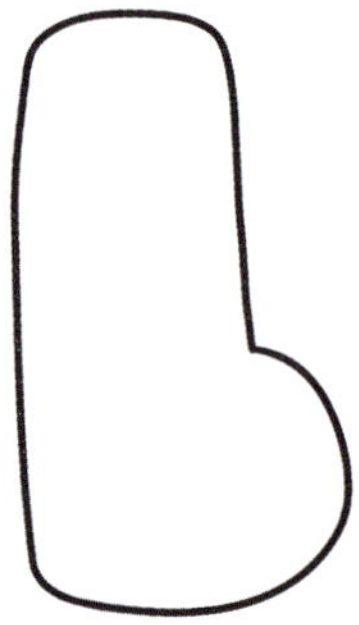

2. Add a curve connecting the ends of the U shape to make a B-shaped body.

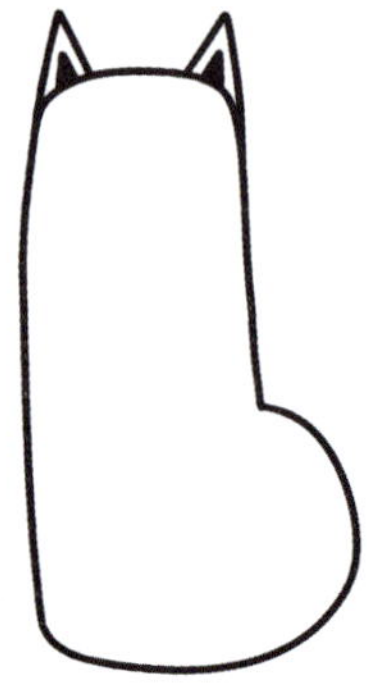

3. Draw two triangle ears, then add two smaller triangles in each.

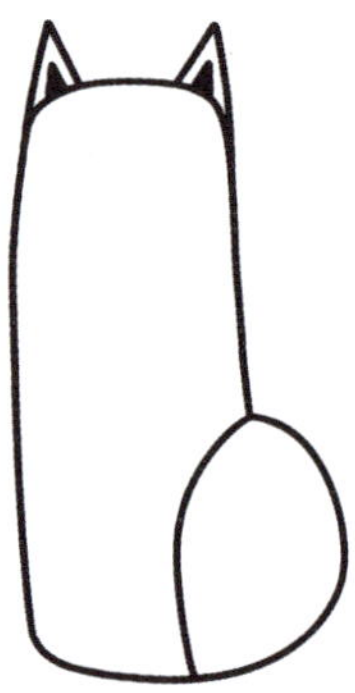

4. Segment off the bump of the B shape with a curved line.

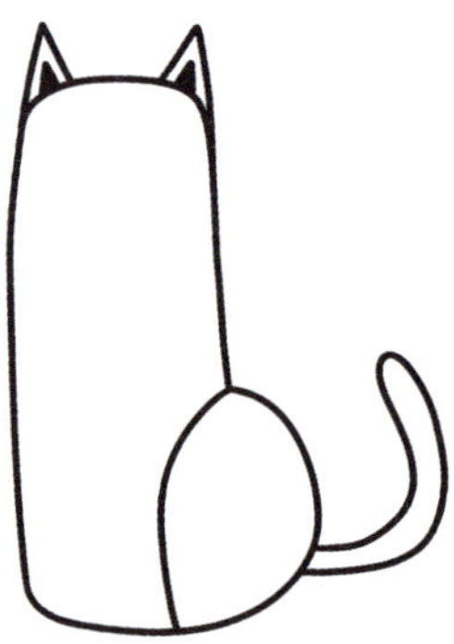

5. Draw a thin, curved tail on the bottom right.

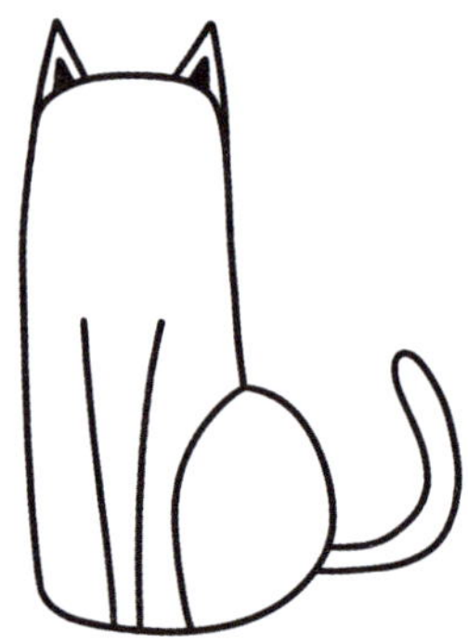

6. Draw two lines inside the body for the front legs.

BE BOLD!

What does your cat get up to? Give your cat a toy like a yarn ball to play with, or dress them up with a collar with their name on it.

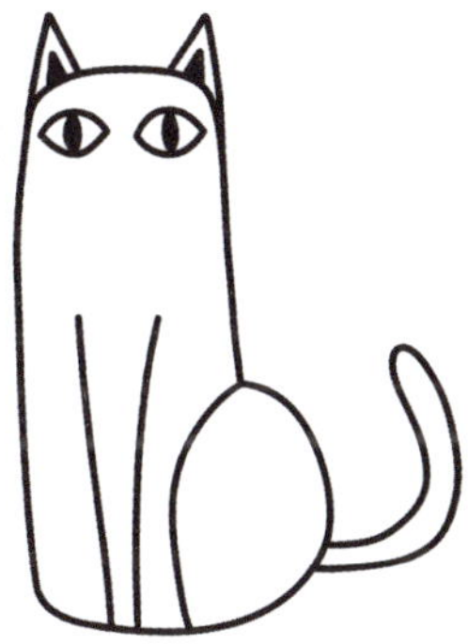

7. Draw two pointed eye shapes with ovals inside.

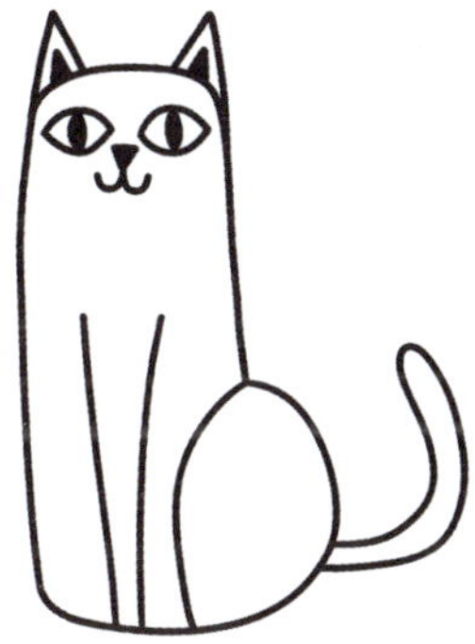

8. Draw a triangle nose and a curved mouth.

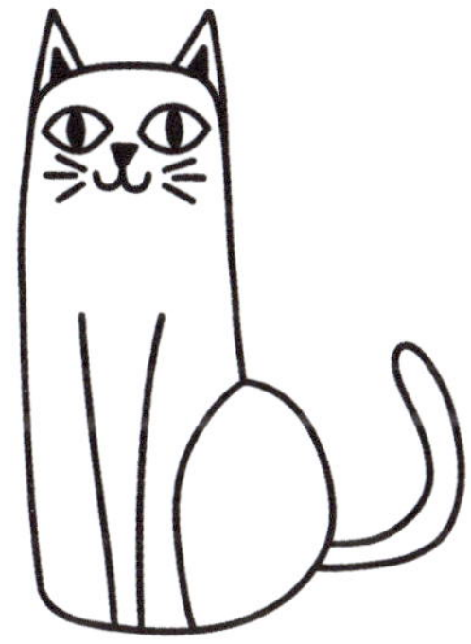

9. Add three short lines for whiskers on either side of the mouth.

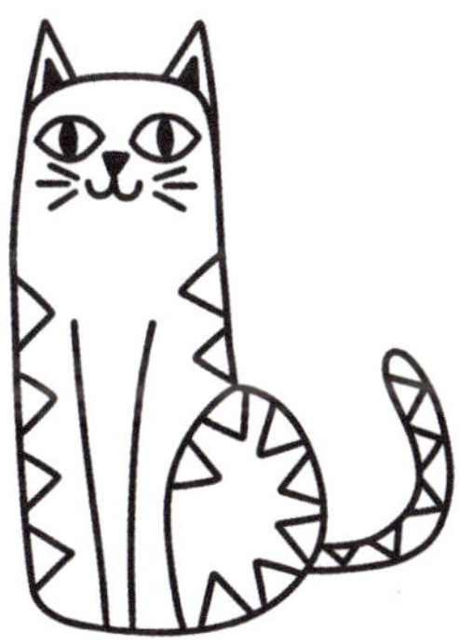

10. Draw triangle shapes along the inside edges of the body and the tail.

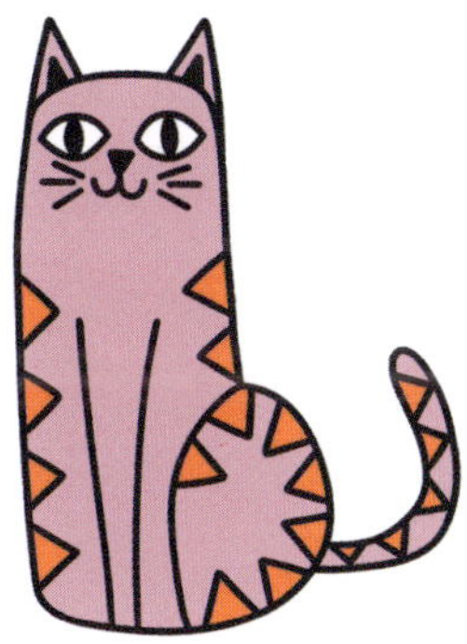

11. Fill in the cat with colors of your choice!

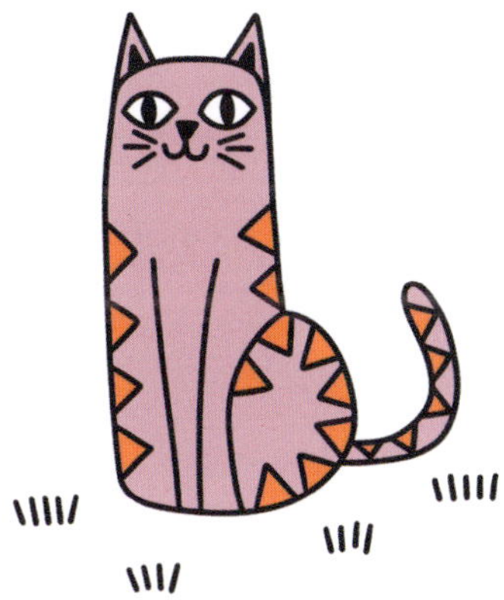

12. Add a few clusters of dashes to make grass surrounding the cat.

DACHSHUND

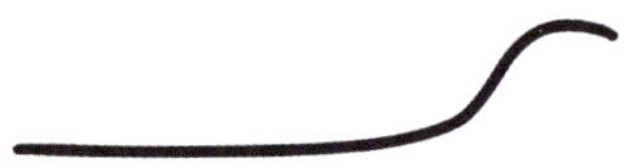

1. Start with a long horizontal line that has a curved bump on the right side.

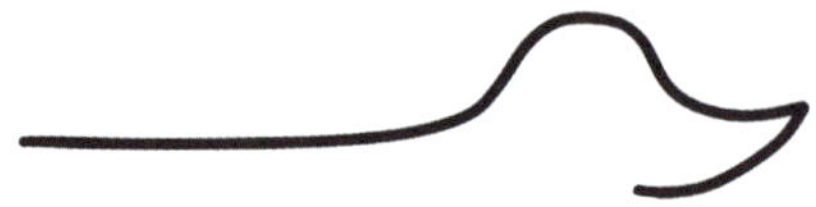

2. Draw a curved V shape for the snout.

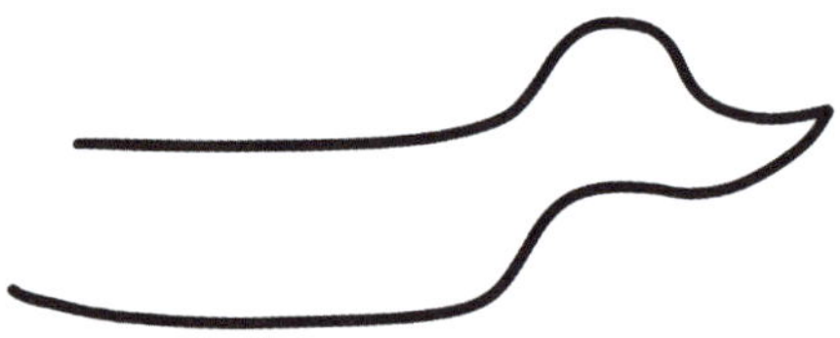

3. Draw a curved line to make the bottom of the body.

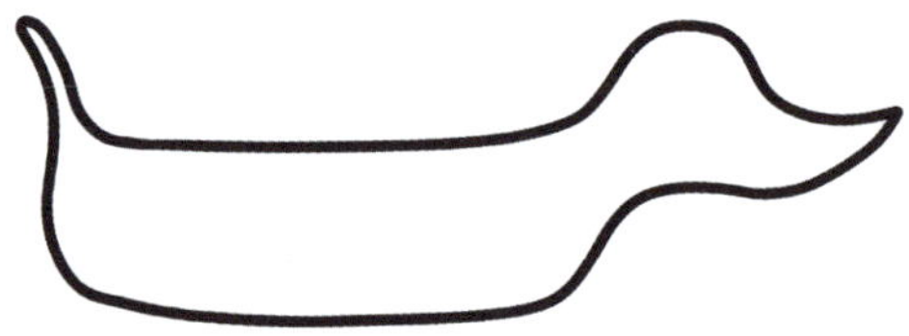

4. Connect your two horizontal lines with a thin, curved tail.

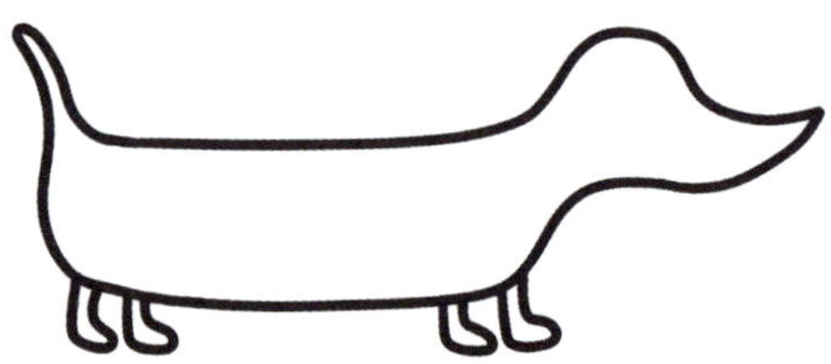

5. Draw four little L-shaped feet under the body.

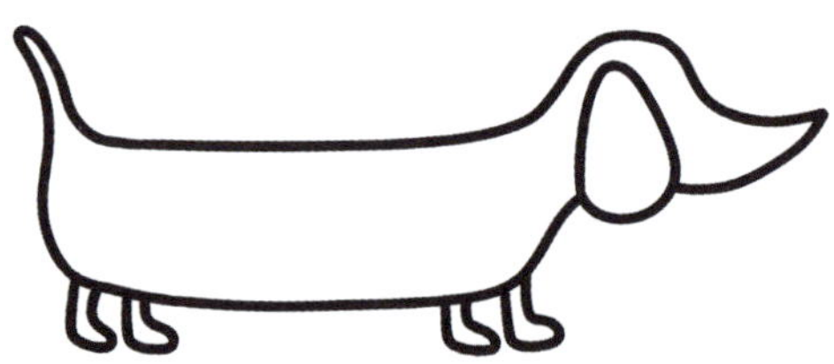

6. Draw an egg-shaped ear.

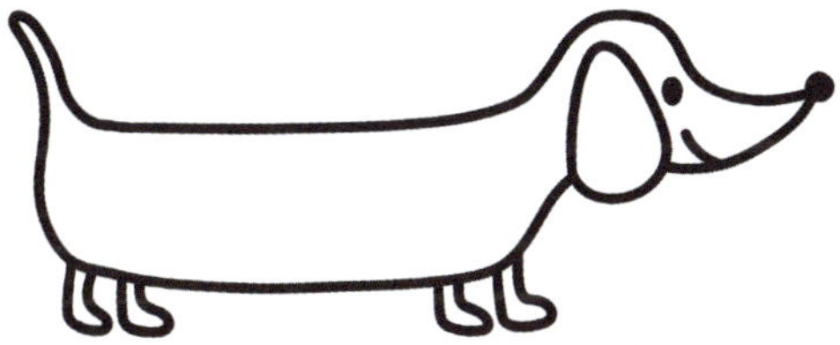

7. Add a dot for an eye, a small curve for the mouth, and a dot for the nose.

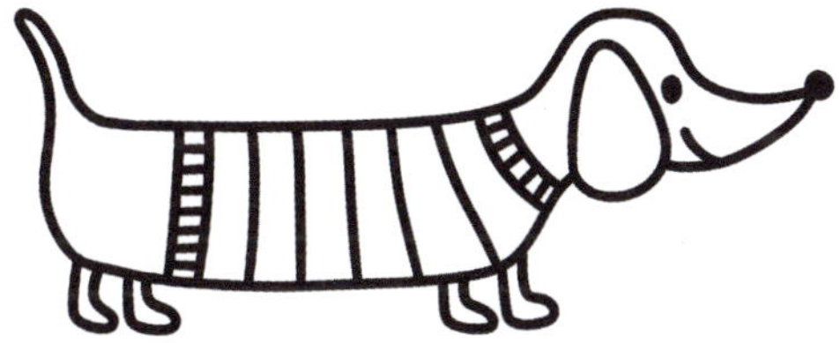

8. Draw a sweater by drawing a series of vertical lines along the body and dashes for stripes at the top and bottom of the sweater.

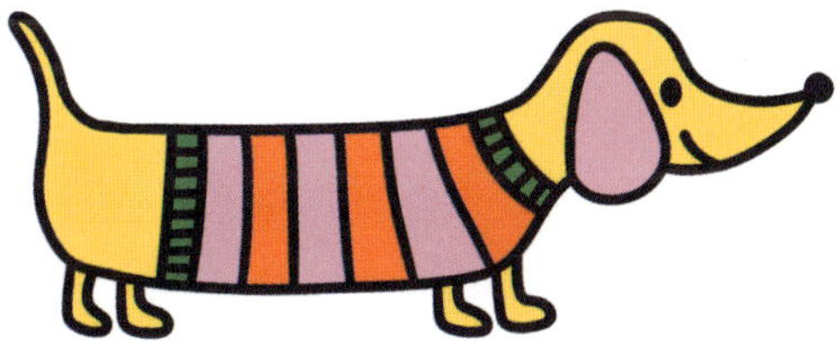

9. Fill in with the colors of your choice!

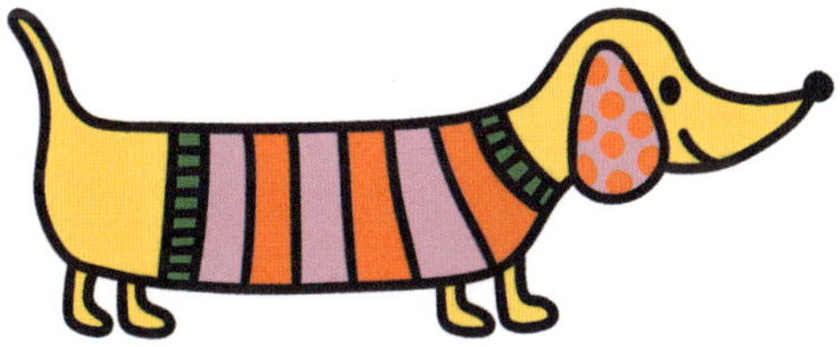

10. Decorate by adding polka dots to the ear.

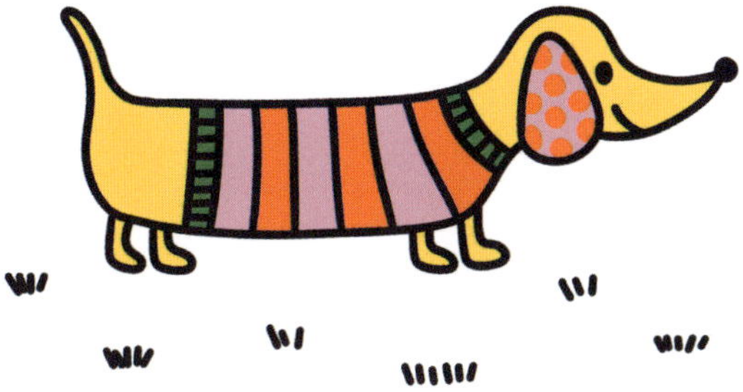

11. Add a few clusters of dashes to make grass.

BE BOLD!

Get creative with clothing. Give the sweater more details—maybe your dachshund is wearing an ugly Christmas sweater for the winter. Or have them wear a raincoat and little boots during a spring rain.

POODLE

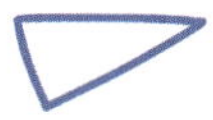

1. Start with a pointed triangle on the far right side of the page.

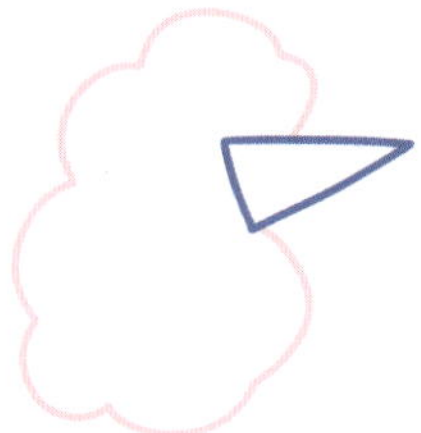

2. Draw a fluffy cloud shape around the base of the triangle for the poodle hair.

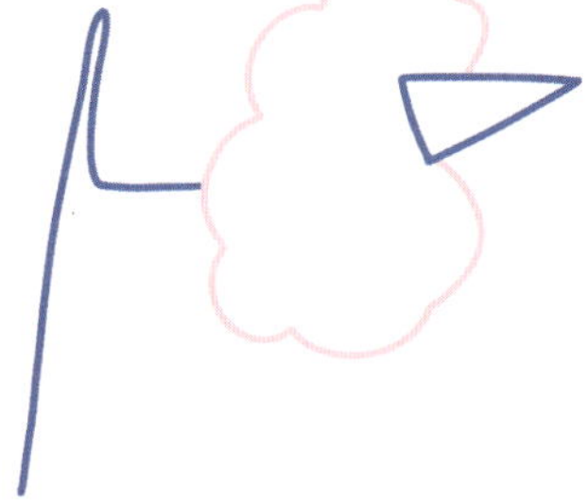

3. Draw a horizontal line on the left of the hair. Then make a tall, thin tail and extend the left side down.

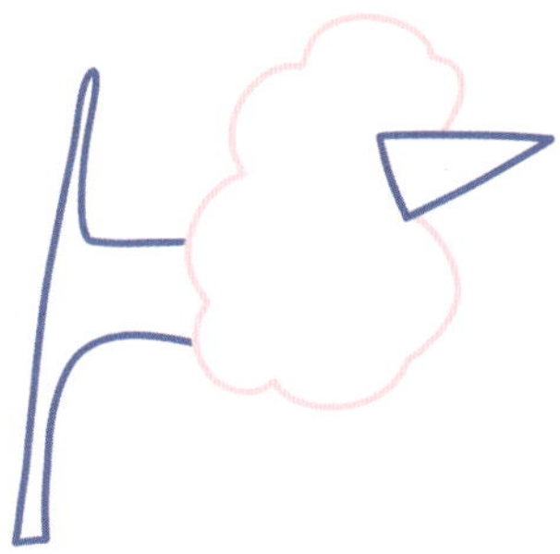

4. Start a thin, rectangle leg. Then draw a curved line connecting to the hair.

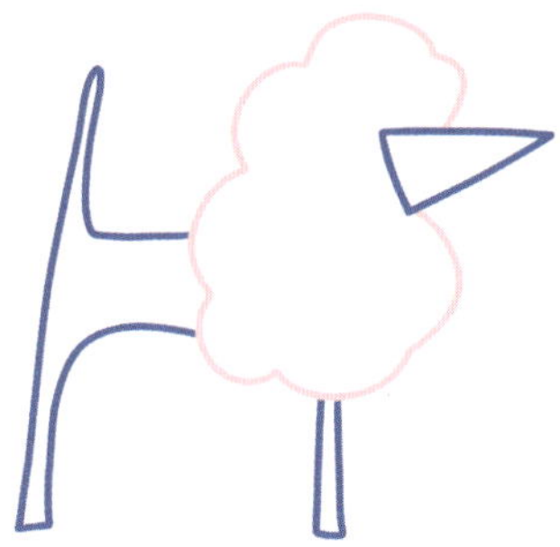

5. Add a long, thin rectangle shape under the hair.

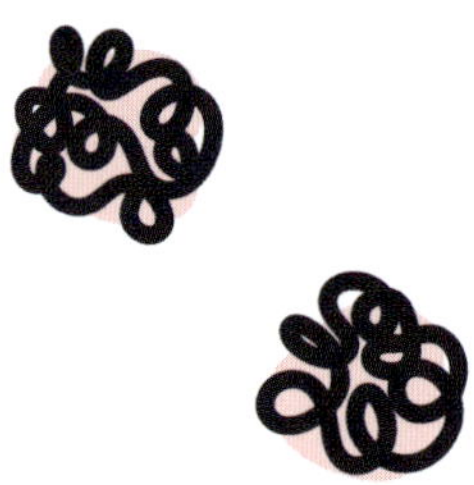

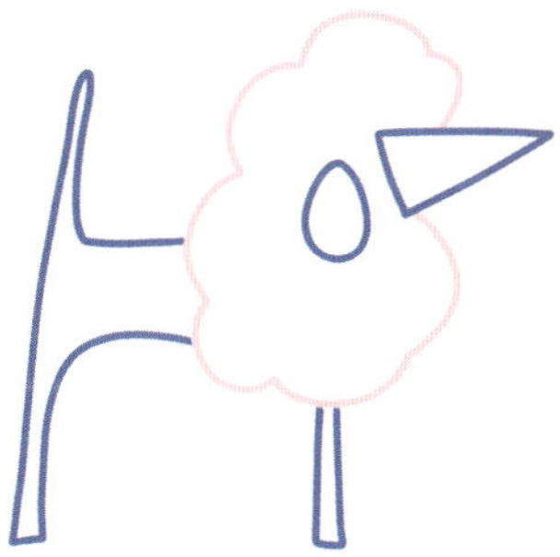

6. Draw a small egg-shaped ear.

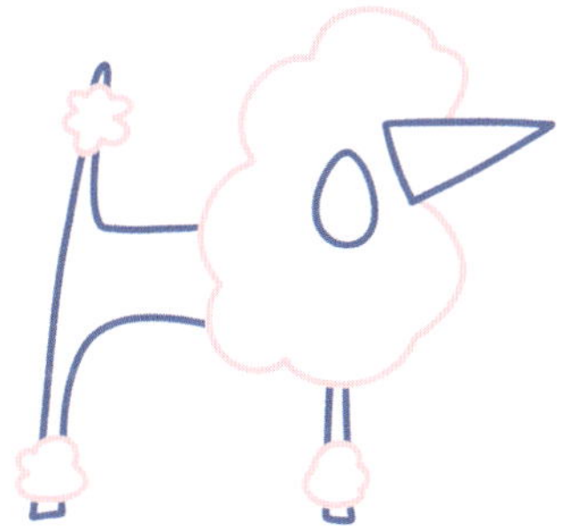

7. Draw additional little cloud shapes at the ends of the tail and both legs.

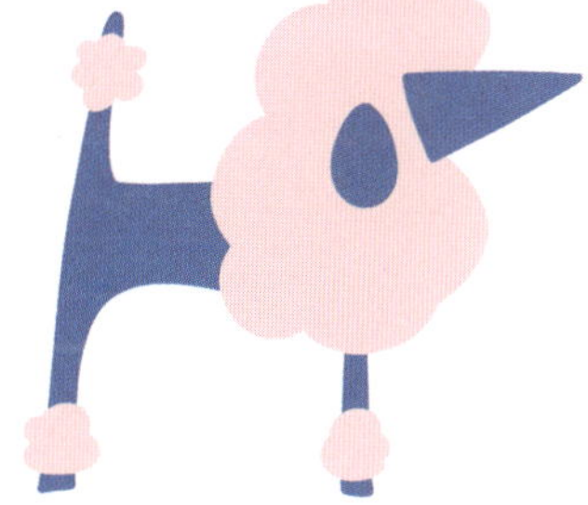

8. Fill in the colors!

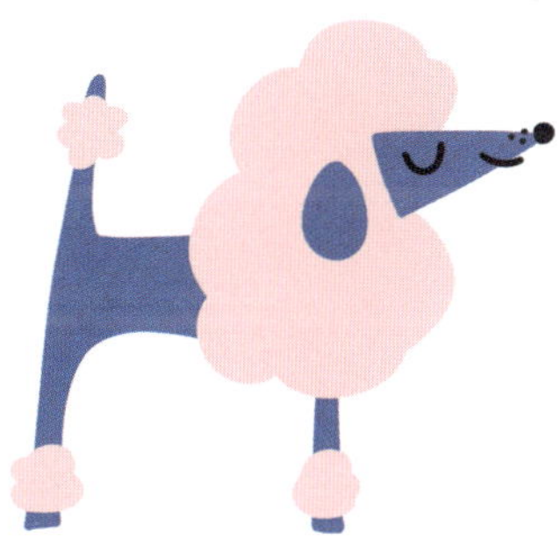

9. Create a face with a small curve for the eye, a shallow curve for the mouth, a large dot for the nose, and a few extra dots for freckles.

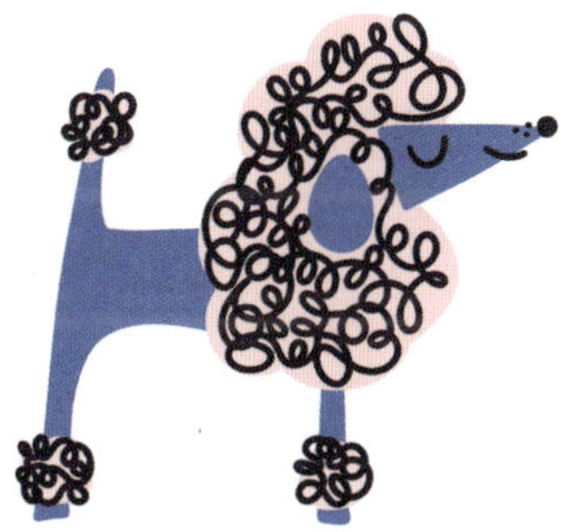

10. Create curly hair texture by drawing a bunch of doodle lines in the cloud shapes.

BE BOLD!

Poodles are known for their fancy hairdos. Get creative with the shapes of the hair around the head, tail, and feet or add a mohawk!

BUNNY

1. Start with an oval in the center of the page.

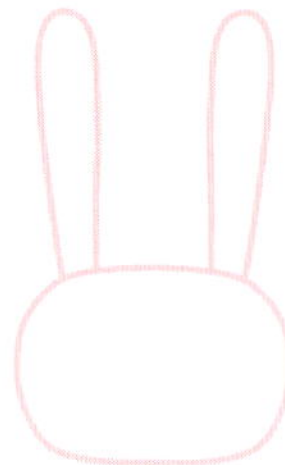

2. Add two extra-long U-shaped ears to the top of the oval head.

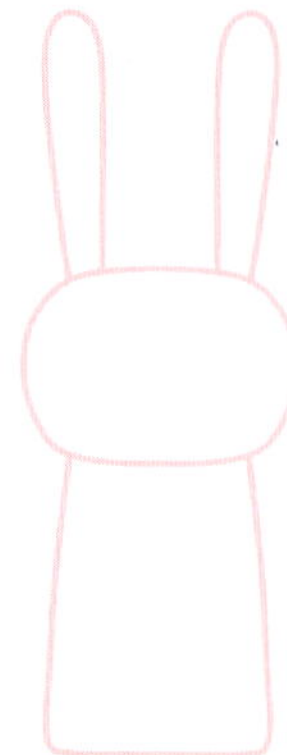

3. Draw a rectangular body that tapers slightly at the top under the oval.

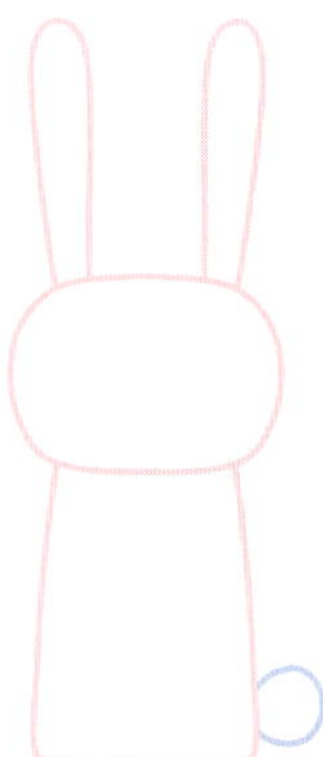

4. Draw a backward C-shaped tail on the bottom right of the body.

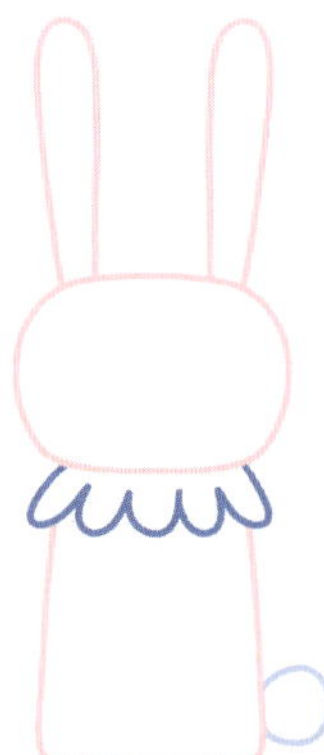

5. At the neck, add a scalloped collar.

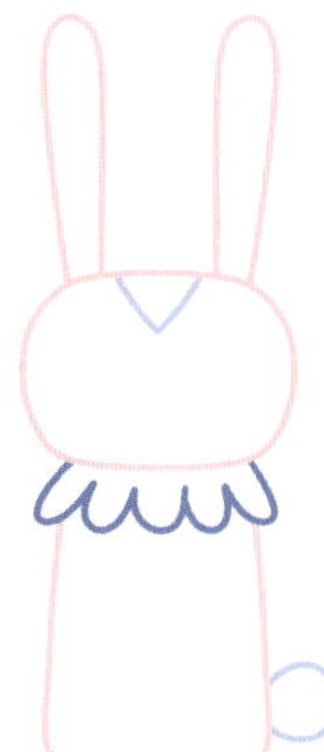

6. Draw a little triangle at the top of the head.

BE BOLD!

Create a scene perfect for spring by drawing a field of flowers around your bunny. Find all sorts of flower options in the Florals & Botanicals section of the book. Or get Easter ready by giving your bunny a basket of eggs!

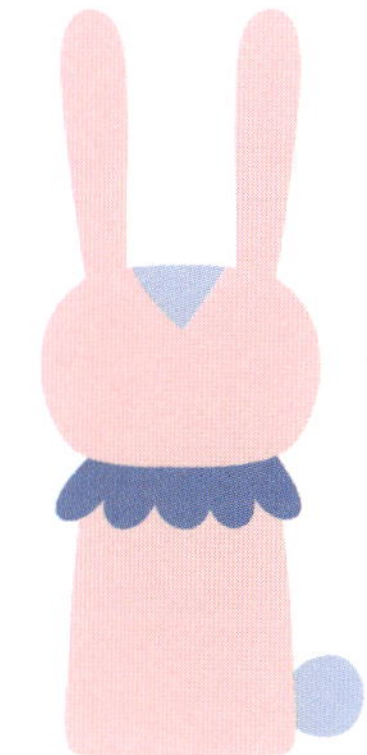

7. Fill in the colors!

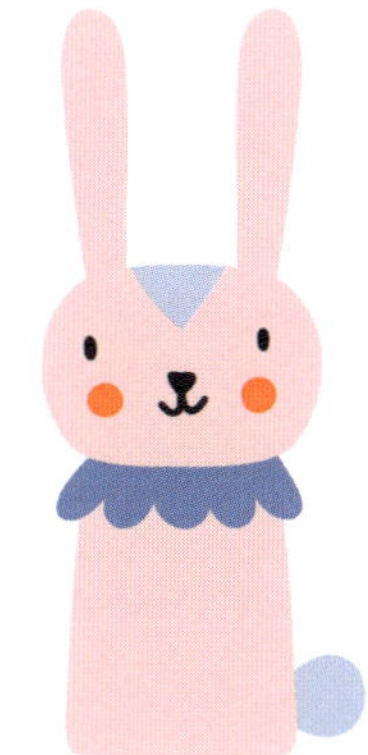

8. Draw two small black ovals for eyes, two circles for blush, and a little heart-shaped nose and a curved mouth.

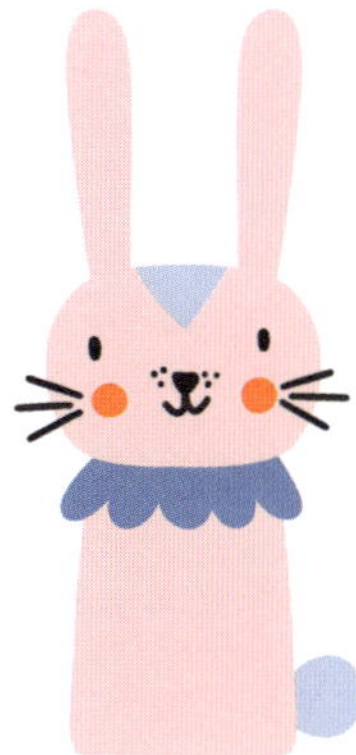

9. Add a cluster of dots around the nose and three long whiskers on each cheek.

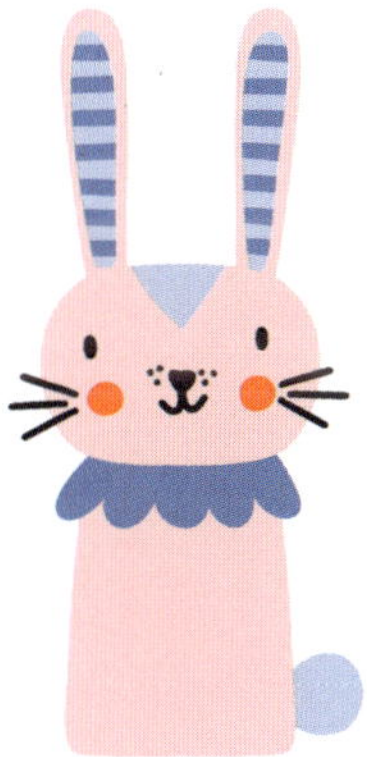

10. Draw a wobbly oval inside each ear and add a series of horizontal shapes for extra decoration.

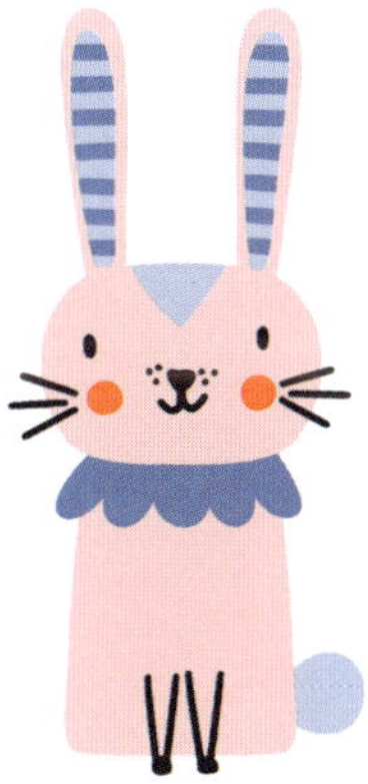

11. At the bottom of the bunny, draw two thin V-shaped legs with dots at the ends for feet.

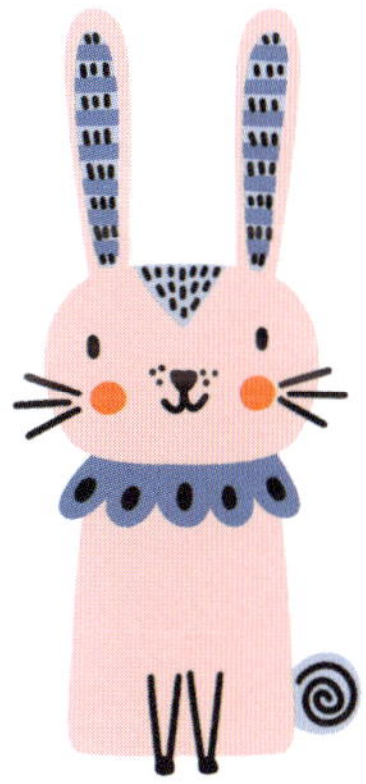

12. Decorate with dots on the collar, a swirl on the tail, and dashes on the ears and the triangle patch on its head.

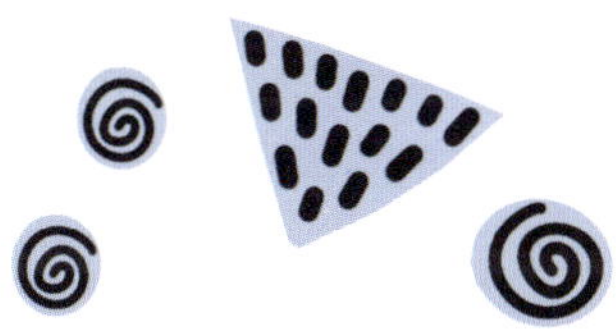

CHICKEN

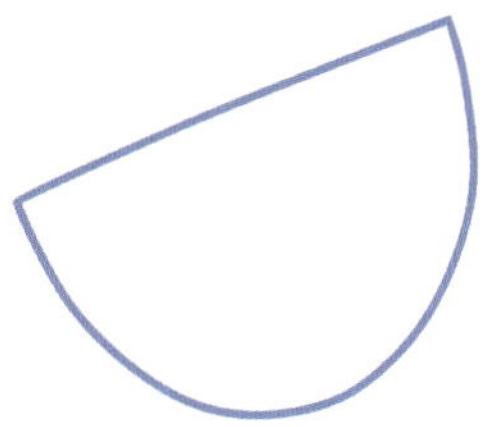

1. Start with a tilted semicircle on the right side of the page.

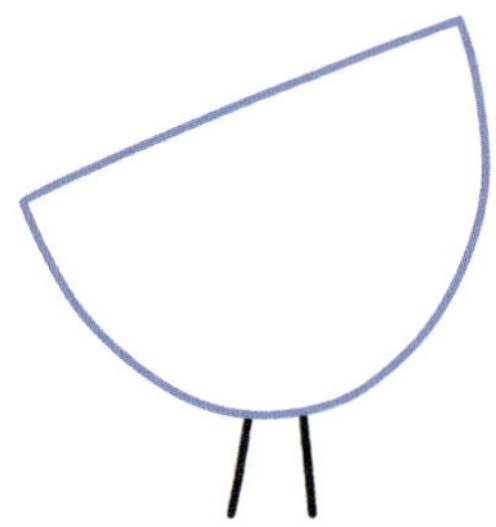

2. Draw two vertical lines, slightly tilted outward, at the bottom.

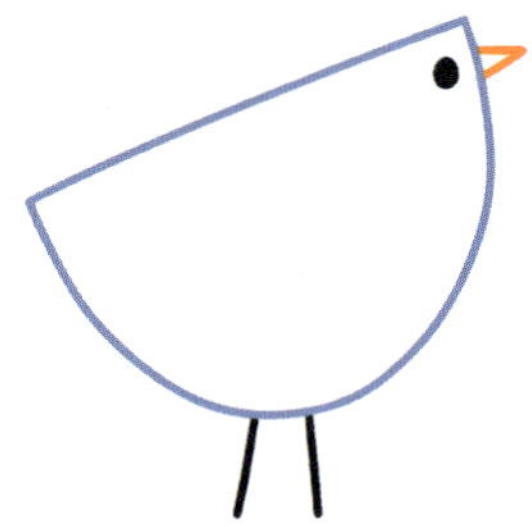

3. Add a black dot for the eye and a small triangle beak.

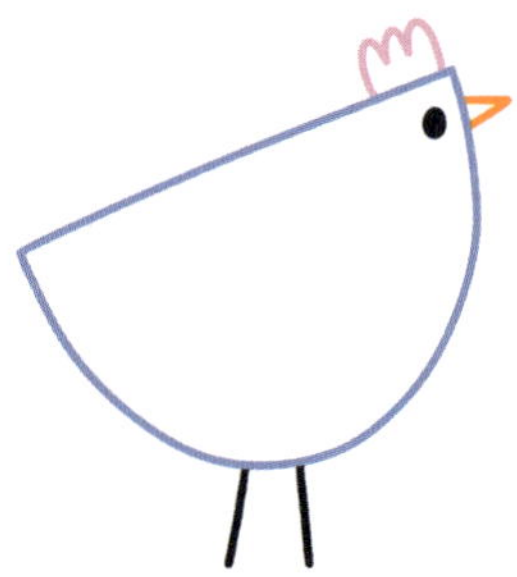

4. Draw the comb with a square with scallops on top.

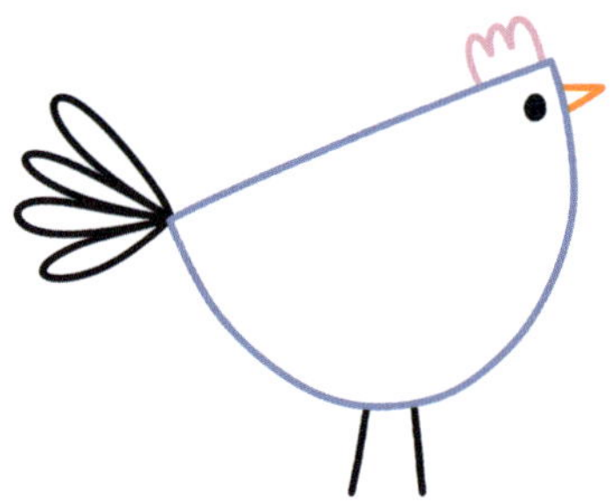

5. Draw four thin teardrop-shaped tail feathers.

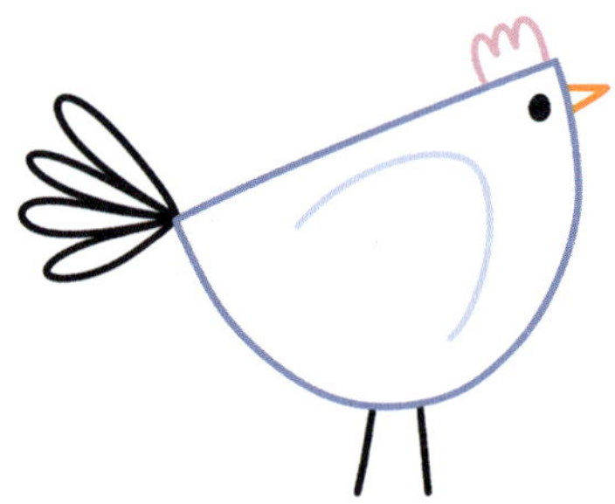

6. Add a U-shaped wing.

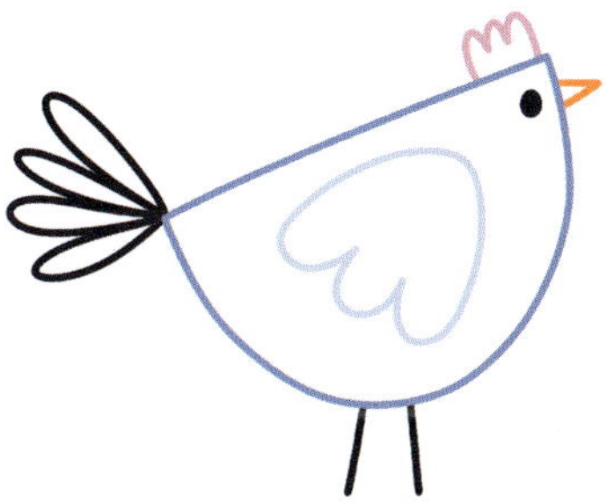

7. Add three scallops to the wing for feathers.

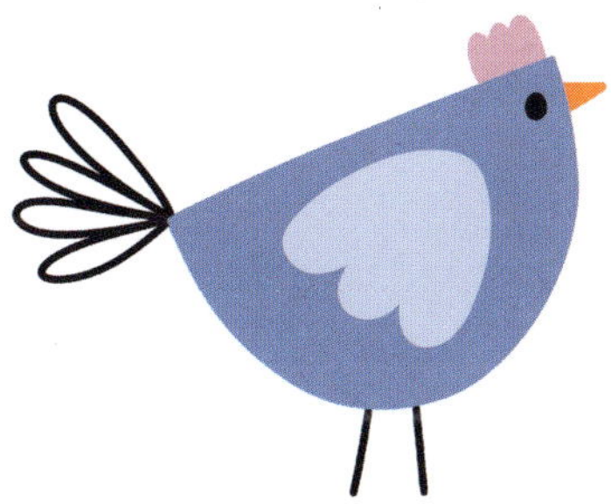

8. Fill in the chicken with colors!

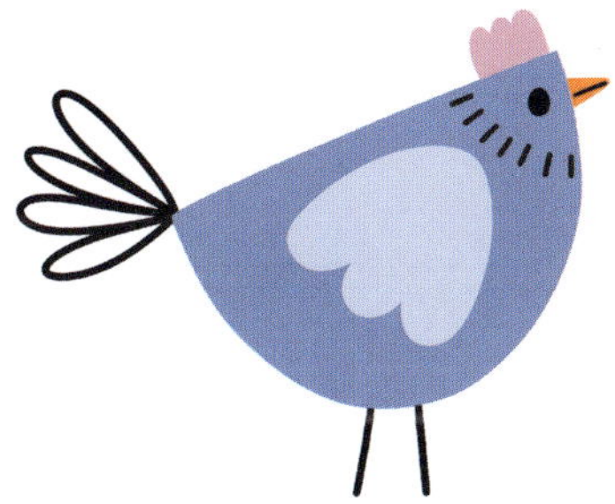

9. Add a black line through the center of the beak and a curved line of dashes around the neck.

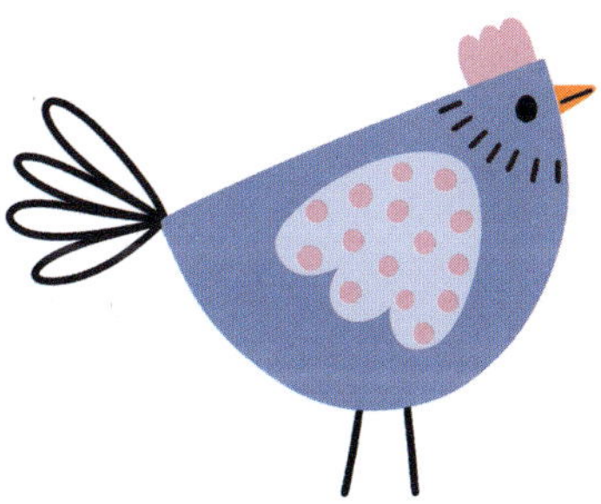

10. Decorate the wing with polka dots.

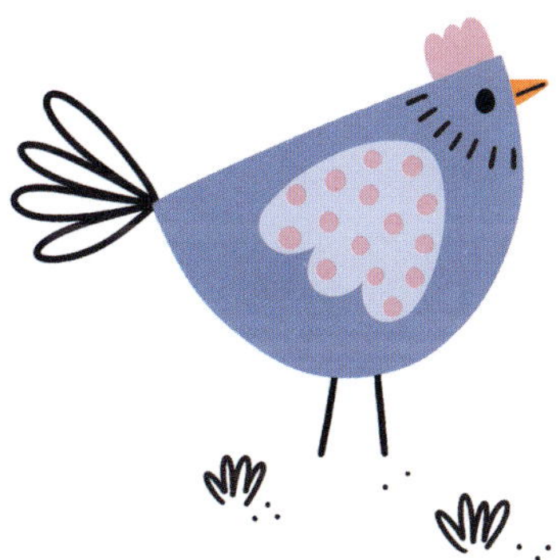

11. Add little clusters of grass and dots around the legs to create the ground.

BE BOLD!

Chickens are often found in groups. Give your chicken some friends by drawing a few more in different colors. Maybe even give them a few eggs to take care of.

SHEEP

1. Start with a large cloud shape in the center of the page.

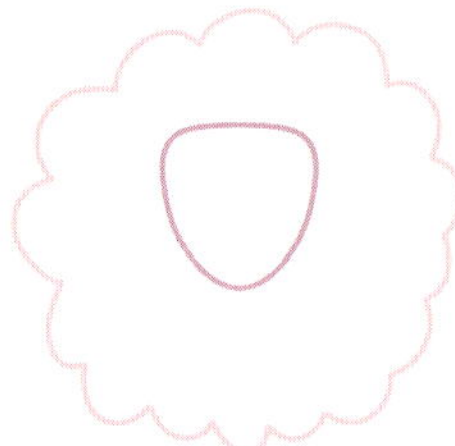

2. Add a rounded triangle with a flat top in the center of the cloud.

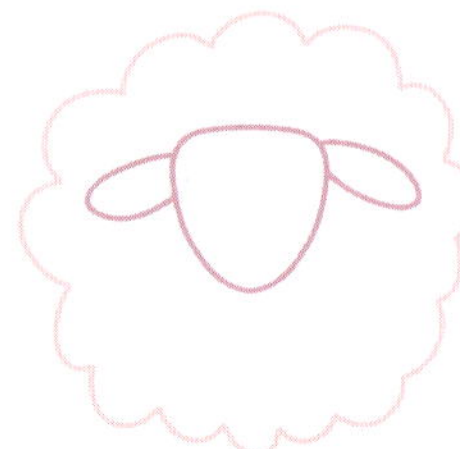

3. Draw two oval ears on either side of the triangle head.

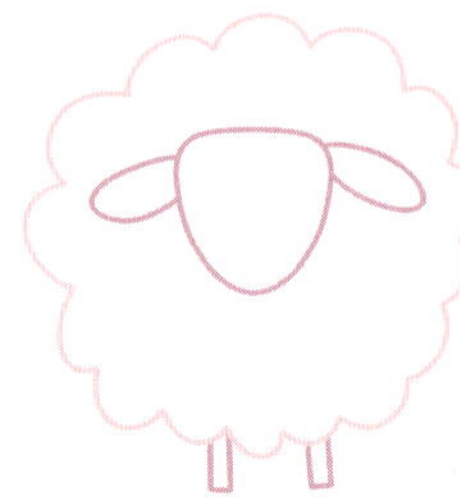

4. Add two small, narrow rectangle legs.

5. Fill in the colors!

6. Add two little triangles to the bottom of each leg for the hooves.

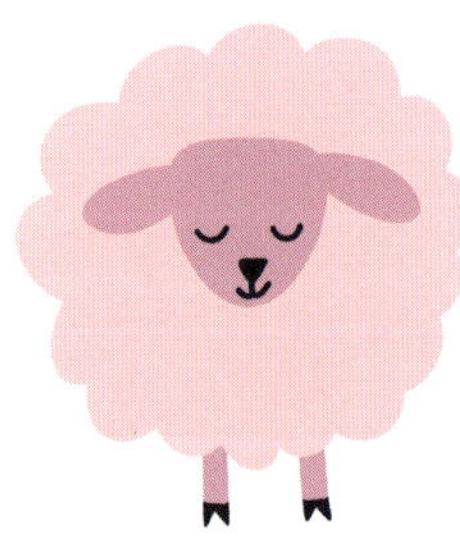

7. Add two curves for eyes, a triangle nose, and a curved mouth.

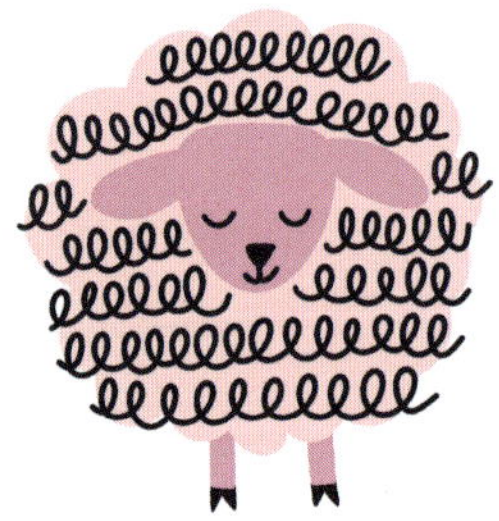

8. Give the wool curly texture by drawing a bunch of swirly lines in the cloud shape.

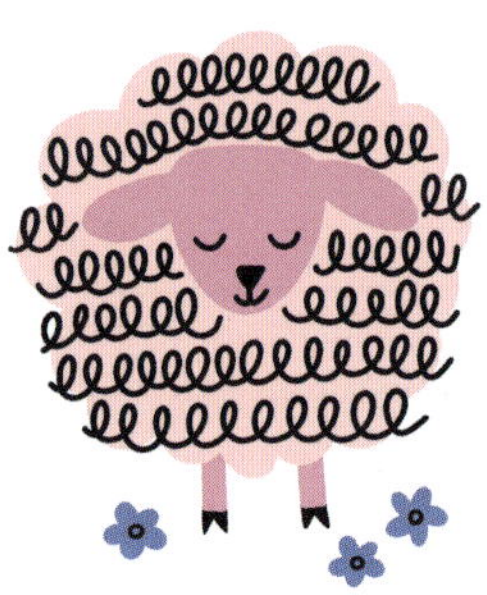

9. Draw a couple of five-petal flowers with a circle in the center around the sheep's feet.

BE BOLD!

Sheep can come in all sorts of natural colors, or they can have their wool dyed to be any color. How many different colors can you make for a single flock of sheep?

BEAR

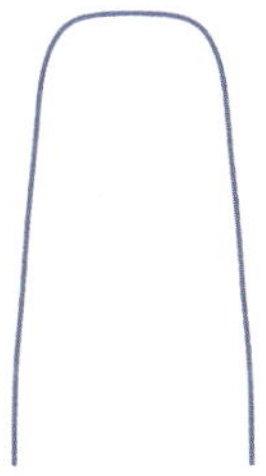

1. Start with an extra-long, upside-down U shape.

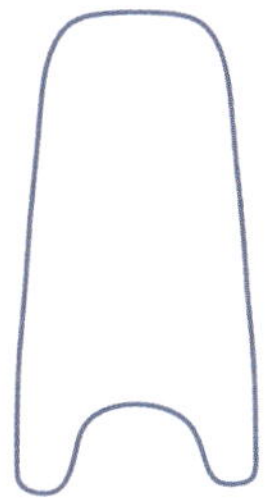

2. Connect the bottom of the U shape with a wavy line that creates two little nubs on each side and an arch in the middle.

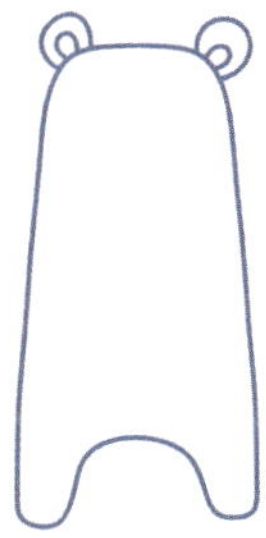

3. Draw two curved ears on the top corners of the bear, then add a smaller curve inside each.

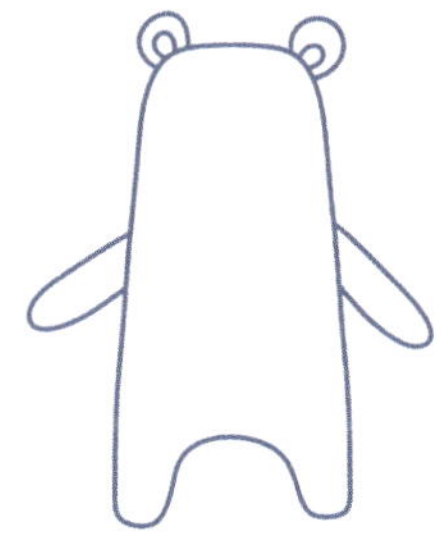

4. Draw one long U-shaped arm on each side of the body.

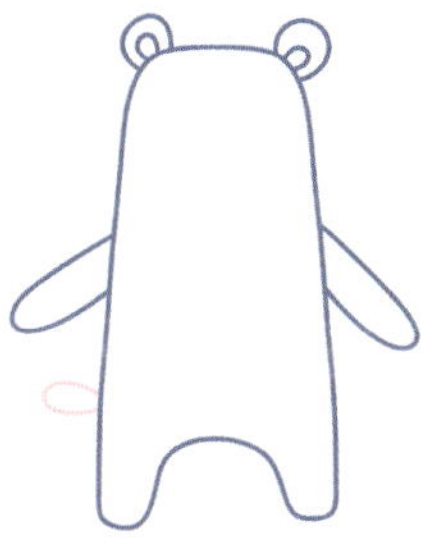

5. On the lower left side, add a little teardrop-shaped tail.

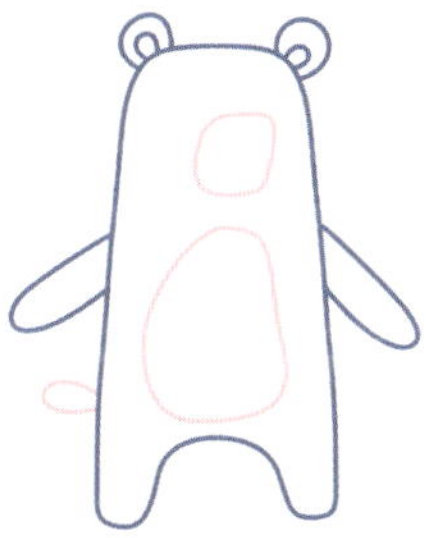

6. Draw a wobbly square for the snout and a wobbly egg shape on the stomach.

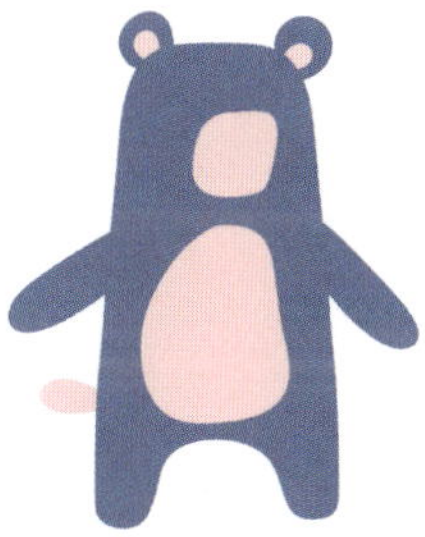

7. Fill in the colors!

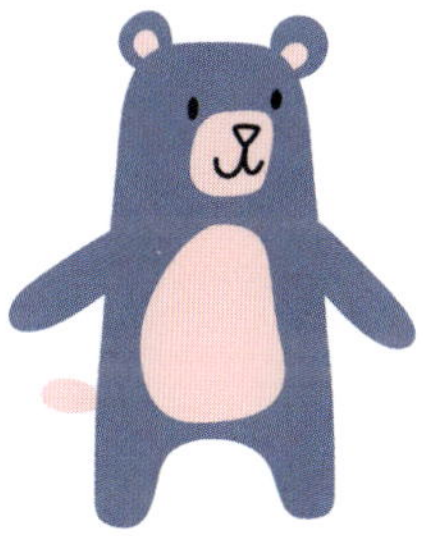

8. Add two black oval eyes, a triangle nose, and a curved mouth.

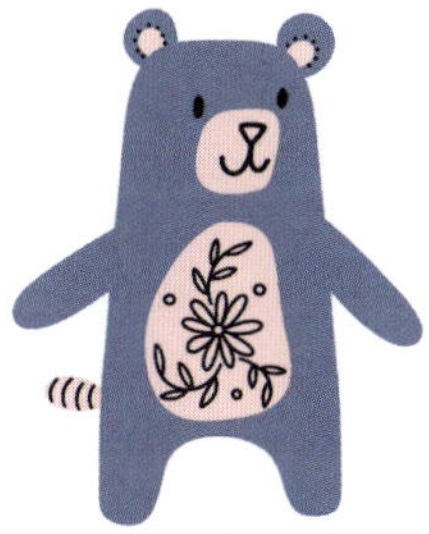

9. Decorate with dots in the ears, curved lines on the tail, and a flower with leaves and circles on the stomach.

BE BOLD!

Do you, or someone you know, have a favorite stuffed bear toy? Make the colors and decorations of your bear match the toy for an extra special drawing.

FISH

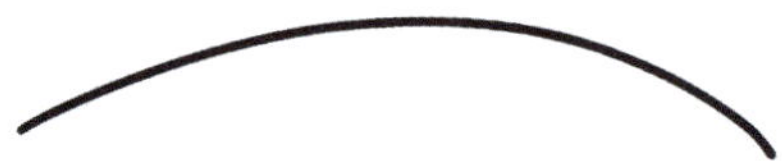

1. Start with a long, curved line.

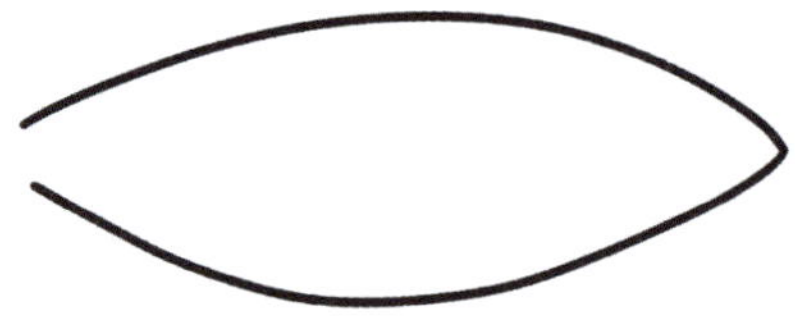

2. Connect another curved line underneath, with the ends on the right connected in a point.

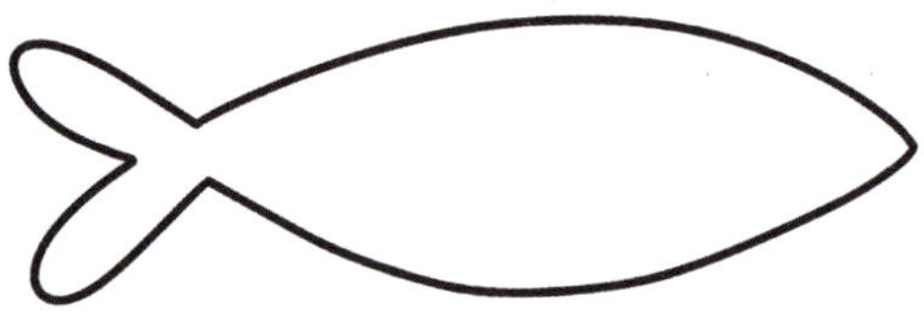

3. Connect the left end with a rounded V-shaped tail.

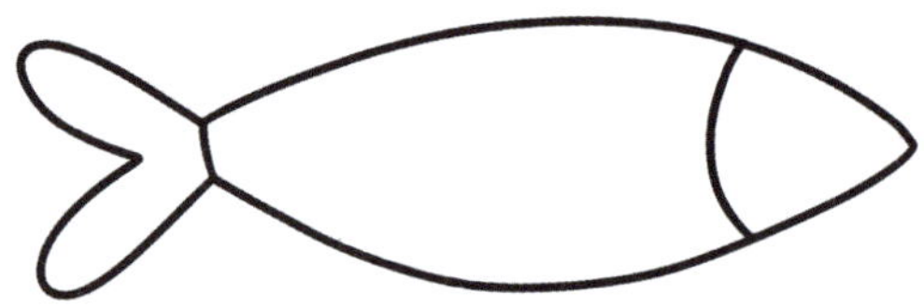

4. Draw a curved line at the top of the tail and another near the right of the fish body.

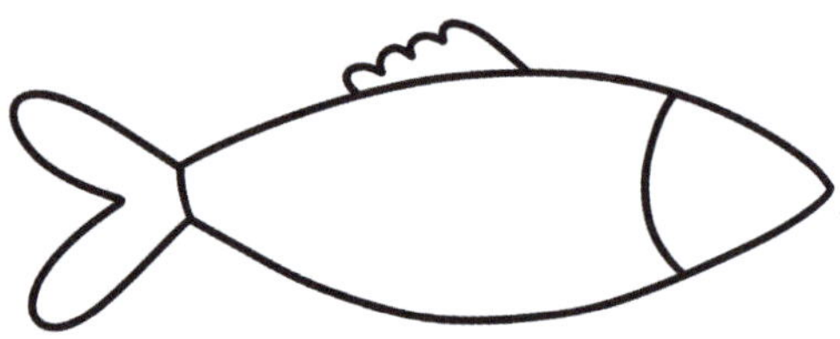

5. Add a scalloped fin shape on top of the fish.

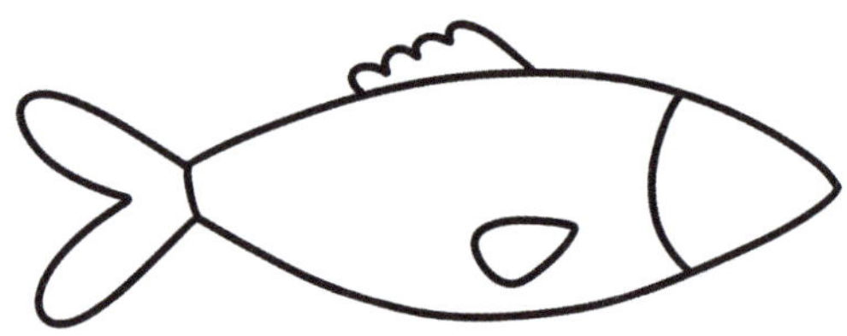

6. Draw a small teardrop-shaped fin near the bottom of the fish body.

BE BOLD!

Complete the scene! Does your fish live in a lake, pond, river, or the ocean? Choose what color the water is and fill in the page with plants and other fishy friends.

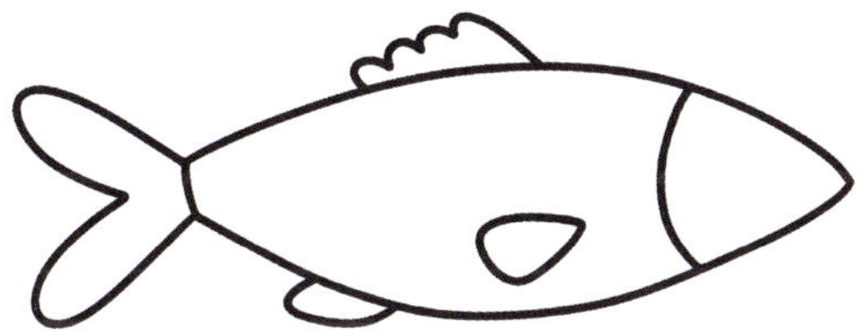

7. Add an elongated U-shaped fin under the body.

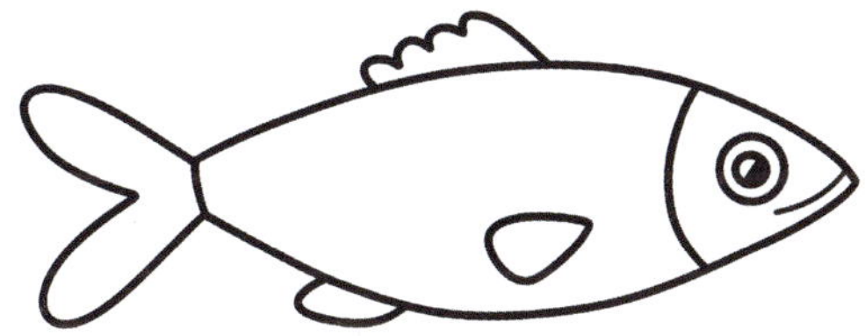

8. Draw a thin, curved mouth and two circles for an eye. Split the center circle of the eye in half and only shade half to create a highlight.

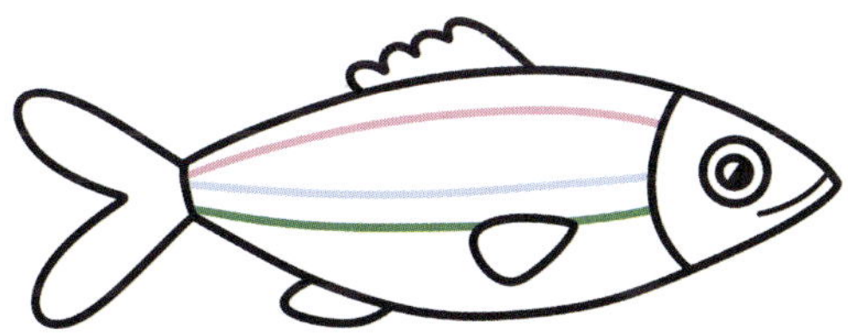

9. Add three curved stripes across the body of the fish.

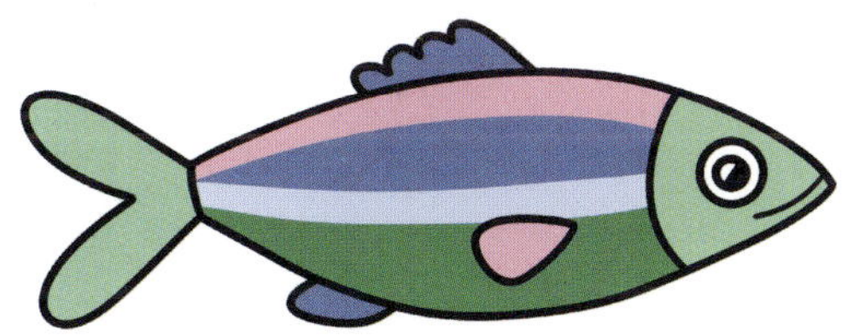

10. Fill in the colors!

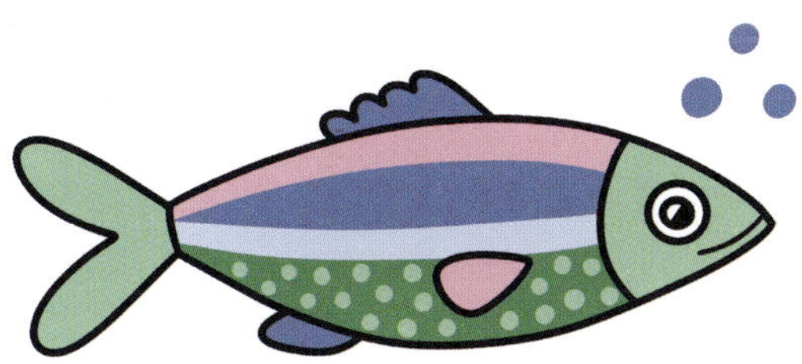

11. Add dots to the belly of the fish and more above the head for bubbles.

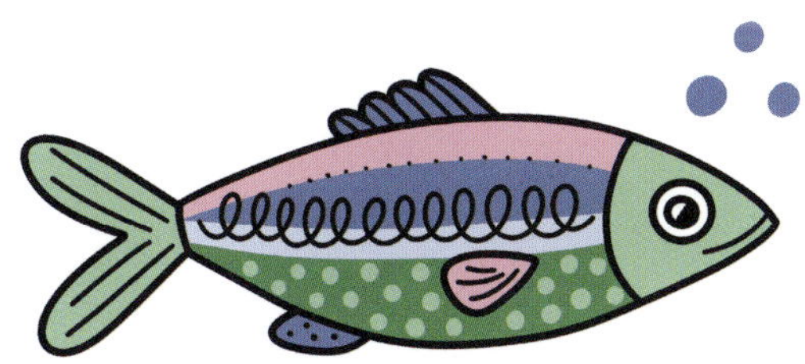

12. Decorate with a series of lines, dots, and swirls for texture on the fins and body.

LOBSTER

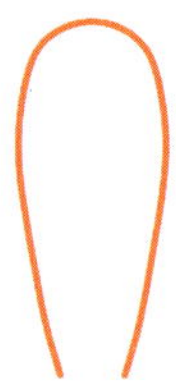

1. Start with a narrow, upside-down U shape.

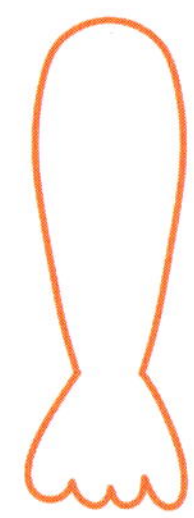

2. Create a triangular tail with a scalloped bottom edge.

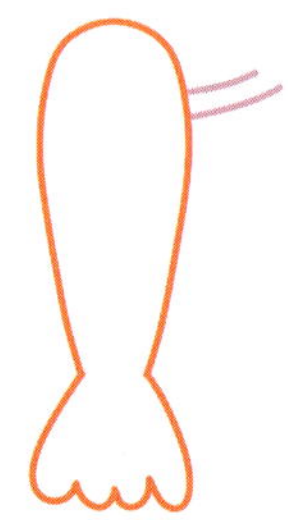

3. Draw two parallel curved lines near the top right of the body.

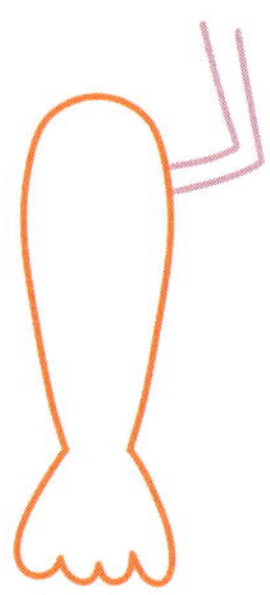

4. Extend the lines up to make a backward L.

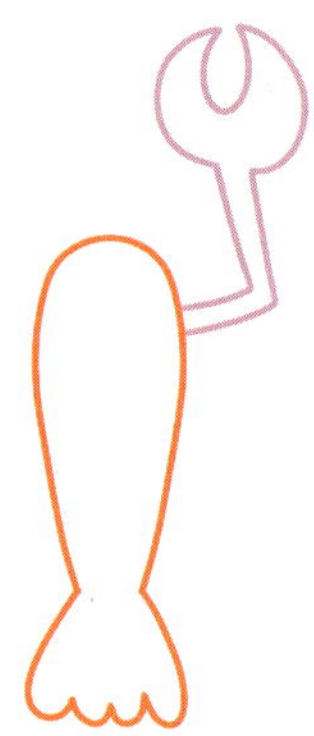

5. Finish the arm with a curved claw shape, using two crescents that connect in the center.

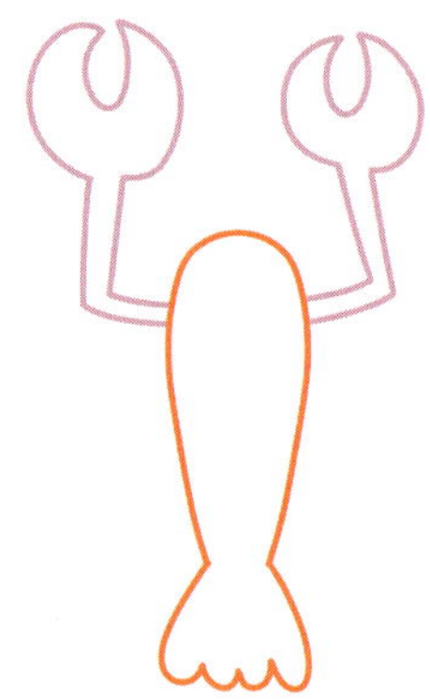

6. Repeat steps 3 to 5 for the left arm.

BE BOLD!

Lobsters come in lots of colors, including blue, green, brown, or even a calico or split pattern. Their shapes also can be different, with spines on their shells or one claw bigger than the other. Get creative with what your lobster looks like.

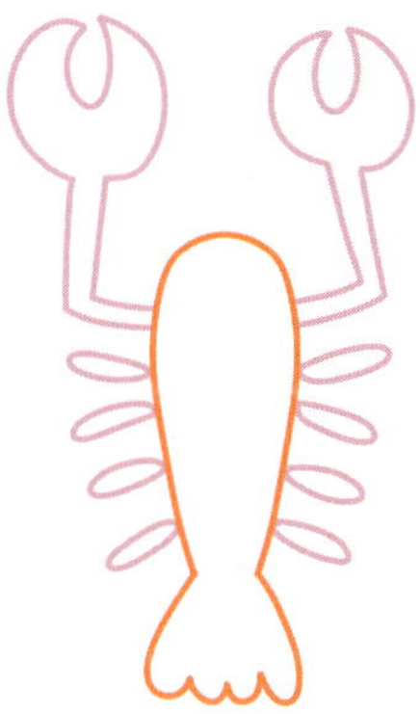

7. Draw four thin ovals on each side of the body.

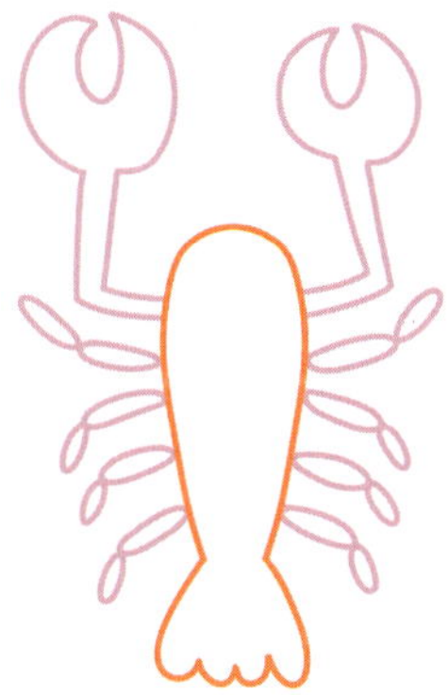

8. Add a smaller oval at an angle to the end of each oval.

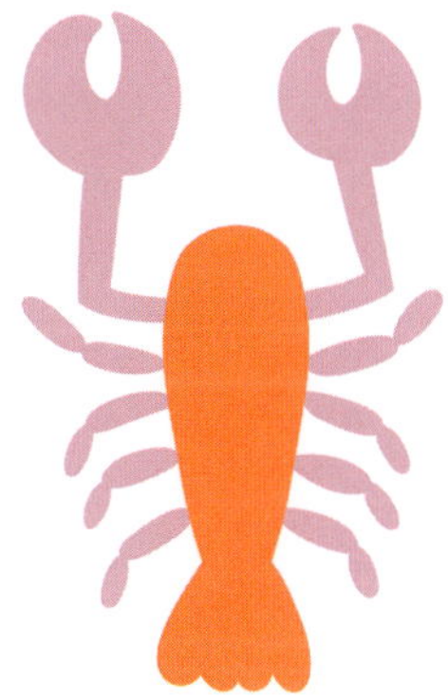

9. Fill in the colors!

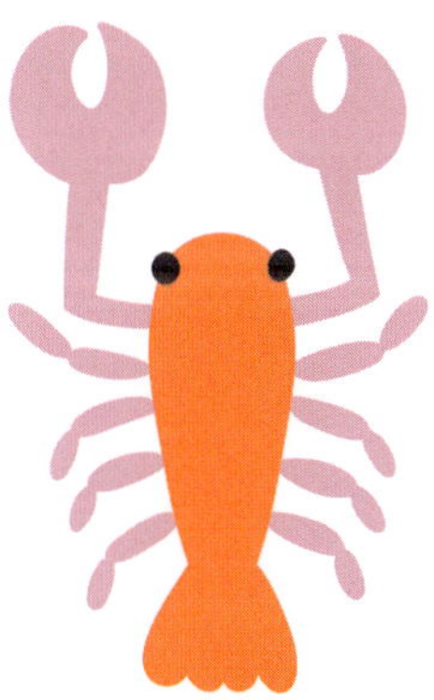

10. Add two black dots at the top of the body for eyes.

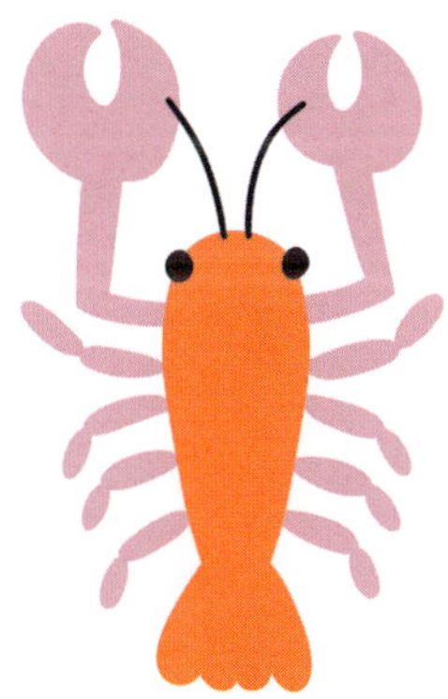

11. Draw two curved antennae at the top of the body, overlapping the claws.

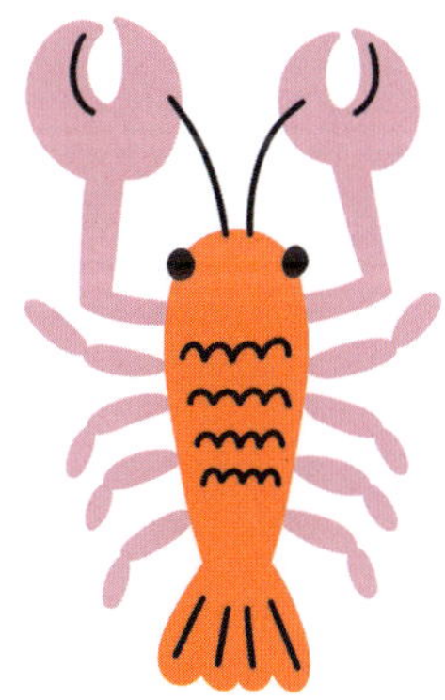

12. Decorate with texture lines on the tail and claws and scalloped lines for the shell on the body.

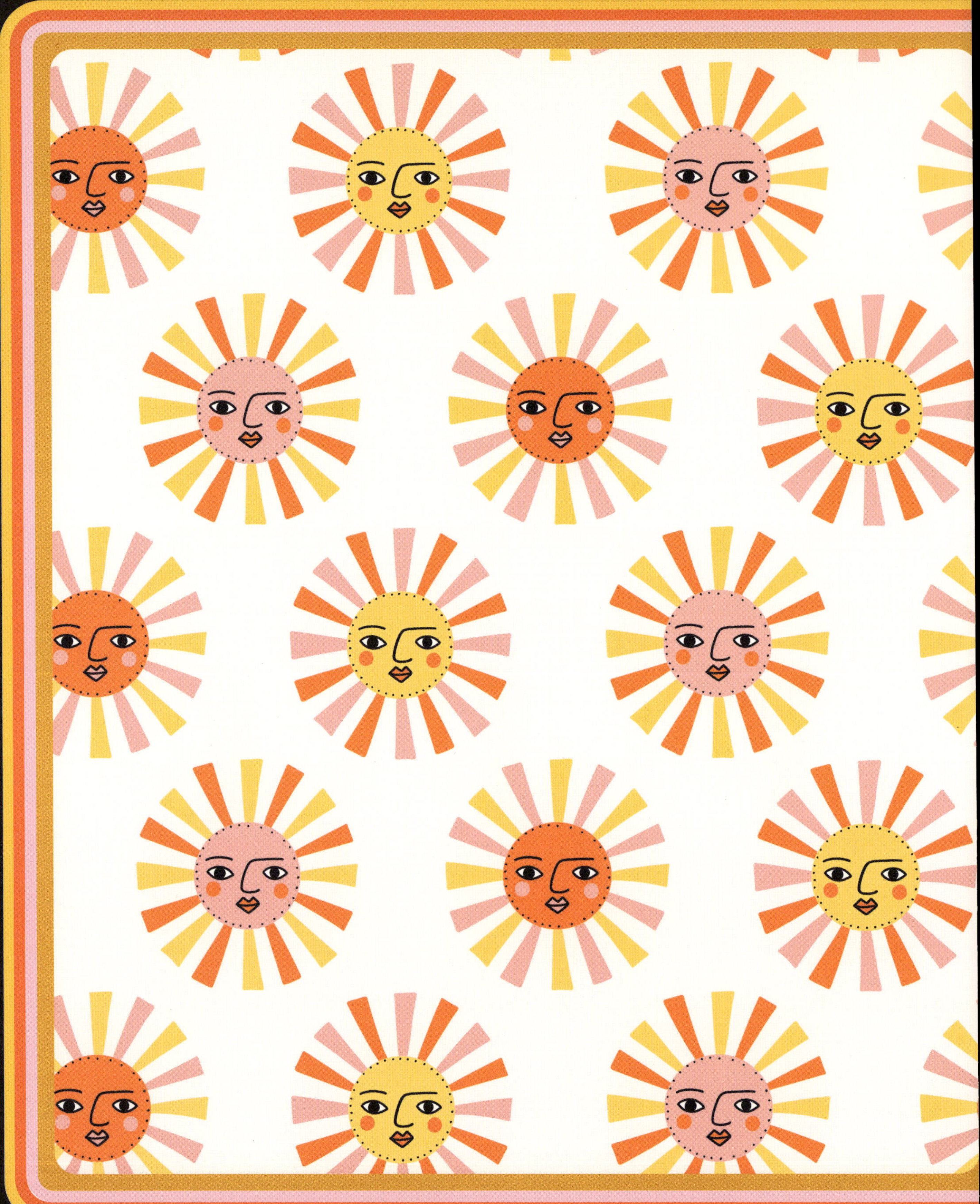

EVERYDAY OBJECTS

ROLLER SKATE

1. Start with a large L-line.

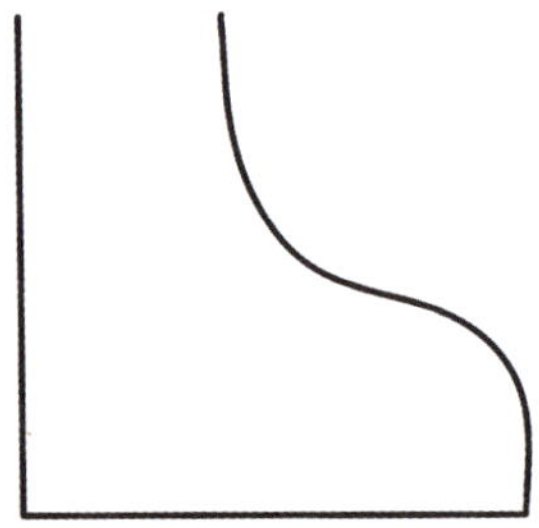

2. Draw a wavy line that connects to the right corner of the L-line.

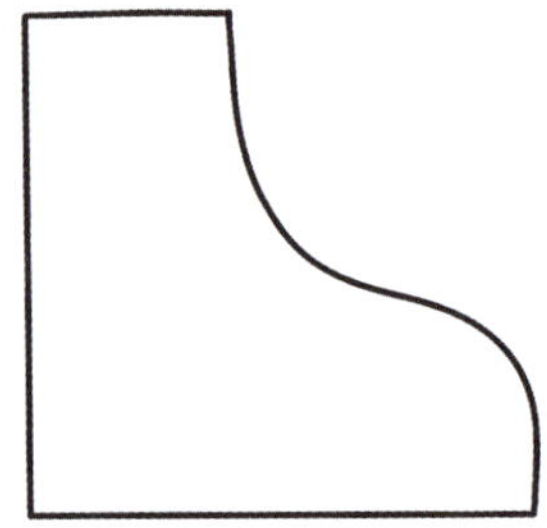

3. Close the top of the skate with a straight line.

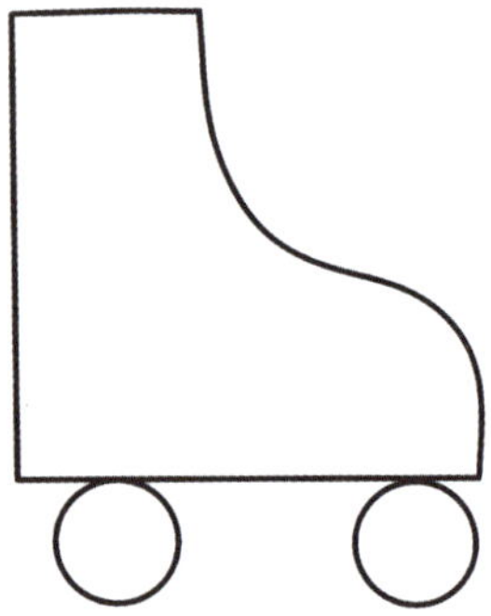

4. Draw two circles to make the wheels.

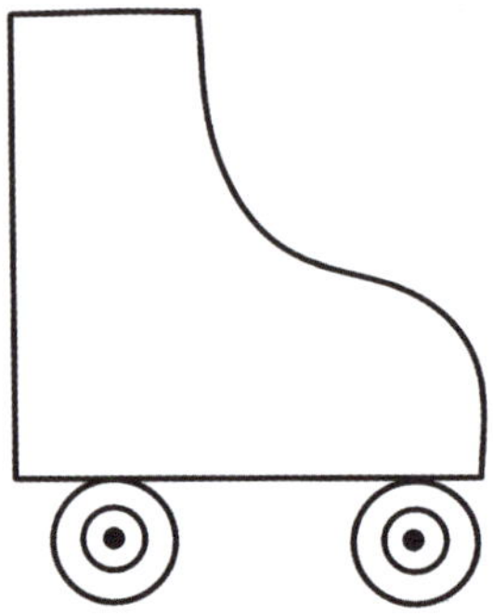

5. Draw a smaller circle and a dot in each circle.

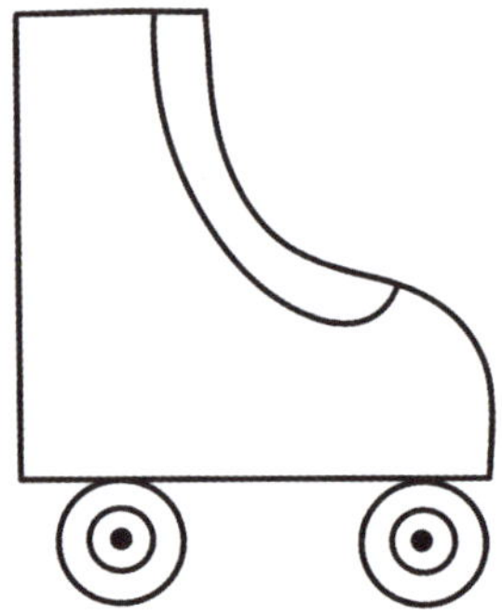

6. Draw a curved line inside the skate to make the tongue.

BE BOLD!

Play around with a variety of colors and decoration items to make the skate match your style. You can even use a bunch of overlapping dots in different shades of the same color to create a "glitter" effect.

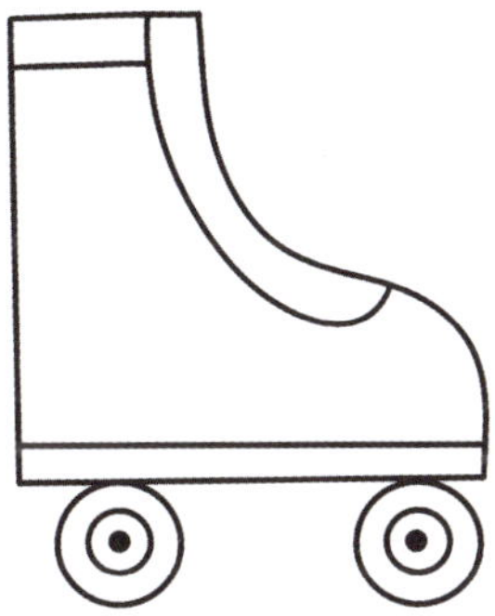

7. Draw a horizontal line at the top and bottom of the skate.

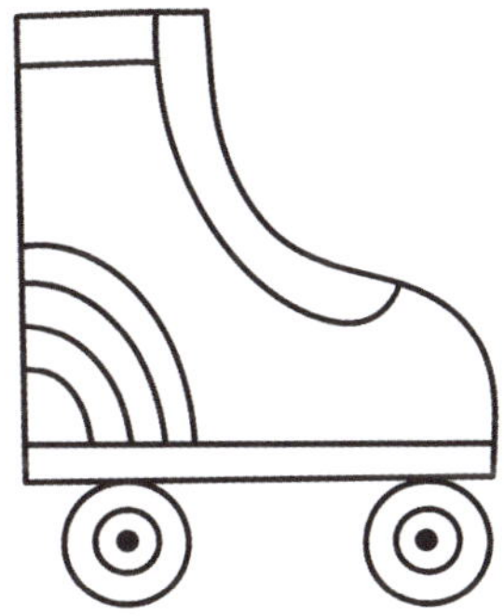

8. Add four curved lines to the bottom left corner of the skate.

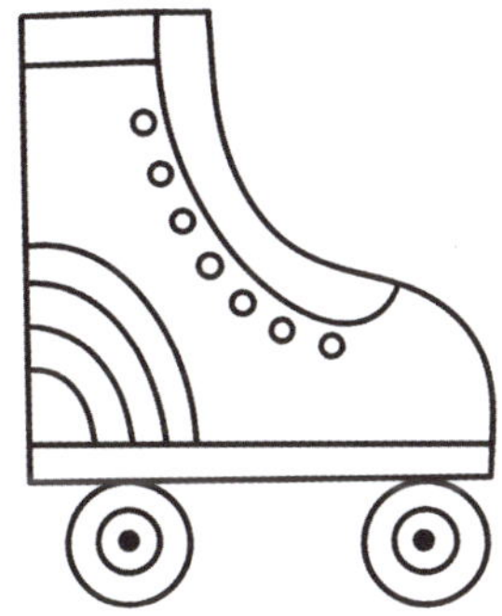

9. Add a series of circles along the tongue for the lace holes.

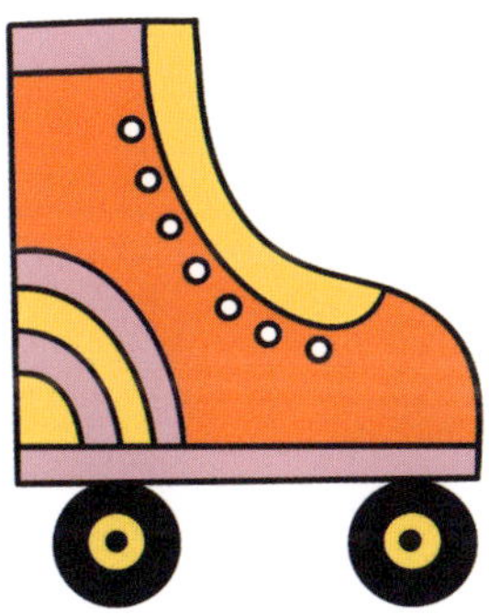

10. Fill in with the colors of your choice!

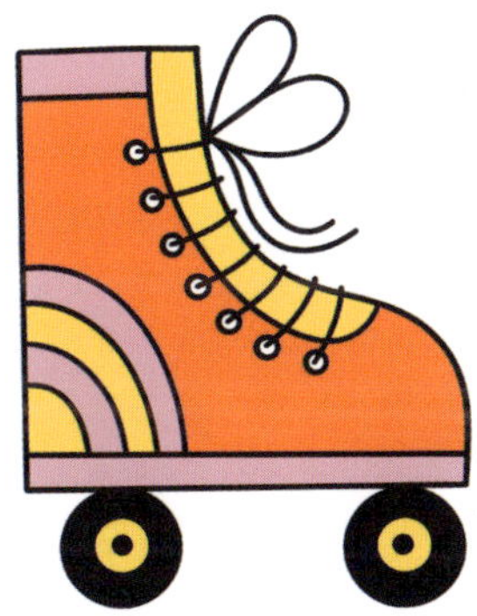

11. Create laces by drawing lines from the circles across the tongue. Draw a bow with two loops and two wavy ends.

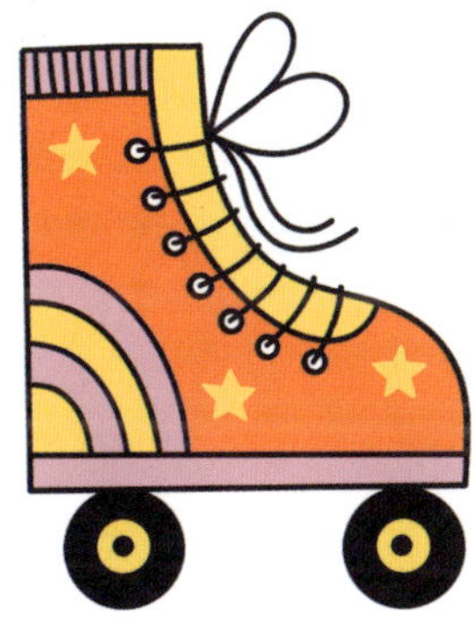

12. Add texture by drawing some stars all over and vertical lines at the top of the skate.

MUG

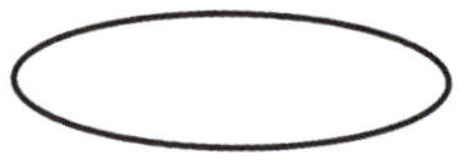

1. Start with a thin oval in the center of the page.

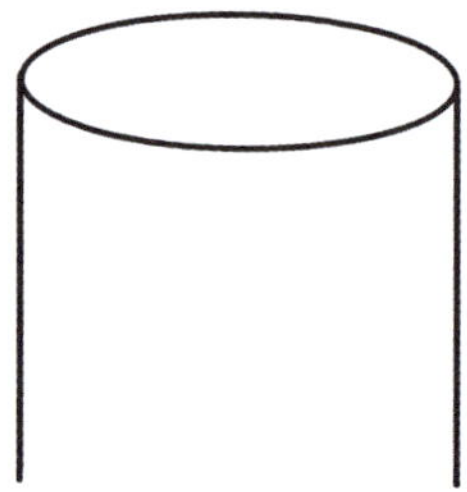

2. Draw two vertical lines down from either end of the oval.

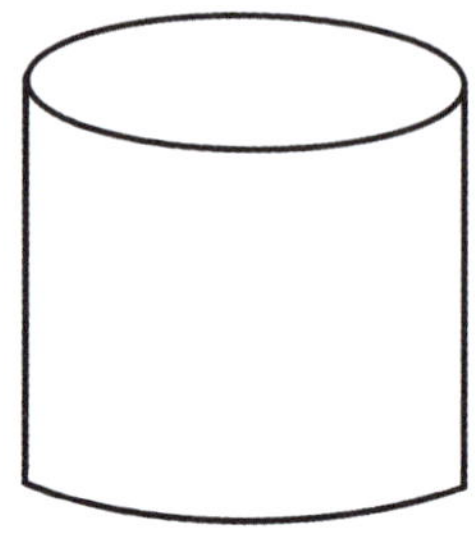

3. Create a cylinder with a curved line at the bottom.

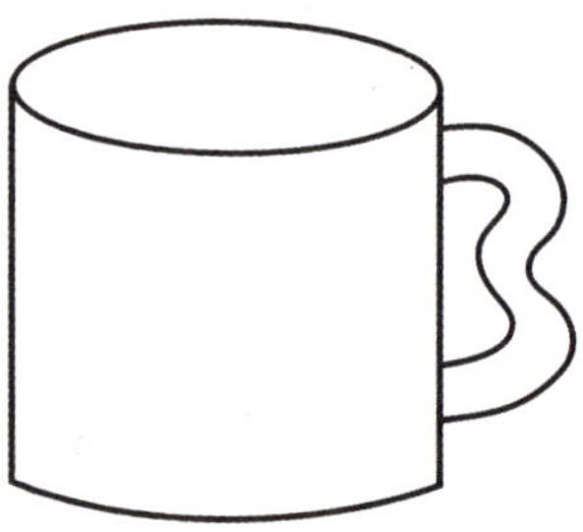

4. On the right side, draw two wavy parallel lines to make the handle.

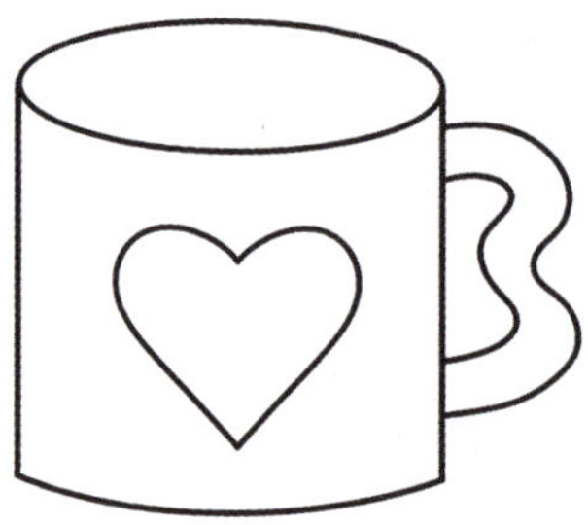

5. Draw a heart in the center of the mug.

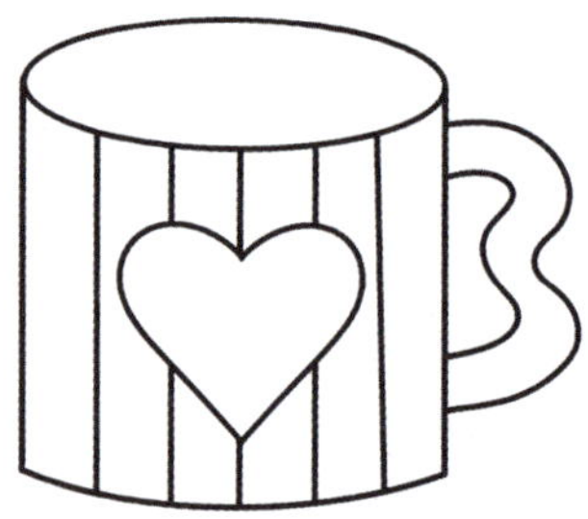

6. Decorate with vertical stripes around the heart.

BE BOLD!

Give your mug a seasonal twist with festive colors, patterns, or a little message.

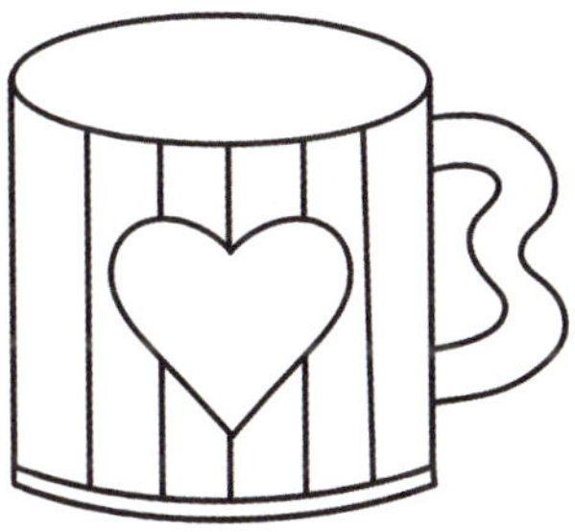

7. Add a thin, curved rectangle along the bottom of the mug.

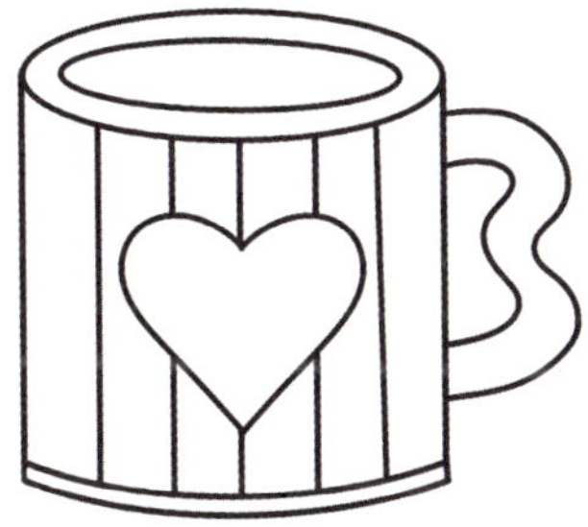

8. Draw a smaller oval in the top oval.

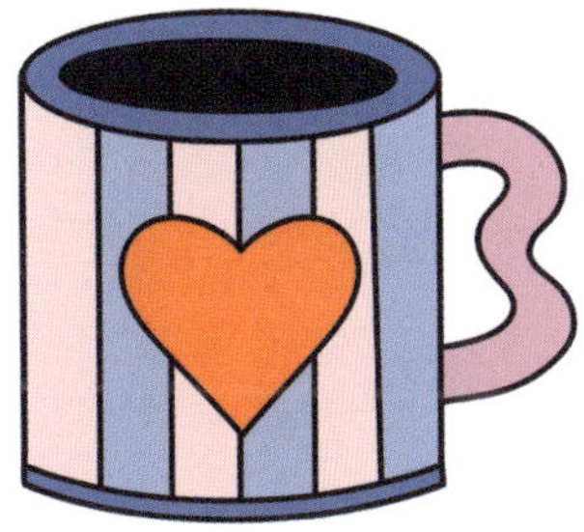

9. Fill in the mug with colors of your choice!

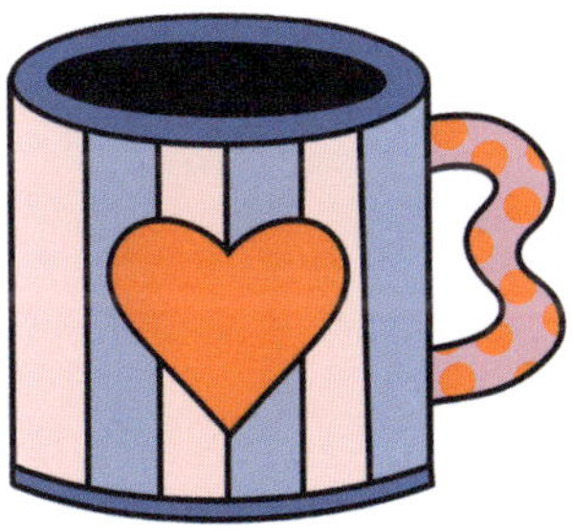

10. Decorate the handle with polka dots.

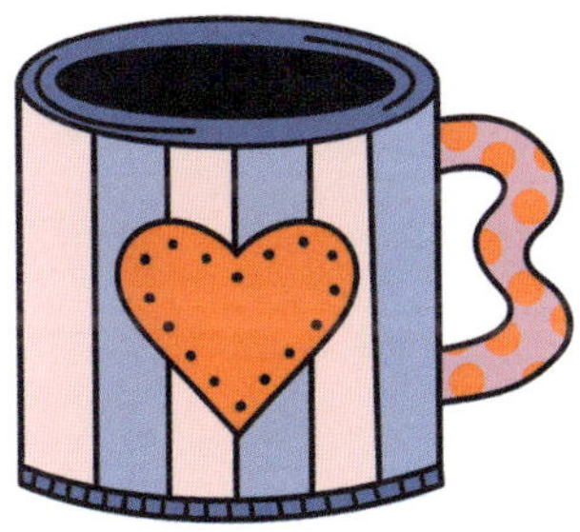

11. Add texture to the mug with dots around the heart, vertical lines on the bottom border stripe, and curved lines on the rim of the mug.

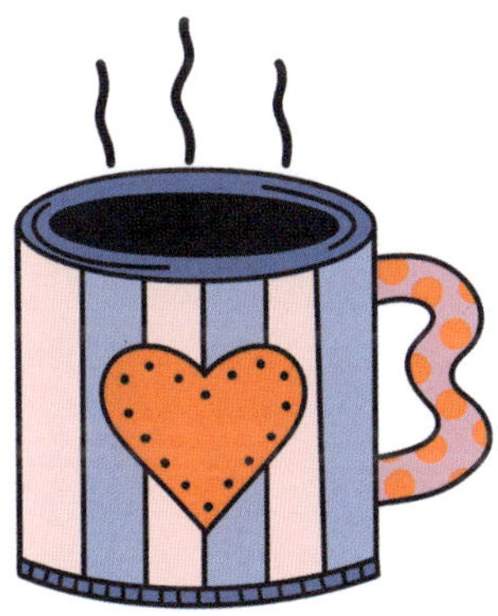

12. Add wavy steam lines above the mug.

TEACUP

1. Start with a thin oval in the center of the page.

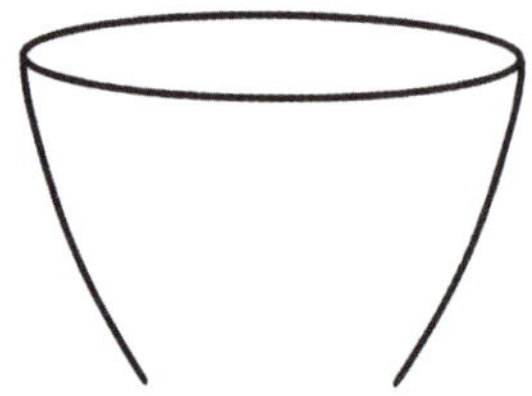

2. On either end of the oval, draw two curved lines that extend down and are slightly angled toward the middle.

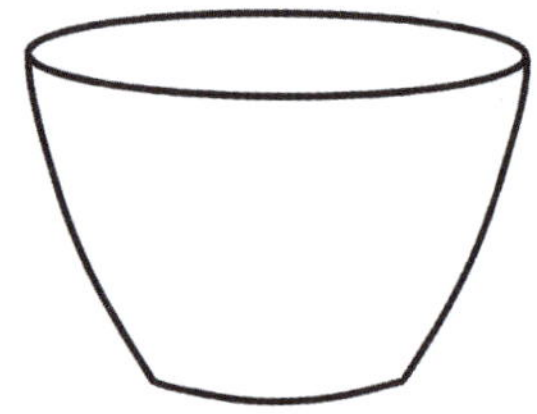

3. Draw a curved horizontal line at the bottom to create a cup.

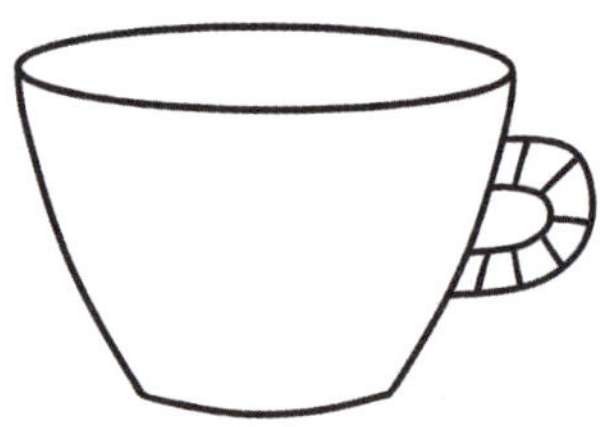

4. Add two parallel backward C shapes to make the handle. Add stripes.

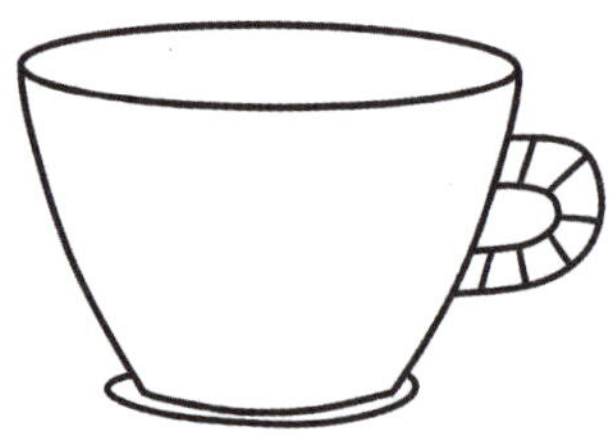

5. Add a thin, curved line around the bottom of the cup.

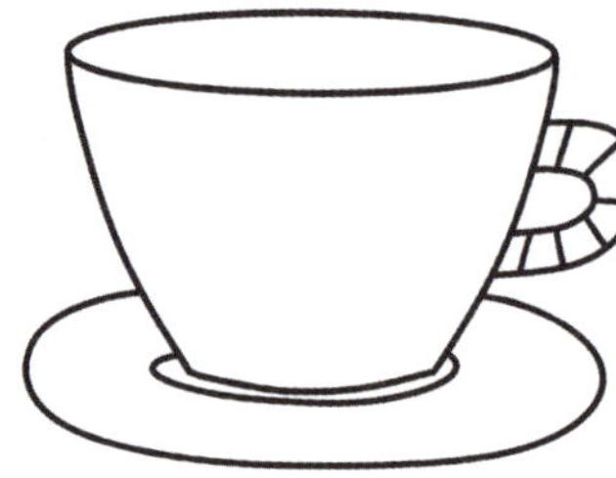

6. Draw a large oval shape around the bottom of the cup for a saucer.

BE BOLD!

Make your teacup more intricate by adding extra details like florals or swirls to the saucer and bowl of the cup. You can even adjust the shape of the handle to make the cup look fancier.

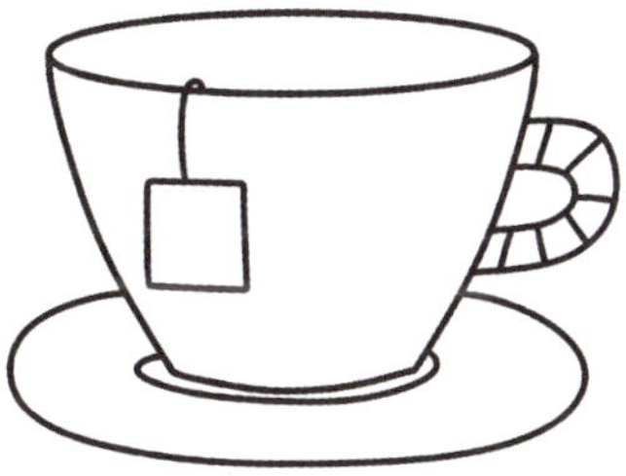

7. Draw a curved line hooked on the top edge of the cup, then add a square at the end.

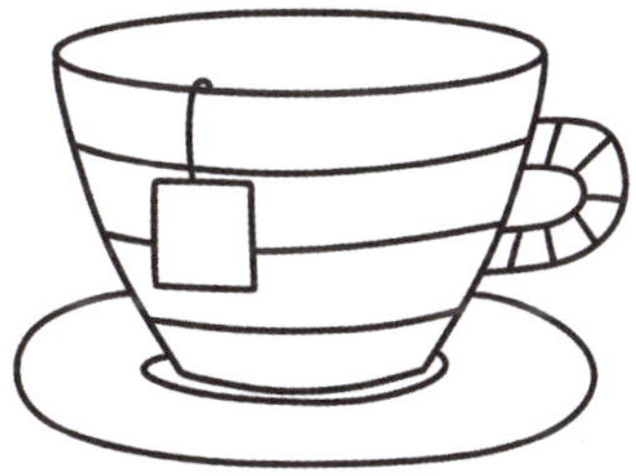

8. Draw a series of curved stripes along the cup.

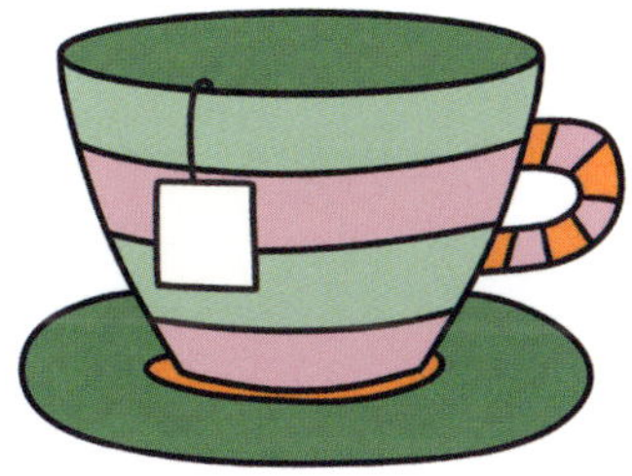

9. Fill in with the colors of your choice.

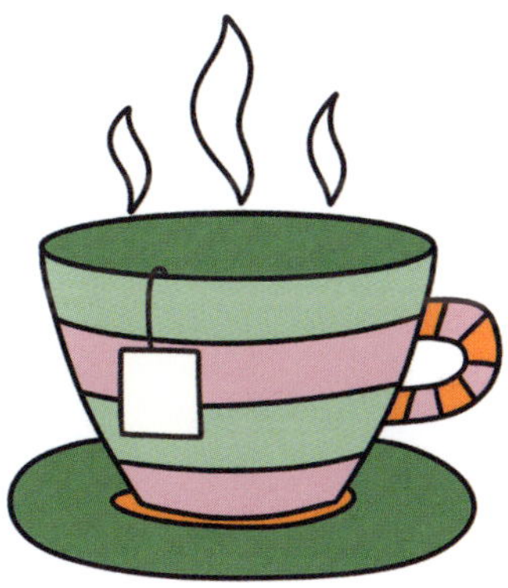

10. Add wavy steam shapes above the cup.

11. Add a heart to the tea bag tag.

12. Add details to the cup with a line of dots on the rim and on the tag, and scallops around the center of the saucer.

TEAPOT

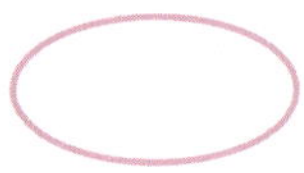

1. Start with an oval in the center of the page.

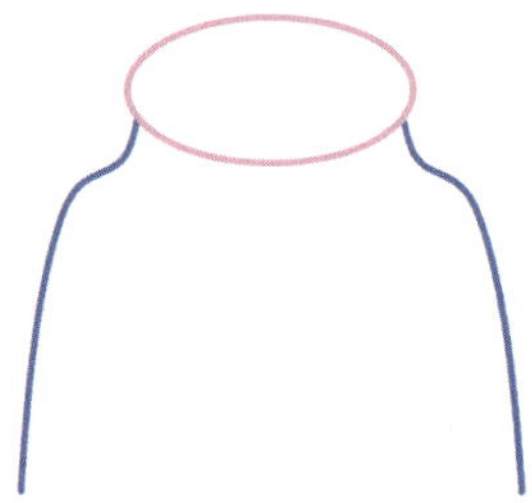

2. Under the oval, draw two curved lines that each have a small bump at the top.

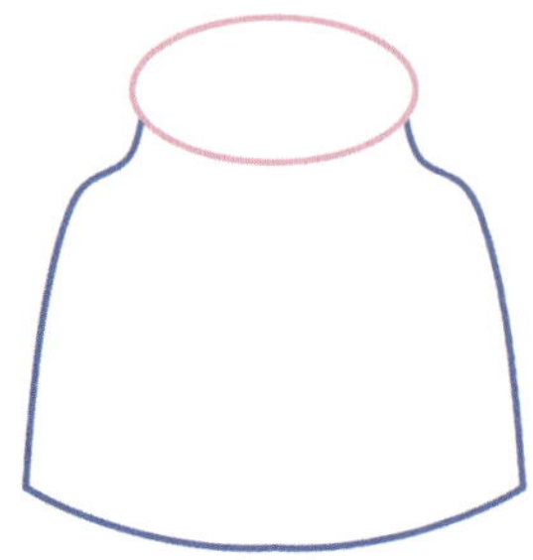

3. Draw a curved line at the bottom to make the body of the teapot.

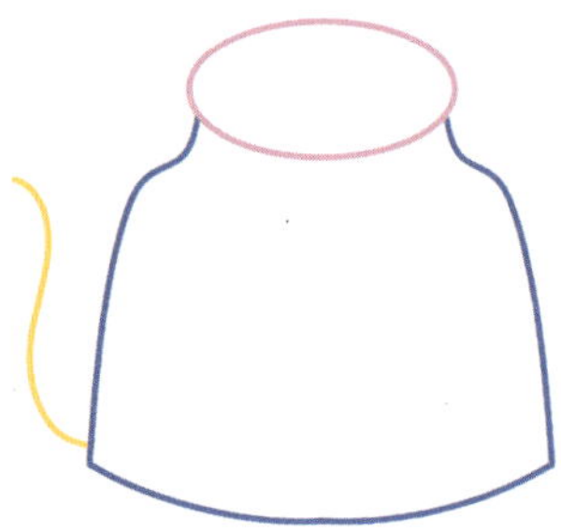

4. Draw a wavy line on the bottom left.

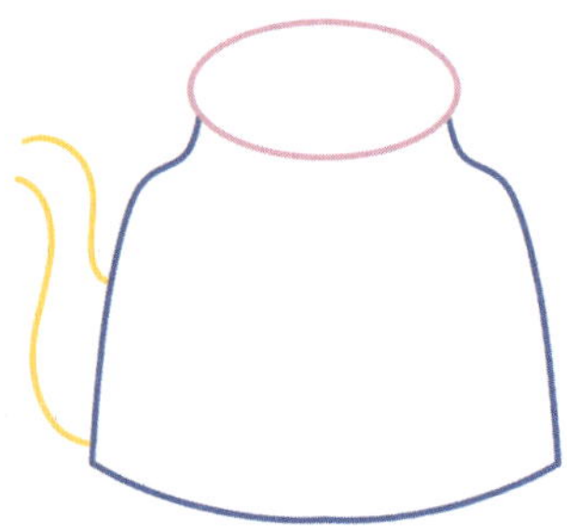

5. Draw a shorter curved line above and parallel to the first.

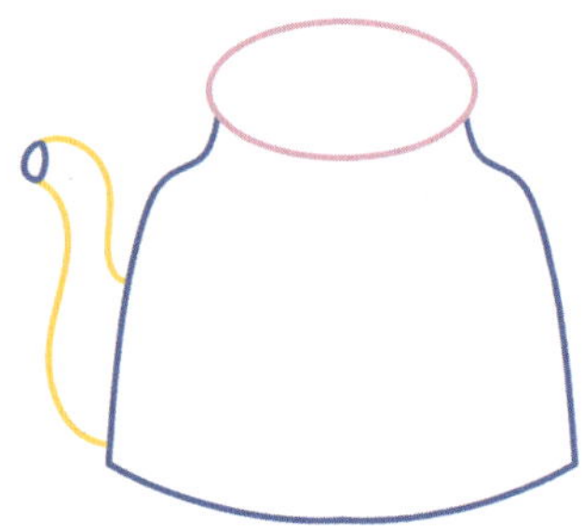

6. Connect the ends of the lines with an oval to make a spout.

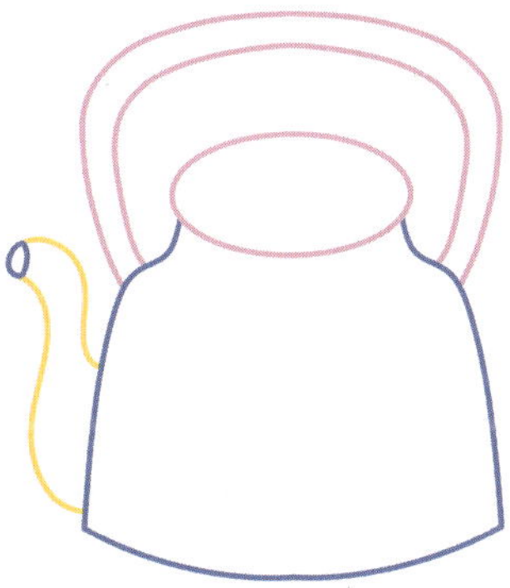

7. Add two parallel wide U shapes on top to create the teapot handle.

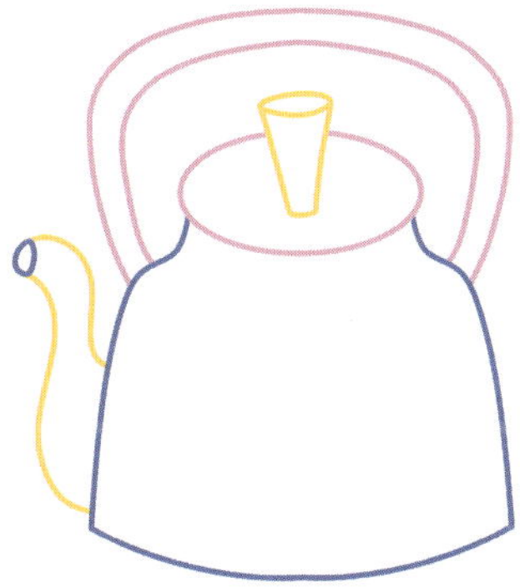

8. Draw a triangular peg shape with a curved line at the top in the center of the oval.

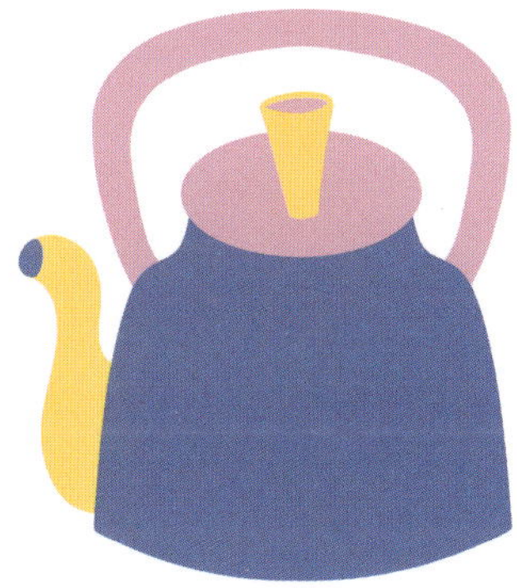

9. Fill in the colors.

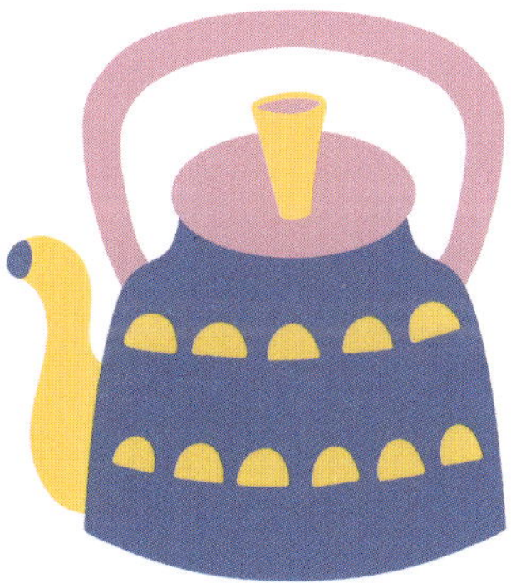

10. Decorate with two lines of uneven semicircles.

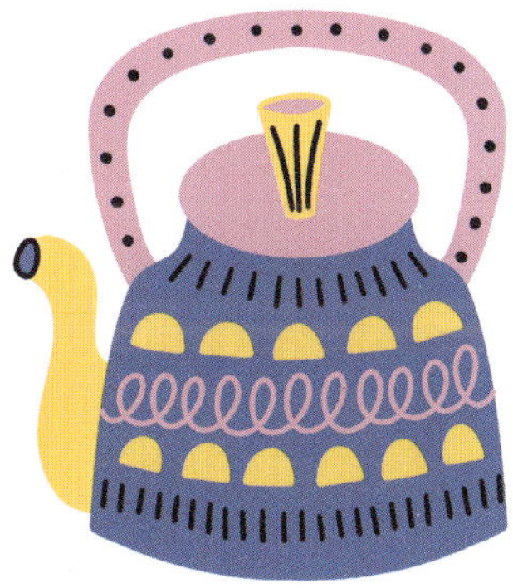

11. Add extra detail and texture with dashes, dots, curved accent lines, and swirly lines.

BE BOLD!

Complete the scene by drawing your teapot pouring tea from its spout into a mug or teacup.

FLOWER VASE

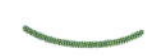

1. Start with a short, curved line in the center of the page.

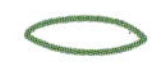

2. Add another curve on top to make a pointed oval shape.

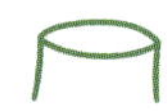

3. Draw two short, curved lines extending down from the points of the oval.

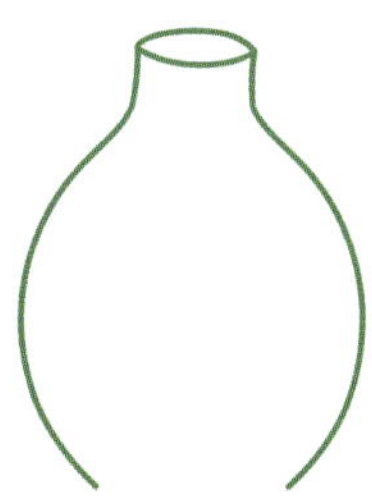

4. Draw two large, curved lines to make the round shape of the vase.

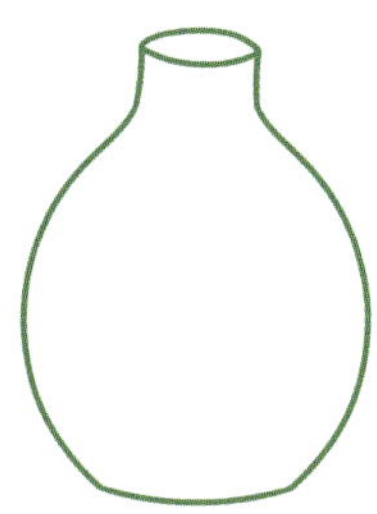

5. Add a curved line at the bottom to complete the vase.

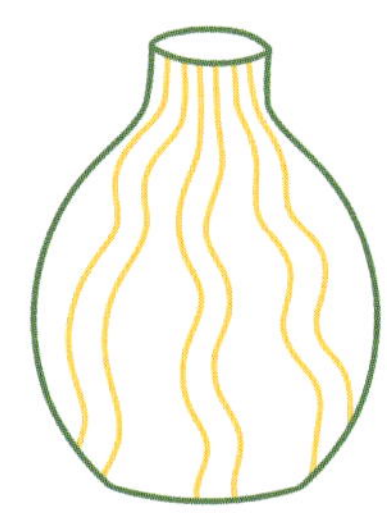

6. Draw six wavy vertical lines within the vase shape to create three wavy stripes.

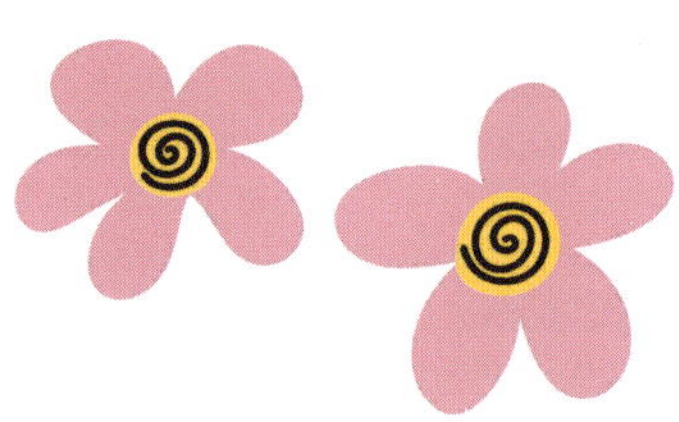

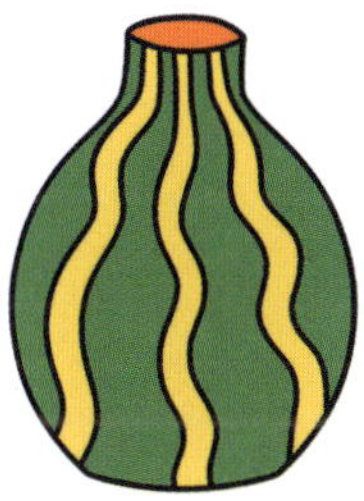

7. Fill in the colors.

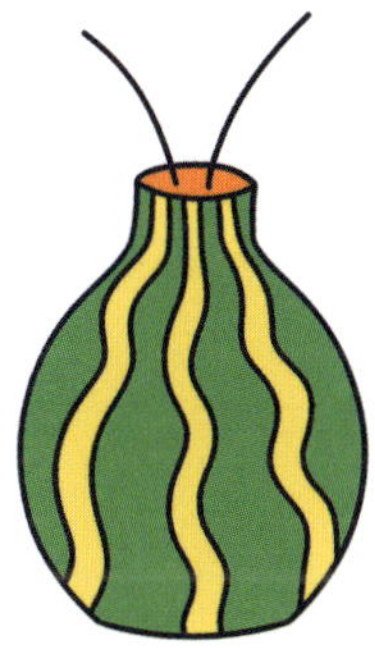

8. Draw two lines curving away from each other at the top of the vase.

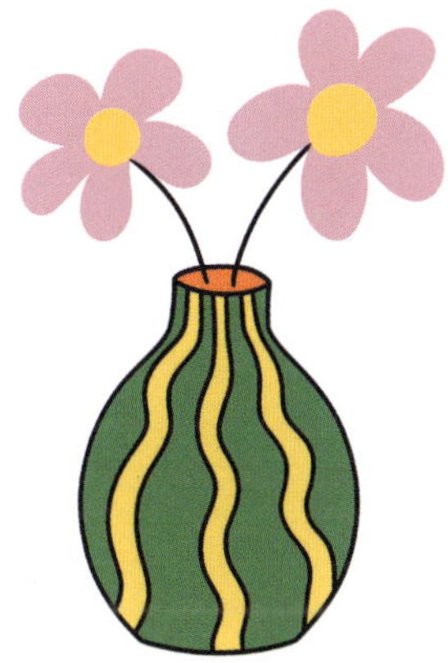

9. Add two five-petal flowers with circle centers at the ends of the lines.

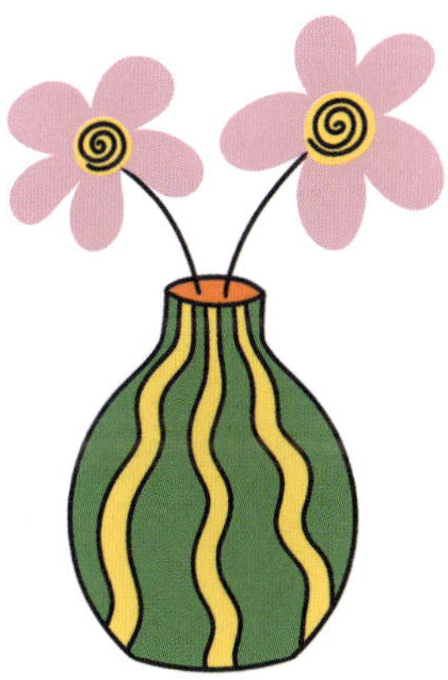

10. Draw a swirl in the center of each flower.

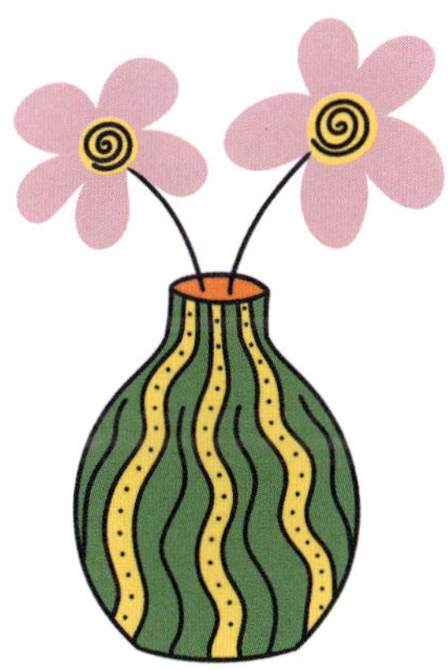

11. Decorate the vase with a series of wavy lines and dots.

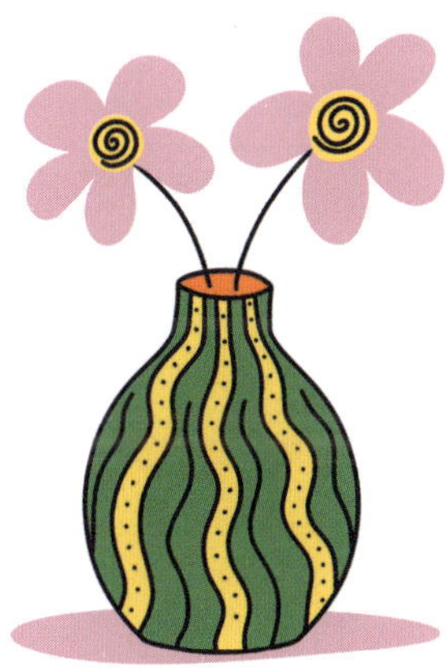

12. Add a pink wobbly shape under the vase to create a shadow.

BE BOLD!

Try putting different flowers in your vase. Check out the Florals & Botanicals section of the book to find all kinds of different flowers you can draw in your vase.

WATERING CAN

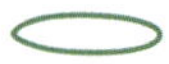

1. Start with an oval near the center of the page.

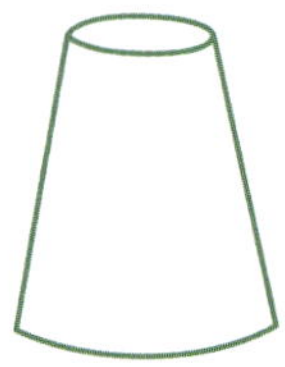

2. Draw two vertical lines, slightly angled outward, and connect the ends with a curved line.

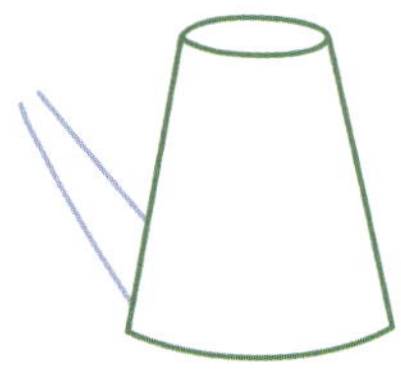

3. Draw two diagonal lines at the bottom left to start the spout.

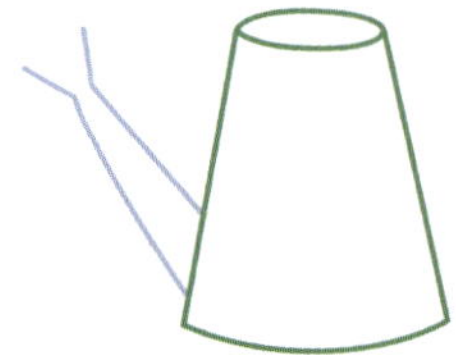

4. Draw two angled lines to make the sprinkler head of the spout.

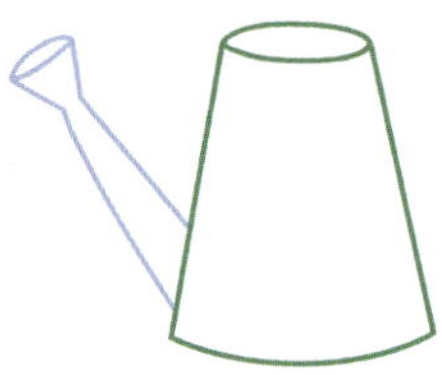

5. Add an oval to close the spout.

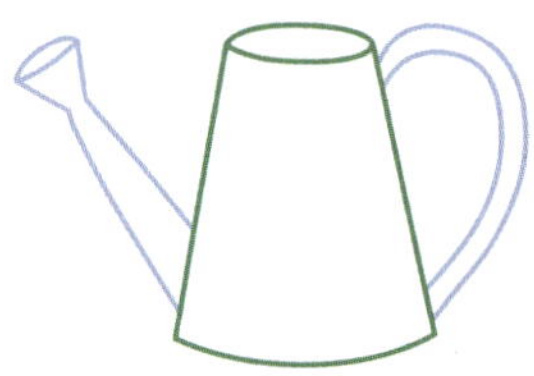

6. Draw two curved, parallel lines on the right to make the handle.

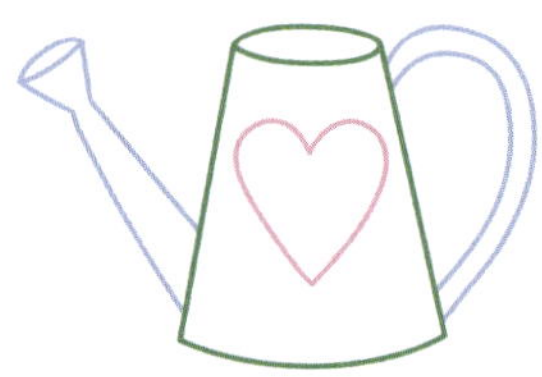

7. Draw a heart on the body of the can.

8. Fill in the colors!

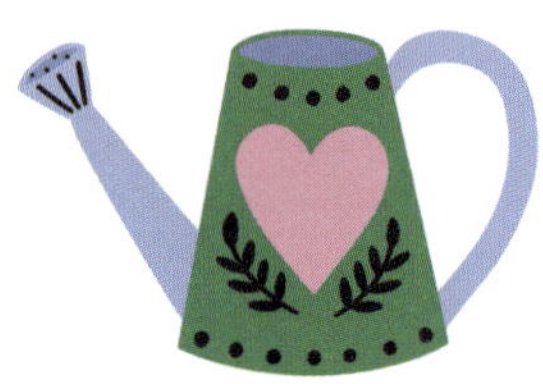

9. Decorate with dots, lines, and branches of leaves.

BE BOLD!

Draw your watering can pouring water droplets onto a garden full of flowers on a sunny day.

BOW

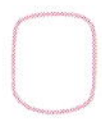

1. Start by drawing a small, rounded square for the center of the bow.

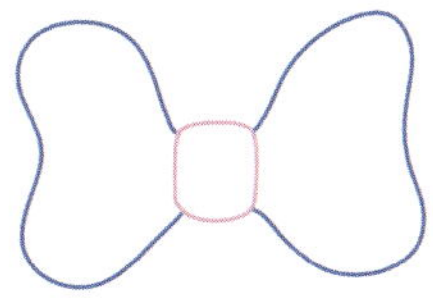

2. Draw two large wavy shapes, like butterfly wings, on each side of the square.

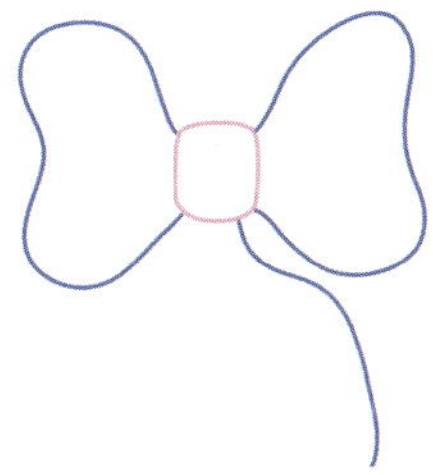

3. Add a long, curved line flowing down from the square.

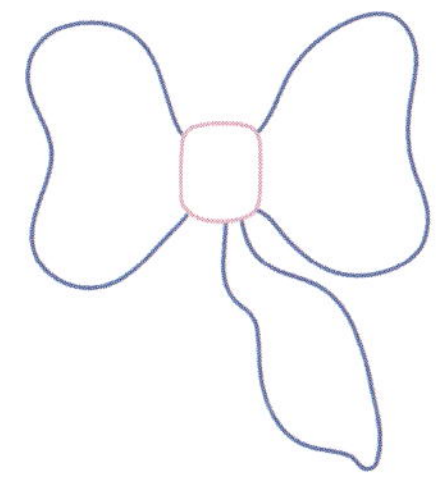

4. Draw a second curved line and connect it to the end of the first to make a ribbon.

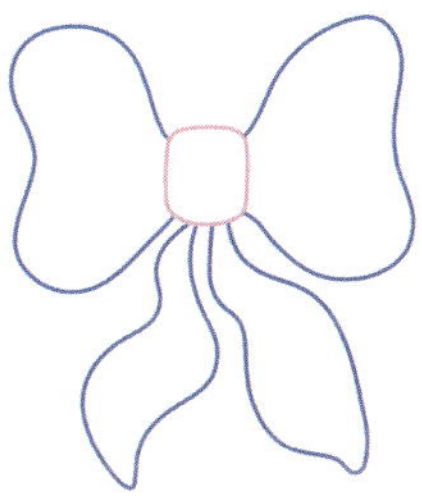

5. Add a second ribbon tail on the left side, making this one different from the first.

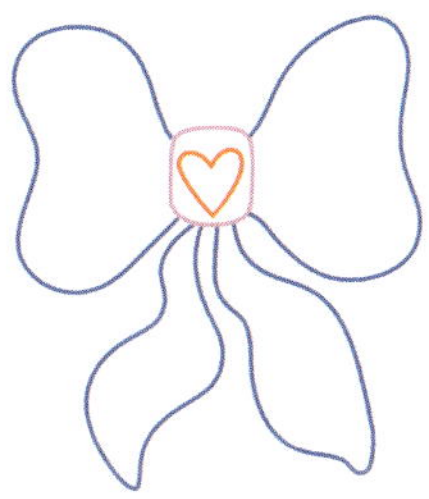

6. Draw a heart in the center of the bow.

7. Fill in the colors!

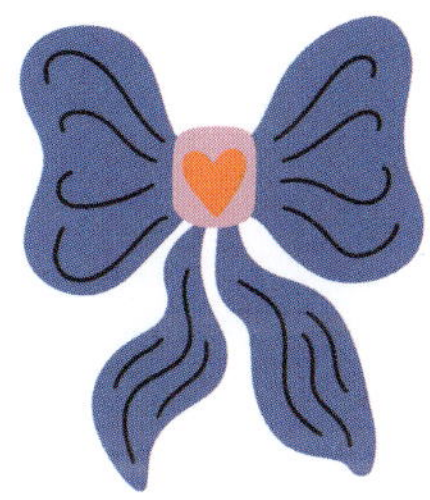

8. Add curved lines inside the bow loops and ribbon tails for extra movement and texture.

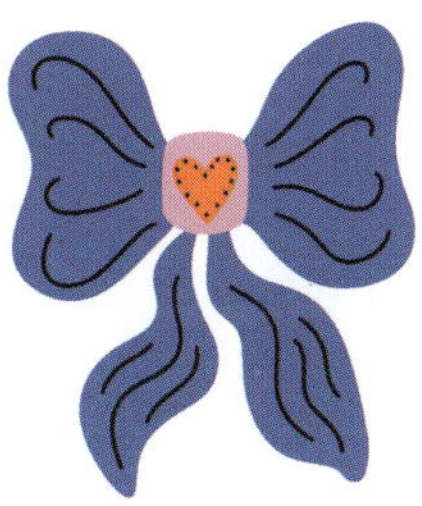

9. Decorate with small dots inside the heart.

BE BOLD!

Try playing with different bow shapes or patterns such as polka dots or tiny stars to make your bow feel full of personality.

CANDLE

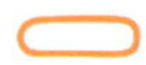

1. Start with a thin, flat oval in the center of the page.

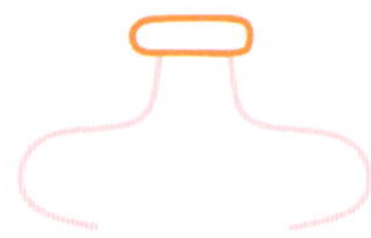

2. Draw two curved lines that start moving vertically underneath the oval and then extend out in a large, curved bump.

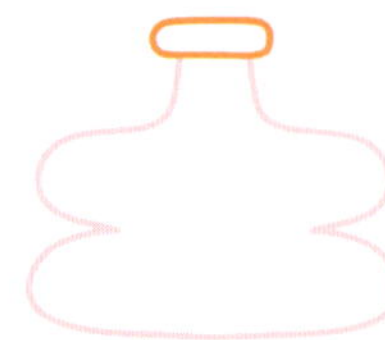

3. Connect the bottom of these lines with a curved line.

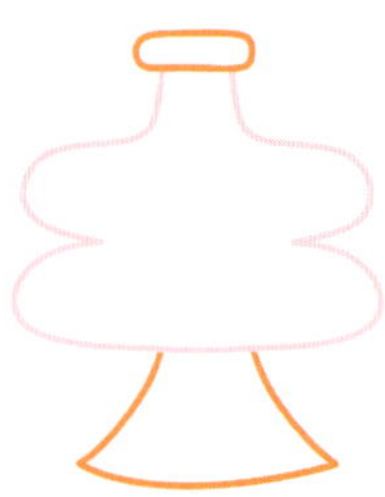

4. Draw a bell-like shape underneath.

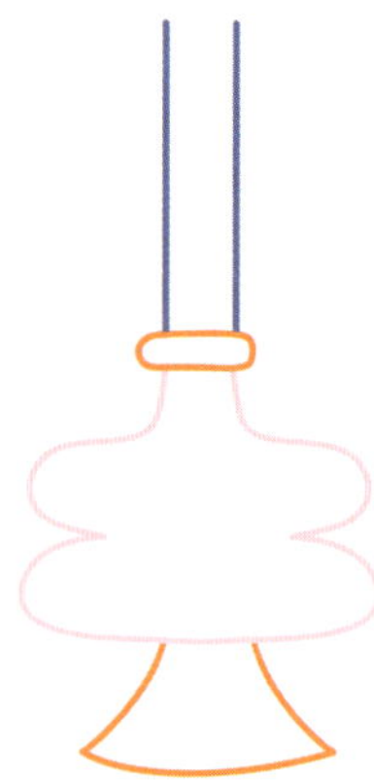

5. Draw two vertical, parallel lines above the oval.

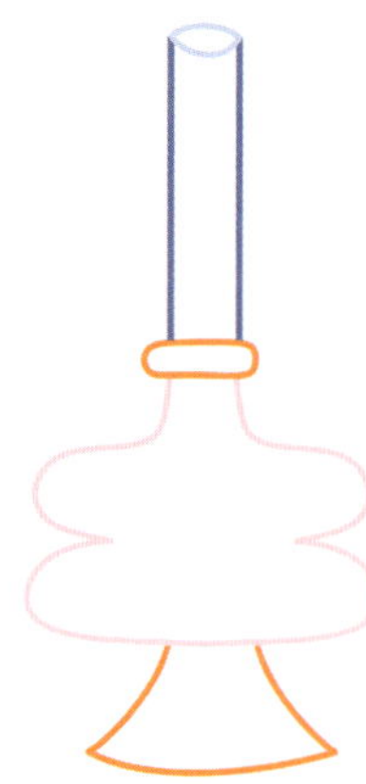

6. Add an oval with pointed ends to the top of the lines.

BE BOLD!

Add extra arms to the candle holder to create a whole, ornate candelabra that can hold lots of candles.

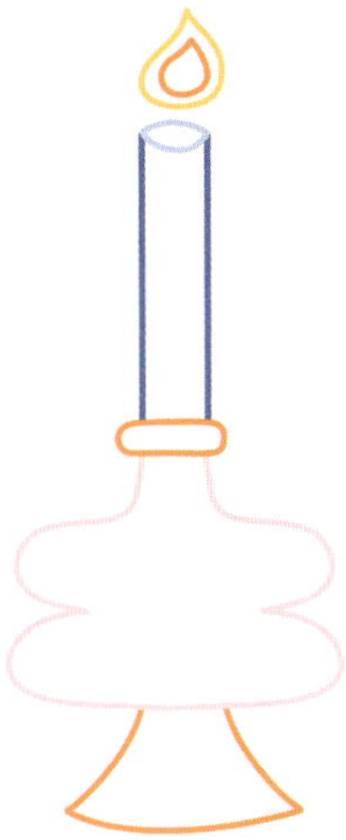

7. Draw two flame shapes, one within the other, hovering above the candle.

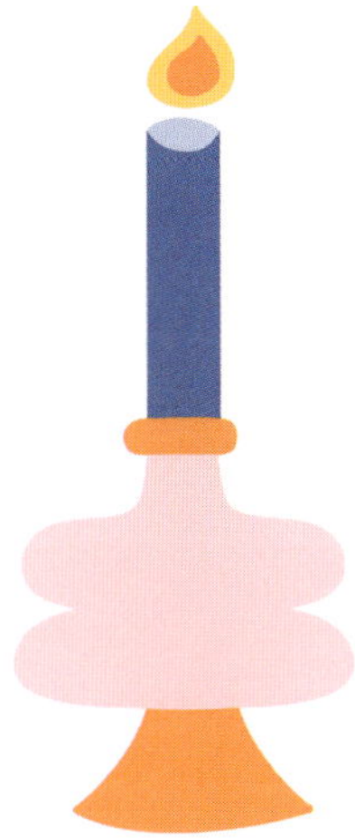

8. Fill in the colors!

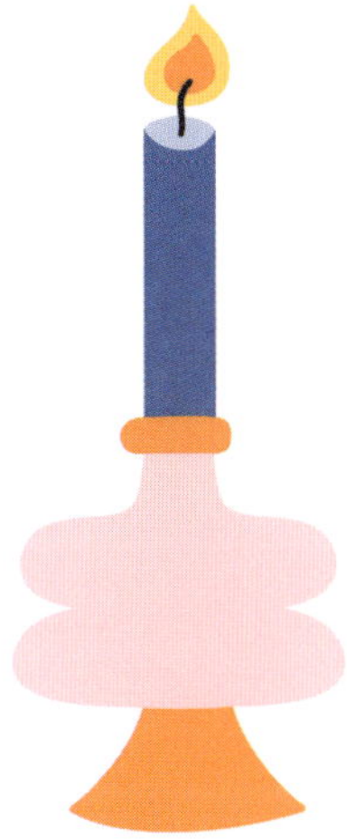

9. Draw a wavy black line between the candle and flame to make a wick.

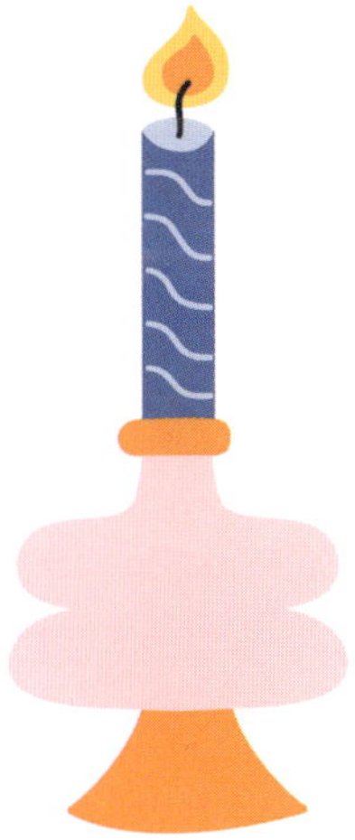

10. Decorate your candle with a series of wavy lines.

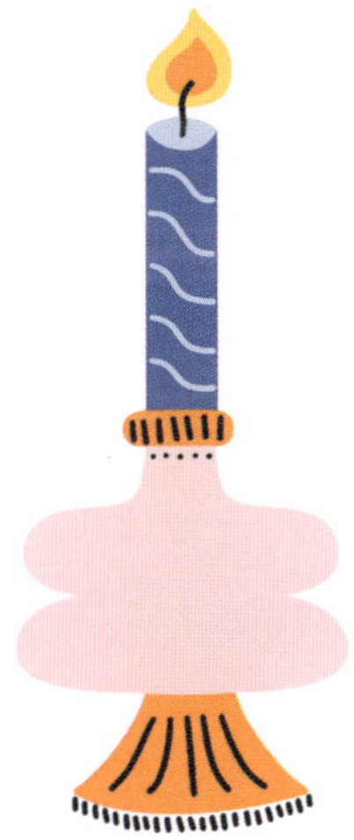

11. Add texture to the candle holder with black dashes, lines, and dots.

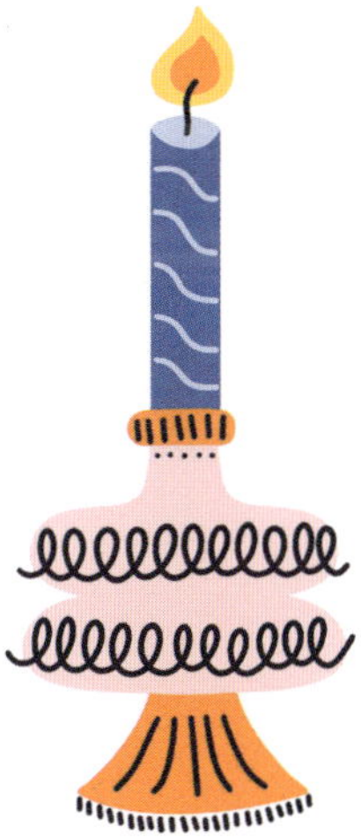

12. Draw swirly lines across the thick parts of the holder for extra decoration.

SUN

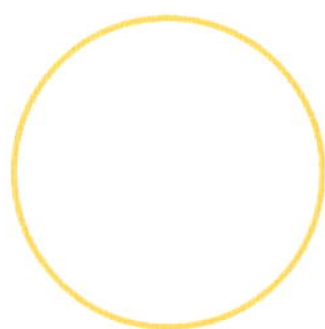

1. Start with a circle in the center of the page.

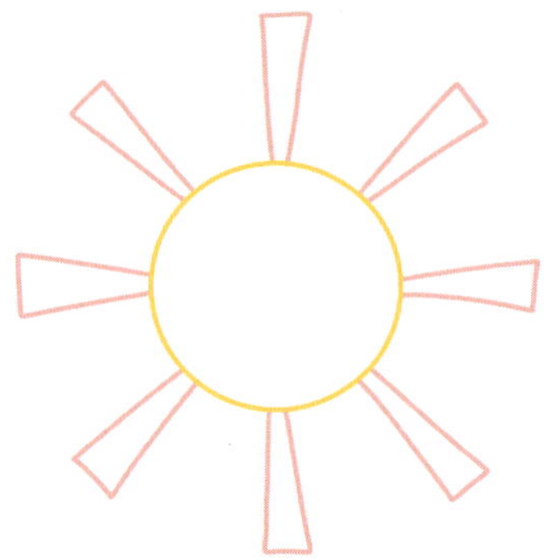

2. Draw eight rectangular shapes evenly around the circle and tapering toward the circle.

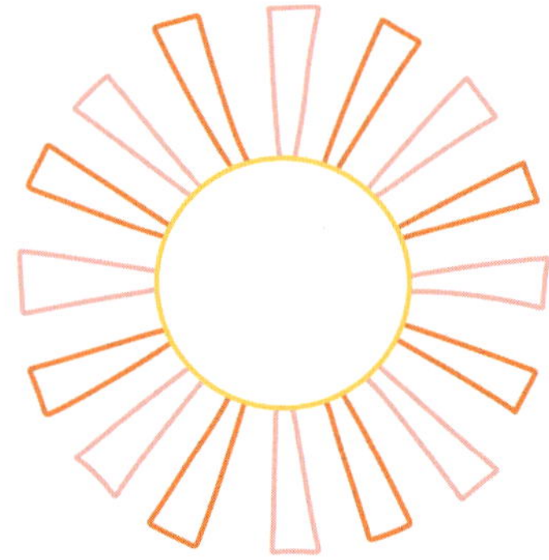

3. Draw eight similar rectangular shapes in between the first ones.

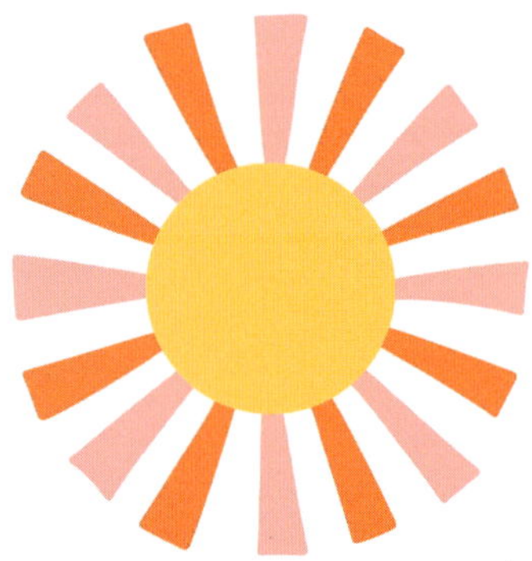

4. Fill in the colors!

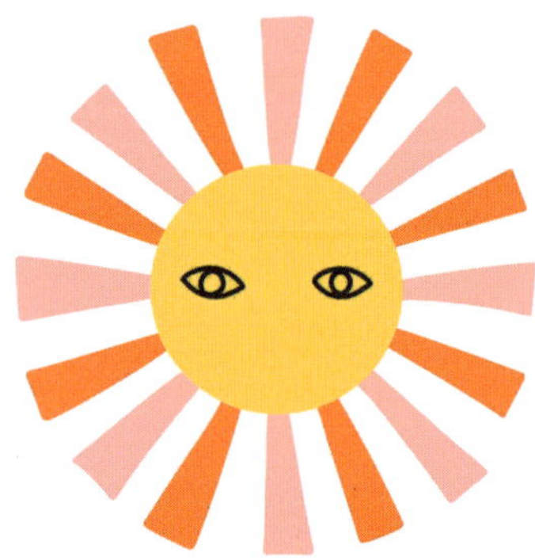

5. Draw two pointed oval eyes with circles inside.

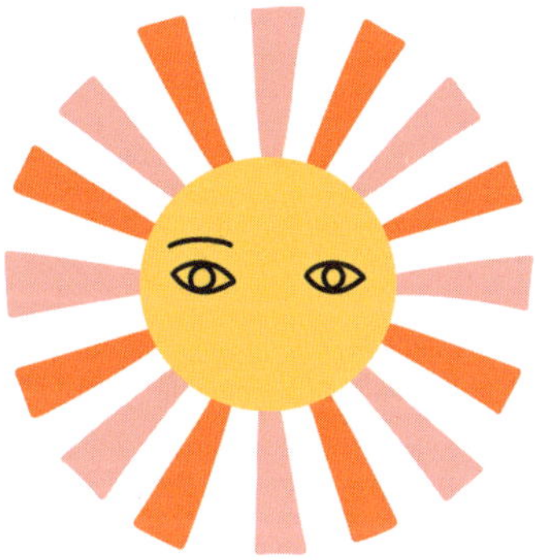

6. Draw a curved eyebrow above the left eye.

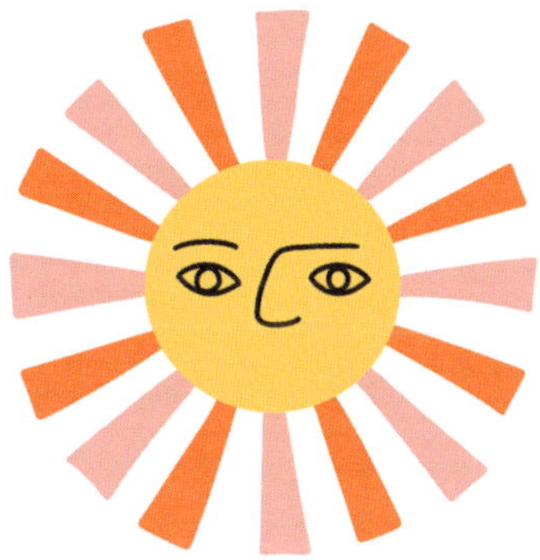

7. Draw a line above the right eye that curves down and up toward the right eye to make the nose.

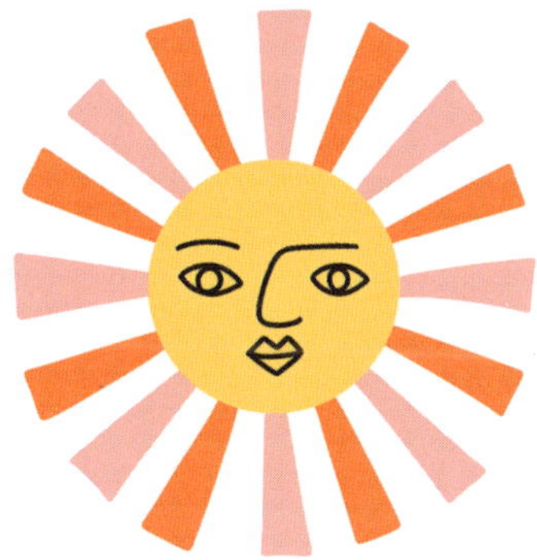

8. Draw a set of pointed heart-shaped lips.

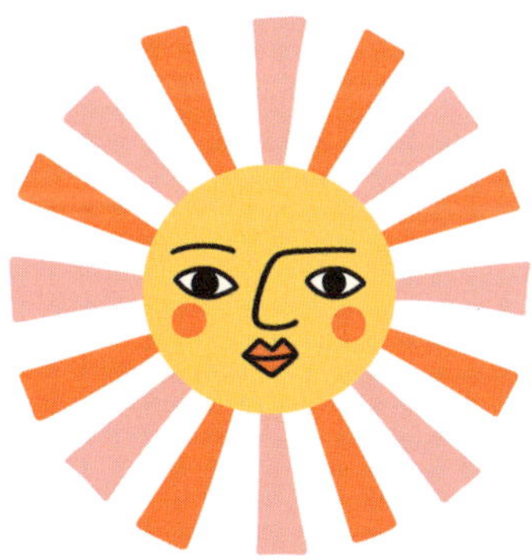

9. Color the eyes and lips and add circles of blush to the cheeks.

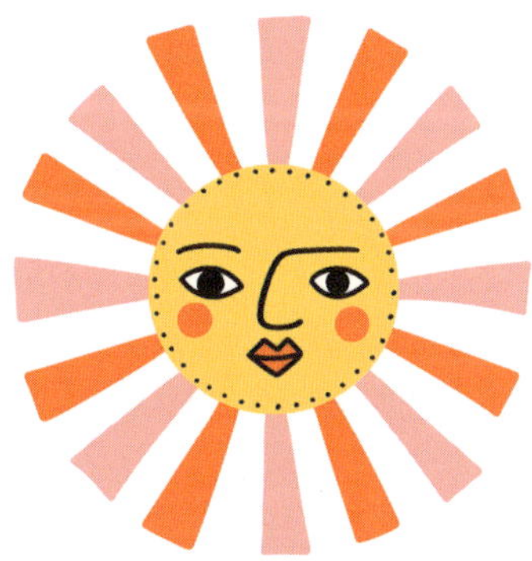

10. Add black dots around the edge of the circle.

BE BOLD!

Draw your sun in the sky surrounded by fluffy clouds or next to its friend the moon to create a cute folk art skyscape.

WEATHER

1. Start with a cloud using a horizontal line and a bumpy, scalloped top.

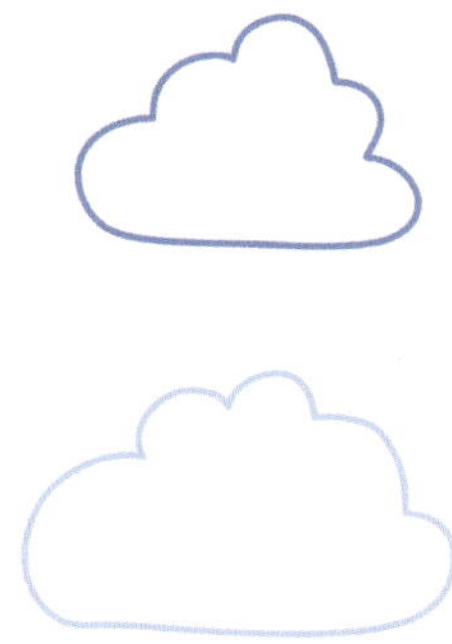

2. Draw another larger cloud below.

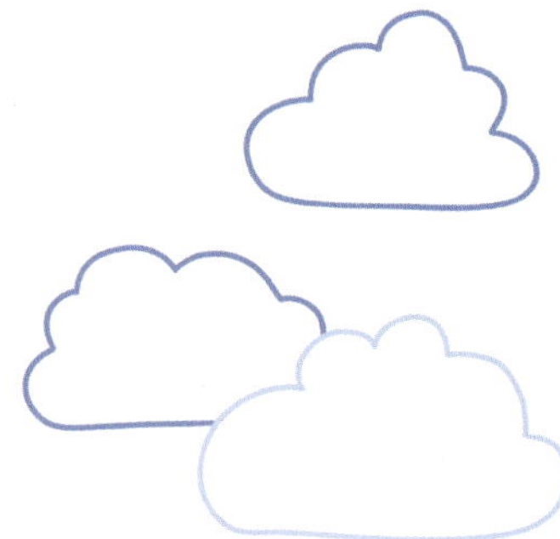

3. Add a third cloud on the left and slightly behind the second cloud.

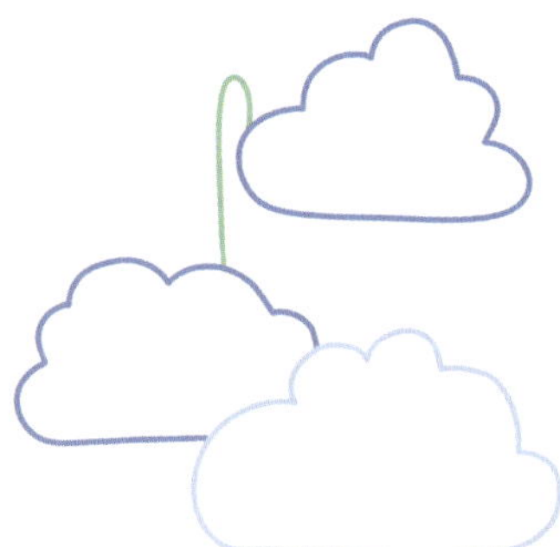

4. Draw a curved line that hooks onto the top cloud.

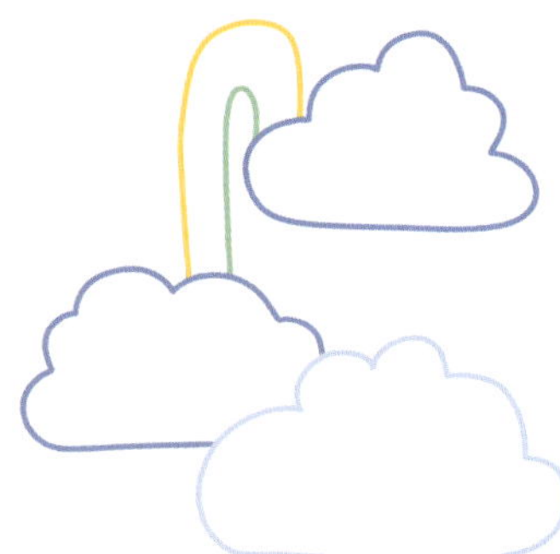

5. Draw another hooked line next to the first.

BE BOLD!

Make your weather scene more extreme by adding some lightning bolts coming down from the clouds, or make it happier by adding a smiling sun above the clouds.

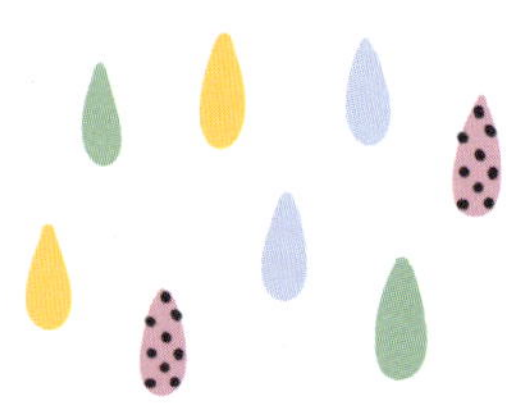

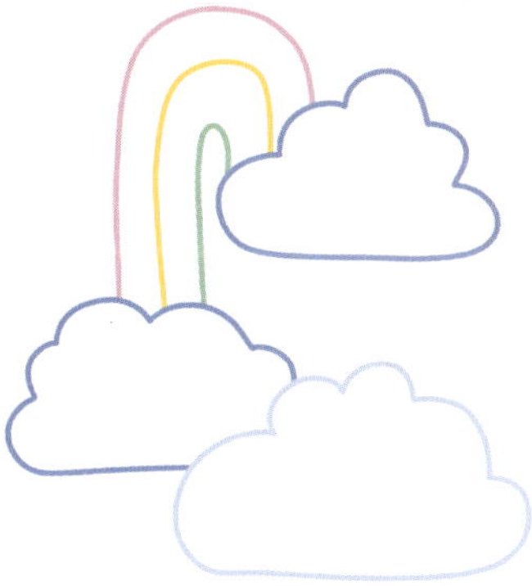

6. Draw a third hooked line.

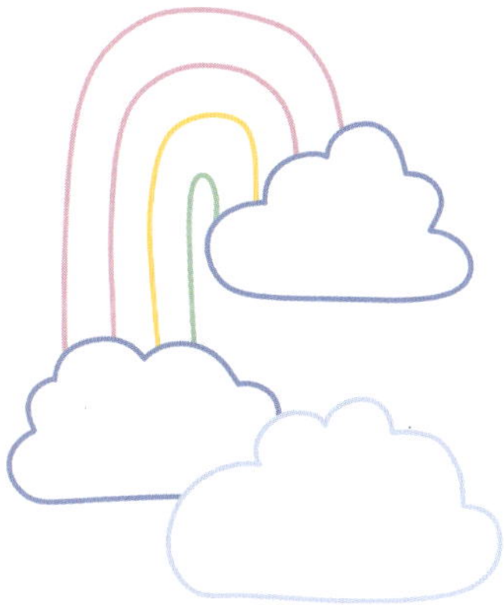

7. Draw a fourth hooked line.

8. Fill in the colors!

9. Add teardrop-shaped raindrops under the clouds.

10. Decorate with dots, scalloped lines, swirly lines, and dashes.

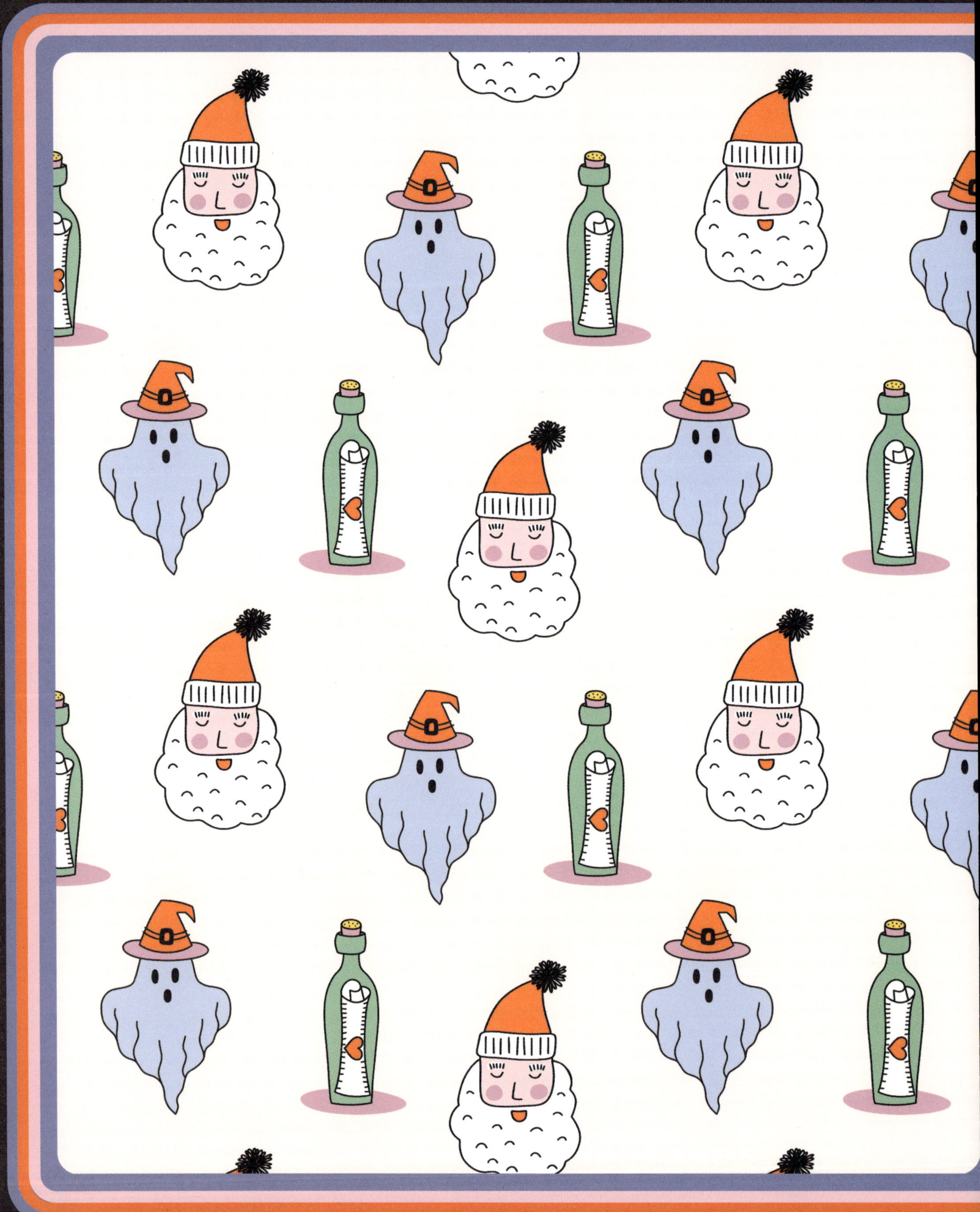

HOLIDAYS

CHRISTMAS TREE

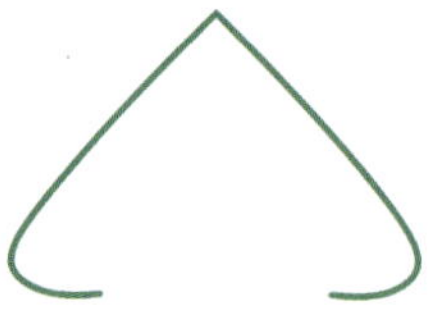

1. Start with a triangular line with rounded bottom corners that is open at the bottom.

2. Draw two curved lines starting at each end of the triangle.

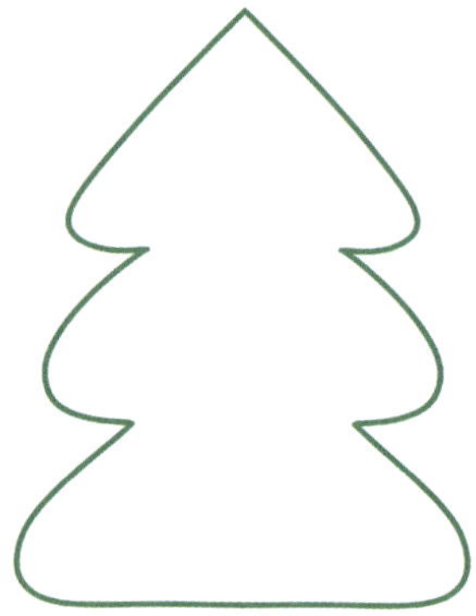

3. Close the bottom of the tree with rounded corners.

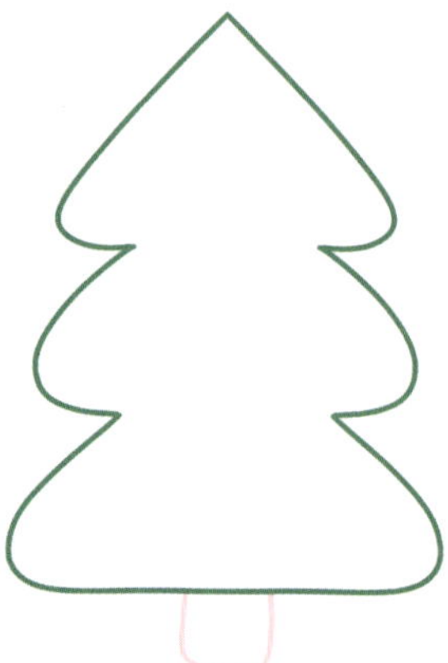

4. Add a rounded square underneath the tree.

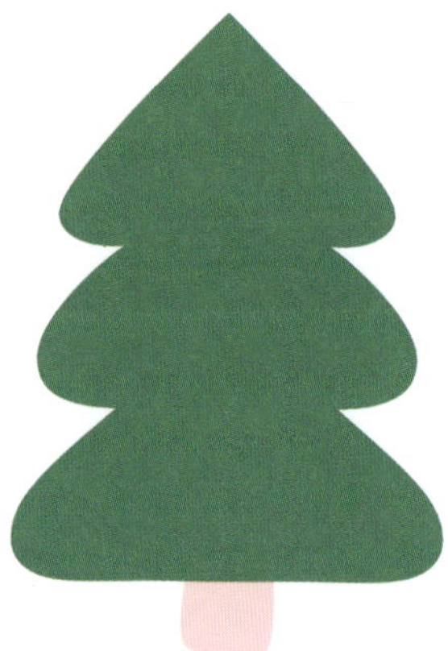

5. Fill in the colors!

6. Draw three hearts down the center of the tree.

7. Draw curved black V-lines underneath each heart.

8. Add a circle at the end of each black line, then draw six oval petals around each circle.

9. Add two to four black oval leaves to each flower stem.

10. Draw some more leaves in the spaces around the hearts and a dot at the top point of the tree.

11. Decorate the tree with more black dots.

12. Add a pointed star shape to the top of the tree.

BE BOLD!

Do you have special ornaments, garlands, or décor on your Christmas tree? Add motifs that look like your favorite decorations to your drawing.

GIFT BOXES

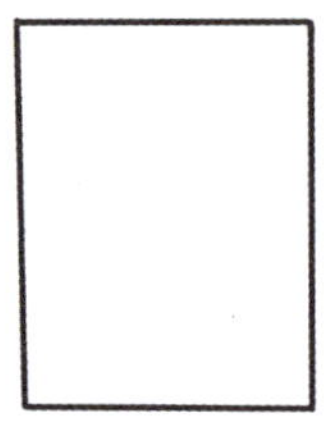

1. Start with a large rectangle in the lower left of the page.

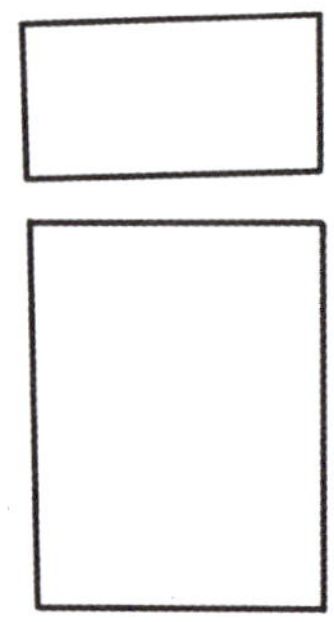

2. Add a small rectangle on top.

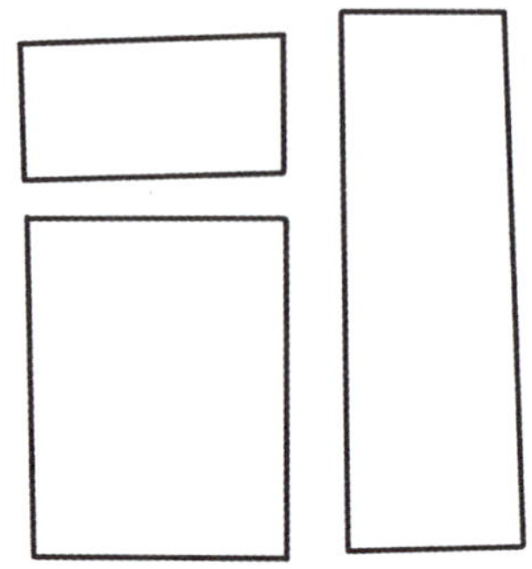

3. Add a long rectangle on the right.

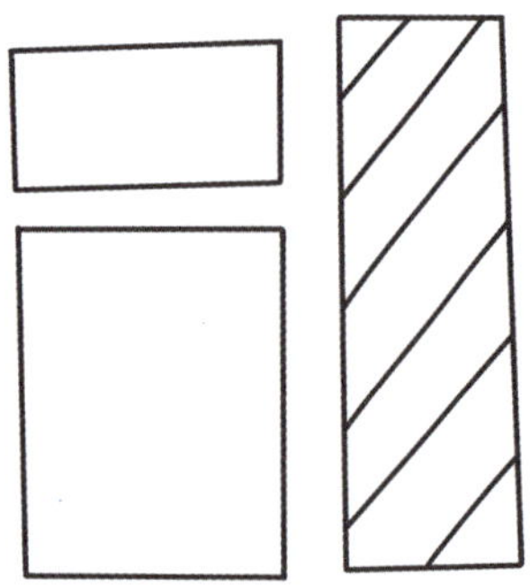

4. Draw diagonal stripes across the long rectangle.

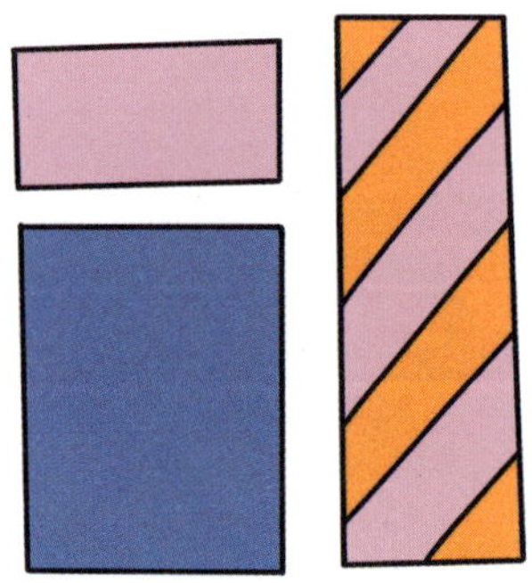

5. Fill in with the colors of your choice!

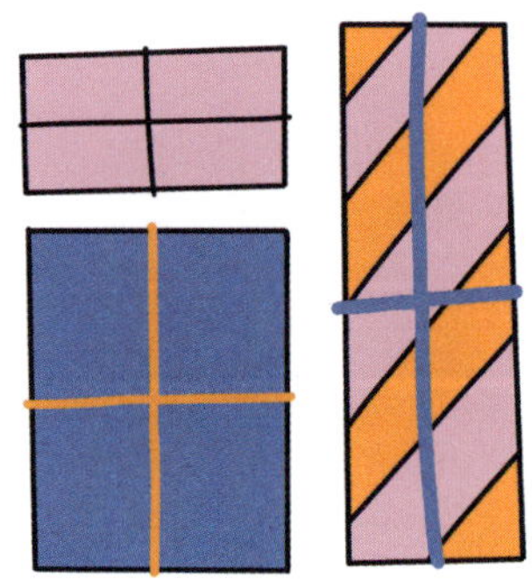

6. Draw crossing lines on each rectangle.

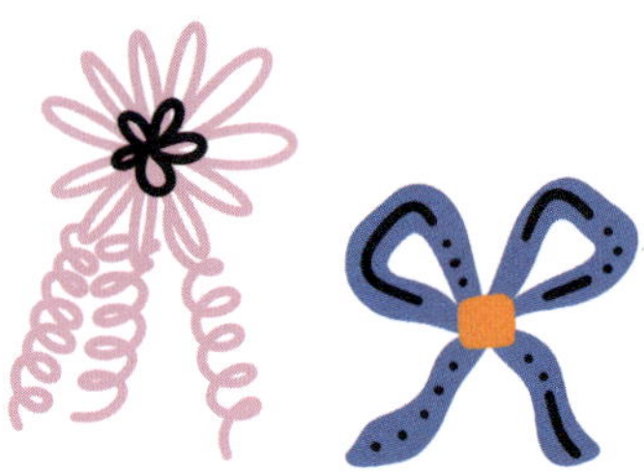

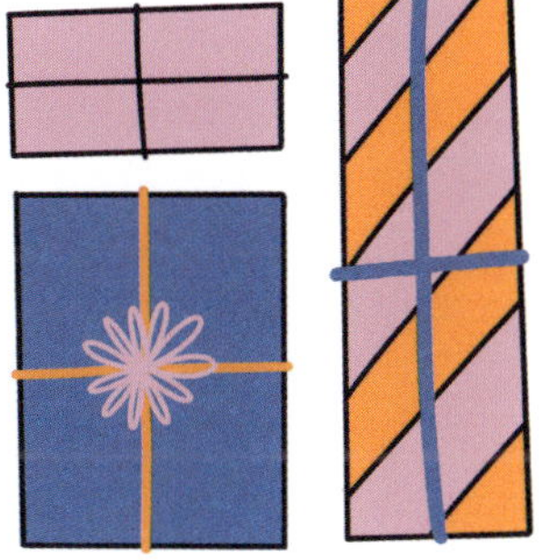

7. Add a fluffy bow to the bottom left rectangle by drawing a series of narrow ovals in a circle.

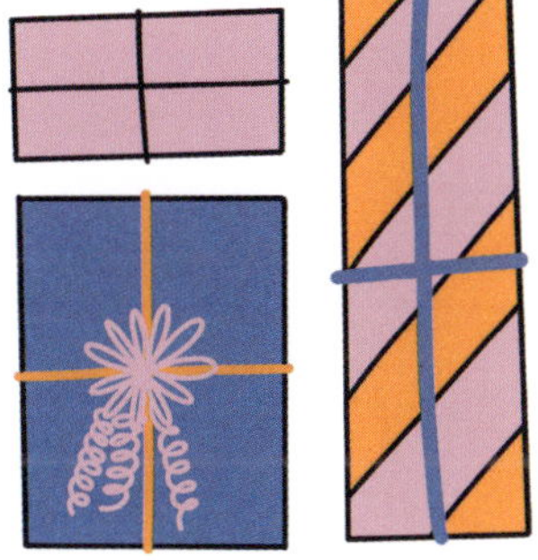

8. Draw trailing swirly lines below the bow to create three ribbons.

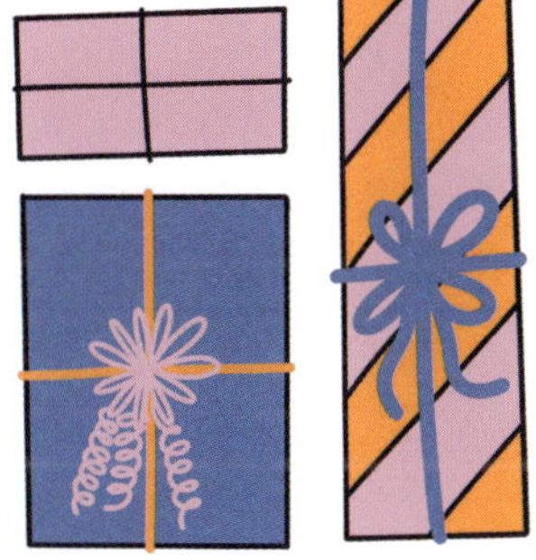

9. Draw four teardrops and two wavy lines on the right rectangle to make a bow.

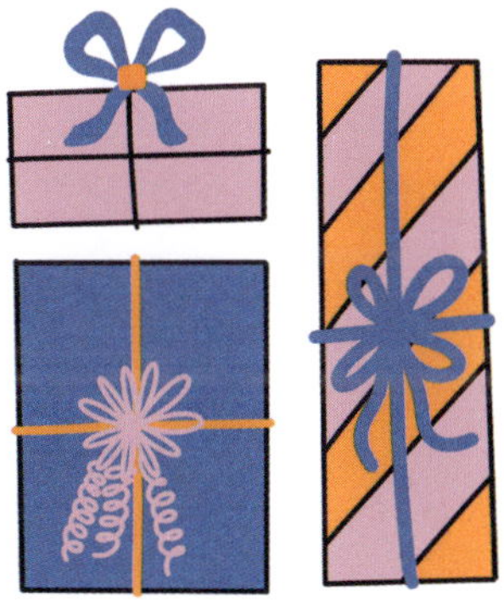

10. Draw a big ribbon bow with two large loops, two thick wavy lines, and a square center on the top left rectangle.

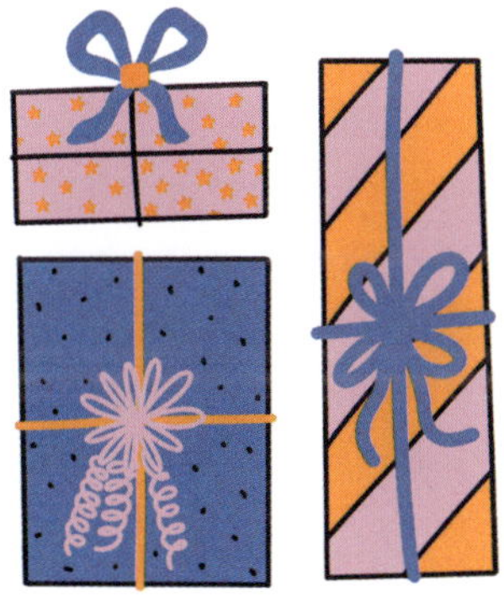

11. Add patterns to the wrapping paper with dots and stars.

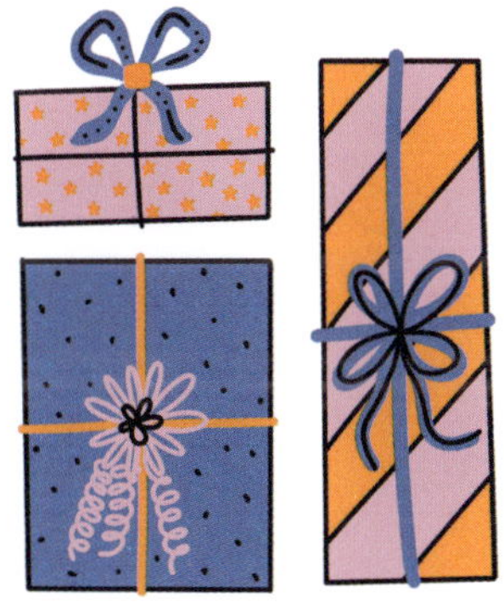

12. Add texture to the bows with black lines, dots, dashes, and additional layers.

BE BOLD!

One of the gift boxes got opened! Draw the toy inside coming out of the box—maybe it's a teddy bear, a box of chocolates, or a new teapot!

UGLY CHRISTMAS SWEATER

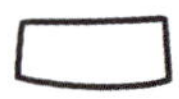

1. Start with a small, curved rectangle near the top center of the page.

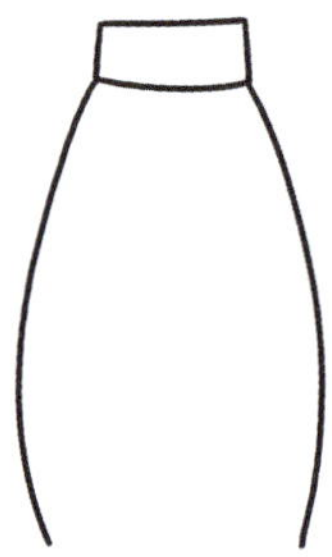

2. Draw two curved lines under the rectangle.

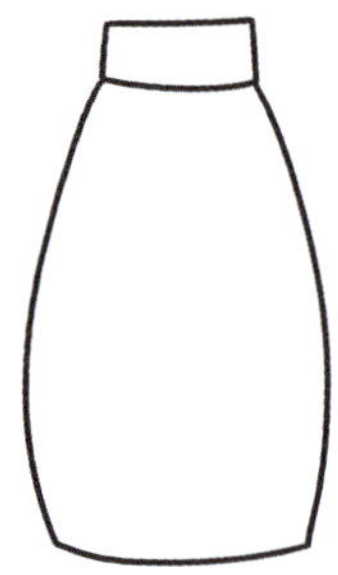

3. Connect the lines with a slightly curved horizontal line.

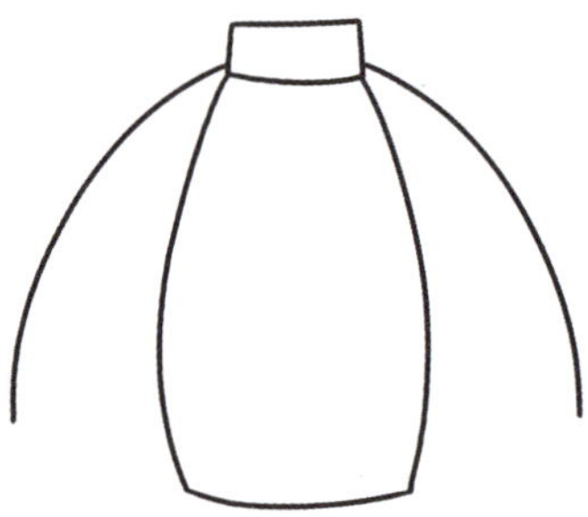

4. Draw two long, curved lines extending from the rectangle.

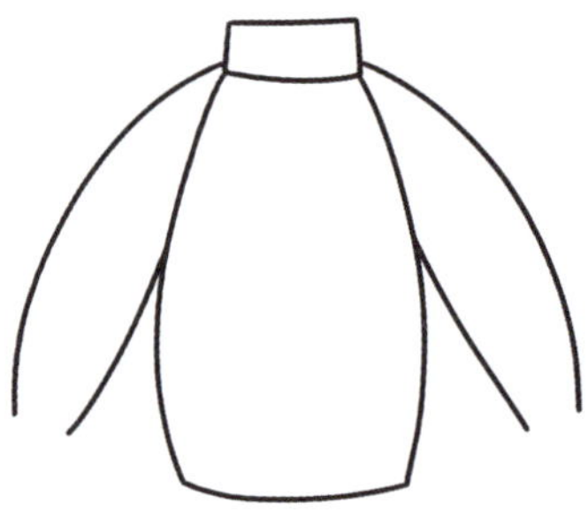

5. Draw two curved lines to make the shape of the sleeves.

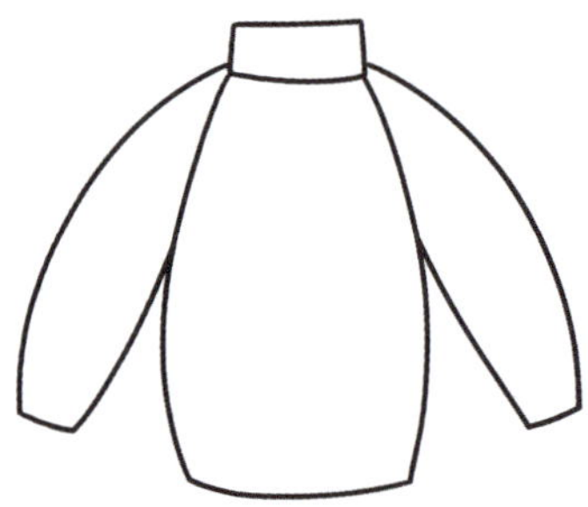

6. Close the sleeves with two straight lines.

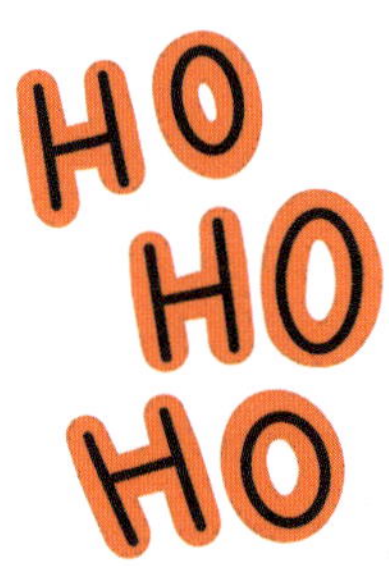

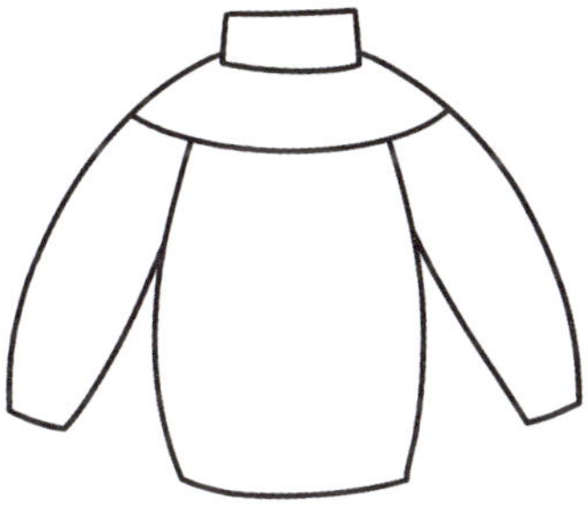

7. Draw a curved line across the top of the sweater.

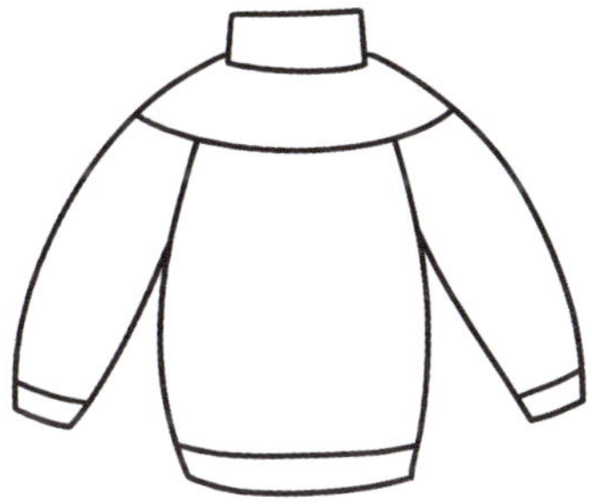

8. Add stripes to the bottom edges of the sweater and sleeves.

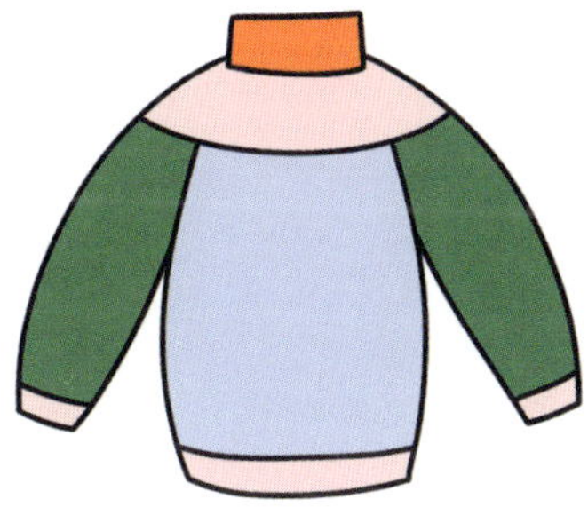

9. Fill in with the colors of your choice!

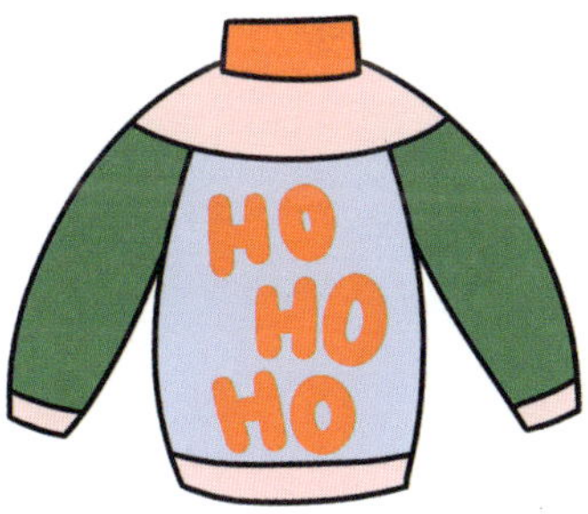

10. Write "Ho Ho Ho" in thick letters on the front of the sweater.

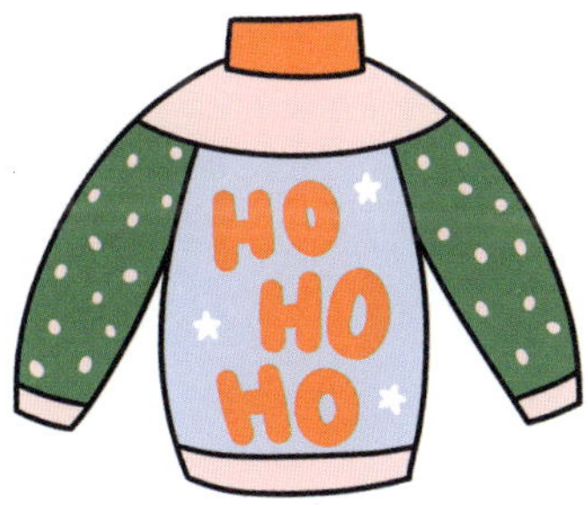

11. Decorate with polka dots and stars.

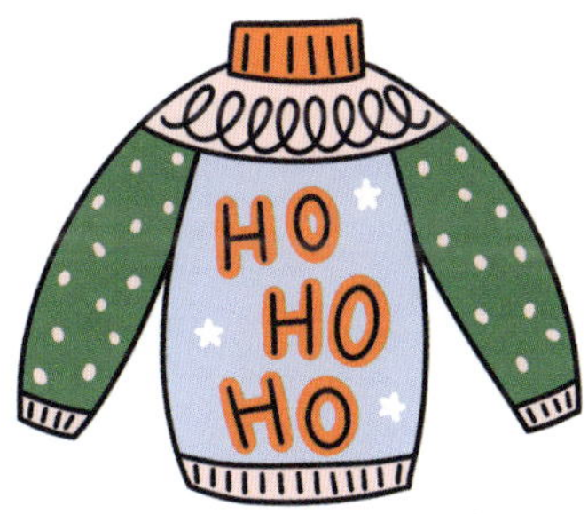

12. Add texture with black dashes, swirly lines, and black tracing in the words.

BE BOLD!

The uglier, the better! Mix patterns, colors, and silly details for maximum festive fun.

CHRISTMAS ORNAMENT

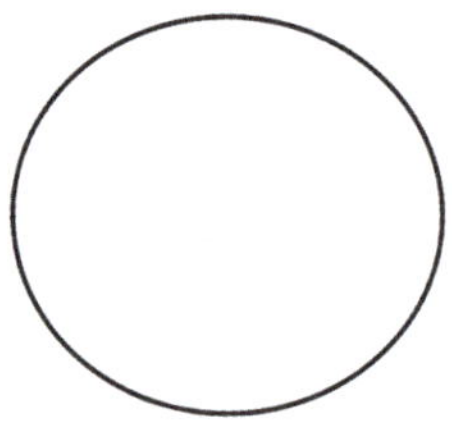

1. Start with a circle near the bottom center of the page.

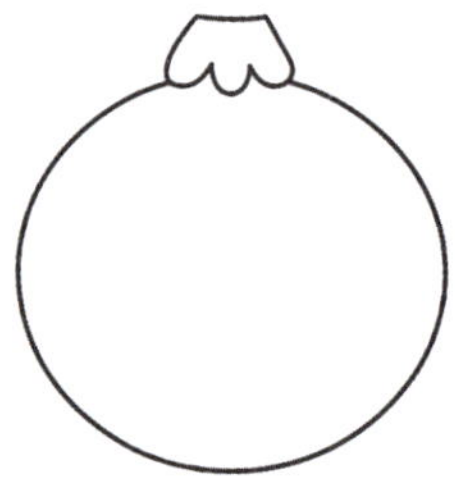

2. On top of the circle, draw the top of a trapezoid with three scallops along the bottom.

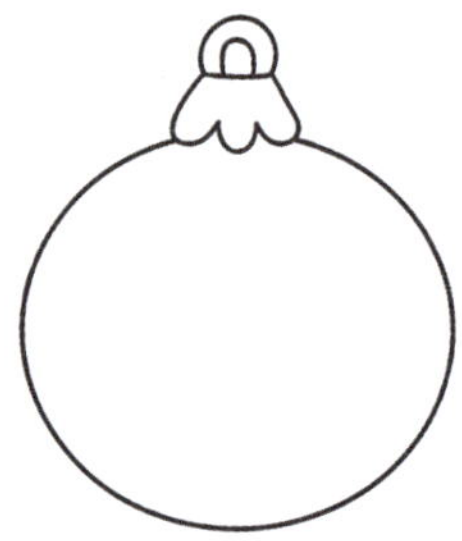

3. Draw two curved lines, one inside the other, on top.

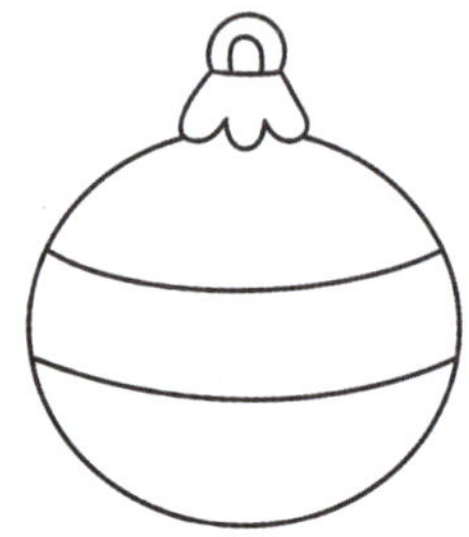

4. Add a horizontal stripe to the ornament with two curved lines.

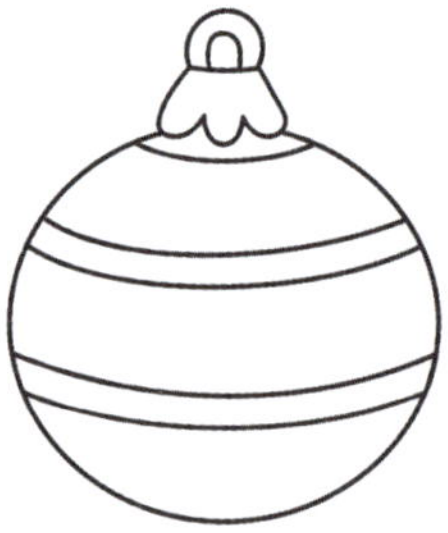

5. Make two thin stripes with curved lines above and below the large stripe, and another at the top of the ornament.

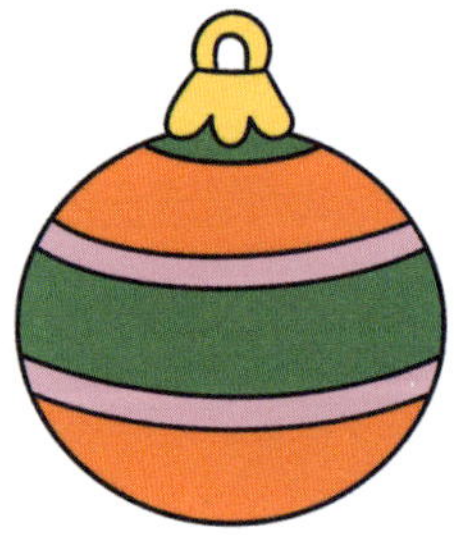

6. Fill in the colors!

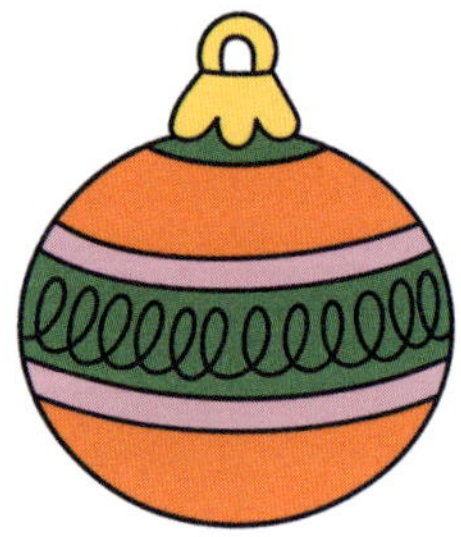

7. Add a swirly line in the middle stripe.

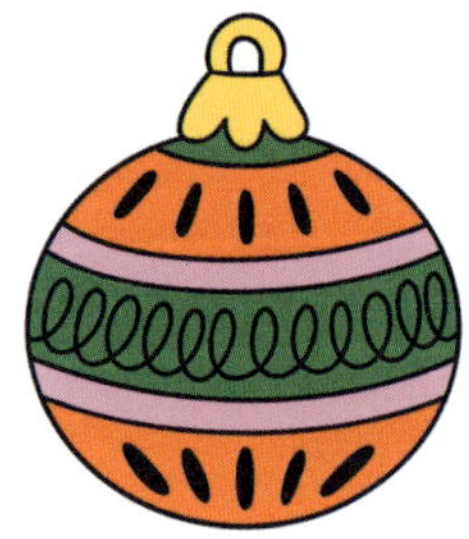

8. Add ovals on the top and bottom of the ornament.

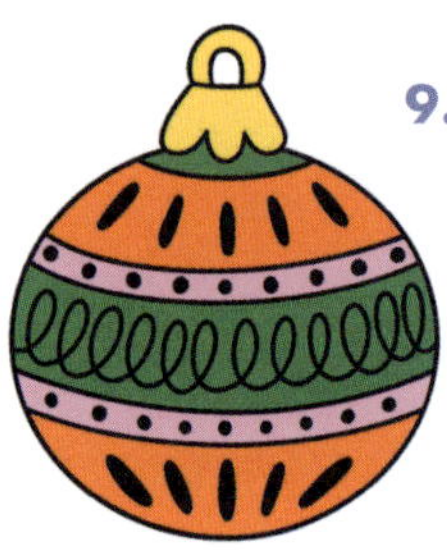

9. Add dots along the thin stripes.

BE BOLD!

Use your favorite seasonal colors to fill in this ornament, such as pastels, metallics, classic green and red, shades of icy blue, and more!

BELL ORNAMENT

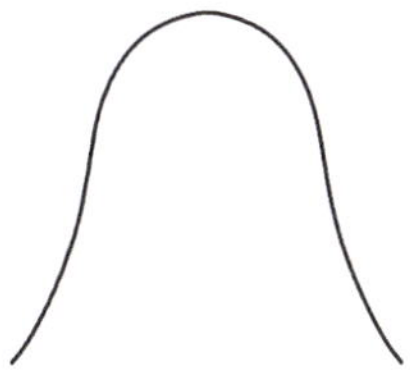

1. Start with an upside-down U-shaped line that extends out at the bottom.

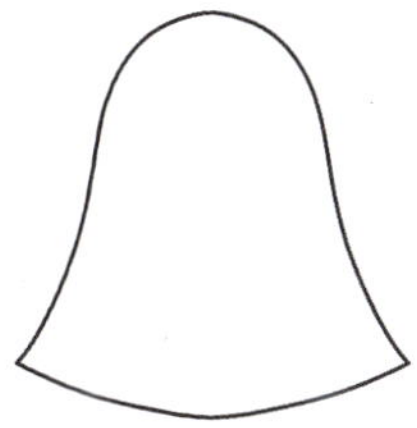

2. Connect the ends of the line with a curved line to make a bell shape.

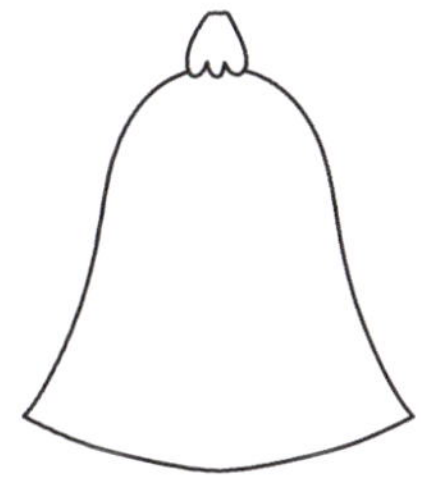

3. Draw a narrow shape on top of the bell with three scallops on the bottom and a flat top.

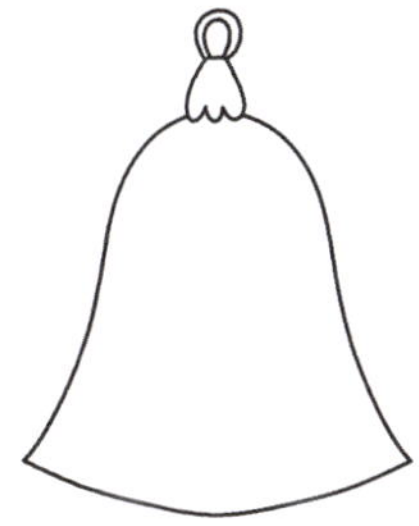

4. Draw two curved lines, one inside the other, on top.

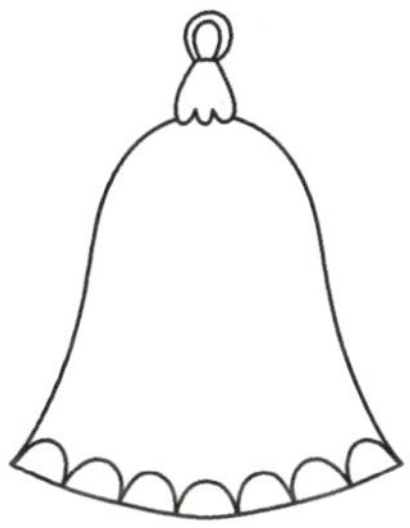

5. Draw a series of semicircles along the inside bottom edge of the bell.

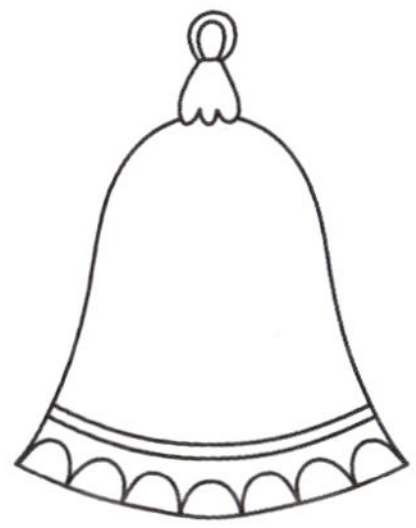

6. Draw two thin, curved lines above the semicircles.

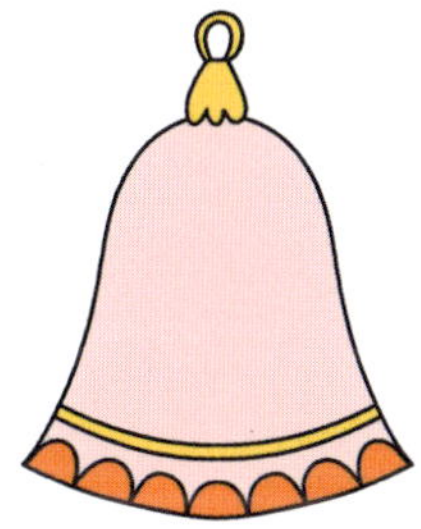

7. Fill in with the colors of your choice.

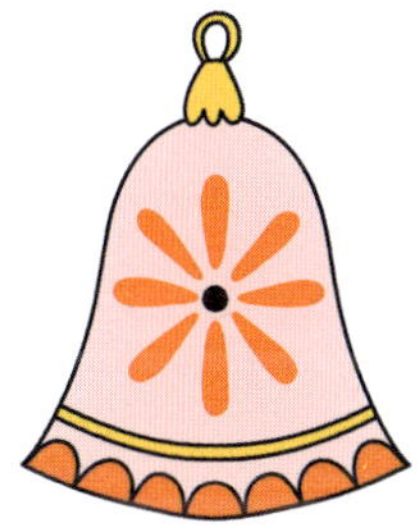

8. Draw a circle in the center of the bell, then surround the circle with eight evenly spaced teardrop-shaped petals.

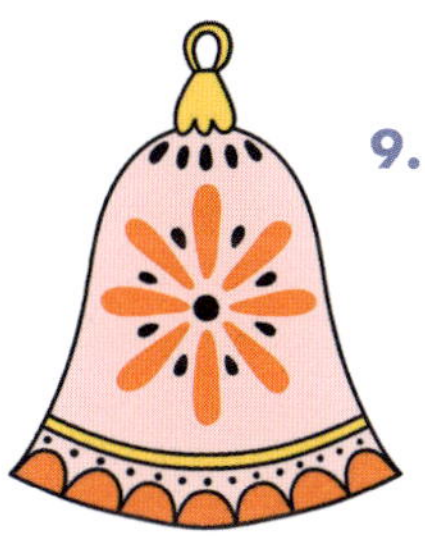

9. Decorate with ovals, teardrop shapes, and dots.

BE BOLD!

What other shapes of ornaments can you imagine? Try a diamond shape, a pointed shape with rounded sides, or a funky bauble shape.

SANTA CLAUS

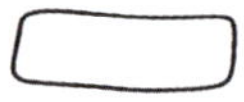

1. Start with a wobbly rectangle just above the center of the page.

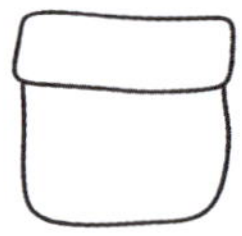

2. Draw a wobbly U shape below the rectangle.

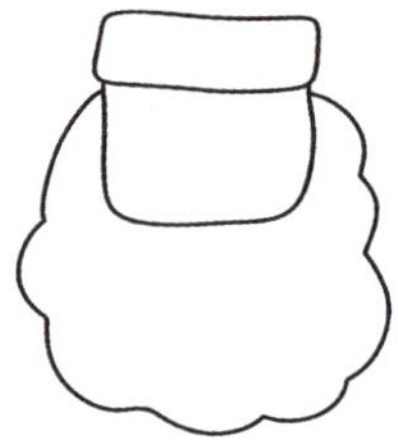

3. Draw a large fluffy cloud shape around the U to make the beard.

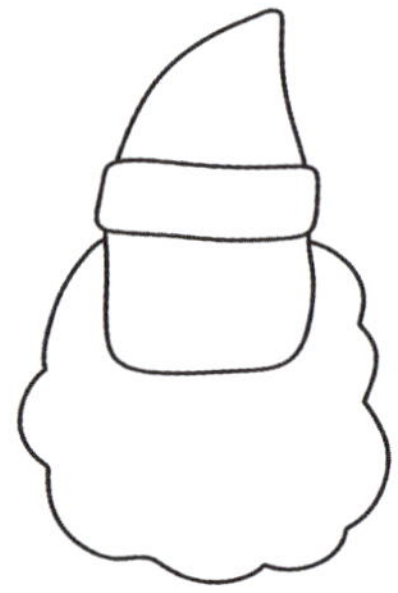

4. Add a curved triangle hat that tilts to the right.

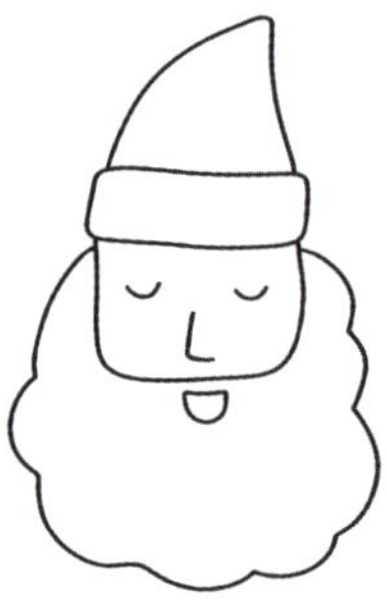

5. Draw two curved eyes, an L-shaped nose, and a semicircle mouth.

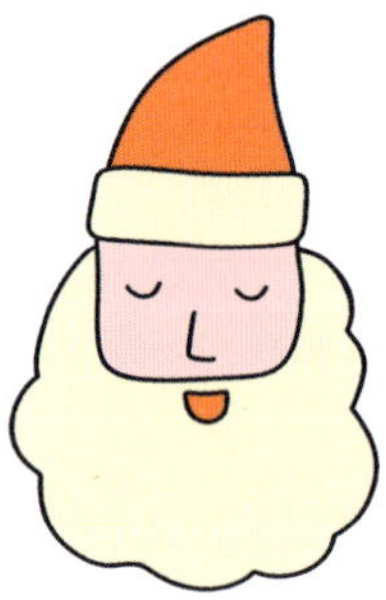

6. Fill in with the colors of your choice!

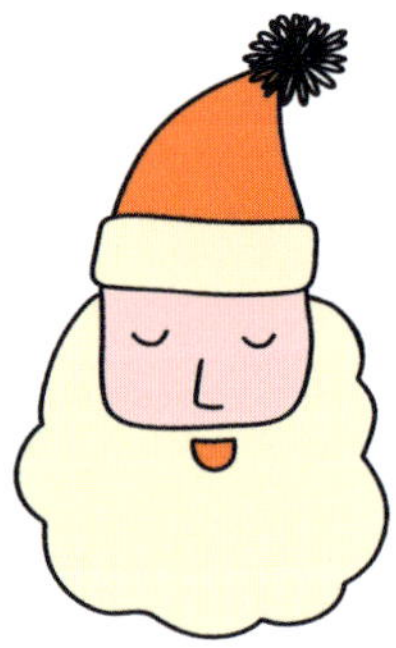

7. Draw an overlapping series of black loops on the tip of the hat to make a pom-pom.

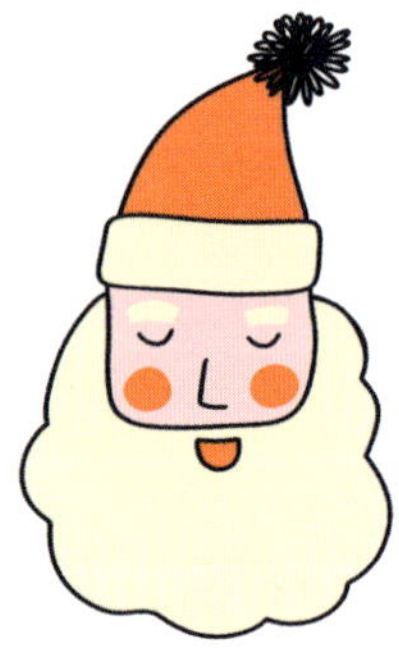

8. Draw two thick rectangle eyebrows and two circles of blush.

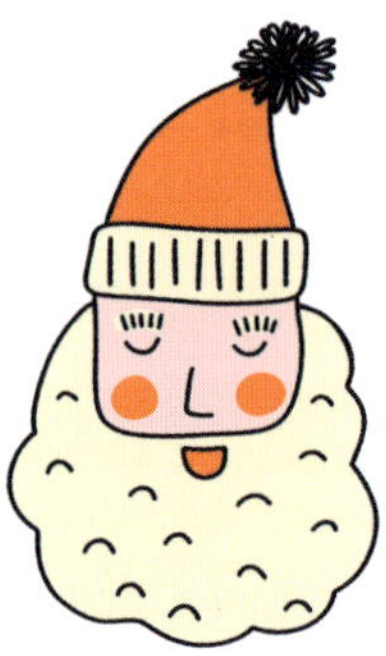

9. Add lines to the hat and eyebrows and small, curved lines in the beard.

BE BOLD!

Draw a frame around Santa with classic holiday motifs like holly, peppermint candy canes, pine branches, and pine cones. You can even include some of the items from your Christmas list.

THANKSGIVING GOURDS

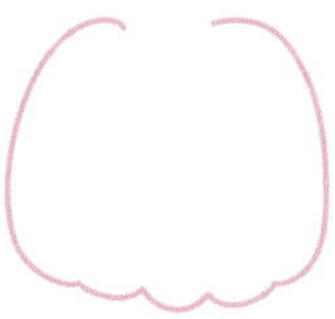

1. Start with a U shape with scallops along the bottom edge.

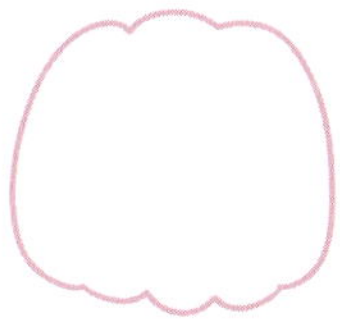

2. Add a small, curved line to close the top of the gourd.

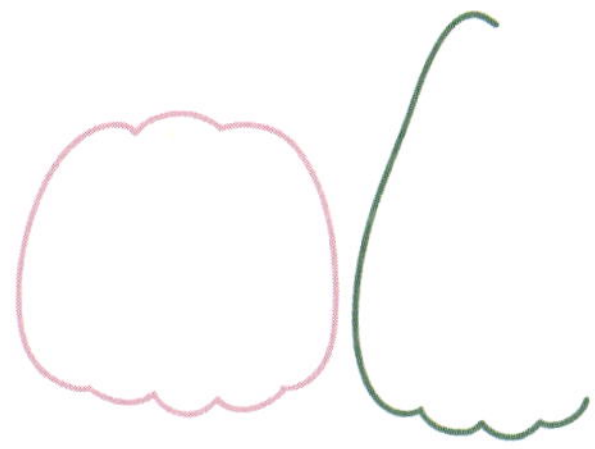

3. Draw a curved L-shaped line with scallops along the bottom edge.

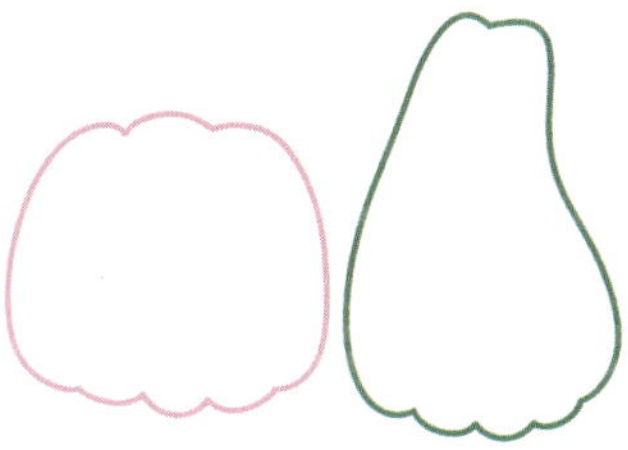

4. Connect a curved line on the right to complete a second gourd.

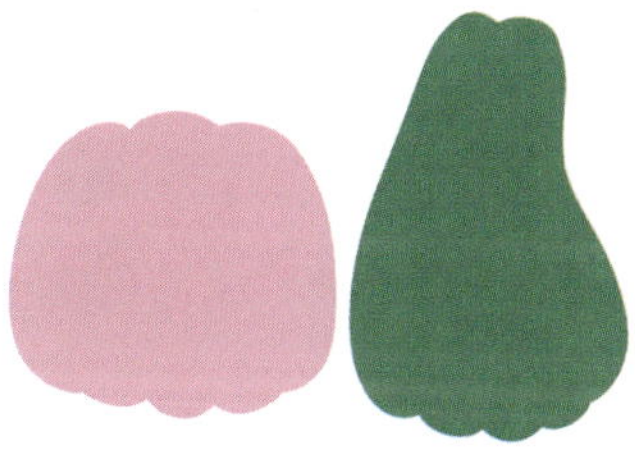

5. Fill in the colors!

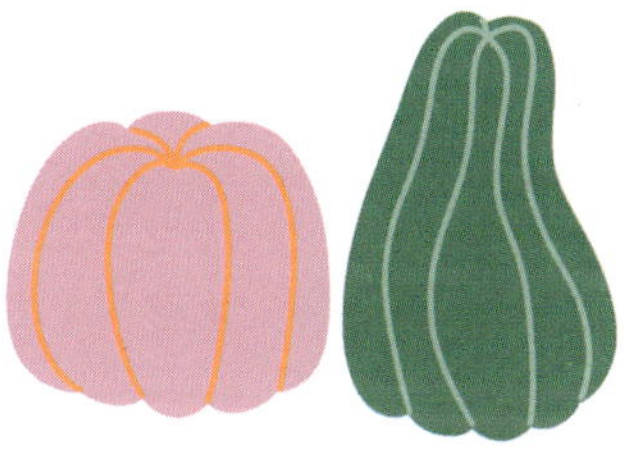

6. Decorate with curved, vertical lines that stem from a center point.

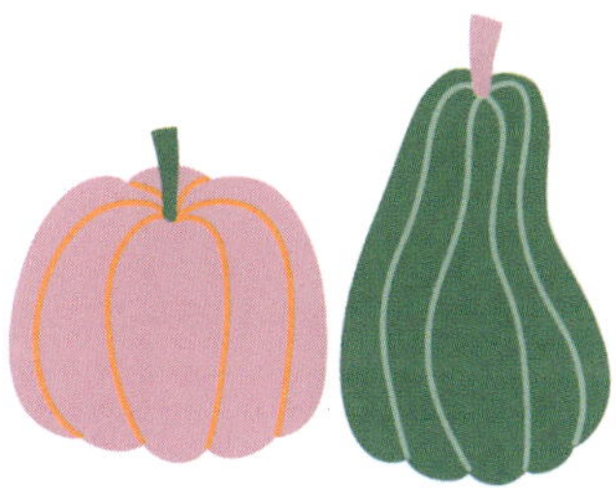

7. Add a tapered stem to the top of each gourd.

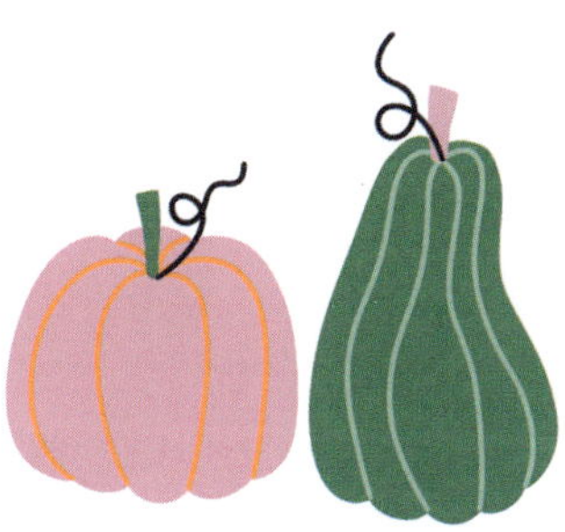

8. Add an extra detail with a curly vine sprouting next to each stem.

BE BOLD!

Build a full Thanksgiving cornucopia by adding fall harvest favorites like apples, corn, pears, and more to the scene.

JACK-O'-LANTERN

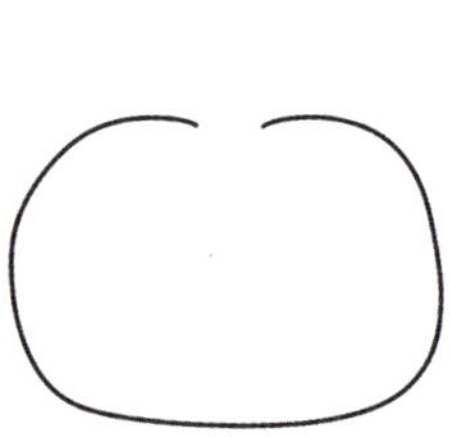

1. Start with a wide oval shape that is open at the top.

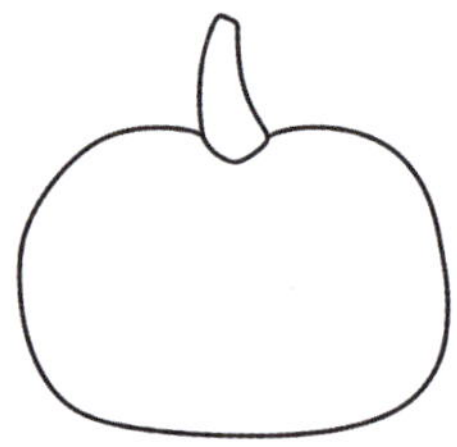

2. Draw a curved stem in the opening.

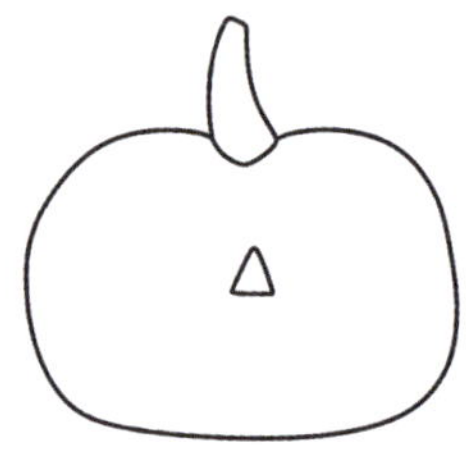

3. Add a triangle to the center of the pumpkin.

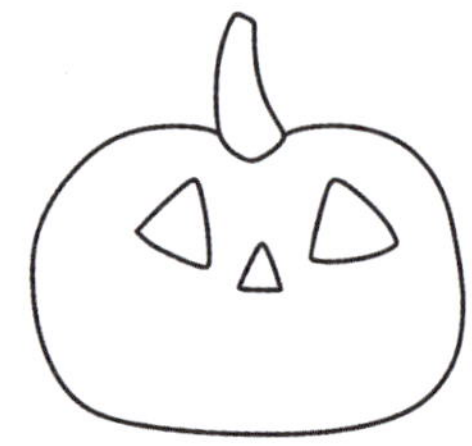

4. Add two larger triangles to make the eyes.

5. Draw a jagged mouth.

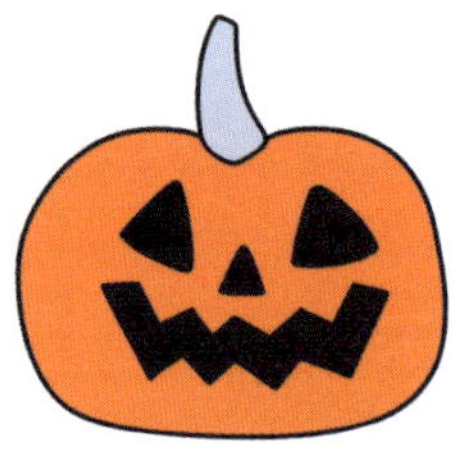

6. Fill in the colors!

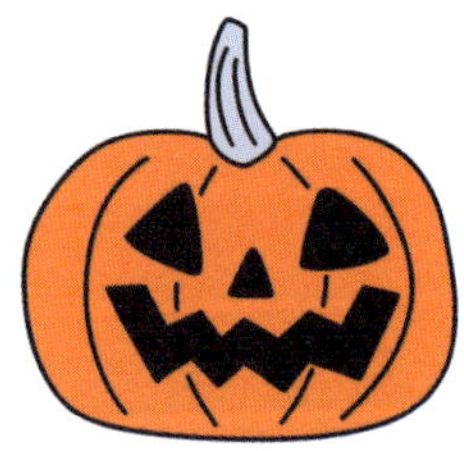

7. Draw some accent lines on the stem and to segment the bumpy pumpkin sections.

8. Make your jack-o'-lantern extra cute by drawing a six-petal flower with a circle center on the top right.

BE BOLD!

There are all kinds of faces you can carve into a pumpkin. Try circle or half-moon eyes, use a square or rectangle for a nose, or create a mouth with buck teeth or sharp fangs.

WITCHY GHOST

1. Start with a curved line near the top of the page.

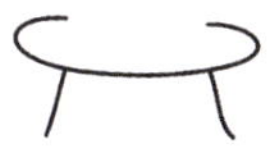

2. Draw two vertical lines underneath that curve slightly outward.

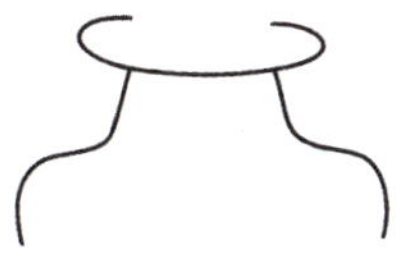

3. Add a curved line to each of the vertical lines.

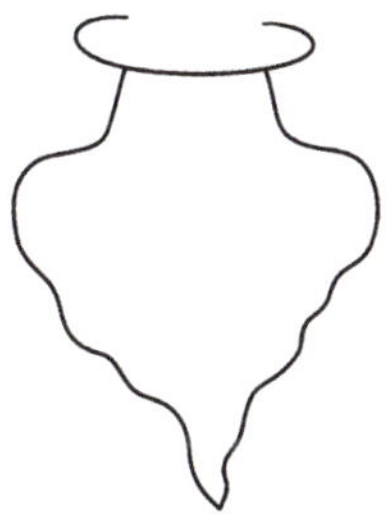

4. Draw wavy lines that angle toward the middle and meet at the end.

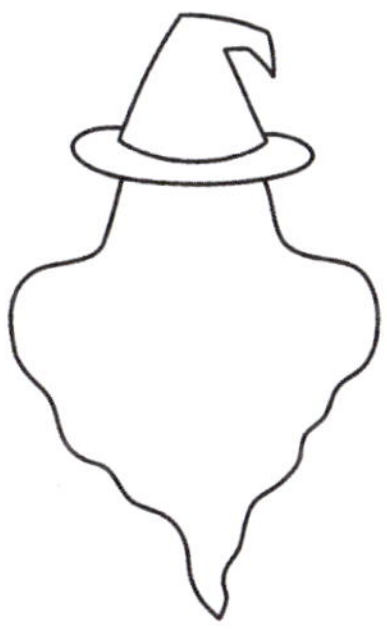

5. Start a triangle hat with a curved base, with a crooked tip that points downward.

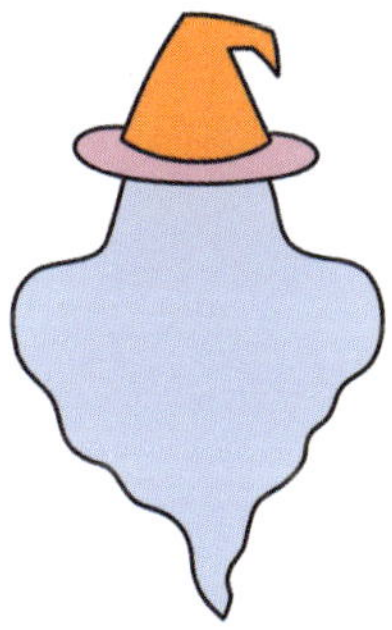

6. Fill in with the colors of your choice!

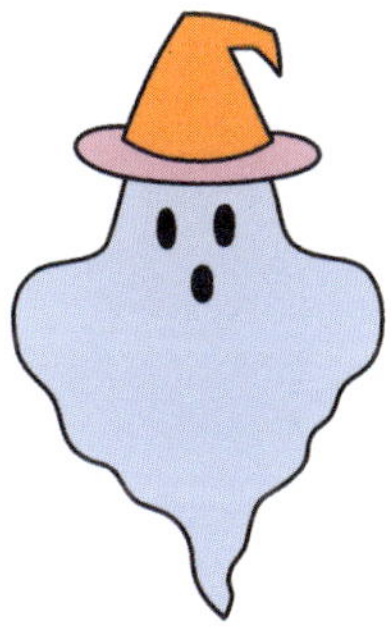

7. Add three ovals for the eyes and mouth.

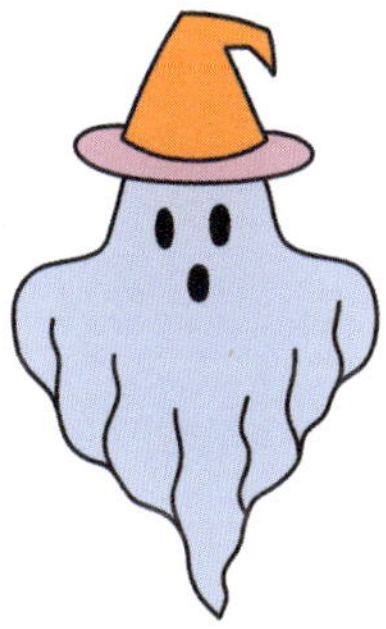

8. Add dimension with wavy lines along the edge.

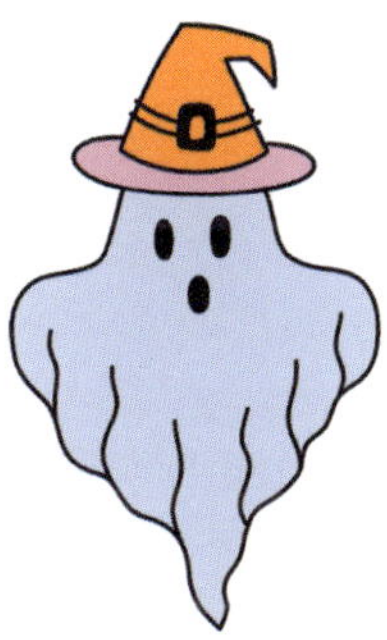

9. Add two curved lines for a belt and a rectangular buckle on the hat.

BE BOLD!

Try different faces on your ghost. Make it happy, scared, or sad. Or try different accessories like a witch's broom, a vampire cape and fangs, or a crown.

CUTE MONSTER

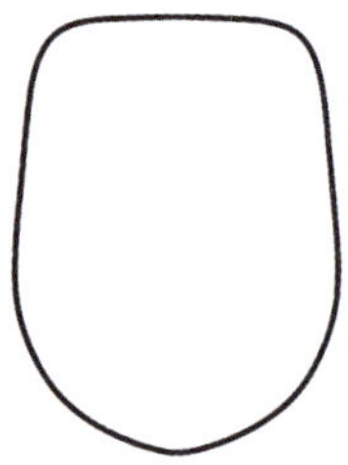

1. Start with a long bulbous shape that has a round point on the bottom and a flat top.

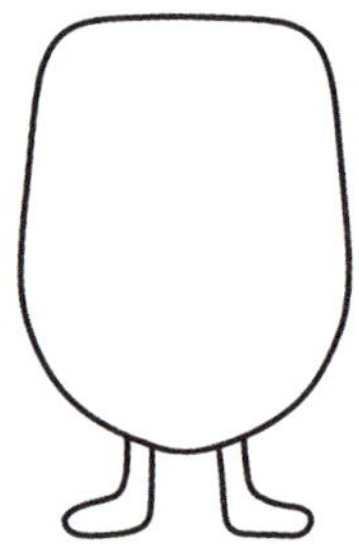

2. Draw two little L-shaped legs underneath.

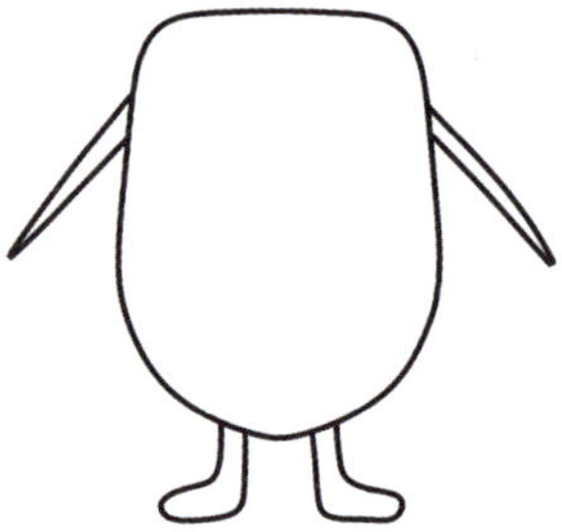

3. Draw two thin, pointed arms.

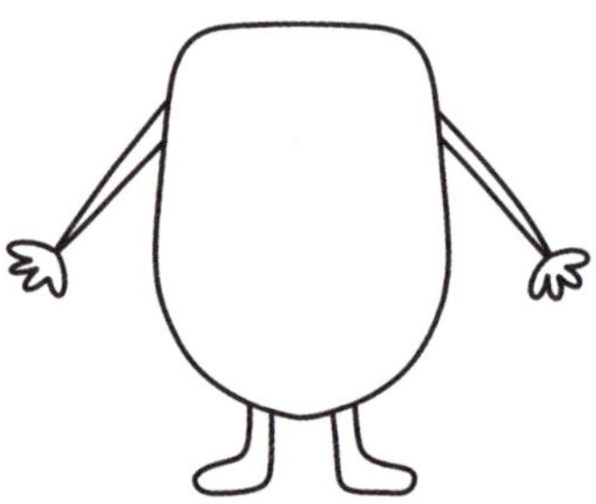

4. At the ends of the arms, draw little four-fingered hands.

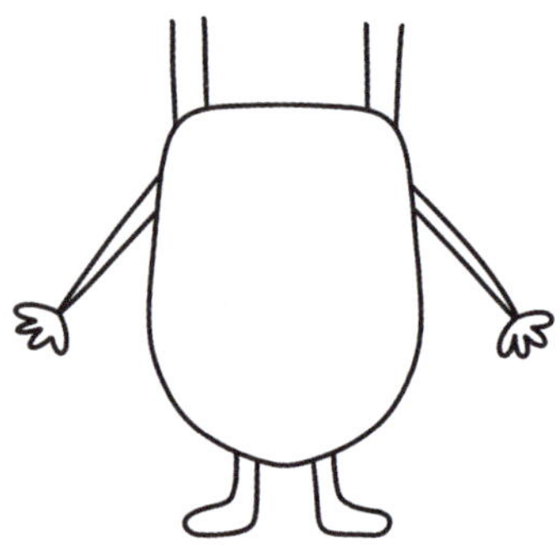

5. On top, draw four vertical lines, two on each side.

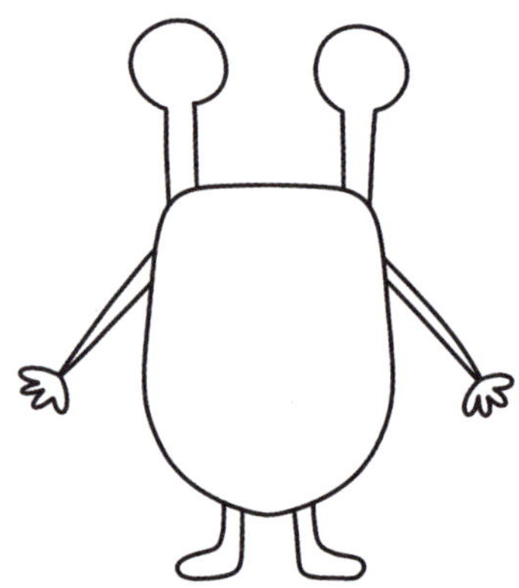

6. Draw a large circle on top of each set of vertical lines for the eyes.

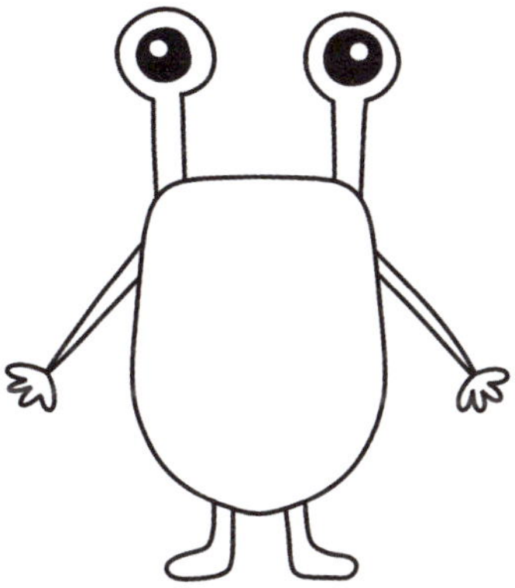

7. Inside the eyes, draw a large black circle with a white dot for a highlight.

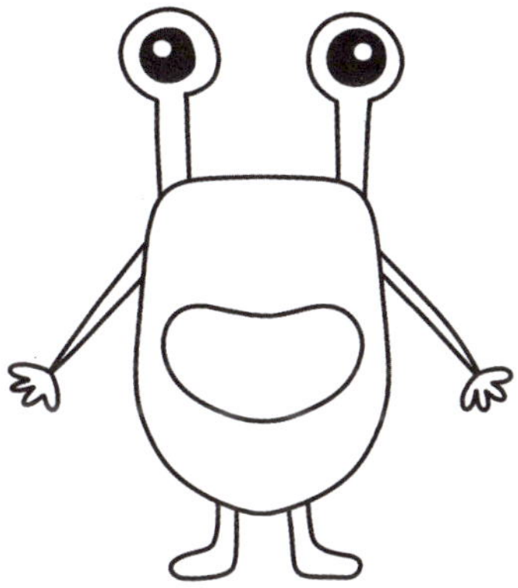

8. Add a large bean-shaped mouth.

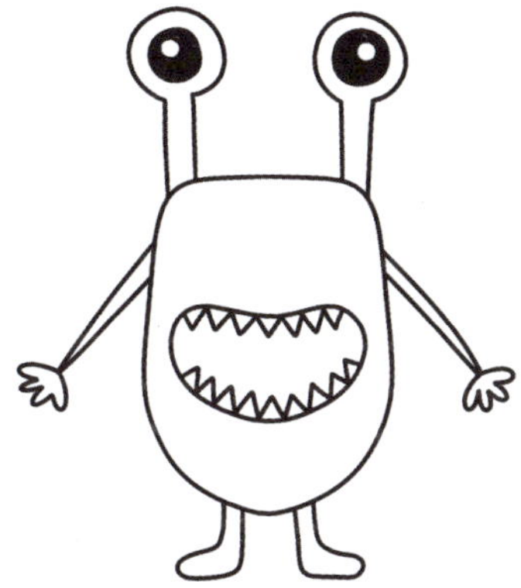

9. Draw a row of tiny, spiky triangle teeth inside the top and bottom of the mouth.

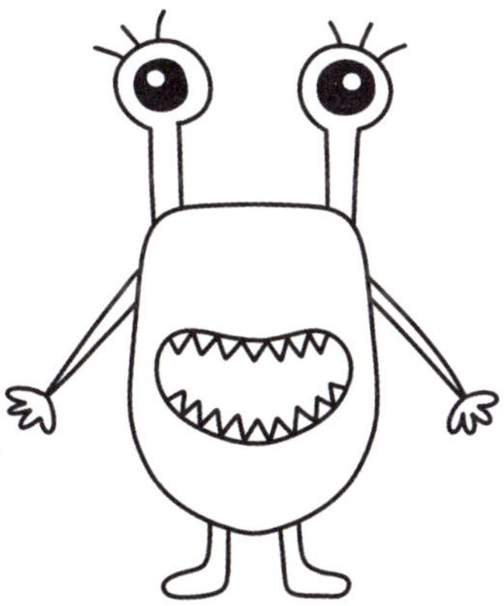

10. Add three curved eyelashes on top of each eye.

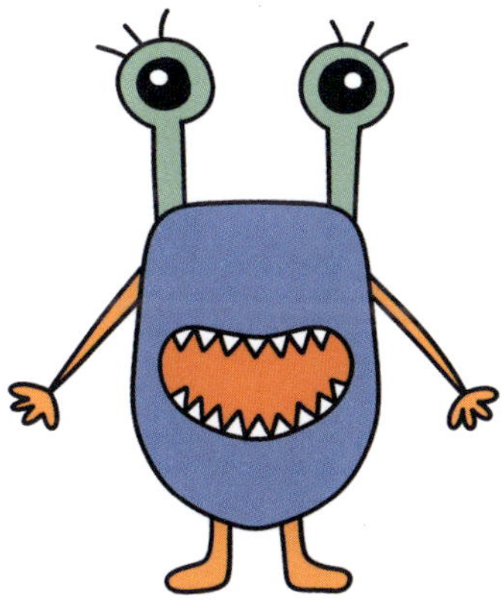

11. Fill in with the colors of your choice!

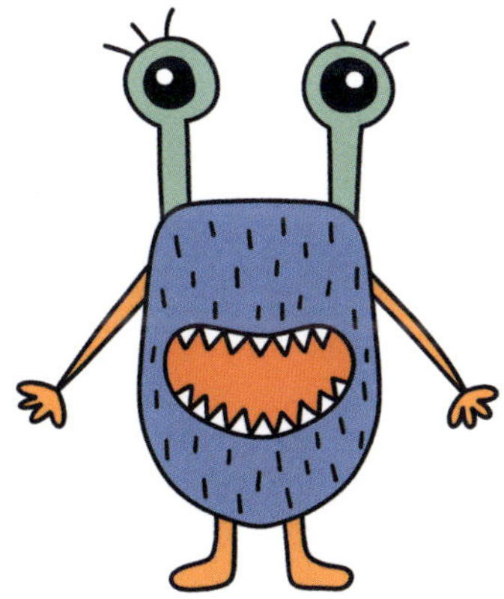

12. Add texture with dashes all over the body to create fur.

BE BOLD!

Monsters come in all shapes and sizes. Change the size of your monster's body, where the eyes go, the size of the mouth, the teeth, and more to make a unique little monster.

VALENTINE'S LETTER IN A BOTTLE

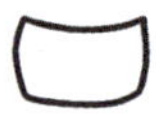

1. Start with a small, curved rectangle near the top center of the page.

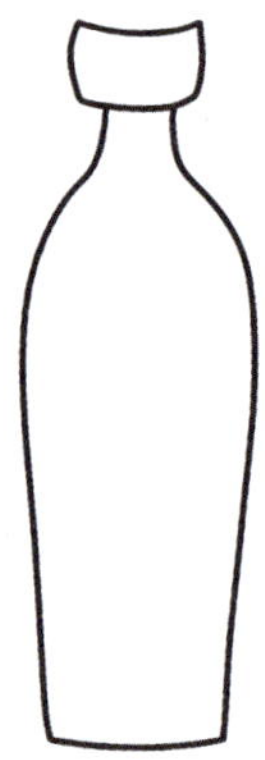

2. Draw a thin bottle using curved lines for the sides and a flat bottom.

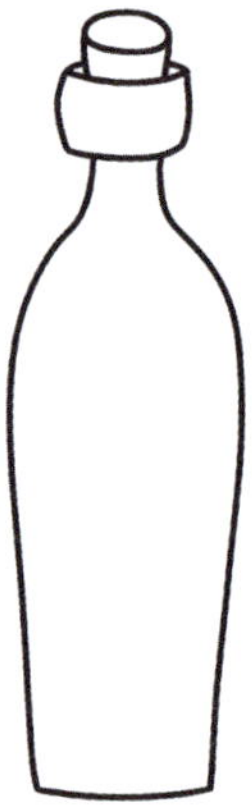

3. Add an oval above the rectangle and connect it to the bottle with two vertical lines and two short horizontal lines.

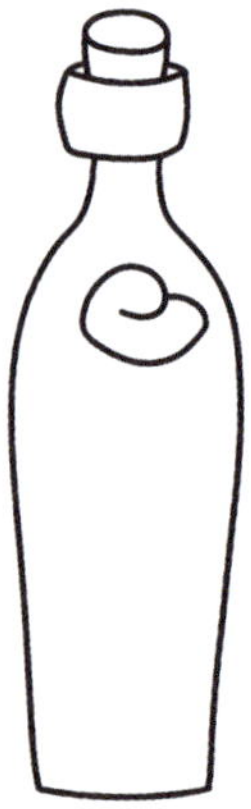

4. Draw a heart-shaped swirl inside the bottle.

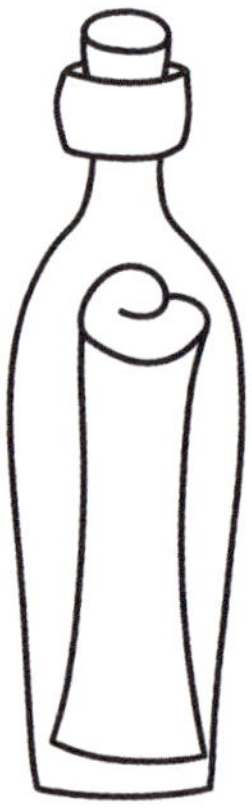

5. Draw two curved, vertical lines and make a flat bottom for the rolled-up letter.

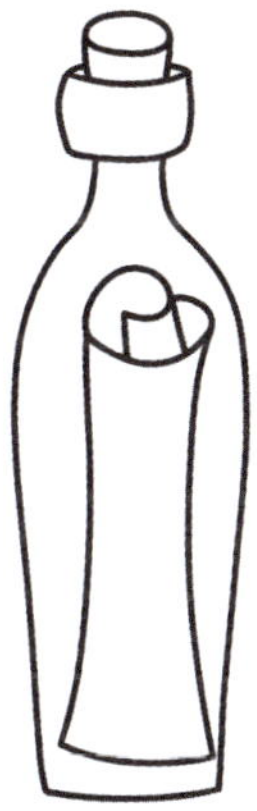

6. Add two lines in the center of the swirl to add dimension.

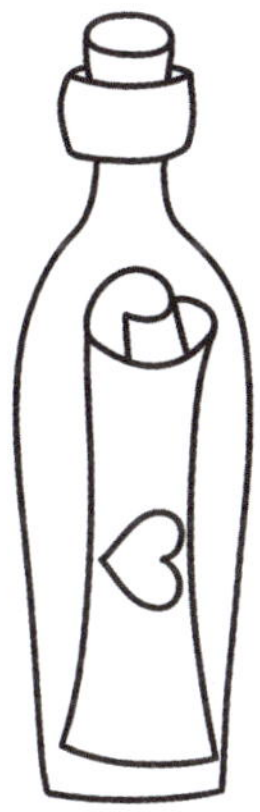

7. Draw a heart on the letter.

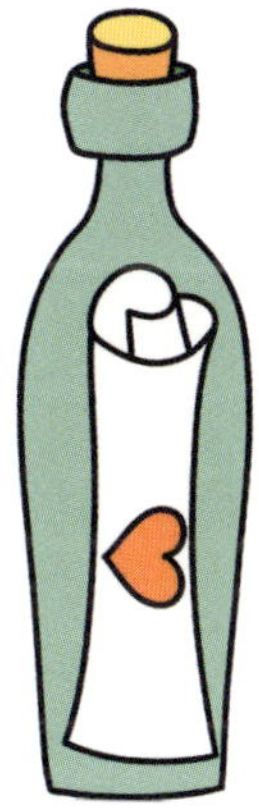

8. Fill in the colors!

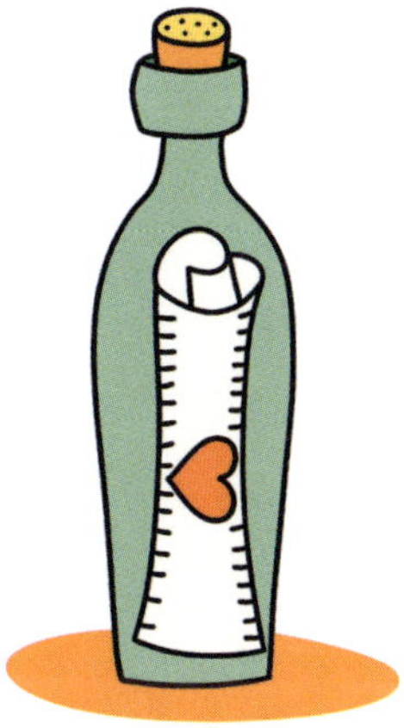

9. Decorate with dots on the cork, dashes along the letter, and an oval shadow under the bottle.

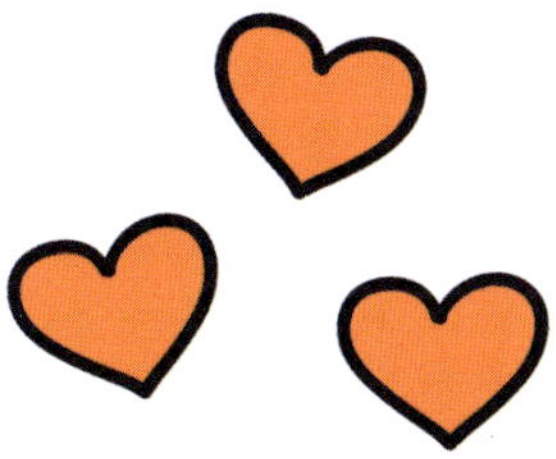

BE BOLD!

What if this love letter got lost and washed up on a beach? Draw what that scene might look like.

VALENTINE'S LOVE BIRDS

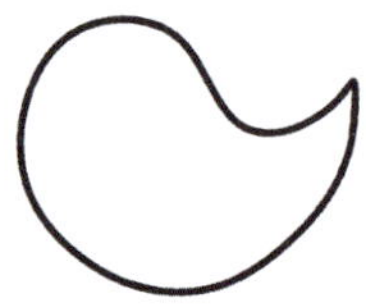

1. Start with a curved teardrop shape on the right.

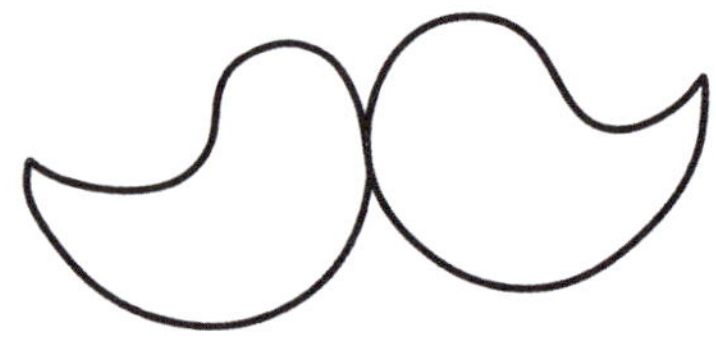

2. Draw a second teardrop shape on the left.

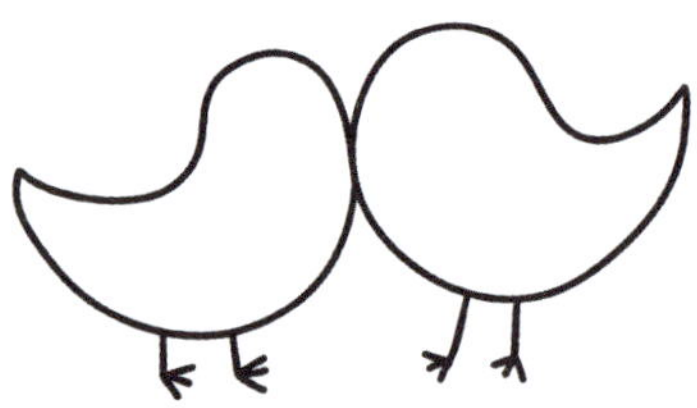

3. Add two short legs with three toes to each bird.

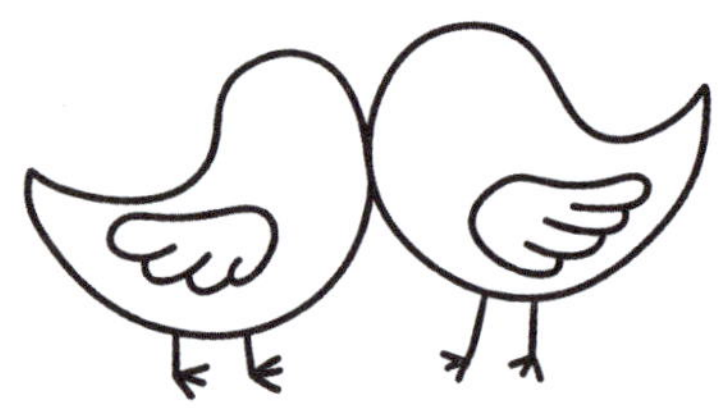

4. Draw a flared wing with four scallops for the feathers on each bird.

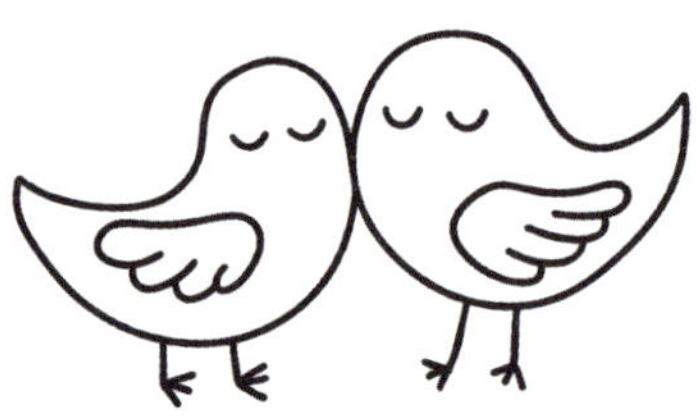

5. Add two curved eyes for each bird.

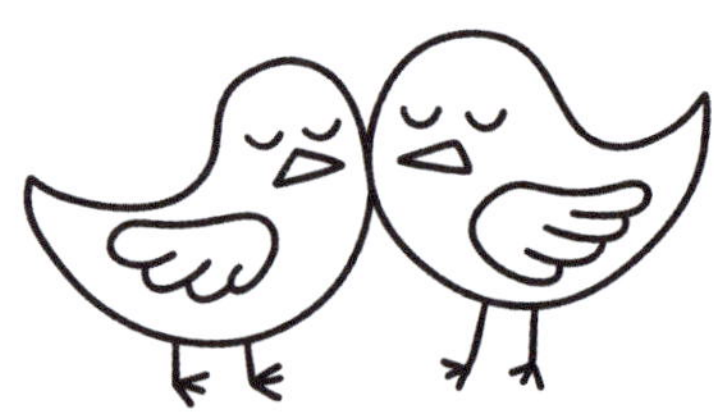

6. Add a triangle beak for each bird.

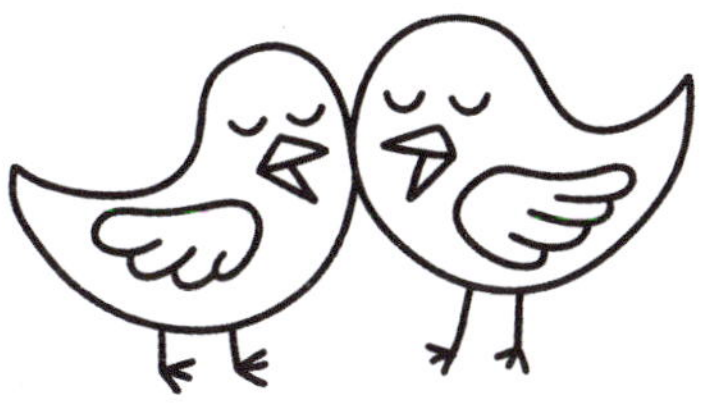

7. Draw a second triangle underneath the first to make an opened beak for each bird.

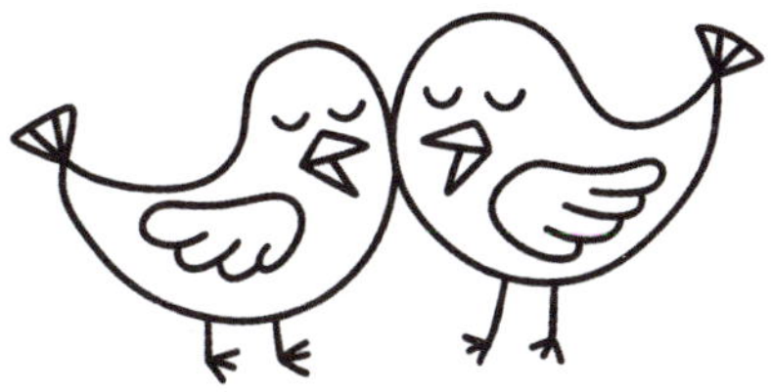

8. Add a triangle tail to each bird with two lines inside to mark the feathers.

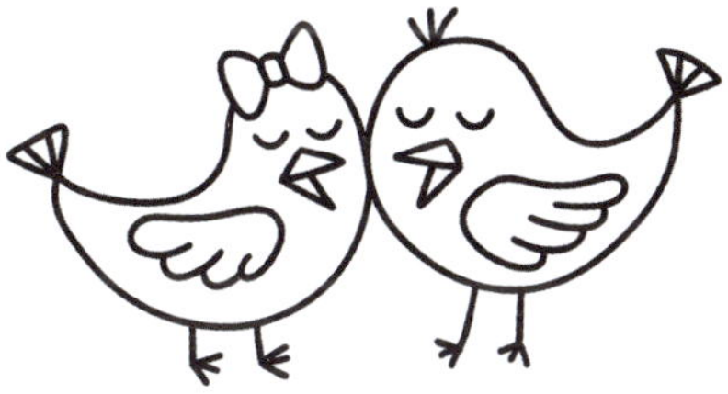

9. Add a bow to the left bird and three lines on the top of the head to the right bird.

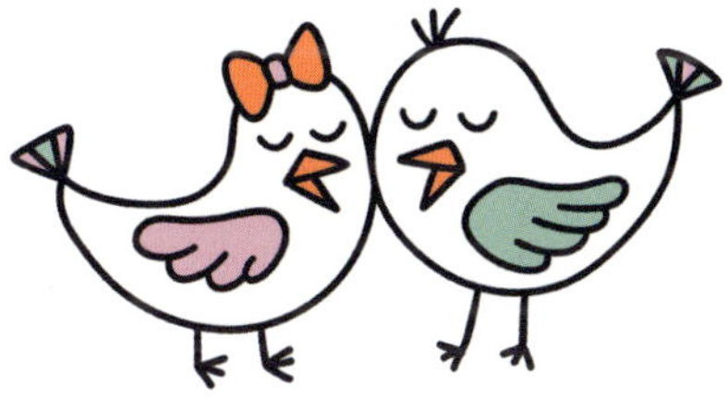

10. Fill in with the colors of your choice.

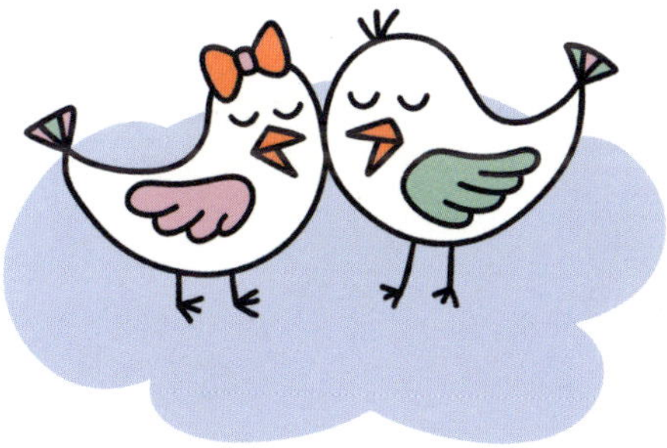

11. Add a cloudlike shape around the birds for a shadow.

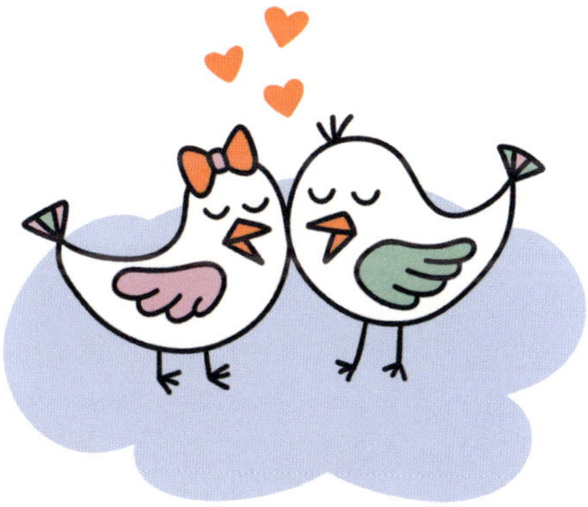

12. Draw three hearts above the birds.

BE BOLD!

What if these love birds had a romantic Valentine's picnic? Draw a table or plate in front of them with whatever you think would be in a romantic bird dinner, such as berries, bread, or bugs—there are no wrong answers.

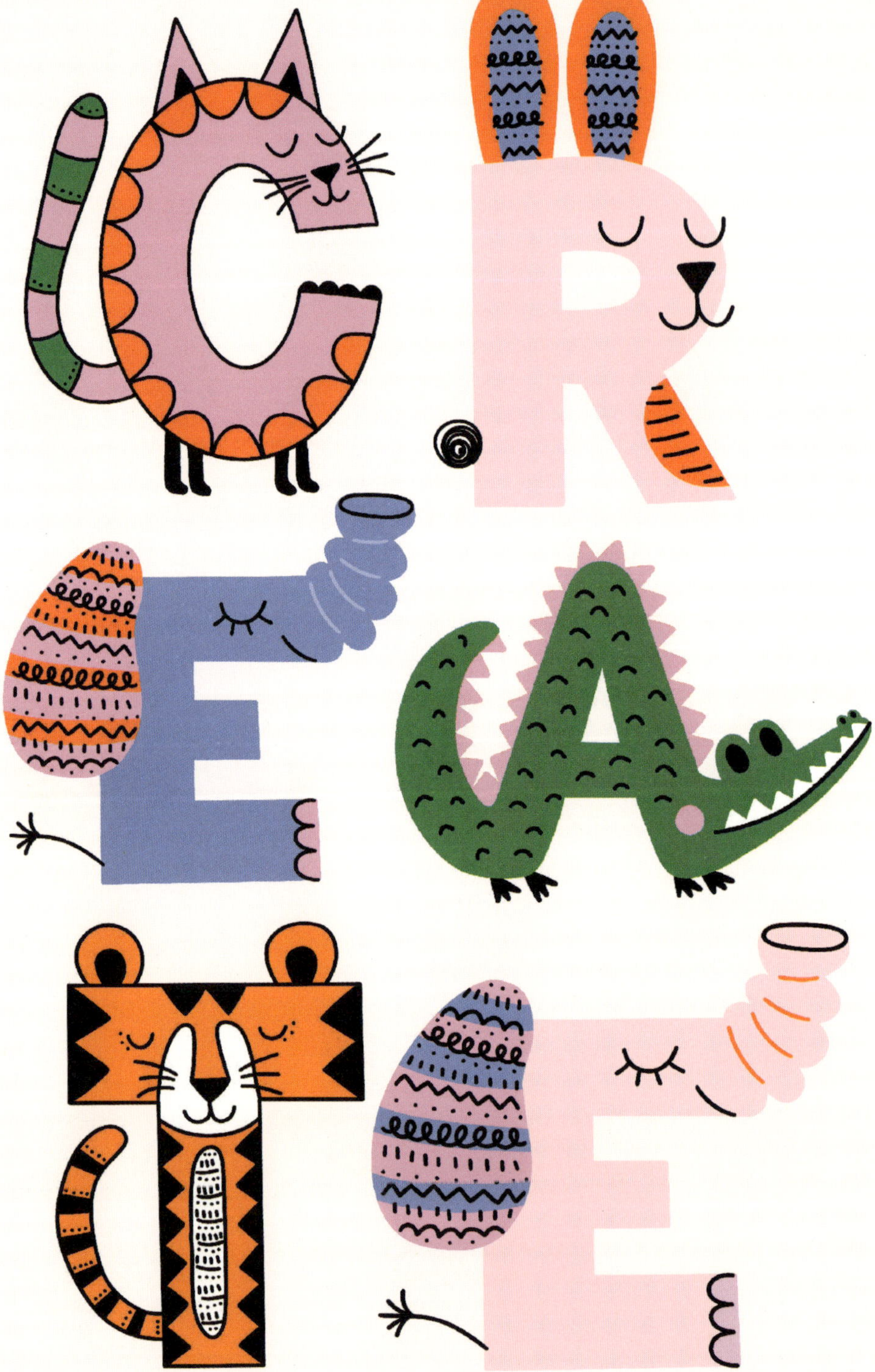
CREATE

LETTERING

FLORAL-DECORATED LETTERS

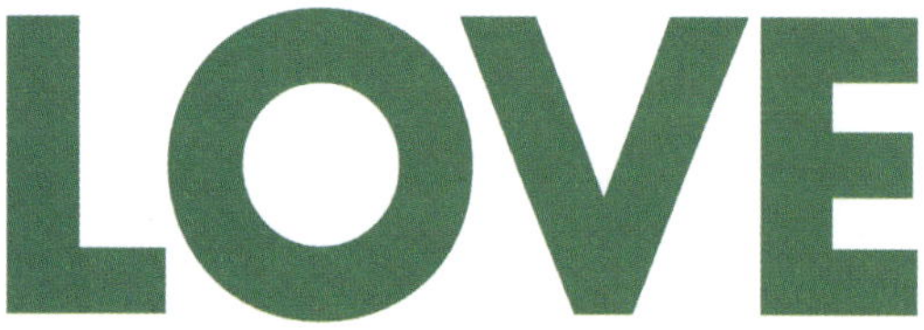

1. Start with the word "LOVE" in big block letters across the page.

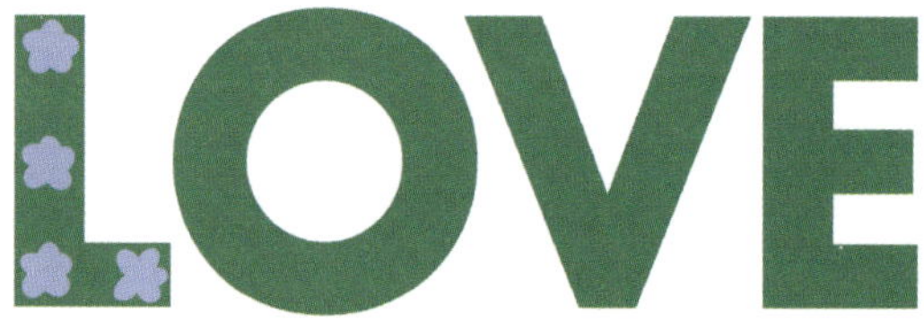

2. Draw four flowers, each with five petals, spaced out evenly within the L.

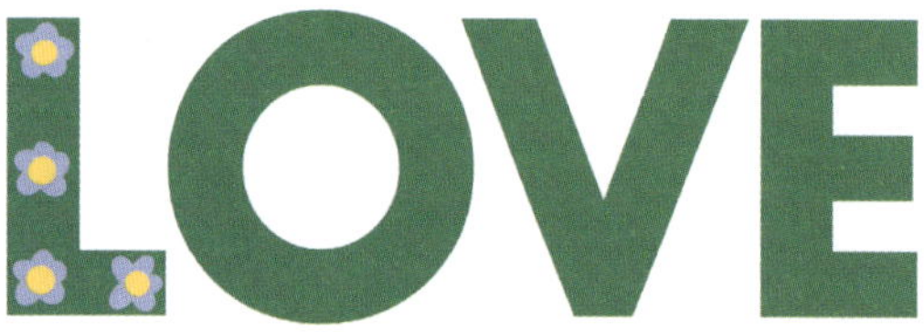

3. Draw a circle in the center of each flower.

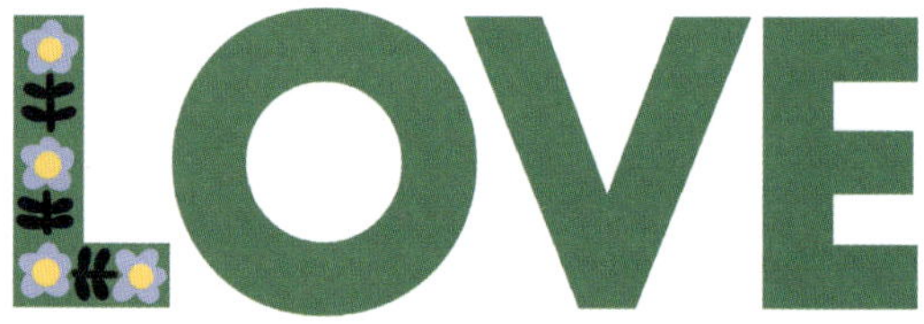

4. Add three stems, each with four teardrop-shaped leaves, in the space between the flowers.

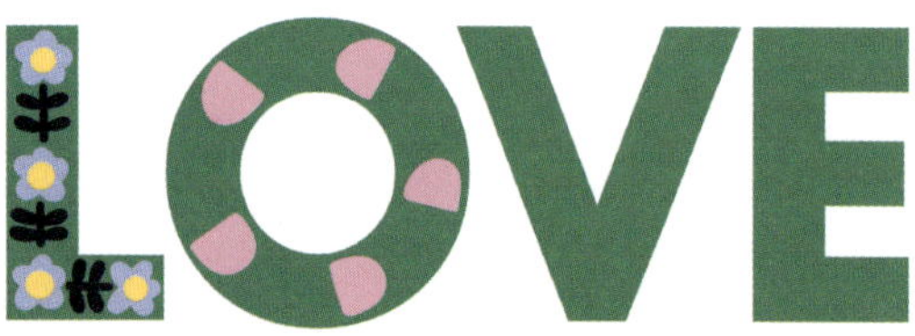

5. Add five semicircles spaced out evenly within the O.

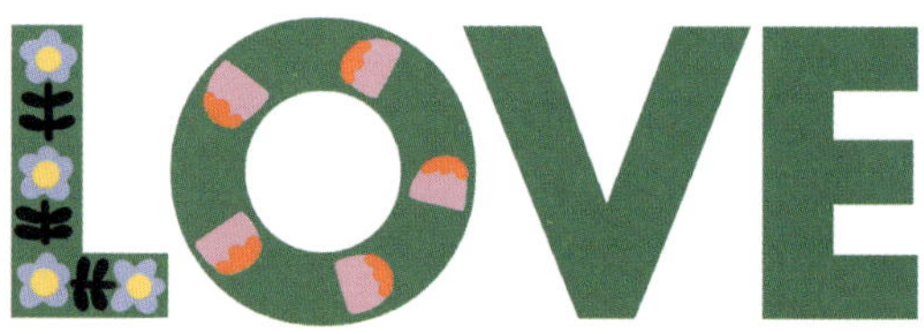

6. Add a scalloped line on the rounded end of each semicircle.

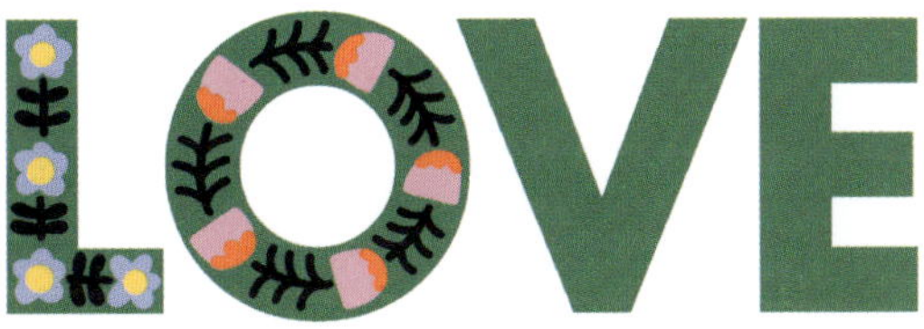

7. Draw five stems, each with six pointed leaves, between the semicircle flowers.

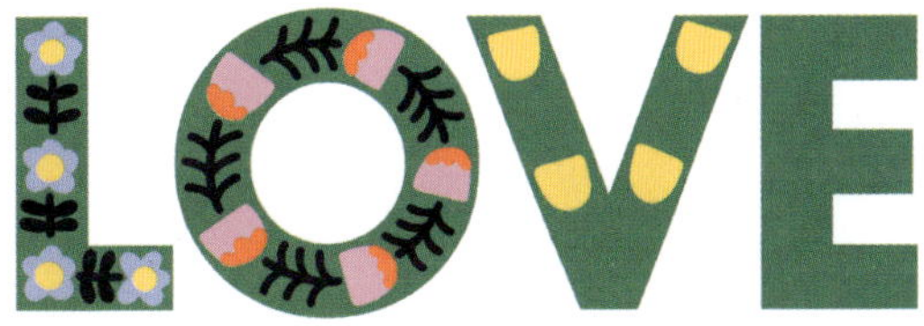

8. Draw four semicircles spaced out evenly within the V.

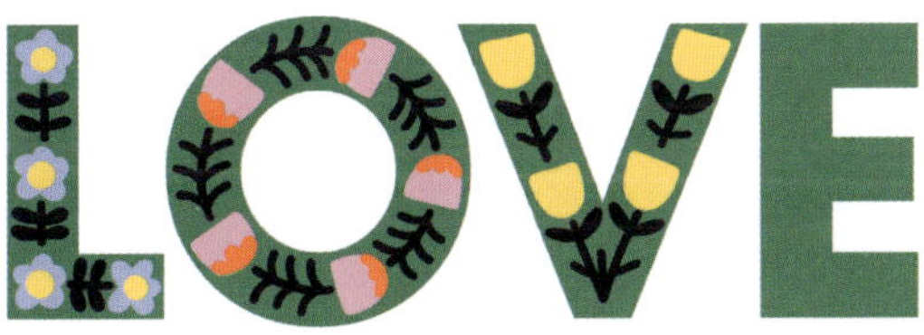

9. Draw stems with two leaf shapes and two stems under each of the four semicircle flowers.

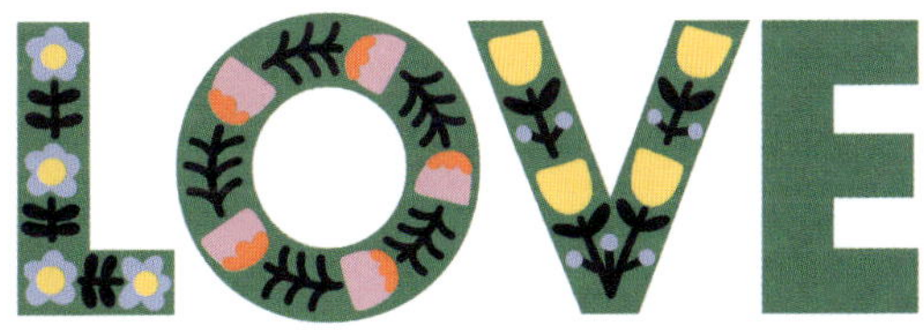

10. Add tiny dots to the stem ends in an accent color.

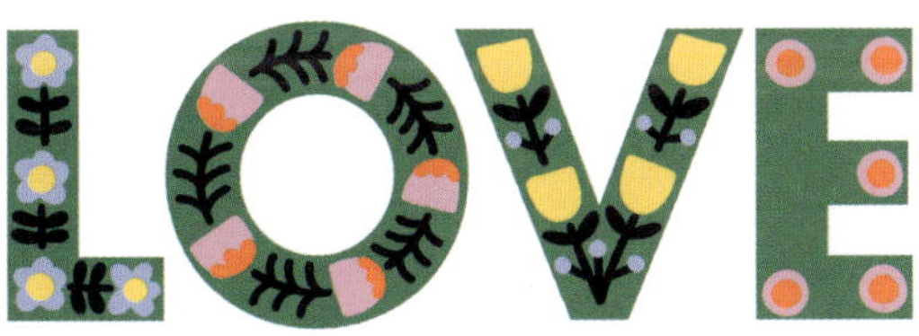

11. Add five circles, with smaller circles inside them, spaced out evenly within the E.

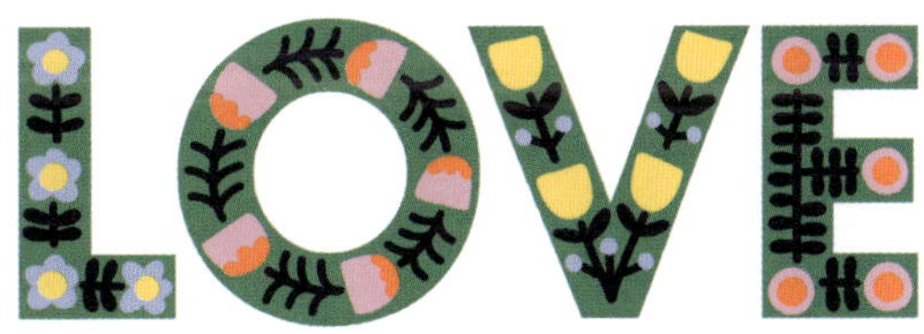

12. Draw stems with lots of straight oval leaves in between the circle flowers.

BE BOLD!

Try longer words like Lovely, Beauty, or Joyful and use a different flower motif in each letter. How many flower motifs can you think of to fill in all the letters?

LETTERS WRAPPED WITH VINES

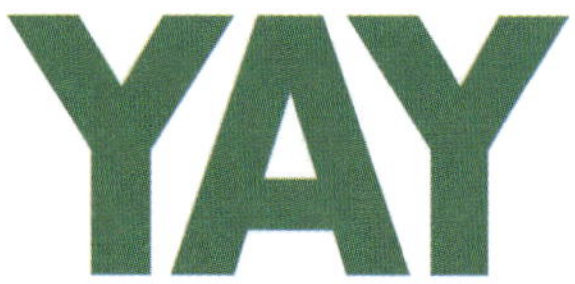

1. Start with the word "YAY" in big block letters across the page.

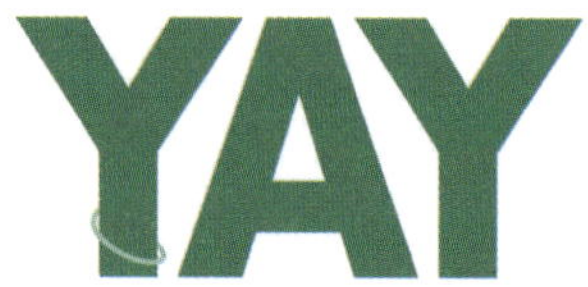

2. Add a diagonal curved line around the bottom of the first Y.

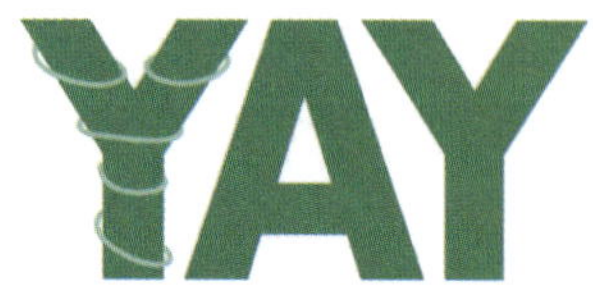

3. Continue to add lines of different lengths around the Y—make some wobbly and some straight—until there are five.

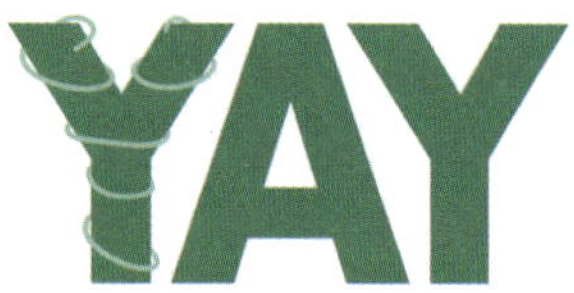

4. Draw two curved lines coming over the tops of the Y.

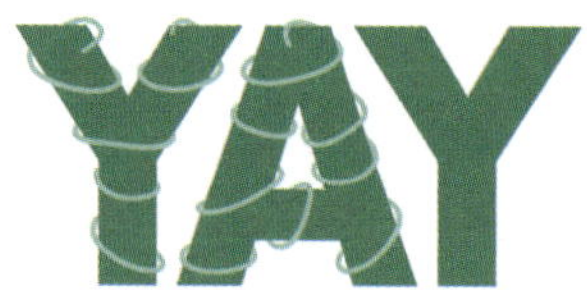

5. Repeat the same process with the letter A, with one curved line coming up over the top.

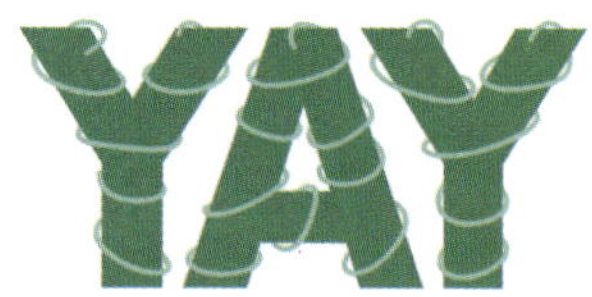

6. Repeat the same process with the last Y, with two curved lines coming over the top.

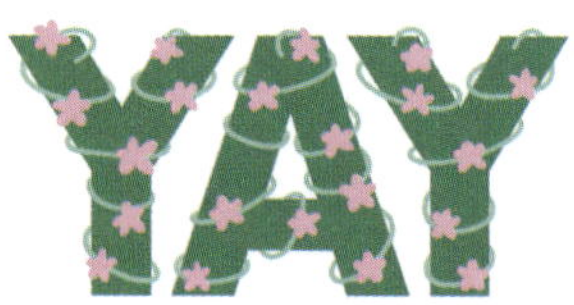

7. Place a five-petal flower over nearly every vine loop and curve, leaving some empty.

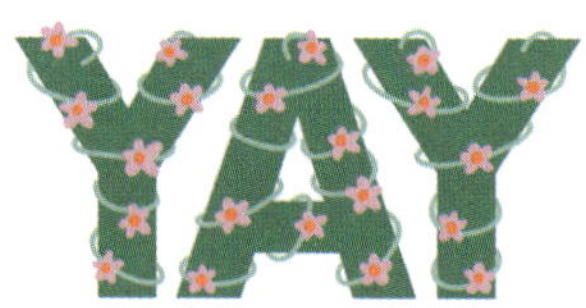

8. Draw a circle center in each flower.

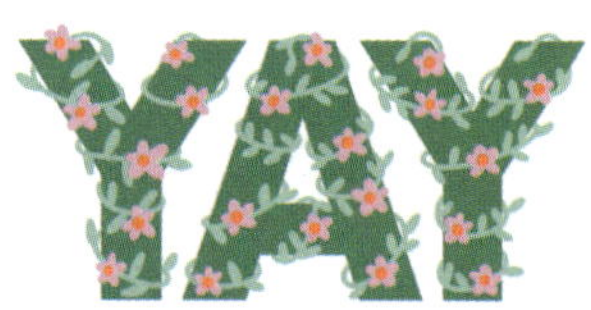

9. Draw little oval leaves in the empty spaces on the vines.

BE BOLD!

What other words can you wrap in floral vines? Try words like Joy, Love, and Happy. Also use different flower shapes with each new word.

COLLAGE-STYLE LETTERS

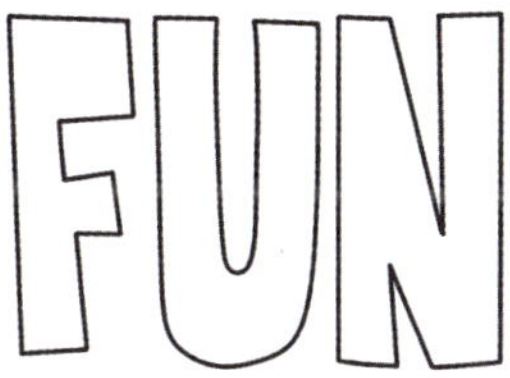

1. Start by outlining the word "FUN" in block letters across the page.

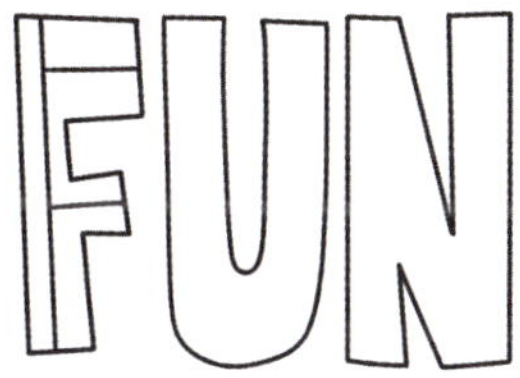

2. Draw a vertical line down the F with a horizontal line in the center of each arm.

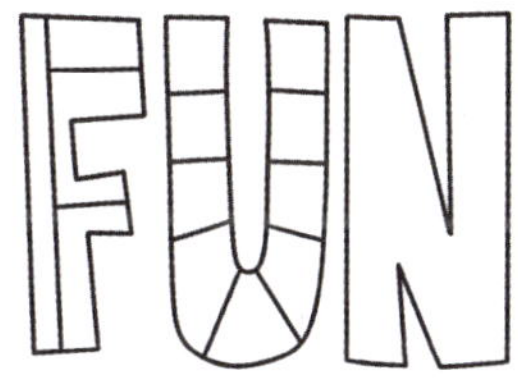

3. Draw lines to create stripes all along the U.

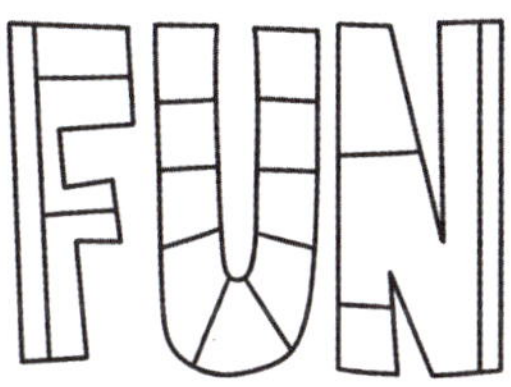

4. Draw a long vertical line down the right side of the N with two horizontal lines on the left side to create two smaller patchwork segments.

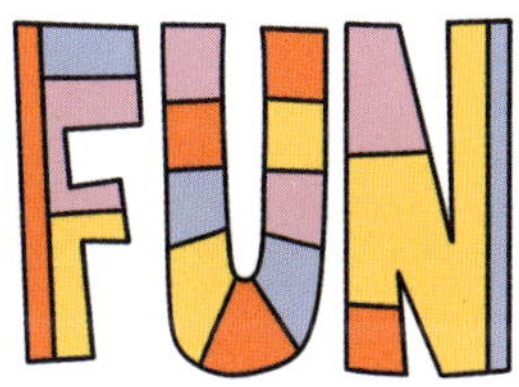

5. Add a different color to each segment.

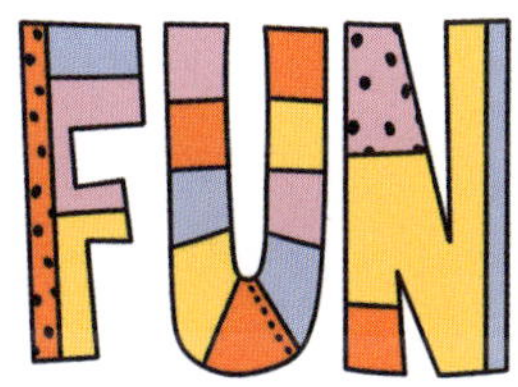

6. Decorate some of the segments with dotted lines and polka dot patterns.

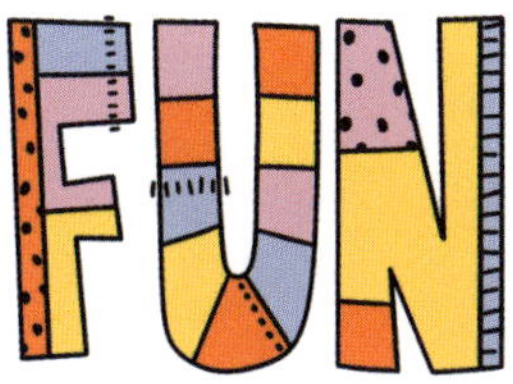

7. Add some lines of dashes to create a more graphic look. Don't be afraid to go outside the lines!

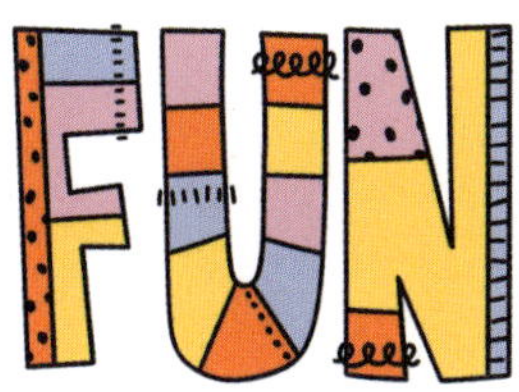

8. Add extra texture with some swirling lines of loops.

BE BOLD!

Create your own unique patchwork by adding special patterns to different segments. Add patterns of hearts, stars, flowers, or little creatures like butterflies to make a unique quilted look.

PATCHWORK LETTERS

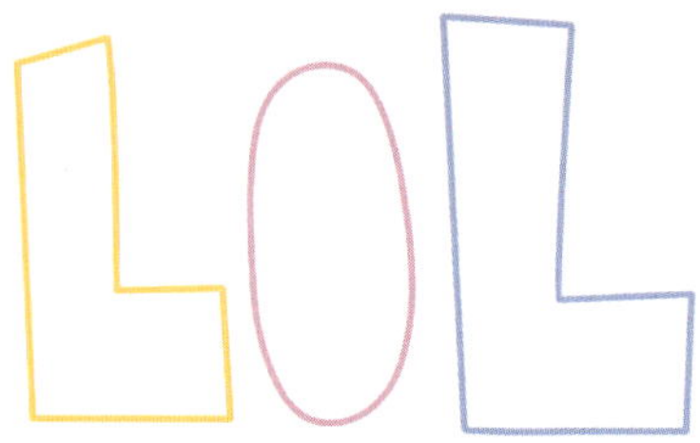

1. Start by outlining the acronym "LOL" in hollow block letters across the center of the page.

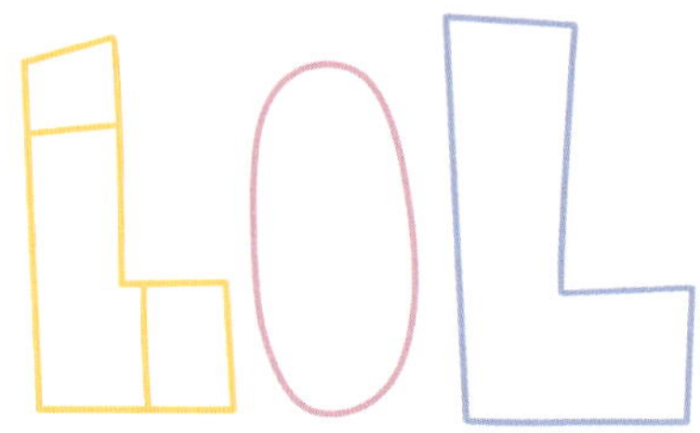

2. Draw a horizontal line near the top of the first L and a vertical line near the bottom.

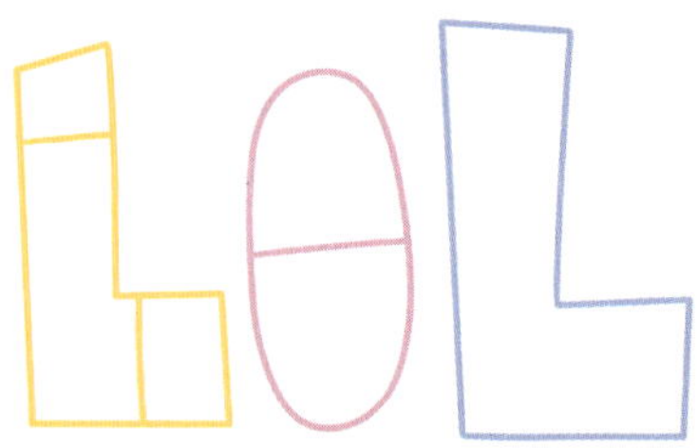

3. Add a horizontal line across the center of the O.

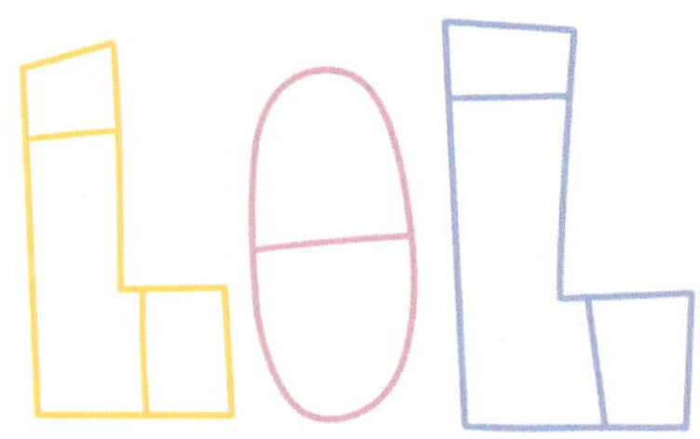

4. Draw a horizontal line near the top of the last L and a vertical line near the bottom.

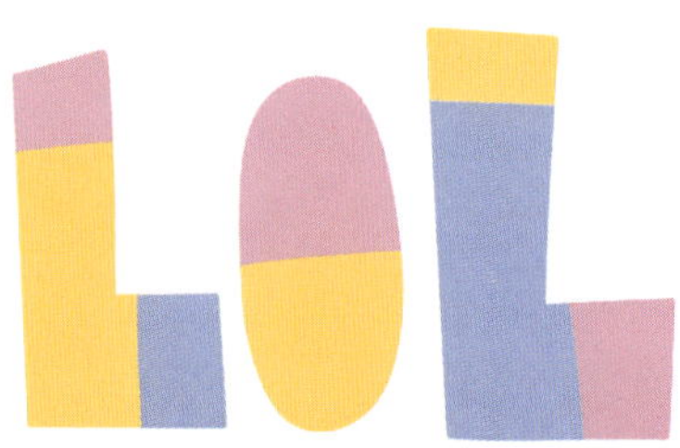

5. Add a different color to each segment.

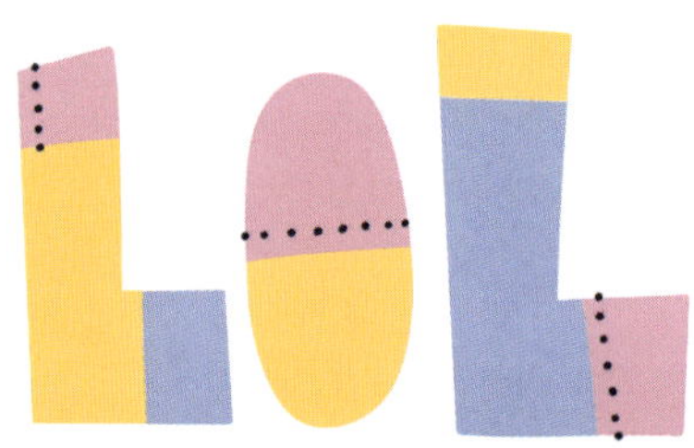

6. Decorate each letter with a short line of little black dots. Don't be afraid to go outside the lines!

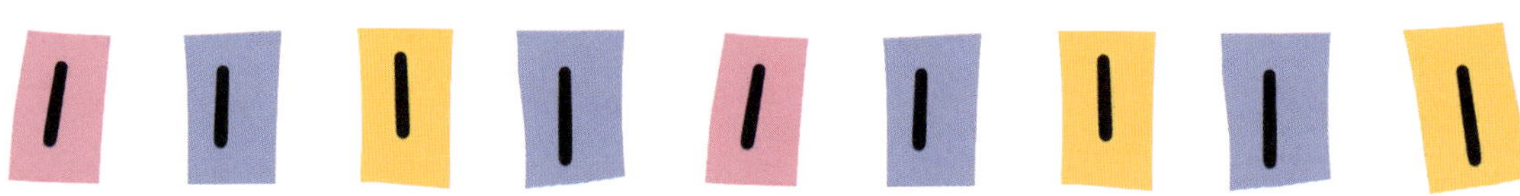

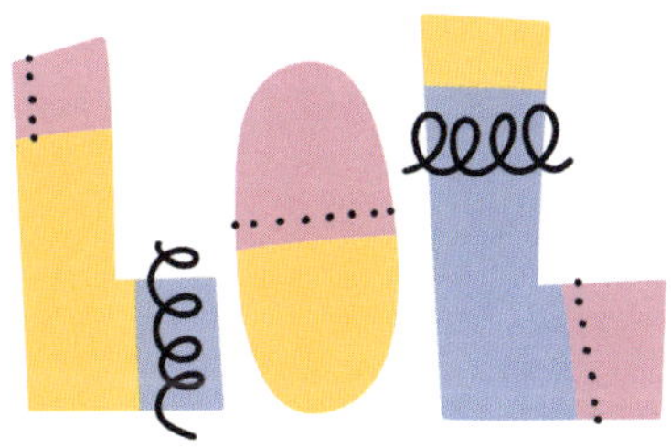

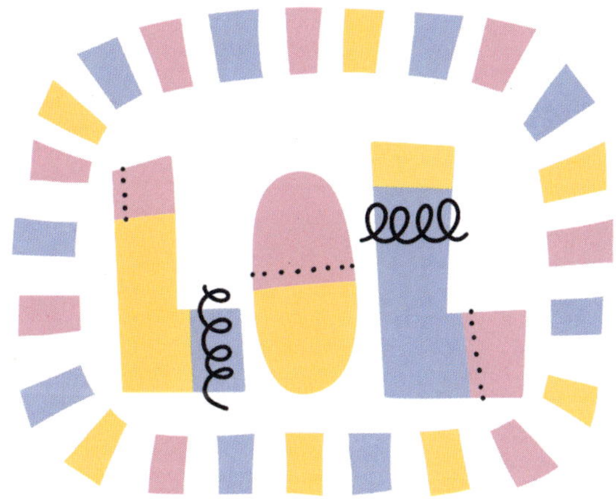

7. Add some texture by drawing some swirling lines of loops.

8. Create an oval frame with imperfect rectangle shapes.

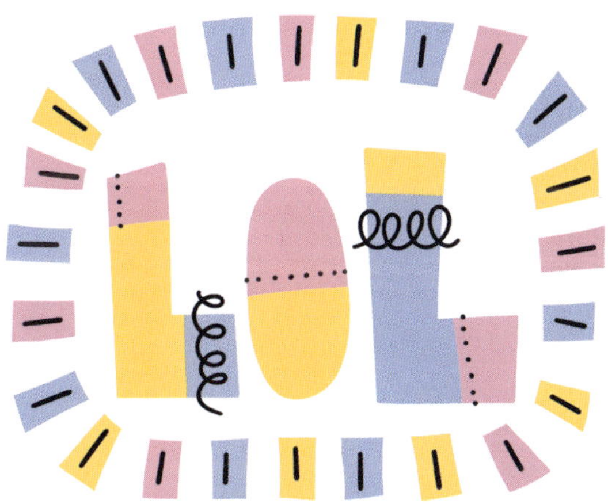

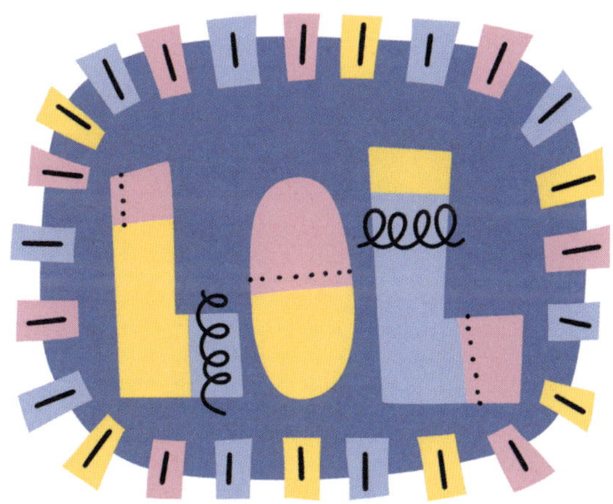

9. Draw a black line through the middle of each rectangle.

10. Create an oval background behind the letters and frame.

BE BOLD!

Go for a retro-style look by adding bold shapes like triangles, squiggles, checkerboard grids, and bright neon colors.

C AS A CAT

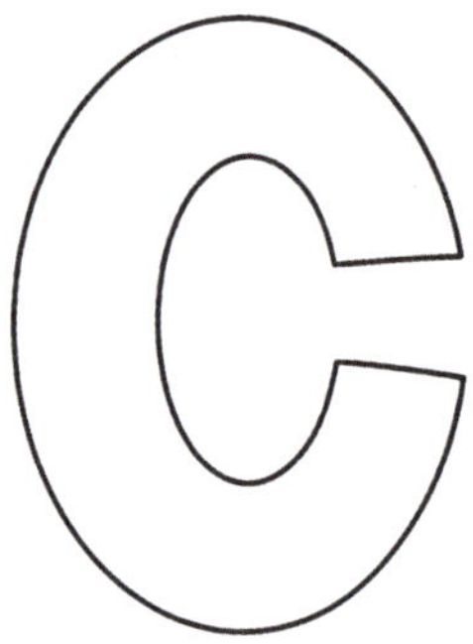

1. Start by outlining a block letter C in the center of the page.

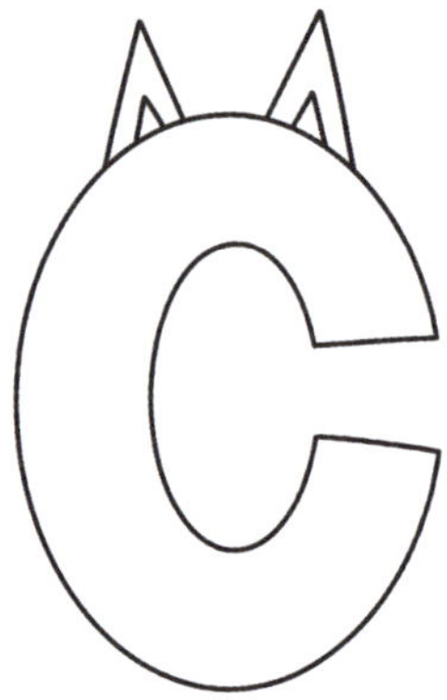

2. Add two triangle ears on top, with a smaller triangle inside each.

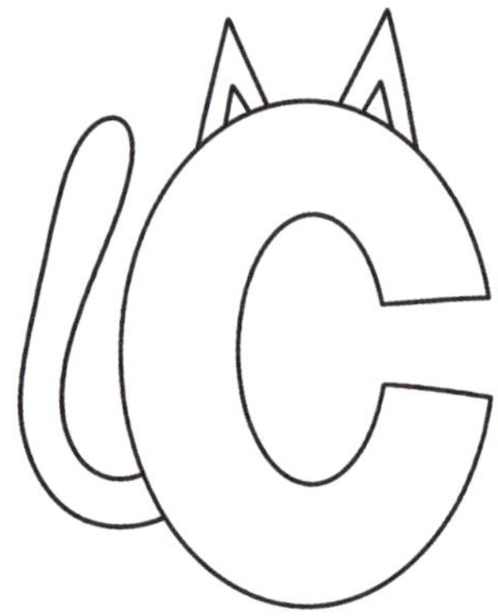

3. Draw a long wavy noodle tail on the left.

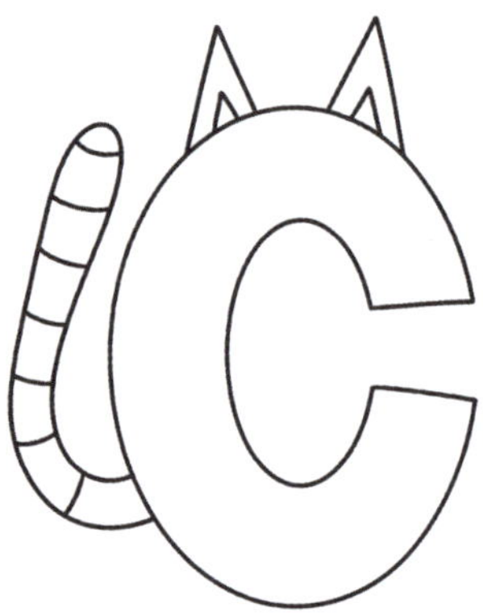

4. Add a series of horizontal stripes to the tail.

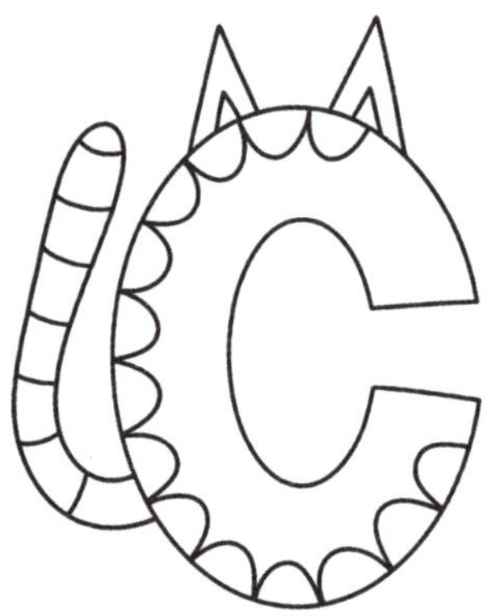

5. Draw a line of semicircles along the outer edge of the C.

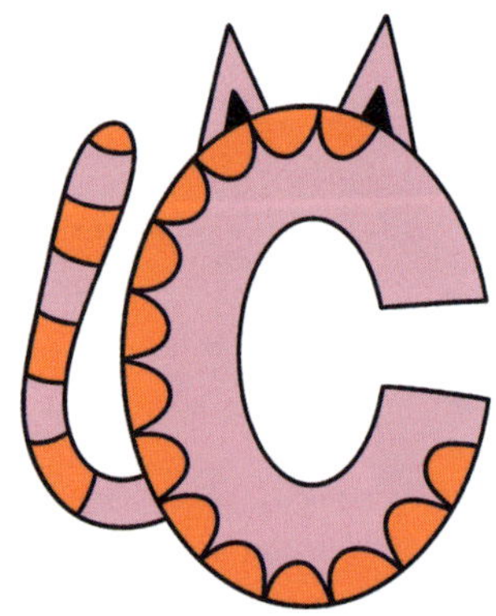

6. Fill in the colors!

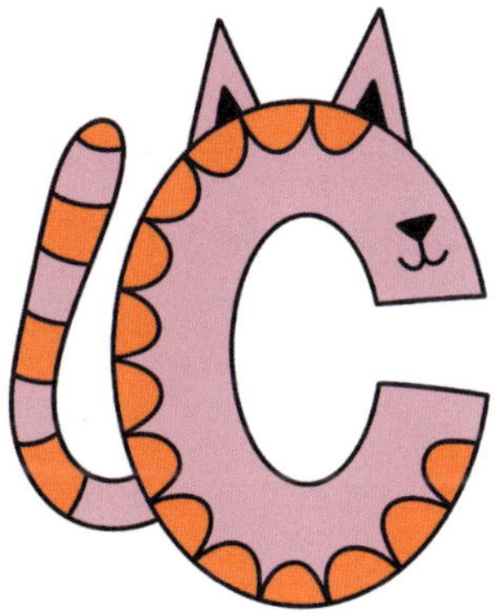

7. Add a triangle nose and little curved mouth to the top right of the C.

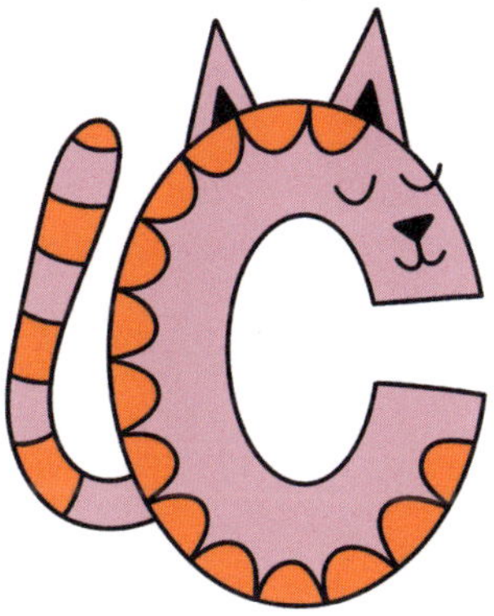

8. Draw two curved lines for the eyes.

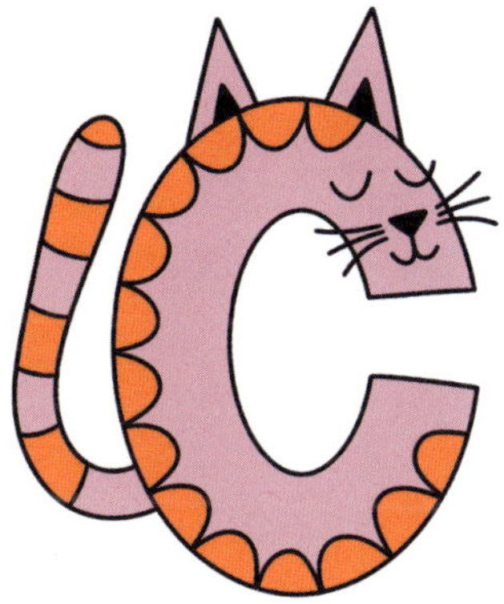

9. Draw three whisker lines on each side of the nose.

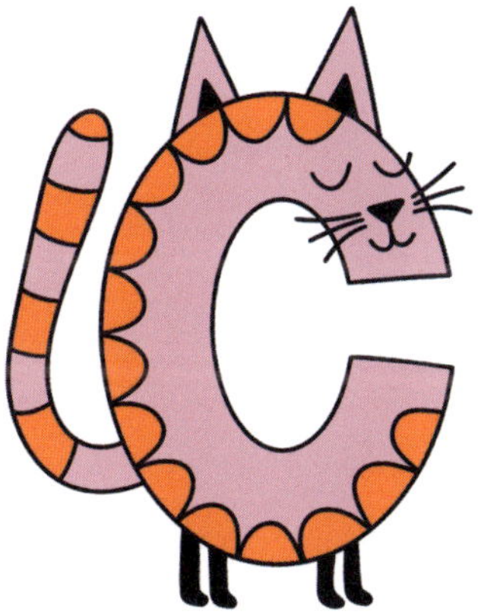

10. Draw four small L-shaped feet, in pairs of two, underneath the C.

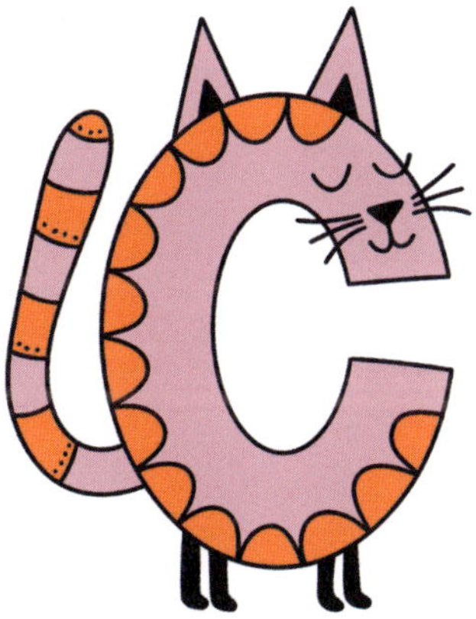

11. Decorate the stripes on the tail with lines of small dots.

BE BOLD!

Try this idea with other animals or objects that start with the letter C, such as crocodile, caterpillar, or carrot.

R AS A RABBIT

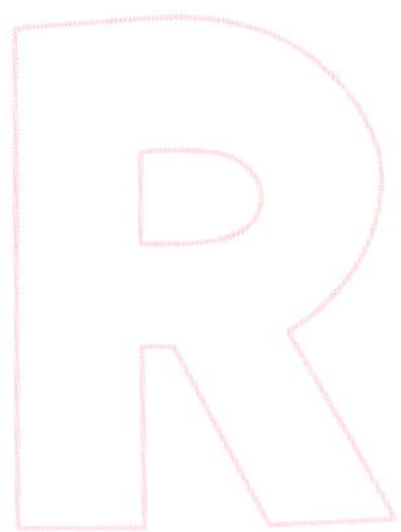

1. Start by outlining a block letter R in the bottom center of the page.

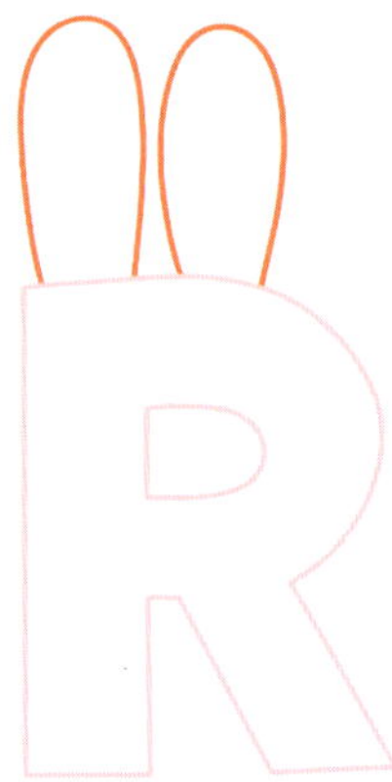

2. Draw two long U-shaped ears on top.

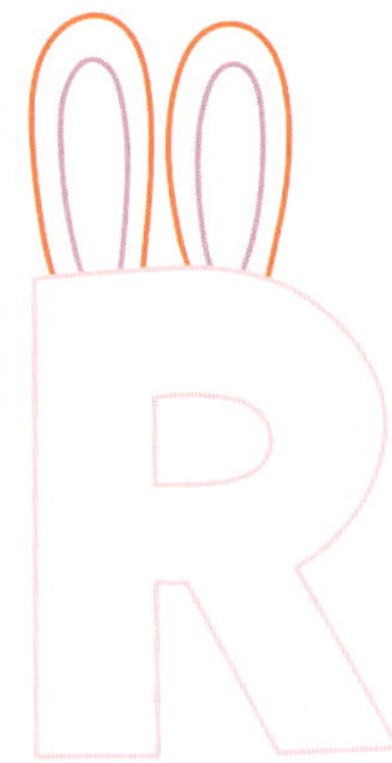

3. Draw a smaller U shape inside both ears.

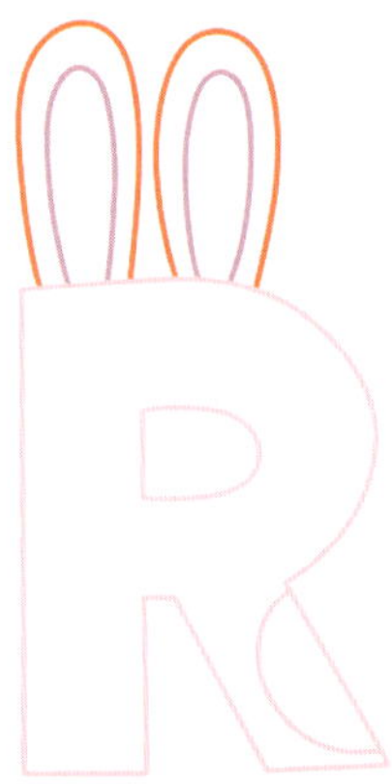

4. Draw a semicircle on the right side of the right leg.

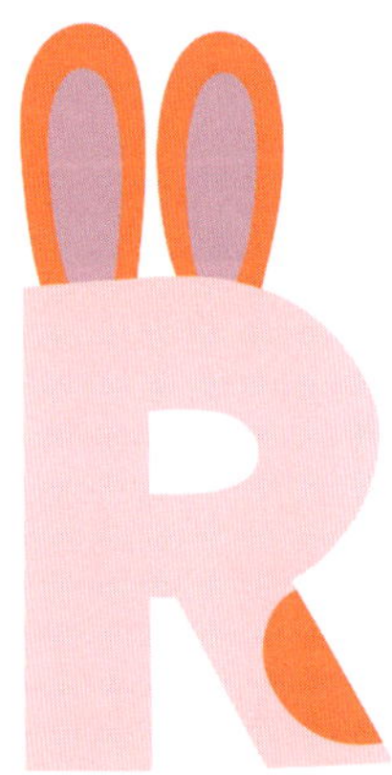

5. Fill in the colors!

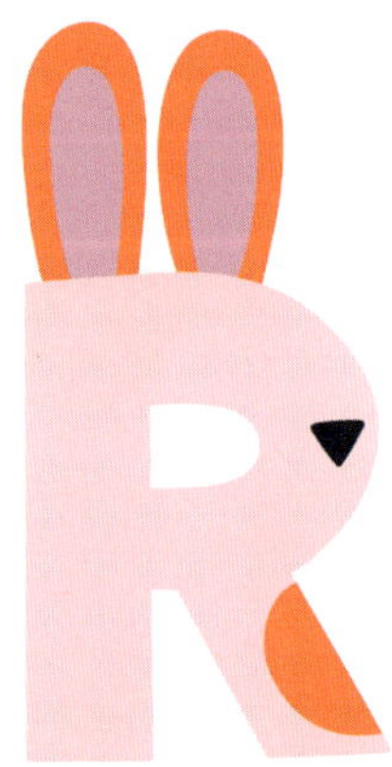

6. Add a black triangle to the center of the R bump.

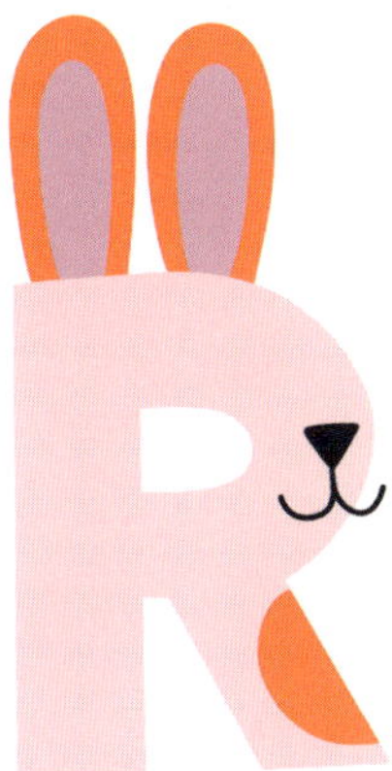

7. Draw a curved mouth underneath the triangle.

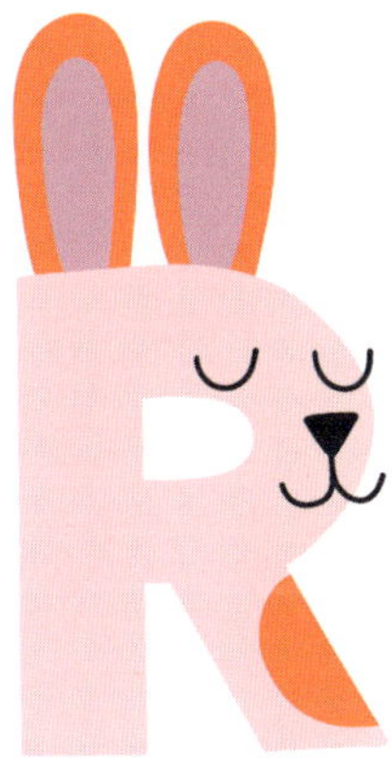

8. Draw two U-shaped eyes.

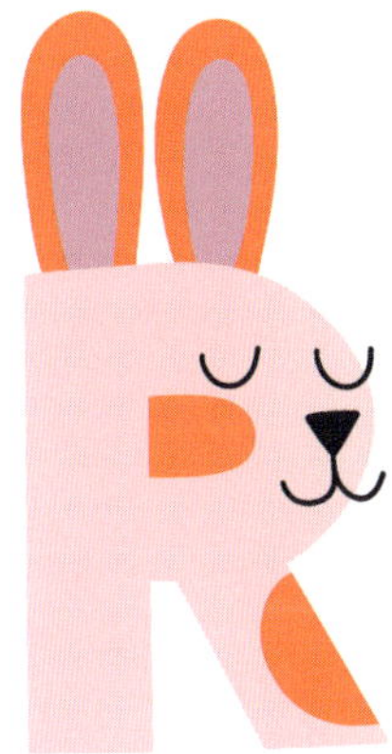

9. Fill in the center of the R with a warm color for the rabbit's cheek.

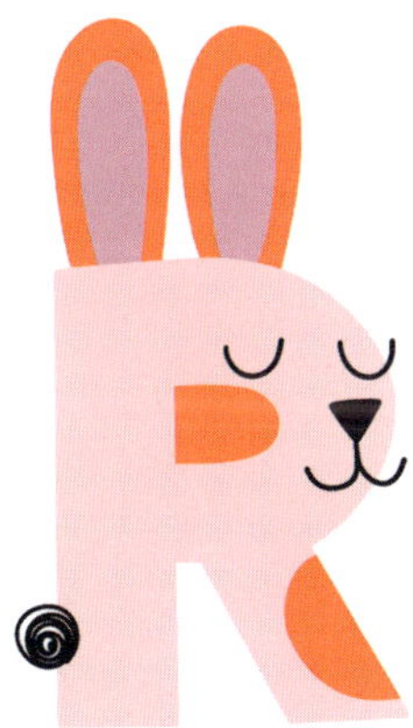

10. Add a swirly circle to the bottom left of the R.

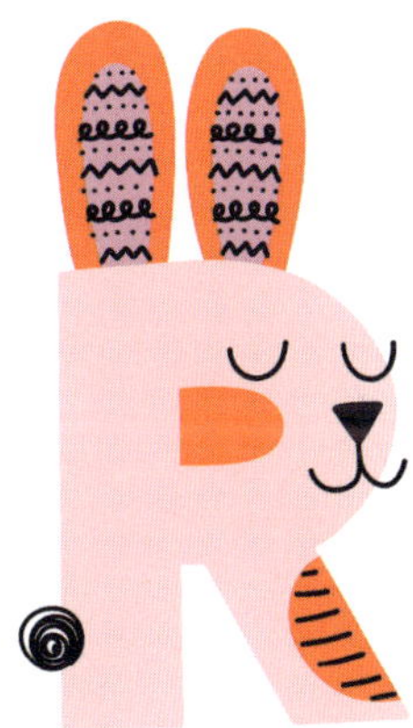

11. Decorate the ears and belly of the rabbit with dots, lines, swirly loops, and zig-zags.

BE BOLD!

Try this idea with other animals or objects that start with the letter R, such as rat, road, or robot.

E AS AN ELEPHANT

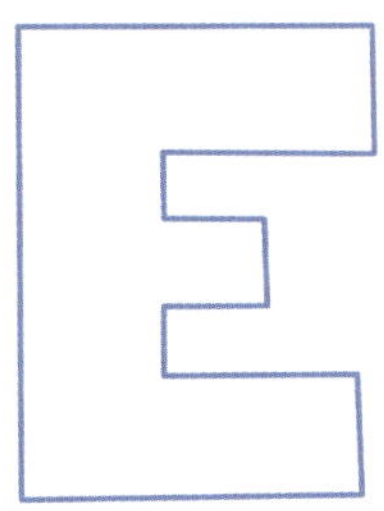

1. Start by outlining a block letter E in the center of the page.

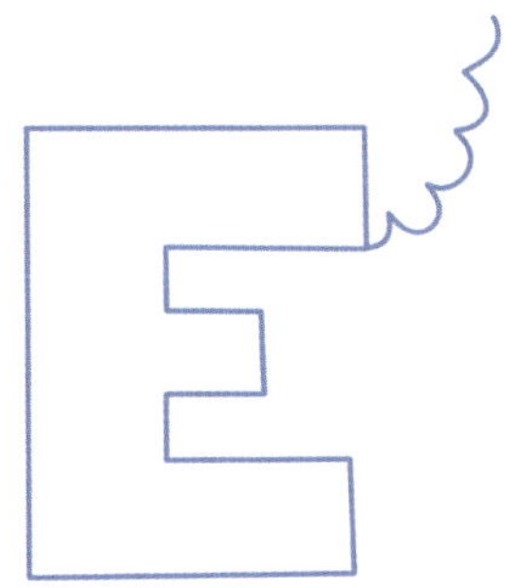

2. Draw a line of five scallops curving up from the top arm of the E.

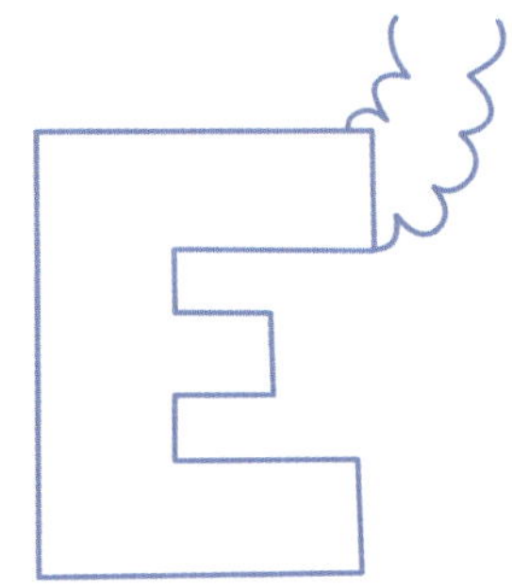

3. Add a line of three scallops from the top of the E, mirroring the first line.

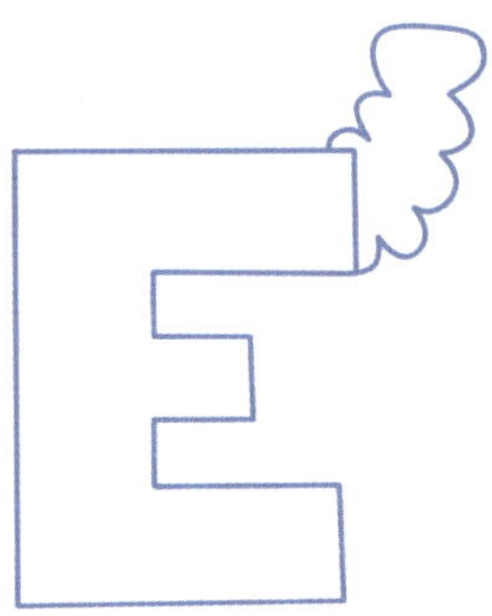

4. Connect the top of the lines with a rounded curve.

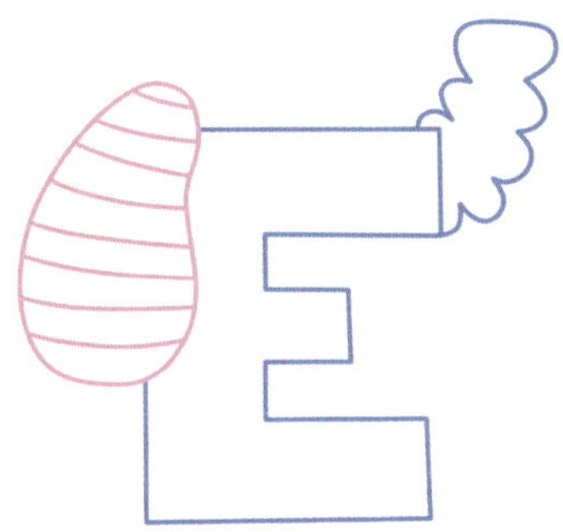

5. Draw a pear-shaped ear on the top left and add a series of horizontal stripes.

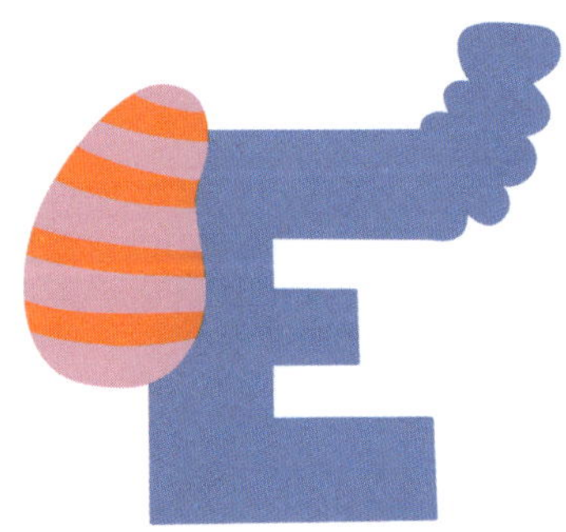

6. Fill in the colors!

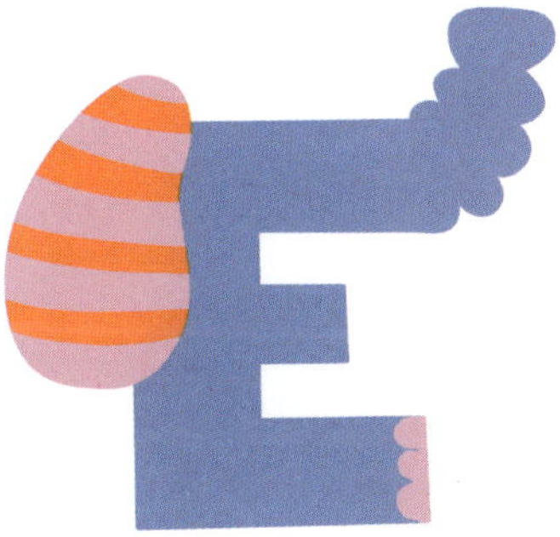

7. Draw three semicircles on the bottom arm of the E.

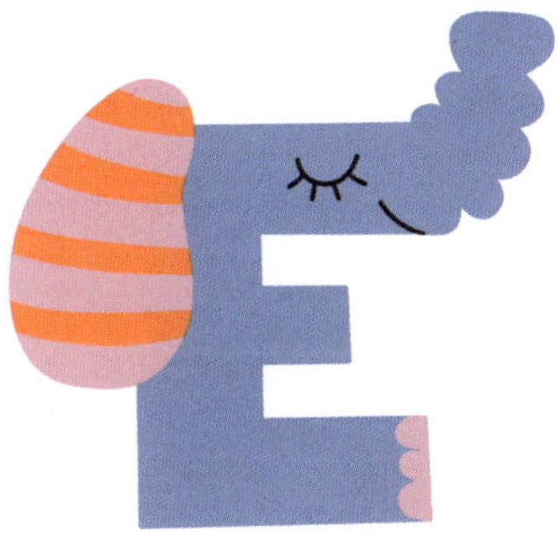

8. Add a small, curved line for the mouth and a U-shaped eye with three lines for eyelashes.

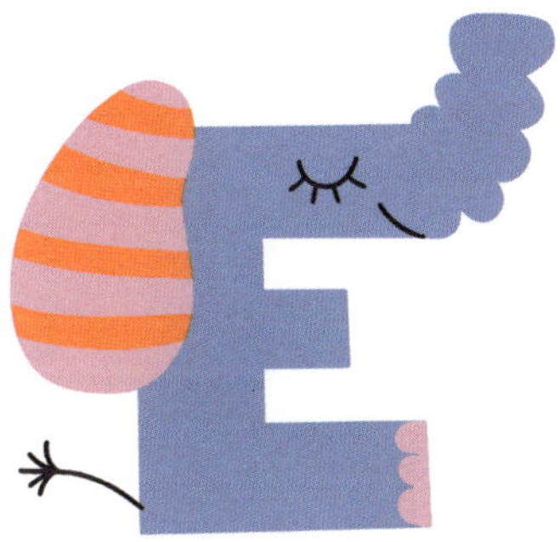

9. Draw a curved black line with five fanning lines at the bottom left of the E for a tail.

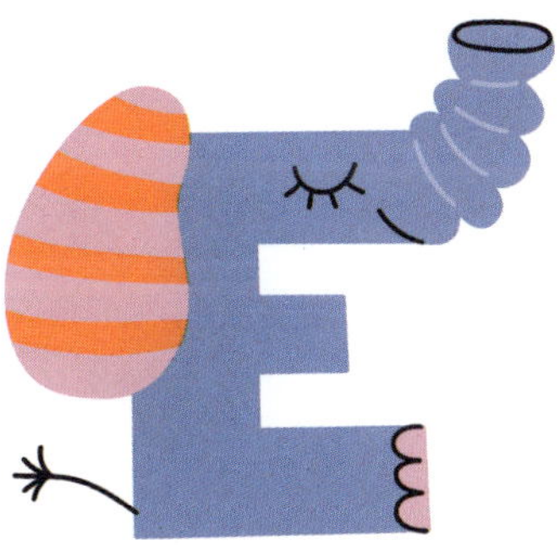

10. Outline the bumps of the toes and end of the trunk in black and add curved lines for the wrinkles of the trunk.

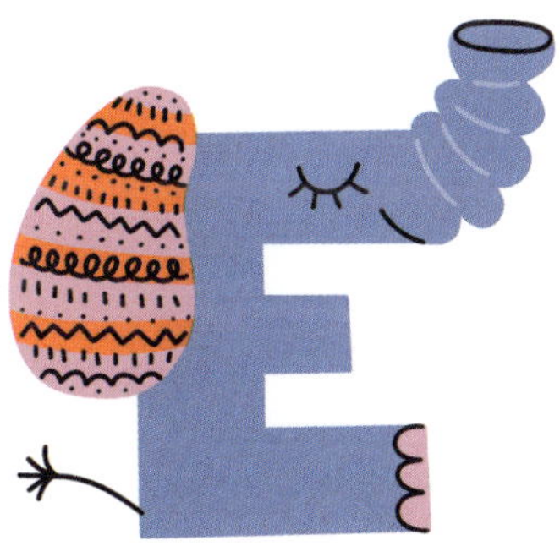

11. Decorate the ear with dots, swirly lines, scalloped lines, dashes, and zig-zags.

BE BOLD!

Try this idea with other animals or objects that start with the letter E, such as eagle, eggplant, or electricity.

A AS AN ALLIGATOR

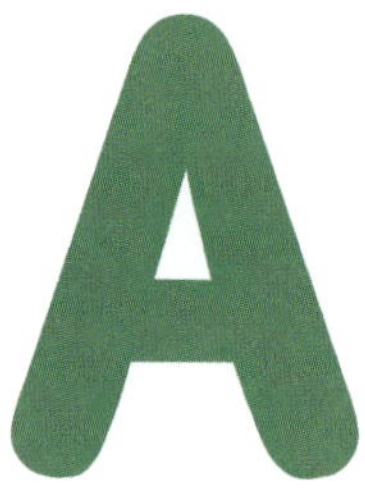

1. Start with a rounded block letter A in the center of the page.

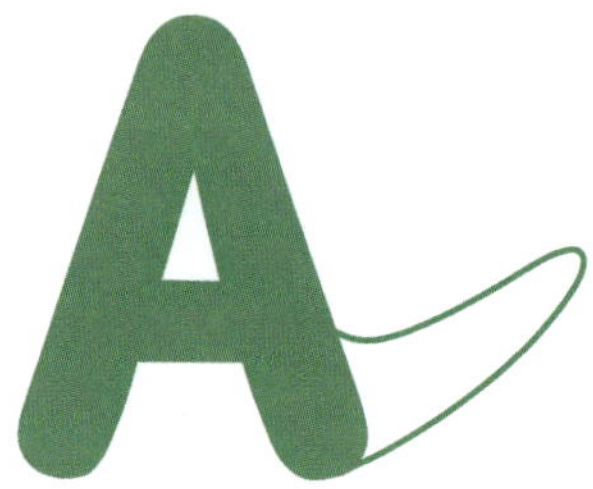

2. Add a curved V shape from the bottom right of the A.

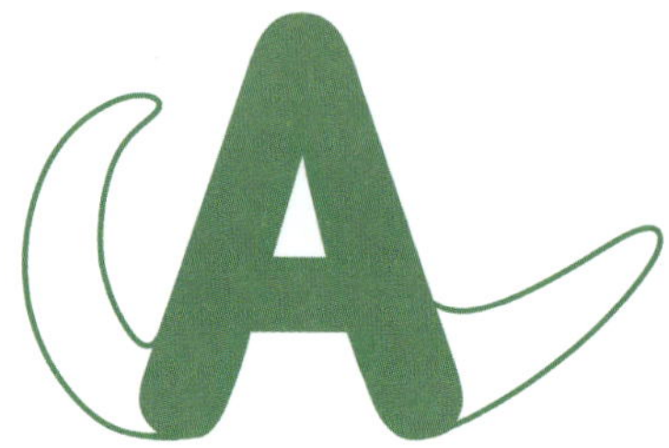

3. Draw a curved C shape from the bottom left of the A.

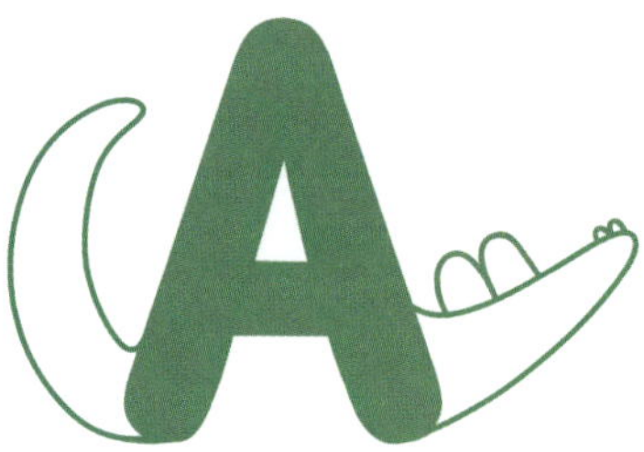

4. Draw two U shapes on top of the V shape with two small bumps at the end.

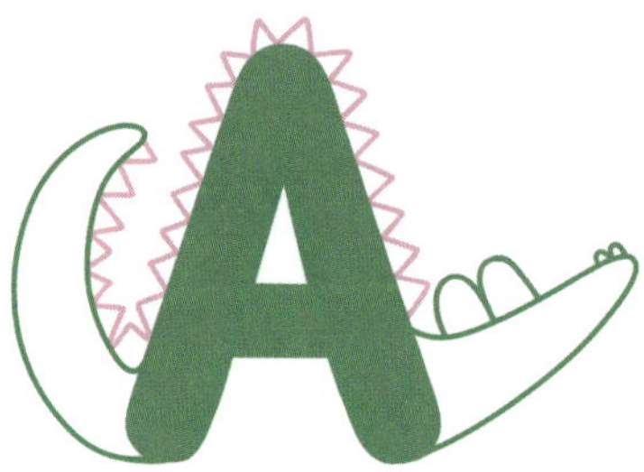

5. Draw spikey triangles along the top of the C shape and the A.

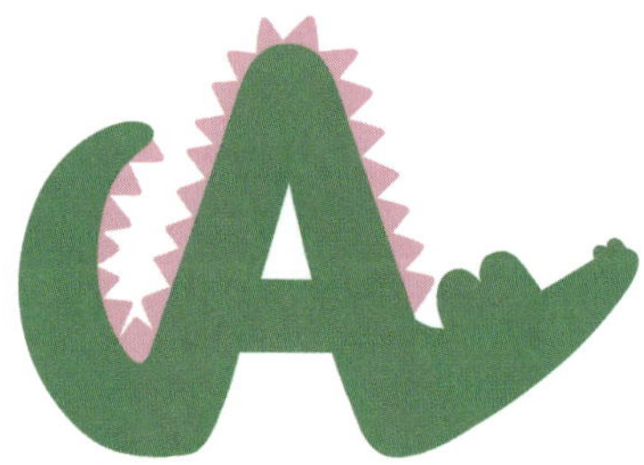

6. Fill in the colors!

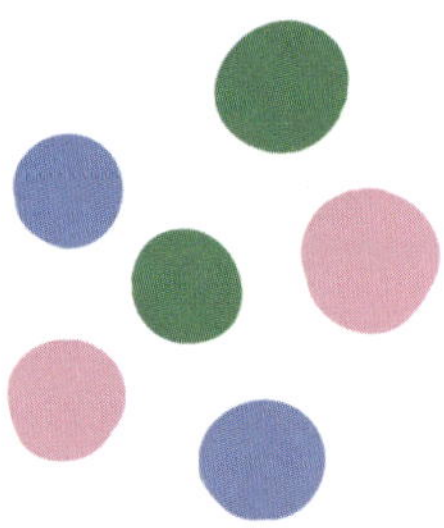

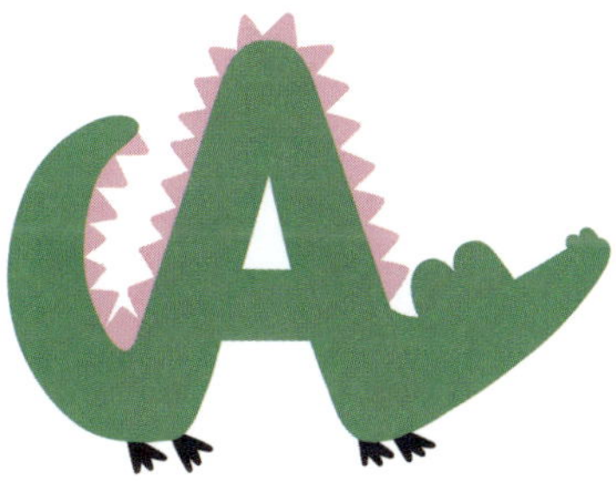

7. Draw two little, three-toed feet under each leg of the A.

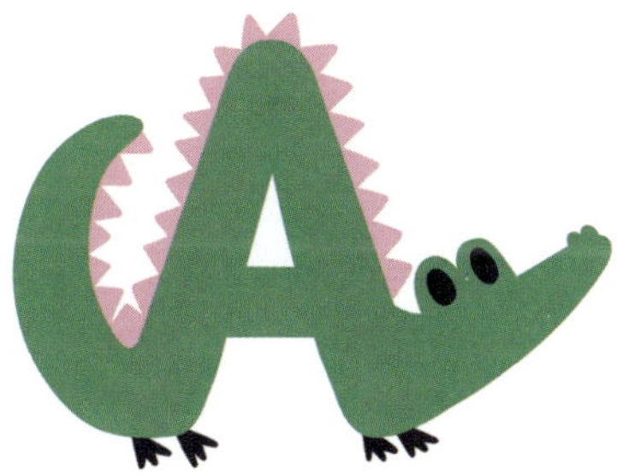

8. Add a black oval to the center of each U shape.

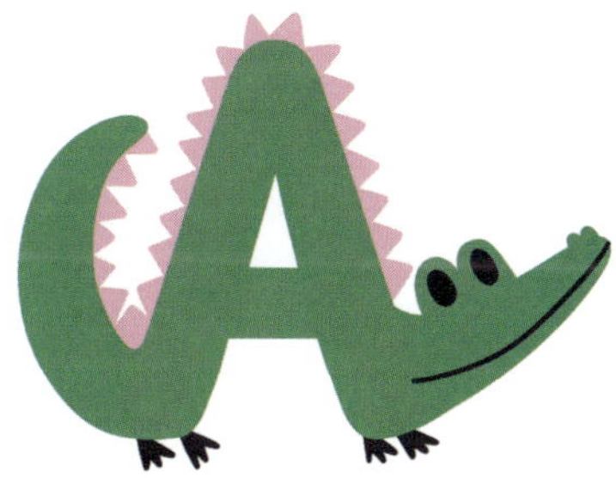

9. Draw a long, curved line through the V shape for a mouth.

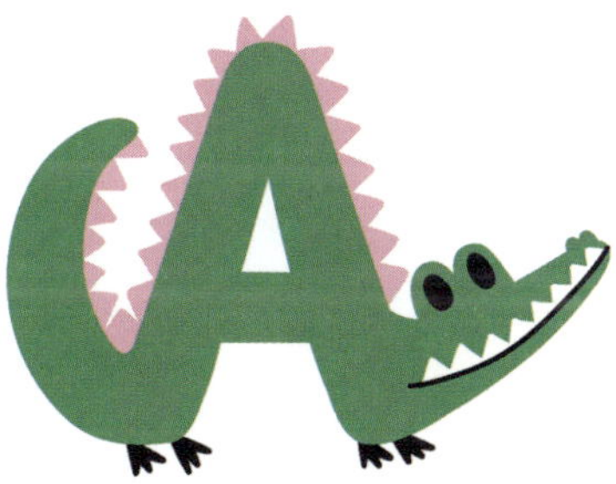

10. Add a line of spiky triangles on top of the mouth line.

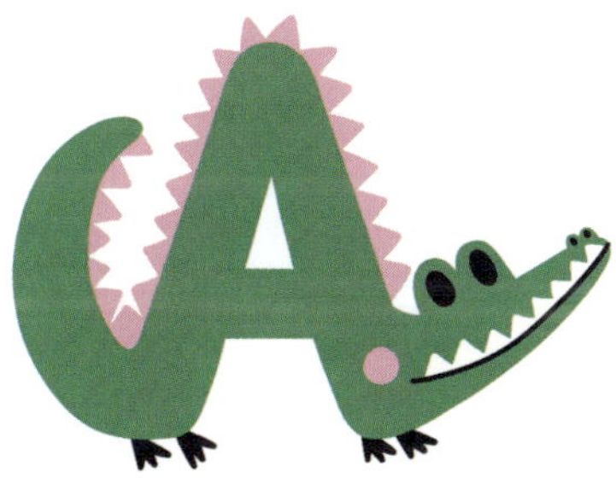

11. Add a circle at the end of the mouth for the blush.

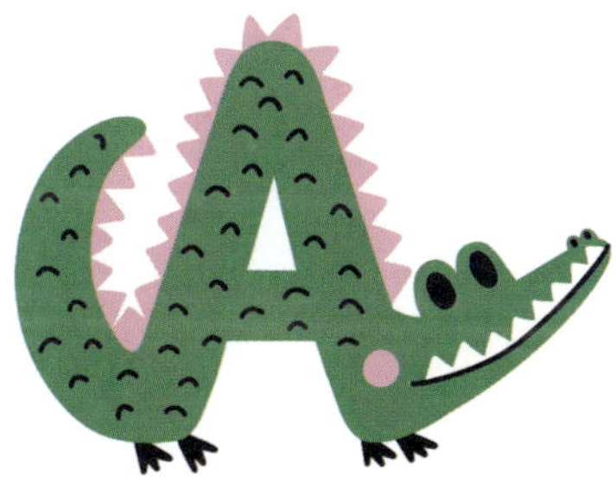

12. Give your alligator texture by covering the body and tail with a series of little curved lines.

BE BOLD!

Try this idea with other animals or objects that start with the letter A, such as apple, ape, or anaconda.

T AS A TIGER

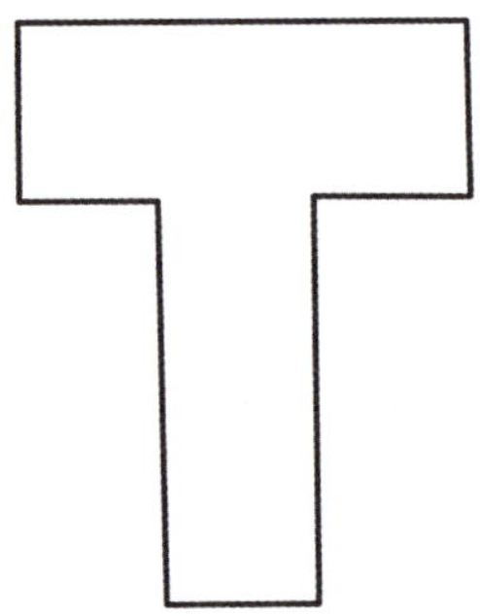

1. Start by outlining a block letter T in the center of the page.

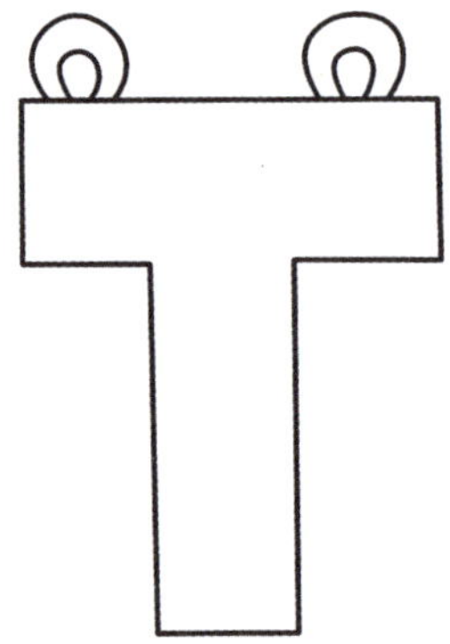

2. Add two round ears on top with two curved lines each, one inside the other.

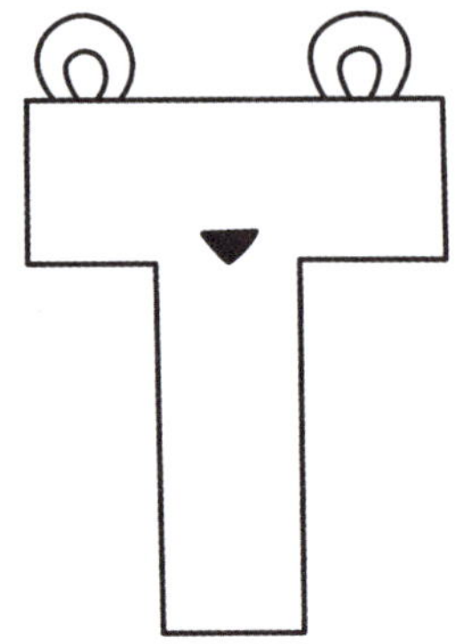

3. Add a wide black triangle to the center cross of the T for the nose.

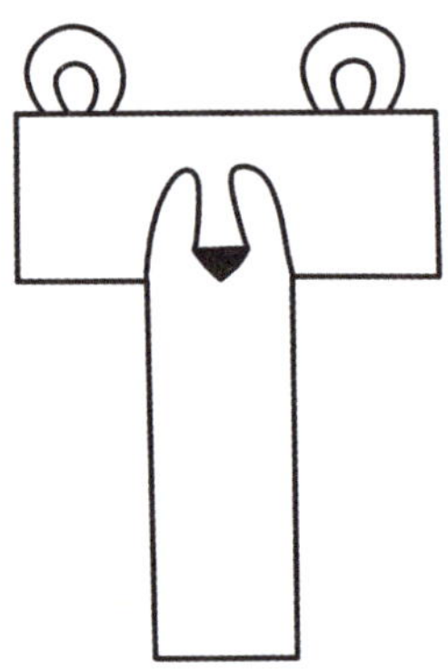

4. Draw two U-shaped lines that touch the top corners of the nose.

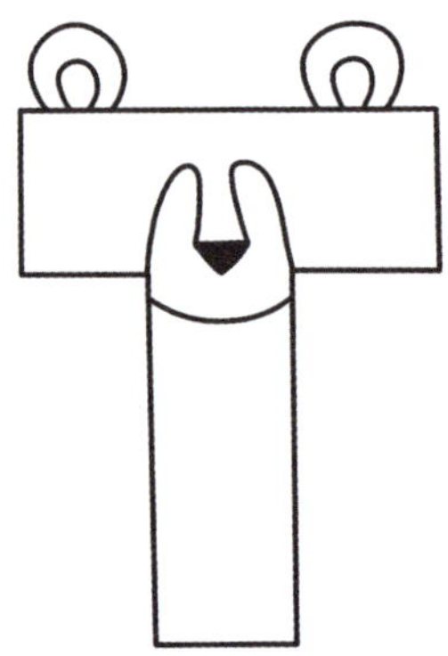

5. Draw a curved horizontal line underneath the triangle.

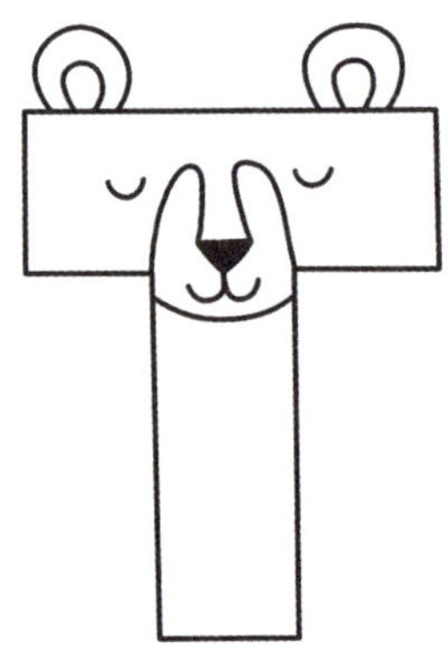

6. Draw a curved mouth under the triangle, then add two small curves for the eyes.

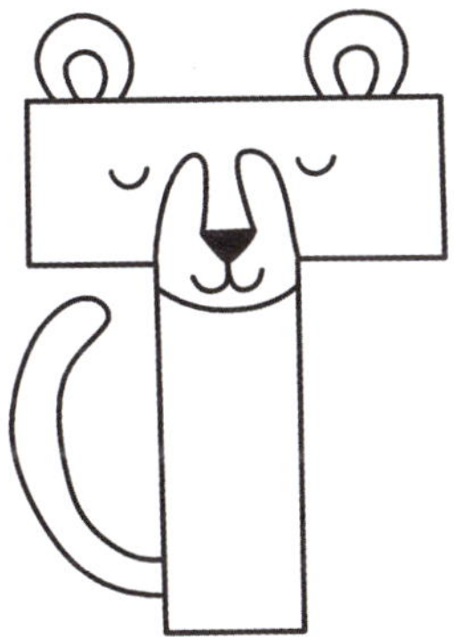

7. Draw a C-shaped tail on the lower left side of the T.

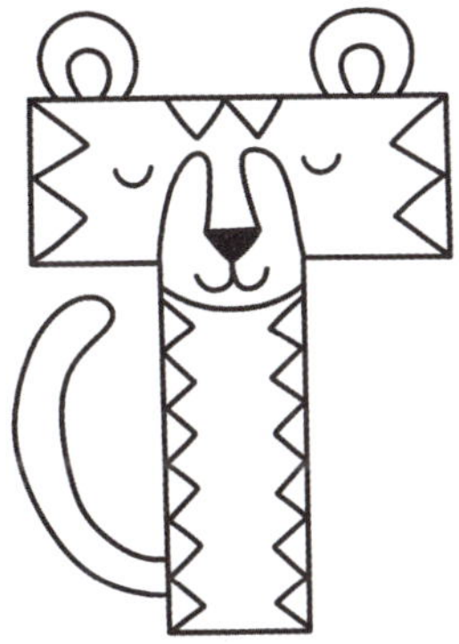

8. Draw triangles on the inner edge of the lower part of the T, on either side of the upper T, and on the top center of the T.

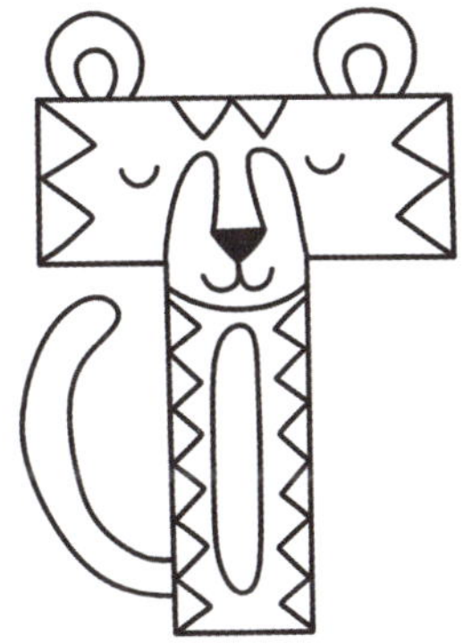

9. Add a long oval to the center of the lower part of the T.

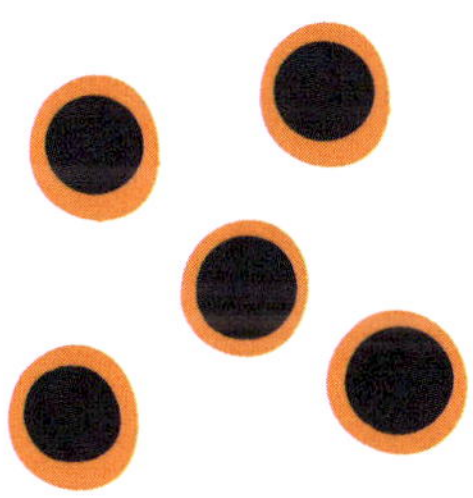

10. Fill in the colors!

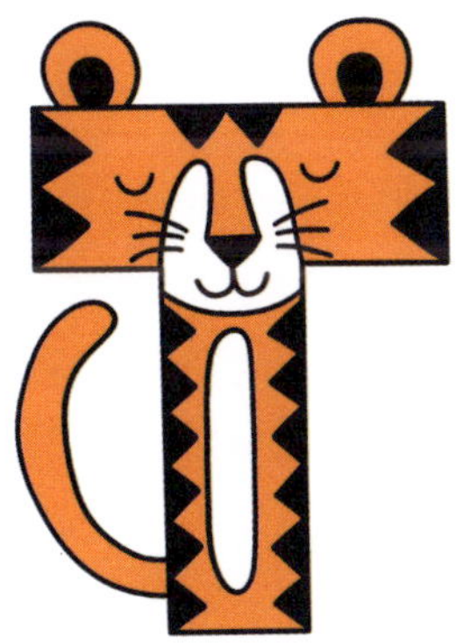

11. Add three whisker lines to each side of the nose.

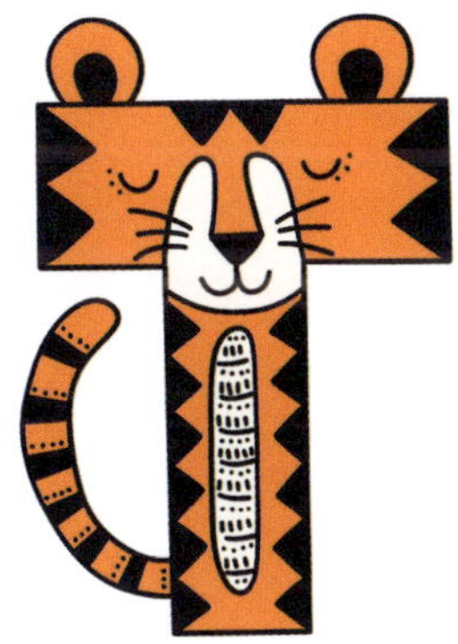

12. Decorate with small black dots, dashes, and lines.

BE BOLD!

Try this idea with other animals or objects that start with the letter T, such as telephone, tree, or tape measure.

BRING YOUR ART TO LIFE

MIX & MATCH

Now that you've drawn lots of playful motifs—flowers, birds, bugs, trees, rainbows, and more—it's time to start combining them! Build a little scene, create a moment, or start exploring layout ideas for a pattern. Try placing different motifs on the same page: a flower with a butterfly, a bird next to a rainbow, a cactus under the sun. Some might naturally belong together, while others that you may not expect to look good together do. A shared color palette or a few simple details can help tie everything in.

Ideas to Try

- **Make a scene:** Choose three to five motifs and arrange them like a tiny illustration.
- **Frame it:** Draw a border using leaves, florals, or repeating shapes.
- **Repeat a shape:** Use the same motif in different colors or sizes to create rhythm or movement.

And don't forget about those little line art details—dots, dashes, textures, and tiny flourishes—we've been using throughout the book. These can work like glue when you're combining multiple elements. Sometimes just a few shared marks are all it takes to make everything feel like it belongs together.

If Working Digitally

In Procreate, try experimenting with:

- Duplicating motifs
- Resizing, flipping, or rotating objects
- Recoloring using Alpha Lock or Hue/Saturation
- Rearranging on different layers to test out compositions

The more you play around with placement and combinations, the more ideas will start to show up—sometimes when you least expect them.

MAKE IT YOURS

Now that you've drawn lots of joyful motifs, it's time to take them one step further and make them yours. These drawings are just starting points. Change them up, play with them, twist them into something new. That's where your artistic style starts to shine through.

Remember the "Be Bold!" prompts? They are here to encourage you to explore, experiment, and let go of perfection. If you haven't tried them yet, go back and give them a go. They're there to remind you that you can always make your own rules.

Ways to Make It Yours

- **Swap the Colors:** Who says a strawberry has to be red? Try pink with blue leaves.
- **Add a Face:** Give your mushroom a personality, or make your sun look sleepy.
- **Exaggerate Shapes:** Make super tall ears, tiny legs, or huge eyes.
- **Combine Motifs:** What if a bird delivers a love letter? Or a fish wears a crown?
- **Add Details:** Try stripes, dots, dashes, checkerboards, stars, scribbles—anything goes.

The more you play, the more your creative voice will start to show up. Maybe it's a certain shape you keep repeating, the way you draw faces, or how you use color. Find your style and watch it develop the more you make your own creations.

CREATIVE APPLICATIONS

You've drawn, colored, and explored, now let's find some fun ways to use your art beyond the sketchbook or tablet!

There are so many ways to bring your motifs into the real world. You don't need fancy tools or a big studio, just a little curiosity and the courage to try. Whether it's handmade or digital, a simple drawing can turn into something joyful and useful.

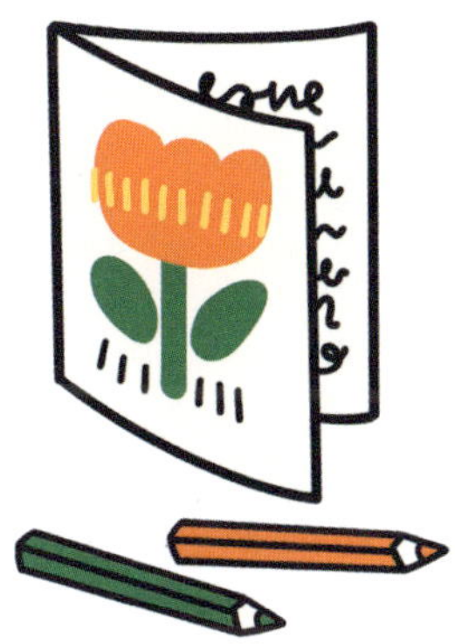

Think beyond the page. Some people turn their motifs into stickers, greeting cards, or wall art. Others explore textile patterns or crafty DIY projects. The key is to play and experiment!

Try This with Your Motifs

- Make a card for a friend using one of your favorite motifs as a sweet and simple way to share your art.
- Turn your drawings into stickers using platforms like StickerApp (www.stickerapp.com) where you can upload your art and get custom stickers printed. Or stay local and look up a printshop near you and ask if they print stickers and stationery. Use your own stickers to decorate notebooks, label jars, or add a cheerful touch to envelopes.
- Use collage techniques by cutting out your drawings and gluing them into your sketchbook. Or design your own journal covers using layered motifs.
- Print your designs on fabric or home décor. Platforms like Spoonflower (www.spoonflower.com) let you upload your art and turn it into fabric, wallpaper, or pillows! It's a great way to see your work come to life in the real world.

Your art doesn't have to be perfect to be meaningful. Don't be afraid to share what you've made or use it to brighten someone else's day.

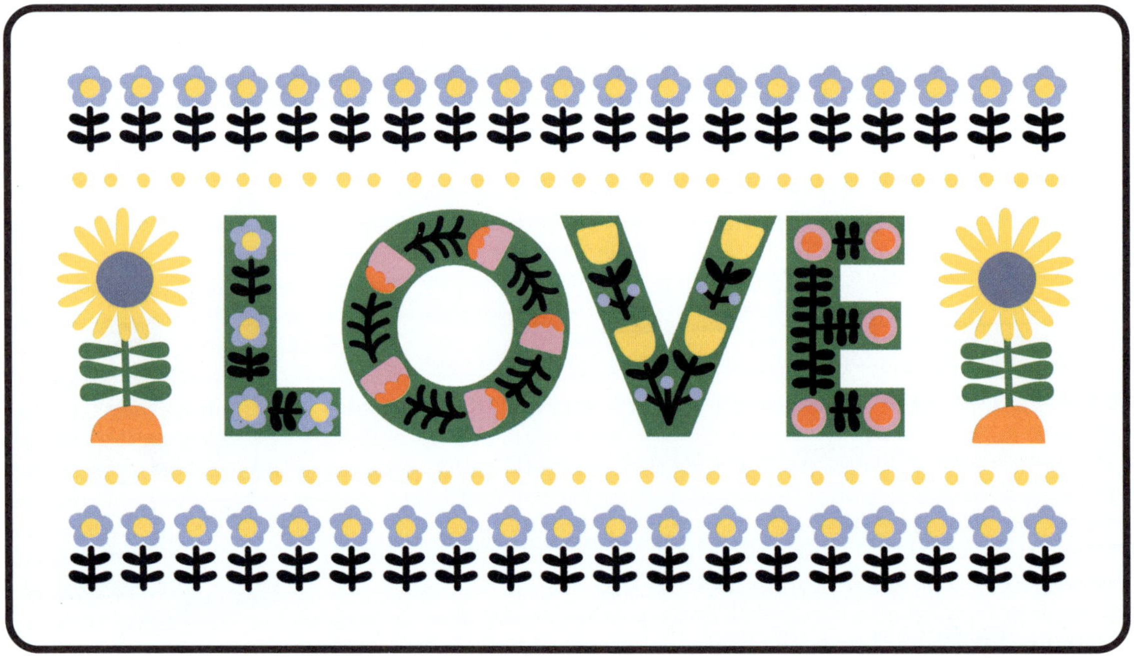

ACKNOWLEDGMENTS

Thank you to my husband Michael—for believing in me even when this dream took time, for giving me the space to create, and for supporting me in so many ways along the journey. Your patience, encouragement, and help made it possible for me to turn what I love into a real path, and I'm really grateful for that.

To my daughter Lily—your creative spirit is one of my greatest inspirations. Watching you dive into arts and crafts with so much joy reminds me exactly why I love making things. Since I create most of my work with kids in mind, you're truly the perfect helper. You're always ready with ideas about what to draw next or what colors to choose—you're the best creative assistant I could ask for!

A big thank you to everyone who supports my work—whether you follow along, leave a kind comment, share my designs, or bring my art into your home. From fabric and wallpaper to prints and playful products, every bit of support means more than you know.

And to the wonderful companies and partners who trust my artwork and help bring it out into the world—thank you. Seeing my designs come to life through our collaborations is something I'll never take for granted.

Thank you all for being part of this creative journey.
Sandra

ABOUT THE AUTHOR

Sandra Hutter is a surface pattern designer and illustrator based in Vienna, Austria. She specializes in creating cheerful artwork in bold and vibrant colors for the things people love in their everyday lives. Her art has been featured on a wide range of products by companies around the world. See more on her website sandrahutter.com and follow on Instagram @sandrahutterdesigns.

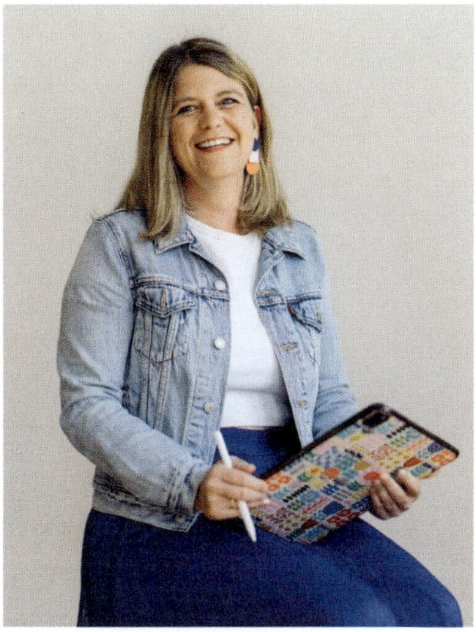

Photo by Marie Bleyer

First published in 2026 by Rock Point, an imprint of The Quarto Group,
135 West 36th Street, 13th Floor, New York, NY 10018, USA
(212) 779-4972 www.Quarto.com

EEA Representation, WTS Tax d.o.o.,
Žanova ulica 3, 4000 Kranj, Slovenia.
www.wts-tax.si

10 9 8 7 6 5 4 3 2 1

ISBN: 979-8-3179-0066-3

Digital edition published in 2026
eISBN: 979-8-3179-0067-0

Library of Congress Cataloging-in-Publication Data

Names: Hutter, Sandra author
Title: Modern folk art / Sandra Hutter.
Description: New York, NY : Rock Point, 2026. | Summary: "In Modern Folk Art, surface pattern designer and illustrator Sandra Hutter guides you through 75 easy tutorials for drawing beloved folk art motifs"-- Provided by publisher.
Identifiers: LCCN 2026006980 (print) | LCCN 2026006981 (ebook) | ISBN 9798317900663 paperback | ISBN 9798317900670 ebook
Subjects: LCSH: Drawing--Technique | Decoration and ornament--Miscellanea
Classification: LCC NC730 .H88 2026 (print) | LCC NC730 (ebook)
LC record available at https://lccn.loc.gov/2026006980
LC ebook record available at https://lccn.loc.gov/2026006981

Group Publisher: Rage Kindelsperger
Editorial Director: Erin Canning
Creative Director: Laura Drew
Managing Editor: Cara Donaldson
Editor: Katelynn Abraham
Art Director: Beth Middleworth
Cover and Interior Design: Kim Winscher

Printed in Huizhou City, Guangdong, China TT062026